robert rauschenberg

robert rauschenberg

breaking boundaries

Robert S. Mattison

yale university press • new haven and london

to my daughter, Anna and my son, Spencer

Designed by Elizabeth McWilliams

Printed in Singapore

Library of Congress Cataloging-in-Publication Data

Mattison, Robert Saltonstall.
    Robert Rauschenberg : breaking boundaries / Robert Mattison.
        p. cm.
Includes bibliographical references and index.
    ISBN 0-300-09931-2 (alk. paper)
    1. Rauschenberg, Robert, 1925 – Criticism and interpretation.
    I.Rauschenberg, Robert, 1925 – II. Title.
    N6537.R27 M37 2003
    700'.92–dc21

                            2002152374

A catalogue record for this book is available from The British Library

Frontispiece: Rauschenberg collecting material for his *Glut* series from a refuse dump in Florida (1986), photo by Darryl Pottorf. © Untitled Press, inc.

contents

acknowledgments

In the spirit of Robert Rauschenberg's art, this book is collaborative. I wish to thank a number of people for their time and expertise. First, my deep gratitude goes to Robert Rauschenberg for allowing me to conduct hours of interviews and for providing the opportunity to spend time in his studio. I owe an enormous debt to David White, Rauschenberg's curator, who provided valuable insights about the art and checked factual accuracy. I would also like to thank Ann C. Barnhart-Park, Trisha Brown, James Dean, Sidney B. Felsen and Joni Moisant Weyl, Bill Goldston and Larissa Goldston, Lisa Hahn, Barry Kew, Billy Klüver and Julie Martin, Gillian Malpass, Elizabeth McWilliams, Michiko Okaya, Nena Ossa, Jennifer Ozdoba, Darryl Pottorf, Katharine Ridler, Nancy Rothberg, Arthur J. and Barbara Rothkopf, Donald Saff, Robert Schulman, Mario Stein, Natalia Swiderska, Kenneth Tyler and Marabeth Cohen-Tyler, and my wife Elizabeth for her support.

introduction

Robert Rauschenberg is one of the most prolific and best-known artists of the post-war period. Both the quantity and variety of his works, created over a fifty-year career, are astonishing. For example, the final American exhibition (1991) of the artist's ambitious Rauschenberg Overseas Culture Interchange (ROCI), consisting of works made in eleven countries, filled all of the East Wing of the National Gallery of Art, Washington, D.C. Rauschenberg's recent retrospective (1998–99), which was a selective look at his career, occupied the entire Solomon R. Guggenheim Museum in New York City, the Guggenheim's branch museum in SoHo, and an additional enormous space borrowed for the occasion, the Guggenheim Museum at ACE Gallery. Nearly five hundred works were included in the retrospective, and it covered over seven thousand linear feet of museum space. At the same time as the retrospective, Rauschenberg had exhibitions of his most recent paintings and prints, and a survey of his photographs at two commercial galleries in the city. The artist Jasper Johns, who is an acute commentator on contemporary art, once said, "Since Picasso, no one has invented more than Rauschenberg."[1]

The sheer volume of Rauschenberg's output is essential to his method of working and his core ideas about art. He believes in unfettered creativity, the importance of instinctive responses, and the power of the moment; censorship and editing are anathema to him. In terms of the critical appraisal of Rauschenberg's work, his enormous productivity has had positive and negative consequences. On the positive side, the quantity and variety of the art indicate the richness of his creative mind, his physical energy, and the enormity of his ambition. On the other hand, some observers are dismayed by the artist's refusal to refine ideas; they question how deeply Rauschenberg has considered the works, both in terms of style and content. Another practical problem raised by Rauschenberg's enormous output is that his individual pieces, or even whole series of works, rarely receive adequate attention. The artist has created so much, in so many media, that even extensive studies of his oeuvre, like the recent retrospective catalogue, give individual projects scant notice.

This book addresses the situations just described in that it features a limited number of Rauschenberg's projects, or ideas, which are investigated in detail. The selected studies approach is modeled on that used for "Old Master" investigations. In such books, the authors have realized that the literature on these artists is so extensive and issues involving their work so complex that focus on particular problems is advantageous.[2] In this book, by looking at a few Rauschenberg projects in depth, his working procedure and the reasoning behind his various artistic choices may be better understood. The specialized chapters allow increased insight into the manner in which Rauschenberg selects and prepares projects, the type of attention he gives them, and the permutations that the works undergo during their creation. The book investigates which ideas Rauschenberg rejects and why, how he uses assistants, advisors, and collaborators, how the pieces are brought to completion, and what are the effects of viewer responses to the art works. Not surprisingly, it becomes evident that Rauschenberg devotes more detailed attention to these undertakings than the literature has indicated and more than the artist himself sometimes cares to admit. Rauschenberg's attitude of laissez-faire creativity and total freedom notwithstanding, he is revealed as adhering to an underlying system of values, both in content and style, which rotates around beliefs that he has developed over his long career. The advantage of the type of investigation in this book is specificity, but the selected studies method also has its limitations. In concentrating hard on particular topics, others are necessarily neglected. One of the important features of the visual arts, and this is particularly true of Rauschenberg's work, is that multiple and even contradictory ideas can be embodied in the same image. Discursive language functions in a more linear fashion; one argument leads to the next and so on. In this study, significant aspects of Rauschenberg's career are highlighted, while others do not receive attention.

The book has been divided into five chapters. The first involves direct observations of Rauschenberg's studio and the ways that he works there. Rauschenberg's large, recently constructed studio on Captiva Island, Florida has been specifically designed to encourage his improvisational art form. Watching Rauschenberg create works provides insights into the chains of associations that lead both to the formal structure and subject matter. In the immediate context of his work space, Rauschenberg reveals the nature of his decision-making process, and this process in turn suggests types of interpretations that are relevant to his art. The first chapter also investigates the concept of lateral thinking and asserts that this mode of thought, which runs parallel to Rauschenberg's own intuitively developed working process, provides a further way to understand his art. Finally, the chapter discusses Rauschenberg's dyslexia and the manner in which this physiological condition has a profound effect on his art and his understanding of the world.

Rauschenberg's physical environment is essential for his art, and the second chapter places him in the context of downtown New York during the creation of his seminal Combines and silkscreen paintings in the 1950s and early 1960s. Using archival photographs, urban historical records, and such unusual documents as reverse telephone directories, which list the businesses surrounding Rauschenberg's various studios, the chapter argues that the Combines were strongly influenced by Rauschenberg's involvement in that multi-ethnic, working-person's neighborhood, where commerce was essential and both the energy and decay of modern industry were evident. At that time, the very existence of Rauschenberg's South Street neighborhood was being threatened by the high-rise buildings of urban renewal. In the face of those changes, the Combines and silkscreens are shown to constitute a plea for city-based and democratic diversity.

By the mid-1960s, Rauschenberg had turned his attention to international issues, and one of his primary interests – that has remained a career-long fascination – became space exploration. The third chapter shows the depth of Rauschenberg's involvement with this theme, which represented to him one of the primary accomplishments of humankind. While the chapter connects Rauschenberg to the popular interest in the "space race," it demonstrates that, far from simply aligning himself with prevalent American perceptions or being a pawn of NASA, as some writers have suggested, Rauschenberg developed his own ideas about space exploration. These beliefs include non-militarism, multinational efforts, emphasis on pure scientific research, connections with the history of human inventiveness, and positive interactions between space technology and the natural world. The space exploration works foster these convictions.

The first three chapters of the book deal sequentially with the artist's creative methods, his connections to the immediate environment (downtown New York City), and one leitmotif (space exploration) that has occupied him throughout his career. Another essential aspect of Rauschenberg's oeuvre is his attitude toward collaboration. Since his early years, Rauschenberg has utilized collaborators from a wide variety of disciplines, ranging from engineering to dance, to enlarge his vision and thrust him into areas he might not otherwise have considered. The collaborators also represent Rauschenberg's desire to involve as many individuals as possible in his art-making processes. Although Rauschenberg favors the term "collaboration," the major impetus in these relationships usually comes from him. The collaborators modify, often according to technical feasibility, his original ideas; certainly the engineers with whom Rauschenberg has worked would not call themselves artists. In contrast, Rauschenberg's relationship with Trisha Brown has been a true collaboration between creative equals. Chapter 4 investigates joint work on five dances that resulted from this twenty-year association. In addition, it traces Brown's and Rauschenberg's common roots to the seminal Judson Dance Theater during the 1960s. While Rauschenberg's dance activities – including choreography, performance, set design, costume, and lighting – have often been treated as peripheral issues in his art, they are actually central to the performance-based nature of his entire body of work. The chapter shows the incisive manner in which Rauschenberg understands Brown's choreographic principles and how Brown and Rauschenberg have evolved mutually through their interactions with each other.

The final chapter explores one of Rauschenberg's most politically charged projects, ROCI/Chile. In 1983, Rauschenberg formally announced at the United Nations the most extensive undertaking of his career: the Rauschenberg Overseas Culture Interchange (ROCI). Eventually, ROCI entailed Rauschenberg working for seven years in eleven different countries, many of which were underdeveloped nations. The artist explored each locale, met with local artisans, and produced a body of work in each that reflected his experiences. Rauschenberg's idea was to establish a greater degree of world communication through art. Perhaps the most controversial of Rauschenberg's venues was Chile. The artist travelled to Chile without fully realizing the degree to which the dictator Augusto Pinochet's repressive policies were tearing the country apart.

When Rauschenberg arrived in Santiago, as he recalled, "Armed soldiers were everywhere, and I was startled by the sounds of gunfire in the streets."[3] While greeted initially by officials from the government and state museum, Rauschenberg soon encountered students and political activists. He often met them secretly in church sanctuaries, where they told him of friends and relatives who had "disappeared." As a result of these experiences and against the advice of his staff, Rauschenberg went on his own to the outskirts of Santiago to photograph everyday life in the slums. He also made the arduous journey to Chuquicamata, 16,000 feet high in the Chilean

Andes. On the way there, he photographed the village life of the Chilean peasants, their folk art, and the natural beauty of the mineral-filled mountains. The copper mines located at Chuquicamata were both the mainstay of the Chilean economy and the location of some of the country's most abusive labor practices. Rauschenberg had himself lowered into a smelter where he photographed cascading sheets of molten copper, an experience he compared to Dante's *Inferno*.

From these experiences, Rauschenberg produced his Copperhead Bite works, a series of large copper panels in which disturbing, and sometimes beautiful, Chilean scenes are combined with tarnishes that have been splashed onto the surfaces as indicators of the artist's emotional response. These works express Rauschenberg's solidarity with the people, and the title of the series refers to a poisonous snake coiled and ready to strike Chile. Despite the controversial character of the works, Rauschenberg was allowed to exhibit them at the Museo Nacional de Bellas Artes in Santiago. Chapter 5 retraces Rauschenberg's movements through Chile during that dangerous period and provides the first detailed investigation of the Copperhead Bite series. Although the ROCI/Chile paintings have political connections not necessarily present in all of Rauschenberg's works, the artist's comment about them stands for his art as a whole and provides a raison d'être for this book. Rauschenberg called them "a needed window on the world."[4]

one   studio practices

I rely on intuition, and it's surprising how much sense there is in intuition.[1]

Critical approaches to Robert Rauschenberg's art have been widely divergent. There is little agreement in the Rauschenberg literature about an approach to his art that best mirrors the artist's own thought processes and working methods. The majority of commentators have viewed Rauschenberg's art as a random accumulation of unrelated objects and images, and the artist himself has encouraged such interpretations.[2] For the earlier writers, Rauschenberg was a symbol of the experimental character of the avant-garde. For them, the modernist proclivity to shock through unexpected effects reached an apex in Rauschenberg's work.[3] The corollary to their attitude was the belief that Rauschenberg's art had an instinctive and uncalculated character. It was not deeply considered or profoundly structured but rather randomly thrown together. As exemplified by Andrew Forge's 1972 monograph on the artist, many of these writers approached their texts in a manner similar to the way they perceived Rauschenberg's art. Their writings have a stream-of-consciousness quality and seem to consist of ideas casually pieced together.

In the more recent, so-called post-modern period, such interpretations of Rauschenberg have acquired renewed significance. For post-modern writers, Rauschenberg's use of found objects and images and the seeming disorganization of his works are benchmarks of the end of the avant-garde. For them, Rauschenberg's art signals the cessation of originality and uniqueness in art works. In their view, Rauschenberg's art centers upon the appropriation of already existing sources in varied combinations. Thus, Rauschenberg's art denies the existence of new and undiscovered content and techniques.[4]

During the 1970s and early 1980s, a third group of art historians took an approach that is diametrically opposed to those just described. Their methodology is based on traditional iconographic studies that claim to reveal a specific meaning for each item used by the artist within a given work. Led by Charles Stuckey's 1977 article "Reading Rauschenberg," these art historians have proposed specific and highly detailed interpretations of individual Rauschenberg paintings.[5] The centerpiece of Stuckey's article was Rauschenberg's painting *Rebus* (1955, private collection). Stuckey attempted to read the painting literally as a rebus, or a picture puzzle, which represents words or syllables by pictures of objects whose names resemble them in sound. For now, it may be said that the article reveals both the seriousness of Stuckey's attempt to interpret Rauschenberg and the profound problems with such a limited, one-to-one, exegesis of his work. Each one of Stuckey's image explanations is open to a variety of counterinterpretations and the final phrase, to which Rauschenberg's images supposedly add up, is mostly nonsensical. It seems very unlikely that Rauschenberg approaches his art in the didactic and literal manner that Stuckey proposes, and in fact Stuckey recanted this methodology in the 1997 Rauschenberg retrospective catalogue.[6]

Given such diametrically opposed approaches to Rauschenberg's oeuvre, it makes sense to try to gain a better understanding of the way the artist actually works. One basis for this understanding is an investigation of Rauschenberg's procedures in the studio and the nature of his working habits. From these observations, it is possible to establish some fundamental ideas about Rauschenberg's creative means and how his mind works. This chapter investigates Rauschenberg in the studio. In addition, it discusses the concept of "lateral thinking" as a parallel to Rauschenberg's mental procedures and as a way of further analyzing his creative methods. Another essential aspect of Rauschenberg's mental make-up will be explored, his dyslexia. This condition has a profound effect on the way Rauschenberg perceives the world and on the manner in which he re-creates these experiences in his art. As a whole, the chapter attempts to grasp more fully the mental states and creative modes that are the foundations for Rauschenberg's art.

The discussion of Rauschenberg's working procedures is based on three days spent with the artist in his Captiva Island studio in 1993. During that period, Rauschenberg was engaged in creating a series of works titled *Scores (Off Kilter Keys)*. Several of these pieces will be investigated in some detail. In addition to this period of observation, both published descriptions and filmed versions of Rauschenberg at work were consulted in order to enlarge, verify, and refine first-hand observations.[7]

×　　　×　　　×

The *Scores (Off Kilter Keys)* (fig. 1) were the first extensive series that Rauschenberg created in his new studio in Captiva. The manner in which he organized both his earlier studios and this one provides essential information about his working methods. In the late 1960s, Rauschenberg purchased a house on the island of Captiva, Florida. The last and best-known of Rauschenberg's New York studios is the former orphanage on Lafayette Street near Astor Place that he acquired in 1965. That building remains the base of Rauschenberg's New York operations, including living quarters for his visits to the city, exhibition spaces to study new and earlier works, offices, and archives. Since 1970, however, Rauschenberg's works have been largely created in Captiva. Rauschenberg left New York partly from a feeling of social malaise and a desire to renew contact with the natural world that was a common occurrence during the late 1960s.[8] He had made several trips to Florida in the two years before his move and on each trip felt that something magical happened. He has recalled:

> I started all these various trips down the East Coast . . . Every time I got to Captiva something very beautiful would happen. Some mind-boggling things – like having to throw on my brakes to avoid turtles crossing the road. It's not like that here now. I have the only jungle left on the place because everything else is developed.[9]

Captiva is a slender barrier island located on the southwest coast of Florida on the Gulf of Mexico. The narrow spit of land extends six miles to the north of its larger neighbor, the island of Sanibel. At the time that Rauschenberg moved there, the island was remote and largely unspoiled, containing fishing villages and a few vacation homes. The causeway had not yet been built connecting Captiva and Sanibel with the mainland, and people still had to take the ferry boat from Fort Myers to reach the islands. Captiva has a subtropical climate and its dramatic vegetation includes royal palms, giant schefflera, and Australian pines. The road along the island was a sand lane, and among the wild creatures that populated the area were manatees, dolphins, great blue herons, loggerhead turtles, and cormorants.

1 Rauschenberg in Captiva studio, Florida with *Scores (Off Kilter Keys)* (1993), photo by the author.

Today, on Sanibel, nature and human development crowd and compete with each other. One approaches the islands through highway construction, automobile congestion, and beach-wear shops with neon advertisements. Beautiful sea birds perch on rusted road construction signs with blinking lights on them. The sea mist gently envelopes a construction derrick near the highway. Crowds of beach-goers stand among the majestic royal palm trees. At the same time, Sanibel and Captiva are known for their pure white beaches, variety of sea shells, their game and bird preserves, and the light blue color of the shallow Gulf of Mexico. Forty percent of Sanibel had been set aside as a nature preserve by the illustrator J. N. (Ding) Darling. The contradictions that are found here between human development and the natural world, technology and the environment, do not disturb Rauschenberg. He has long been a strong advocate of balanced use of the islands so the natural habitats are not damaged, yet Rauschenberg believes that nature and human development must co-exist. He does not find that nature and technology are irreconcilable forces but believes that they can, when properly managed, reinforce each other. The search for a sympathetic relationship between technology and nature has been one underlying theme of Rauschenberg's work and, as will be seen in Chapter 3, is a dominant concern in his space exploration works.

The hot subtropical climate of Captiva suited Rauschenberg, who had been brought up in Port Arthur, Texas near the other side of the Gulf of Mexico. Shortly after moving to Captiva, he bought a second adjoining property in 1971 and turned the house on that land into a print atelier. Two years later, he acquired the house next door to his and, with the help of friends, converted it into a painting studio. The property currently comprises 35 acres and has ten buildings including a new residence, as well as houses for guests and assistants. The buildings include a small structure, the "fish house," built in 1948 by Ding Darling on pilings over water; the artist uses it as a private retreat. Its simple design set against the backdrop of sea and sky make it look like the images in some of Rauschenberg's most serene paintings,

and Rauschenberg goes to the "fish house" when, as he has said, "I have to be absolutely alone and surrounded by peaceful thoughts." The most recent addition to the property is an extensive new studio complex, which was designed by Rauschenberg and the artist Darryl Pottorf, who is Rauschenberg's studio assistant (fig. 2). The complex was conceived in 1991 and completed in 1993. This building is the culmination of ideas Rauschenberg has developed about his working environment that extend back to his first studios in New York during the 1950s. Its structural design and the way that the artist uses it add significantly to the understanding of his art.

While Sanibel is crowded with tourists, Captiva has become an enclave for the very rich, and huge mansions sit on lots that are only feet larger than the houses themselves. In contrast, Rauschenberg's land remains a hidden retreat at the end of the island. Despite the number of buildings on the property, Rauschenberg has kept the landscape natural, and thus his studios are surrounded by the indigenous jungle consisting of palm trees, sea grapes, and casuarina trees. The jungle is dense and grows up close to all of the buildings; Rauschenberg refuses to cut down trees even to yield a view of the water. The dirt road at the entrance is named after his cherished dog of the 1970s, Laika, who in turn was named after the first dog in space. One travels onto the property and through it via rutted dirt roads. Small animals run across these paths, and the immense palm trees tower overhead. The dominant impression given by Rauschenberg's Captiva compound is that the artist's building projects have not disturbed the natural environment and that Rauschenberg's cherished ideal of the co-existence between human beings and nature is a reality, at least here.

The new studio is an enormous structure, 17,000 square feet. From the outside it looks like the late International Style, and at the same time its form of architecture has some connections to the simple proportions of Spanish-American buildings whose roots can be traced to Florida's colonial past. The influence of Rauschenberg's friend, the architect Renzo Piano, is also apparent. Clear geometry, forthright use of materials, open interior space, and particularly the sensitivity to lighting conditions

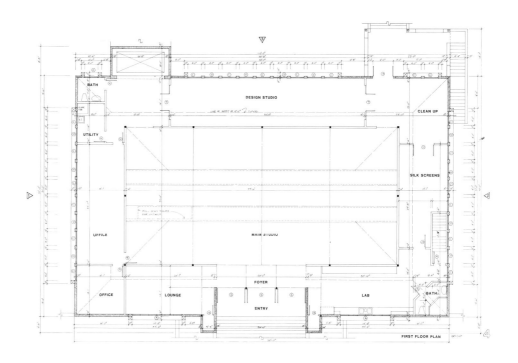

in the interior resemble Piano's De Menil Collection gallery and the Cy Twombly gallery in Houston. The steel structure of the studio is covered in white stucco, while the steel sheeting on the roof remains exposed. A hip roof at the center is surrounded by multiple, single-pitch roof lines, and the building extends outward in varying trapezoidal shapes that indicate on the exterior its various work areas. One climbs two short flights of stairs to the monumental entrance, which extends twenty feet from the body of the building. It consists of a square portico whose interior walls slope inward toward the glass doors leading into the central work room of the studio. Turning around, one looks to the "fish house" on stilts in the water and toward the gulf beyond.

Despite the studio's scale – Rauschenberg's assistants call it the Taj Mahal – and the complexity of its systems, this new atelier is actually a culmination of studio arrangements that the artist has developed over many years. Understanding the layout of the studio and the manner in which it is used yield clues to Rauschenberg's working methods (fig. 3). The largest and most important space in the building is the main painting room at its center. This space is an enormous 80 feet long and 40 feet wide; it is 30 feet high, culminating in a pitched roof that is ringed by skylights. The space itself encourages epochally scaled works. The interior is all white, and the steel beams that support the roof and tie the structure together are exposed. Above these beams, one looks up to the full height of the pitched roof. This room, like the whole building, emphasizes structural clarity.

Nearly all of the wall space of the enormous central room is reserved for hanging works, and natural light is provided by the clerestory windows ringing the roof. Because of the angle at which these windows are set, they largely reduce the effects of direct light from the hot Florida sun, and there is also a ring of track lights. As mentioned earlier, a view to the outdoors is provided through the entrance to the structure, whose deep portico also avoids the effects of direct sunlight. The central studio room contains four flatbed tables on which the artist works. Each of these is

16 feet long and 8 feet wide and results from combining four smaller metal tables and attaching a continuous flat linoleum surface. (This unbroken absolutely smooth surface is essential for the execution of Rauschenberg's silkscreens.) All of the tables are on rollers so that they can be easily moved about the studio. Flexibility of design is a keynote of the studio as it is generally of Rauschenberg's work. In addition to the tables, there are four large metal rolling racks which contain holders for brushes and approximately forty bottles of acrylic paint arranged in tiers on each rack. The paint itself is placed in chromatic order, and each bottle is numbered for identification. The colors are the intense hues that Rauschenberg favors in his work, and many of them are mixed by the paint company to Rauschenberg's specifications. The studio also contains a large-screen television that is usually tuned to news shows, documentaries, or the artist's favorite soap operas as he works. The television provides one way that Rauschenberg brings the outside world into his studio. He thrives amid distractions, and it is noteworthy that though he seems to be using the television only as background noise he can give, at any point, fairly detailed accounts of the shows. Rauschenberg's mind works in such a way that he characteristically divides his attention between many tasks.

The first element that stands out about the central studio is its size. On the whole, Rauschenberg prefers large-scale works, so that each piece creates its own environment. He thinks of this scale as being related to the energy of modern life. The sheer size of the studio space not only allows the artist to work big but it encourages him to design works on a monumental scale. In the central studio room, Rauschenberg can work on multiple pieces at once: all four tables may be filled with projects and other partially completed works can hang on the wall. The artist views his works as continuous and related experiences (fig. 4). He typically switches rapidly from one work to the next and often will repeat a successful motif in several works. The extensive wall space allows him to hang an entire series at once and thus to relate all of the completed pieces to ones he is still executing. These cross references between works are essential to understanding Rauschenberg's art. Thus, in this space, all the ideas for a series are available visually at one time for the artist. The immediacy of this information is essential for his working procedures.

An important issue related to Rauschenberg's desire to surround himself with an entire series of contemporary works is the fact that he keeps virtually no earlier examples of his art either at his studio or at his house. All series, soon after completion, are shipped off the island. Works not sold during an exhibition are stored in New York. When asked about this practice, the artist indicated that he found the past inhibiting. He said, "What interests me is the here and now." He took me by the shoulders and continued, "Reality is you and I here at this moment."[10] Rauschenberg's focus on the present is a key feature of his creative attitude. He views his concentration on contemporary events, his response to new materials and situations, and his interest in instinctive responses as ways of avoiding repetition and conformity in the work and keeping the work alive to new occurrences. Rauschenberg is constantly redefining himself through his works and in relationship to new experiences. His art does not plumb the depths of personality but instead responds to constantly changing exterior events.

Two other aspects stand out about Rauschenberg's main studio room. One is his interest in lighting conditions. The space has been painstakingly planned so that both daylight and artificial illumination can be carefully controlled and varied. The artist spoke repeatedly and with great sensitivity about the subtle play of light and shadow over the *Scores* as viewed at different times during the day and night. The neatness and careful organization of the studio is also notable. While Rauschenberg deliberately creates an impromptu appearance to much of his work, his approach to the creative process is methodical, and earlier commentators on his studio practices have confirmed this.[11] The studio itself is extremely clean, with all surfaces carefully arranged for the day's work, and completed or partly completed works are carefully hung. The rolling racks for paints, brushes, and other tools are arranged so that colors are instantly available. It appears essential to Rauschenberg's creative method that he has organized all aspects of the studio to foster the easiest possible access to materials and tools and thus to make "spontaneous" creation more possible. While seemingly a paradoxical situation, the studio organization actually makes practical sense. The artist said of his studio methods, "Everything I can organize I do, so I am free to work in chaos, spontaneity, and the not yet done."[12] Thus Rauschenberg's main working space is geared to large pieces, to the interrelationship between different pieces, to the movement of the artist from one piece to the next, and to the rapid access to materials and implements.

The subsidiary rooms surround the main area and support its function. These include machine shops, storage areas for silkscreens, a packing and shipping zone, a washing room to clean the silkscreens, a computer room, a small gallery, and kitchen. The main studio is actually on the second floor of the building. The first floor, which functions like a basement, is occupied by the machine shops, silkscreen storage, and packing areas. The machine shops are extensive. Wood, aluminum, steel, and plastic can all be worked. Both arc and acetylene welding are done there and large cutting and finishing machines for all these materials are present. Rauschenberg currently has three full-time artist technicians employed in the machine shops, and all of the highly finished aluminum panels for the *Scores* were prepared in these shops.

The machine shops allow Rauschenberg to realize even the most complex design ideas right at his studio. He has placed a premium on the promptness and efficiency with which his objects can be fabricated. With the aid of the in-situ machine shops, Rauschenberg can invent elaborate designs and count on their execution without becoming bogged down in the long construction process himself. For some artists, the execution of every aspect of their works from start to finish is essential, but for Rauschenberg it is an impediment to the speed and freedom of creativity. Since the beginning of his career, he has relied on technical collaborators to help with his projects. Later on, I shall discuss such examples as Rauschenberg's involvement with engineers during his Experiments in Art and Technology, his relationship with officials at NASA in his space exploration works, and his use of a team of preparers for the Rauschenberg Overseas Culture Interchange. Rauschenberg relies on his collaborators to provide not just technical solutions but also insights into the possibilities and limitations of materials that will often profoundly influence the outcome of the works.

Loading docks are connected to the machine shops via sliding steel doors so that works may be easily shipped from that area. As mentioned above, Rauschenberg makes a creative point of keeping nothing but the most recent work at his studio, so the immediate departure of finished pieces is not just a convenience but a necessity for the artist for his continued creativity. The lower level of the studio also contains Rauschenberg's silkscreen storage racks. The silkscreen process will be discussed later, but I note here that the screens contain photographic emulsion images that Rauschenberg transfers to his works. The screens are framed, and they range in size from 2 to 5 feet on their longest side. They are relatively delicate and are stored carefully on their framed edges in specially designed racks. Each screen is numbered and the rack slots have corresponding numbers for quick reference. Currently, Rauschenberg has about five hundred screens available. Most of their imagery comes from photographs that the artist has taken himself, and a majority of those photographs that he has recently used derive from ROCI. Thus they depict scenes from all over the world. The numbers on the screens are coordinated with books containing the photographs, arranged by the country in which they were taken, that are kept in the main studio room.

The connection between the studio above and the silkscreen storage space below is provided by a high-speed freight elevator. Rauschenberg's assistants emphasized

that a special high-speed unit was selected for the building. The arrangement of spaces allows Rauschenberg, when working in the studio, quickly to thumb through his reference photo books and select an image he wishes to include in a work. He gives its number to an assistant who goes immediately to the storage racks to find the corresponding screen which can be rushed to the artist on the fast elevator. This systematic approach permits the artist to work as swiftly and as instinctively as possible.

On the main floor, the central studio is ringed by support facilities one of which is a washing room for the silkscreens. In order to be re-usable, the screens must be cleaned immediately after use. The acrylic paint is washed out of the pores of the screens using high-pressure hoses. For this purpose, Rauschenberg has constructed a tiled room thirty-foot square with four pressurized hoses and sizable floor drains. Thus the screens may be cleaned for immediate re-use with a different color on another work or returned to storage. The main floor also contains an elongated corridor that is used as a gallery to hang smaller works and thus to experiment with their arrangement for future exhibitions. There is also a galley kitchen.

Rauschenberg and his assistants will spend up to twelve hours in the studio, and they can prepare meals as they work. Conviviality and even playfulness are essential to Rauschenberg's working method and to his relationship with his assistants. The helpers are all relatively young and most are aspiring artists themselves. Many of them come from nearby areas, and a number of them have studied at the University of Southern Florida which has a strong art program. Rauschenberg has worked with the core group of helpers for several years so there is an easy familiarity. In addition, during a night of work, former assistants and close friends will stop by the studio. Far from disturbing the artist's concentration, they seem to add to his creative energy (fig. 5). There is a constant running banter between Rauschenberg and the assistants, jokes are exchanged, small talk made, and amid all of this seemingly unrelated activity ideas about the works are generated. At the same time, there is much efficiency in the manner that the assistants work with Rauschenberg. They seem to be able to anticipate his requests and to keep his creative process moving smoothly.

Each assistant is familiar with a variety of the different techniques and materials that Rauschenberg uses including metal fabrication, silkscreening, computer imaging, and electrical wiring. When Rauschenberg comes up with a new idea, they eagerly research the possibilities for its execution. Over his long career, Rauschenberg has also developed an extensive network of specialists in a wide variety of fields who are more than keen to investigate technical solutions to his ideas. By picking up the telephone, he can often start a process of research into materials and techniques that will be critical to the execution of a work.

Another important room in the studio complex is an extensive computer facility with a mainframe, six terminals, and a number of printers, including a recently invented Iris unit. So far, Rauschenberg has shown no particular interest in operating the computers, but their possibilities greatly interest several of his assistants. Currently, the assistants are digitalizing Rauschenberg's photographs using a flat-bed scanner. This process has produced some surprising results, and such surprises through the use of new technologies have always been a mainstay of Rauschenberg's work. At the same time that the *Scores* were being created, Rauschenberg's assistants began printing some of his digitalized photographs on the Iris printer. This device allows color prints of the photographs to be made on a scale up to five feet. Immediately, the artist liked the grainy character of these large prints which fell somewhere between photographic realism and abstraction. Initially, Rauschenberg had several prints interspersed and overlapped on a single sheet of paper, but he later discovered that dyes used by the printer were vegetable-based and thus water soluble. From this information, he developed the idea of re-working the photographic images with water and brush, essentially treating the prints like watercolors. This discovery has yielded some fine works that combine the grainy photographic images with personal hand-worked surfaces; they are in some respects large-scale heirs to Rauschenberg's transfer drawings of the 1950s and 1960s. There is a powerful and interesting interaction in these recent works between the gritty realism of the photographs and the rich sensuality of their hand-painted surfaces. Since the visit to Rauschenberg's studio being described here, such digitalized reproduction and transfer methods have become as frequent as silkscreening in his works.[13]

Structurally, the most unusual aspect of Rauschenberg's new studio is that it is intended to withstand the direct impact of a hurricane. The building is supported on steel pilings that are sunk deep into the subsoil of the island. The upper floor is constructed with heavy-gage metal walls. By contrast, the walls on the bottom floor are very thin. The idea is that, as water surges over the island, these bottom walls would be knocked out, and the water would pass without resistance between the massive piers of the building. The machine shop would be lost, but the structure would survive. Rauschenberg has even spoken of weathering a hurricane in the building. In an emergency, leaving Captiva via the narrow bridge connecting it to Sanibel would be very difficult. The studio has its own emergency electrical generator and might provide a safer refuge than being caught while trying to evacuate to the mainland.

Rauschenberg's new studio may be intricate but it is basically an elaboration of the way he has organized earlier studios. The first studio that he built in Captiva, dating to 1970, is an elongated two-story structure, which in turn is based on the lofts he occupied in New York City. In the earlier Captiva studio, the art works were made in a rather large (30 × 40 feet) continuous space on the second floor. Silkscreens were washed on an open porch at the end of the studio, and the machine shop was directly below on the first floor. The major advantage of Rauschenberg's new studio is the efficiency it allows him while working. The entire configuration has been carefully calculated to enhance the artist's methods. Rauschenberg's creation of the *Scores (Off Kilter Keys)* exemplifies the manner in which he uses this new studio and reveals some of his artistic procedures.

*　　*　　*

Some general comments on the *Scores* are in order. The series consists of twenty-five large silkscreen paintings on aluminum panels that Rauschenberg created during the fall and winter of 1993, and the works were exhibited in the Leo Castelli Gallery in New York during the spring of 1994. The series was extensive enough that Castelli utilized both his West Broadway gallery and a space on nearby Thompson Street. The individual *Scores*, which are titled by Roman numerals, are all quite large, the most sizable being six by fourteen feet. All of the works in the series consist of multiple aluminum panels cut in various geometric shapes and attached together. The panels are hung on the wall and project outward from it in various three-dimensional configurations. Each of the panels has an ivory-white enamel surface that has been sprayed onto the metal panels. In each, some of the panels are filled or partly filled with painted silkscreen images, and others are left white. During his career, Rauschenberg has frequently created works that both hang on the wall and project from it. His most celebrated art works, the Combines of the 1950s, often did precisely this. For Rauschenberg, such creations stand between the two-dimensional character of painting and the three-dimensional nature of sculpture. As suits Rauschenberg's drive for inclusiveness, they break traditional boundaries between these types of art. More importantly for the artist, the works extend assertively into the viewer's space, and they thus engage the viewer more actively with them.

Within the limitations of the *Scores'* geometric design, it is surprising how varied they are. For instance, number XVI (see fig. 13) consists of four surfaces connected in an X configuration projecting off the wall. Its white sides face outward and the rear sides of the X are covered with silkscreen imagery. The viewer has to stand beside, not in front of, the work to see this imagery. Number xiv consists of three trapezoidal panels joined together and set vertically into the corner of the room so that it forms an irregular vertical pier rising in that corner. All exterior surfaces are covered with painted silkscreen images. One example is a large flat panel with a projecting trapezoidal box in its center, another is a horizontal three-sided polygon, and so on.

Rauschenberg often begins a series of works with a single general idea; the concept is then expanded and modified as the series proceeds. The underlying notion for the *Scores* is that the spectator must move around each work to see all of it. The viewer's movements determine how much is seen and in what order, so that the viewer creates her individual impression of the work. Rauschenberg's idea of allowing the viewer to engage with the works while at the same time maintaining the integrity of his original creation is a delicate balance that the artist seeks in his most successful pieces. None of the *Scores* can be viewed wholly from a single point in space or at a single moment in time, and a number of the works reveal particular surprises in the dramatic contrast between white and colorful, image-filled panels as one moves around them. Rauschenberg originally intended much more of the surface area of each work to be covered with silkscreen painting, and the reasons why he changed his mind will be explored below.[14] In any case, Rauschenberg actively encourages the viewer to become part of the work and thus to "finish" it through her physical interaction with it.

The idea of asserting viewer interaction relates to Rauschenberg's interest in Marcel Duchamp, and to his friendship with both the composer John Cage and the painter Jasper Johns, all of whom have engaged in related practices. In a variety of creative manners, Rauschenberg has sought throughout his career to activate viewer involvement. A few examples include *Charlene* (1954, Stedelijk Museum, Amsterdam) in which the umbrella attached to the surface was originally intended to be spun, *Interview* (1955, Los Angeles Museum of Contemporary Art, The Panza Collection) in which the doors may be opened and closed to reveal art works by Rauschenberg and other artists, *Black Market* (1961) in which spectators were encouraged to remove and replace the objects in an open briefcase, *Soundings* (1968, Museum Ludwig, Cologne) in which the sounds and illumination of chair images on plexiglass panels are determined by the noises viewers make as they pass by the piece, and the *Bifocals* series (1982) that contains different images on opposing sides of the works. More recently, Rauschenberg has created *Synapsis Shuffle* (2000, Whitney Museum of American Art, New York), consisting of fifty-two panels that selected viewers will be invited to arrange in different orders (like shuffling a card deck) for varied exhibitions. Thus, the work is intended to reveal something of the viewers' aesthetic sensibilities as well as those of the artist.

Like the interactive and fluid situations mentioned above, even the title of the *Scores (Off Kilter Keys)* series has varied meanings. As Rauschenberg utilizes visual puns throughout his work to enlarge their suggested content, so he prefers titles with multiple connotations. To score relates to getting a goal in sports, and I shall show that Rauschenberg loves the action-filled character of the various sports that appear with frequency in his art. To score is also a slang term for sexual activity; the vitality and energy of sex is a recurrent theme for the artist. The most direct and obvious connection, however, with the title *Scores* is a musical score, and the subtitle *Off Kilter Keys* refers to piano keys and simultaneously to the irregular geometric shapes of the works.

The historical connections between modern art and music are extensive. As one single significant example among many possibilities, Wassily Kandinsky's seminal *Improvisations* and *Compositions* were thus titled so as to make clear their connections to the abstract qualities of music. Rauschenberg has had a long interest in music and has stated his belief that "art like music should happen through time."[15] This statement reveals his belief that art consists of a relationship between the work and the viewer that unfolds over a duration, a principle that is at the heart of the *Scores*. While Rauschenberg was creating the *Scores*, he was in fact creating his first piece of improvised music on an electronic keyboard. His musical score was recorded and accompanied the performance of the dancer Trisha Brown's solo piece *If You Couldn't See Me*, for which Rauschenberg also designed the costume, as well as provided the suggestion that Brown dance the entire piece with her back to the audience. This dance and the other collaborations between Rauschenberg and Brown will be discussed extensively in Chapter 4.

The composer to whom Rauschenberg has been closest throughout his career is John Cage. The seminal connection between Rauschenberg and Cage occurred at Black Mountain College in 1952. There, Rauschenberg created his most innovative set of paintings up to that time, the White Paintings, a group of works with uninflected white surfaces, and these in turn influenced Cage's important musical score *4′33″*. That composition consisted of the pianist opening the keyboard cover to signal the beginning of the piece and closing it to mark the end. The score consisted of the random noises made by the audience and the surrounding environment in the duration between those two events. As I shall show, Rauschenberg made a surprise decision to leave a large percentage of the surfaces of the *Scores* white, rather than painting silkscreen images on them. The title subsequently chosen for the series is a direct homage to his interaction with Cage and a reminder of his own early, important White Paintings.

*   *   *

Rauschenberg worked with his assistants on the shape configurations for the twenty-five *Scores*. His goal was to create a wide variety of surfaces that projected at multiple angles from the supporting panels so that the viewer would be encouraged to approach the works from different angles and would not be able to see all of the surfaces from any one position. After having made these basic decisions, Rauschenberg turned the actual manufacture of the panels over to his assistants. The aluminum panels were meticulously fashioned, attached together and sprayed with paint in the machine shop of Rauschenberg's new studio complex, the first large-

6 *Score XXIV (Off Kilter Keys)*, 1993, acrylic and enamel on aluminum, 96 $^1/_4$ × 206 $^1/_4$ × 31", collection of the artist.

scale project executed there. The color was carefully selected. Rauschenberg sought a color that would be reflective yet also contain the warmth that he prizes in the southern light of Florida. In fact, the artist originally contemplated calling the series "Ivories," a reference to the colloquial term for piano keys, because of the color of the panels.[16]

The manufacture of the panels took two months, and all were completed before Rauschenberg began to work on them again. This approach provided the artist with a variety of choices once he began to paint the panels – maximizing options is essential to Rauschenberg's working method. While the panels were being fabricated, Rauschenberg had little to do with them. He remained involved in other projects, particularly the large watercolors produced from digital photographs printed on his new Iris printer. On one level, Rauschenberg's absence from the manufacturing stage of the works is reminiscent of the traditional Old-Master use of studio assistants to fulfill the more mechanical aspects of a work's preparation. Rauschenberg's attitude, however, more closely reflects his belief in collaboration as an essential aspect of art making. Typically, he seeks advice and input at all stages of the creative process. In fact, with the *Scores*, the studio assistants made design changes in several pieces when the artist's models proved technically unworkable.[17] Rauschenberg readily and easily accepted these changes as resulting from the dictates of the materials which he considers an integral part of the artistic process. For Rauschenberg, such interaction introduces new ideas into the art and increases its freshness. He regards the technical problems that different materials present not as impediments but as inspiration for innovative solutions.

Once the manufacture of the *Scores* panels was completed, all of them were moved into Rauschenberg's painting studio. Rauschenberg had already spent some time surveying the panels and had four of them placed horizontally on the large tables so he could begin painting them. I accompanied Rauschenberg on the fifth of approximately twenty days that he painted the *Scores*. Rauschenberg arrived at the studio in late-afternoon in November.

Typically, Rauschenberg has more assistants in the studio than he physically needs to execute the works; this time he had five individuals with him. The additional people seem to contribute to the common energy of his creative process. The atmosphere became charged as Rauschenberg entered the studio, and he was clearly eager to get to work. Lights were switched on to augment the late-afternoon daylight and the television was turned on. Everyone began to talk more quickly. Rauschenberg gestured toward the different *Scores* that were completed or near completion and talked about their progress. Amid the light conversation and the jokes and drinks being poured, Rauschenberg walked quickly among the works and then began to spend more time concentrating on one particular construction. Slowly and perhaps unconsciously this one occupied his attention. It became *Score XXIV (Off Kilter Keys)* (fig. 6). Rauschenberg strode around the shaped panel, sizing it up with his eyes. He commented on the beauty of the piece in its pristine state, noting the fall of light on it from the windows above. He said, "Look at the colors of the shadows. It's so perfect that it is hard to do anything more to it."

This *Score* consists of four rectangular panels which abut one another. From left to right, the first panel is entirely flat. The second panel has an irregular three-sided polygon on its surface, and the third has a two-sided polygon. Both polygons run vertically the height of the panels. Laterally, each polygon occupies approximately one third of its panel. The first is wider at the top and tilts to the left. The second is wider at the bottom and slopes right. On the fourth panel a single metal sheet projects outward at a ninety-degree angle, while in the vertical direction it is also oriented toward the left. The flat surfaces of *Score XXIV (Off Kilter Keys)* are white but sections of the projecting planes had already been painted in single hues according to Rauschenberg's instructions. The polygon to the right features blue and red surfaces, while that in the center has a light red – almost salmon – color. The extended panel to the far right has one half of its inner face painted yellow, and the outer face is light blue. Rauschenberg stared at the panels and said, "They're like dancers." Then he added "Tall, graceful, female dancers." Such associations form the types of connections between abstract forms and concrete experiences in everyday life that the artist often makes; they are among the essential ingredients of his art.

Rauschenberg quickly went to the photographic file arranged on shelves along one wall of the studio. The file consists of approximately twenty ring-bound notebooks of black and white photographs taken by the artist. As mentioned earlier, the majority of these are from ROCI. This multi-country multimedia project absorbed

the artist from 1983 until 1991, when he traveled to eleven countries and made and exhibited works. (The overall concept of ROCI and one of these projects, ROCI/Chile, will be discussed in Chapter 6.) ROCI has provided a rich source for Rauschenberg's imagery. Several hundred of the photographs he took on those trips were selected to be turned into silkscreens, and each book contains the label indicating the country from which its photographs came. In ROCI, the photographs were used country by country as Rauschenberg executed works related to each area. Now, the artist feels free to mix the images from many countries in a single work (fig. 7). He believes that such a mixture is a continued realization of his dream of global communication through art.

Rauschenberg thumbed quickly and seemingly at random through the ROCI/America book; he did not follow a linear order as he went through the pages. As he did so, one of his former assistants, who had just dropped by, was talking of his recent wedding and laying out wedding photographs on an adjacent table. Rauschenberg glanced at these out of the corner of his eye when suddenly he came across a photograph in his file book of a cast concrete statue of Botticelli's *Birth of Venus* (after 1482, Uffizi Gallery, Florence). Perhaps the wedding photographs sparked a connection with the goddess of love. In any case, this concrete Venus represents precisely the use of the fine arts by popular culture that interests Rauschenberg. He did not object at all to the fact that one of the most perfected painted images of the Italian Early Renaissance had been made into a cheap garden ornament, rather he found her re-creation in concrete a sign of the coarse and humorous energy of popular culture, an observation that led him to photograph the cheap statue standing in front of a local shop. When the artist re-appropriated her into *Score XXIV (Off Kilter Keys)*, making comparisons to females from different parts of the world, he created the amalgam of high and low culture that is one of the touchstones of his art.

He called out the number indicated on the photograph of Venus, and his assistants rushed to the freight elevator to get the matching screen from first-floor storage. The screen arrived within two minutes. It is framed in wood, and about four feet square. By this time, Rauschenberg had already rolled over one of the portable racks with paint jars, brushes, and squeegees on it.

When the screen arrived two assistants carefully placed it on the far right panel over the section that had been painted yellow. Rauschenberg studied it intensely and adjusted its position so that only the part of the image with the concrete sculpture made contact with the panel. The screen was shifted at a slight angle so that the image complemented the irregular angle of the projecting polygon. Asked about his choice of the Venus and her placement on the bright yellow panel, Rauschenberg quipped "She's my dancing partner," and then added "She's trapped by her beauty, but we're going to make her modern and free her." Rauschenberg grabbed a jar of gray pigment.

With two assistants anchoring the screen, Rauschenberg applied the paint with a putty knife in heavy dabs on the upper edge, then taking a squeegee pulled it authoritatively down the surface in one smooth quick movement. The screen was lifted and the image of Venus emerged (fig. 8). Rauschenberg indicated that he wanted to apply the paint one more time to intensify the color contrast, and the screen was carefully laid down again. When it was lifted the second time he smiled, obviously pleased with the results. The sureness of Rauschenberg's hand is evident in these procedures. He knows exactly where he wants the image placed, which colors to choose, how much paint to apply, and the degree of pressure necessary to saturate the screen. To fade the image at its edge, his hand lifts at precisely the correct moment. During the time I watched Rauschenberg work with the *Scores*, no screen was rejected once it was chosen, and no image was wiped out once applied. Although Rauschenberg modifies the works with additional images and paint application, he seldom revokes a decision once it is made.

Looking at the Venus, Rauschenberg suddenly began to talk about his travels in Japan. She might have reminded him of the fascination with re-creating masterpieces of Western art in Japan. This Japanese predilection was the subject of the artist's humorous *Japanese Recreational Clayworks* of 1982, which he manipulated and added to images of famous Western art works that had been reproduced by a Japanese company in ceramic. Rauschenberg has made several trips to Japan, the first in 1964 as the lighting and set designer during the Merce Cunningham Dance Company's world tour. He has an instinctive fascination with Japanese art, and he is particularly interested in how the traditional culture has mixed with modern Western civilization. He finds nothing wrong in this mixture; in fact, he sees it as epitomizing the interaction of diverse societies in the modern world, an idea expressed throughout the *Japanese Recreational Clay Works*.[18] But for the moment, Rauschenberg was thinking about Japanese women. He said that while he was interested in their traditional rituals he found the restrictions put on women's behavior "very upsetting."

In the middle of this thought, Rauschenberg seized the ROCI/Japan book of photographs. He quickly found an image of geishas applying their make-up and

8   Detail of fig. 6.

9 *Happy Birthday Baby Leech/ROCI Japan*, 1984, acrylic and fabric on canvas with gold-leafed bamboo poles, rope, and straw brush, 116 × 137 ½ × 64", collection of the artist.

ordered the appropriate screen. Clearly, the discussion of female freedom and social confinement led him to think of this photograph. It is indicative of the way that Rauschenberg's mind works that he was able to remember this photograph among the dozens contained in the book. Rauschenberg placed the screen at the bottom left-hand side of the projecting left polygon. Interestingly, he chose to paint the screen in a somber black tone, as opposed to the colorful costumes worn by the geishas. If one comes upon *Score XXIV (Off Kilter Keys)* from the left side, one thus sees the geisha image and the Venus silkscreen opposed to one another. As mentioned earlier, one of the overriding concepts with the *Scores* is viewer position. The works all read differently depending on how one approaches them and the path in which one walks around them. In the ROCI series, the geisha photograph was used in *Happy Birthday Baby Leech/ROCI Japan*, 1984 (fig. 9). There, it provides a strong juxtaposition to the large colorful Japanese calligraphy taken from a fabric banner and the equally vibrant abstract paint marks by the artist. The geisha silkscreen is set near an image of floor-stand fans with price tags attached as seen in a store. Circular shapes are repeated from the fans to the rounded hairdos of the Japanese women. Their juxtaposition suggests that the geishas are also like commodities to be sold. The transferral of the geisha image to *Score XXIV (Off Kilter Keys)* demonstrates Rauschenberg's natural tendency to recall earlier images and to use them with related intent.

After silkscreening the geisha photo, Rauschenberg's mind again began to wander and the conversation was less focused. As he chatted, he pulled down the ROCI/Cuba book and began to turn its pages. Suddenly, he stopped at one of the photographs and said, "This is right."[19] The picture shows farm workers riding in and on top of an enclosed wagon of the type that might be used to haul livestock. Rauschenberg

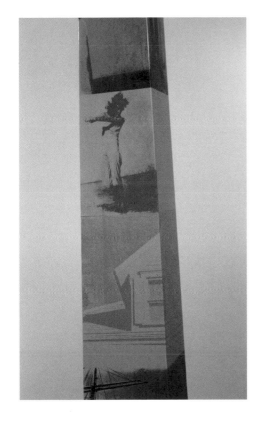

ordered this screen, it quickly arrived, and he placed it directly above that of the geishas. When the image is seen in its cropped state, the vertical slats of the wagon make it look like a prison – a theme that complements that of the "captive" geishas. The screen was then taken away to have its paint removed by the hoses in the washing room.

Directly after painting the screen of the farm workers and wagon, Rauschenberg went with deliberateness to a separate group of photo books and after ten minutes of searching found a photograph of Trisha Brown. The relationship between Brown and Rauschenberg, which will be discussed in Chapter 4, is extensive. They met and collaborated on projects associated with the Judson Church dance group during the 1960s. Since 1978, Rauschenberg has been chairperson of the board of the Trisha Brown Dance Company, and he has designed the sets and costumes for six of Brown's dances. For Rauschenberg, Brown epitomizes the modern, independent, creative woman. The photograph that he selected catches her in the middle of a powerfully extended gesture. The silkscreen, although not the largest in *Score XXIV (Off Kilter Keys)*, is the most dynamic because of its red hue (fig. 10). It is placed near the center of the composition on a diagonal line that leads from the geishas below to Venus above. Brown acts as an anchor for the different conceptions of women and enhances Rauschenberg's original observation that the panels of *Score XXIV (Off Kilter Keys)* look like dancers.

Rauschenberg was so taken with the photograph of Brown and its power that he immediately included it in two other *Score* compositions that were on other tables in the studio ready to be painted. Rauschenberg's re-use of the Brown image in several works allows the viewer to compare and contrast its meanings in different contexts. A visual environment filled with repetitions and variations in which the context of visual images is constantly changing is a significant part of Rauschenberg's world-view. Returning to *Score XXIV (Off Kilter Keys)*, Rauschenberg commented wryly that Brown needed "something to dance on." He selected a photograph of the dormer window of a house and had his assistants fetch the screen, which he painted in bright yellow pigment. I mentioned to Rauschenberg that in his watershed print *Autobiography* (1968), he depicted himself performing in the dance *Pelican* in a similar manner above the rooftops of Lower Manhattan. Rauschenberg seemed amused and remarked, "Well, artists should fly, after all."[20]

Rauschenberg had by then been working five hours, and everyone was tired. By consensus, he and the assistants decided it was time to go back to the house for dinner. There, the atmosphere continued to be festive, and more drinks were poured. Rauschenberg's main living quarters are on the second floor of the house he built in 1989 overlooking the Gulf of Mexico. The central room is about fifty feet long and is an unbroken space except for a galley kitchen at one end. Lengthwise, the room runs parallel to the coastline and beach outside, and it contains sliding glass doors and a porch that extend along its entire water side. From there, one can look beyond the lush green palms and other tropical plants to the beach and crystal blue water of the gulf. Rauschenberg's living space is sparsely decorated with an Oriental-like simplicity. Painted all in white, its furniture consists of only two white leather

11 *Score XVIII (Off Kilter Keys)*, 1993, acrylic and enamel on aluminum, 96 × 84 $^1/_2$ × 13 $^1/_4$", collection of the artist.

couches and a large white linoleum and metal work-table which can be used either for dining or as a place on which to spread out papers or small art projects. There are always fresh flowers, simply arranged, around the room, and it usually has a small selection of the artist's most recent works either hanging on the walls or standing on the floor. That night, Darryl Pottorf had brought fresh fish and started to cook it in a sauce that contained various tropical fruits and herbs. Rauschenberg, who loves to cook, eagerly began to cut mangos for the sauce. I talked with him of Trisha Brown. I had just seen a rehearsal of her dance *Set and Reset*, and I commented on the inventiveness of the dancers' moves. In Brown's piece, when one dancer contacts another, he/she sets that dancer into motion. I said that the dance reminded me of a wonderful, free-form machine. Rauschenberg responded that he thought that Brown sometimes regarded the body as a machine, and he believed this viewpoint allowed her to explore basic physical forces in a manner that avoided traditional dance choreography. Rauschenberg spoke of his own love for simple machines and of the inventiveness that is involved in making them. He reminded me that his favorite figures in history include the inventors Leonardo da Vinci and the Wright Brothers.

The conversation had significance; after dinner Rauschenberg returned to work on the *Scores* while I went back to my hotel. When I saw *Score XXIV (Off Kilter Keys)* in the morning, I noticed that Rauschenberg had added three silkscreen photos of bicycles on the outside of the right-hand panel. They complement the image of Trisha Brown on the opposite side of the central panel. (In *Autobiography*, Rauschenberg placed an upturned motorcycle wheel next to a print of his skeleton, suggesting the similarity between machine and body.[21]) In *Score XXIV (Off Kilter Keys)*, Brown's modernity is enhanced by the machines that surround her. Despite Rauschenberg's preference for Brown as the image of modern woman, *Score XXIV (Off Kilter Keys)* is not polemical. Rather, in keeping with the artist's viewpoint, it presents variety and alternatives to the roles for women in the modern world. It does not make judgments or propose solutions, and as a whole Rauschenberg's work concerns openness to new experiences, not imposed solutions.

The other part of the dinner conversation that was striking was Rauschenberg's poetic description of the white panels in the *Scores*. In subtle terms, he talked of different colors enhanced by the reflected lights and the shadows that fell across the panels as he and his assistants moved around the pieces in the studio. When I saw Rauschenberg the next day at noon, he had unexpectedly decided that much of the surfaces of the *Scores* should remain white. The decision came as a surprise to him because initially he had planned to cover most of them with silkscreen imagery. He said that only later had he realized that the white surfaces encouraged even more viewer interaction with the works because they were constantly changing in response to their environment and to the people who walked around them. As mentioned earlier, Rauschenberg's decision connected the *Scores* with his early White Paintings (1951) that featured entirely unmodulated white surfaces.

Over the next two weeks, Rauschenberg worked on the *Scores* in a similar manner. Extensive areas of white surface continued to dominate the works. Many of the *Scores* seem to revolve around an overall theme. For instance, *Score XVIII (Off Kilter Keys)*

(fig. 11) is a work with architectural associations – its two projecting polygons are like structural piers. The silkscreens chosen by the artist involve buildings. Architecture and the urban environment have long been essential themes in Rauschenberg's work, as shall be seen in Chapter 2. In *Score XVIII (Off Kilter Keys)*, old and new buildings are contrasted along with details of buildings that reveal varied architectural styles. An upper photograph of a steel-grid skyscraper under construction is set against a lower image of traditional stone ornamentation. Located in the center of the work is modern architectural decoration, featuring diagonal stripes on a building facade with an exotic palm plant in front of it. To the lower left, Rauschenberg

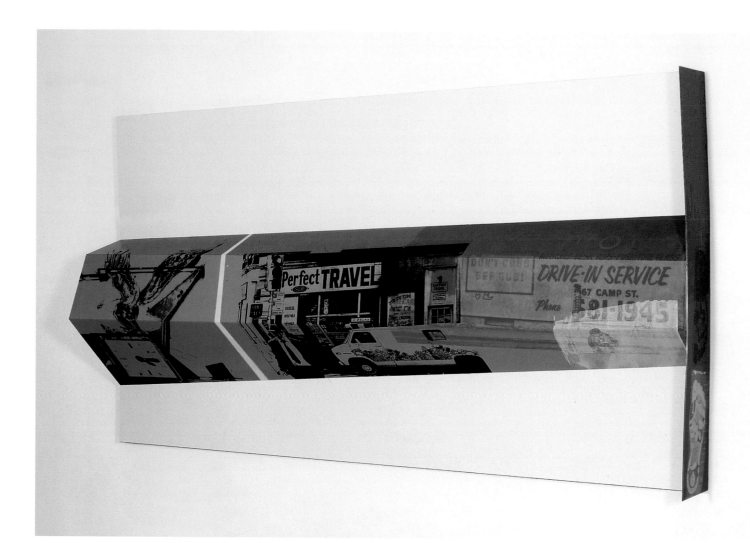

12 (*above*)   *Score XXI (Off Kilter Keys)*, 1993, acrylic and enamel on aluminum, 45 $\frac{1}{8}$ × 96 $\frac{1}{2}$ × 13", Private Collection.

13 (*facing page*)   *Score XVI (Off Kilter Keys)*, 1993, acrylic and enamel on aluminum, 60 $\frac{1}{8}$ × 84 $\frac{3}{8}$ × 47 $\frac{1}{4}$", collection of the artist.

painted silkscreen images of bricks to create a transparent cube. This cube, called the Necker Cube, creates spatial reversals. As will be discussed later in this chapter, such reversals are particularly difficult to resolve visually for someone with Rauschenberg's condition of dyslexia. The Necker Cube undermines the clarity that we sometimes associate with architecture and emphasizes the artist's interest in the urban environment as a fluid, changeable, evolving experience.

Score XXI (Off Kilter Keys) (fig. 12) consists of a three-sided tube-like form, set against a flat plane. The tube angles upward left to right and thus implies motion, which is also the subject of the silkscreens that have been painted on it. They consist of a photograph of a sculpted eagle (flight) above a clock (passage of time) to the far left, a store facade with the sign "Perfect Travel" in the center, and a sign for "Drive-In Service" to the right. Implied and actual motion have been leitmotifs of Rauschenberg's career beginning with his *Automobile Tire Print* (1953; San Francisco Museum of Modern Art) and *First Landing Jump* (1961; The Museum of Modern Art), both discussed in Chapter 2, and continuing through such works as *Revolver* (1967, collection of the artist), a work in which the electrically driven, circular discs actually rotate. In *Score XXI (Off Kilter Keys)* the suggested motion of the tube, however, is suddenly stopped in its tracks by a projecting plane on its right end – such surprising reversals are a theme of Rauschenberg's art.

The most spatially assertive is *Score XVI (Off Kilter Keys)* (fig. 13). Here, the four panels form an X configuration. Projecting outwards, it appears that the panels are flying off the wall. Facing this *Score* directly, the panels are pure white, yet the color is elusively modulated by the angular play of shadows caused by the protruding surfaces. Also, because of their angles, the planes do not read as rectangles but rather as parallelograms spreading like wings at their outer edges. As one moves around to the edge of *Score XVI (Off Kilter Keys)*, the silkscreen panels appear in vibrant green and blue hues on one side and orange and yellow hues on the other. On the left side, Rauschenberg has repeated the eagle and clock motif from *Score XXI (Off Kilter Keys)*. The spread wings of the eagle and the extended hands of the clock are like the X pattern of the overall work. The other silkscreen images include a variety of spatial systems – ropes, pulleys, scaffolding, high-tension lines, furled fabric secured with a knotted cord, and a curtained doorway. The movement suggested in *Score XVI (Off Kilter Keys)* is not the ground-driven motion of the previously discussed *Score* but that of flight. Everything in the work seems to soar, and one is reminded of Rauschenberg's career-long interest in flight, which extends from the photographs of parachutes in his early Combines through his space exploration works discussed in Chapter 3.

*　　*　　*

What conclusions can be reached from these observations of Rauschenberg's studio and his work on the *Scores*? Rauschenberg's studio building has been organized for maximum speed and flexibility in working procedures. The large, central studio room allows the artist to engage in projects of nearly any desired size and to surround himself with an entire series, creating an environment of related pieces. The support facilities around the studio room permit materials and tools to be delivered to the artist with maximum efficiency. His high-speed elevator for rapid delivery of silkscreens is but one example of the design. The extensive workshops that are part of the studio complex permit Rauschenberg both to work with a wide range of materials and to cut down on the time in which those materials can be assembled either by the artist or by his assistants.

Traditionally, Rauschenberg has created art works that are complex in terms of numbers of materials as well as the constructive process required to assemble those materials. Simultaneously, he emphasizes speedy, intuitive realization of his projects. The complicated assembly that many of his works require and the rapidity with which the artist feels he needs to work in order to keep fresh ideas flowing can counteract each other. Rauschenberg's new studio represents a concerted effort to accommodate these contradictory goals. Paradoxically, a good deal of organization is required for the artist to act in as intuitive a manner as possible. Corresponding to Rauschenberg's studio environment is his method of working. Rauschenberg deliberately courts spontaneous and reflexive modes to his art. This understanding of the world is grounded in his belief in the power of the present moment and in the significance of fortuitous occurrences, which keep his art open to fresh types of thinking and allow him constantly to reinvent his personality through the creative process. Everything that Rauschenberg does encourages such openness to unexpected possibilities. He chooses to work in a noisy, active environment with a great deal of physical stimuli present. At Captiva, his assistants and the televisions provide some of these necessary distractions. Rauschenberg tries to reflect in his working environment aspects of a world that is complex, intricate, and multifarious; it is a world in which we are continuously faced with many choices and alternatives rather than clear answers.

The artist lays out multiple works simultaneously so that he can switch from one piece to another in order to stimulate himself with fresh problems. The silkscreen process, as he has organized it, is a rapid way to produce a large number of images. Rauschenberg allows the more mechanical and time-consuming aspects of constructing the works to be done by assistants. He tries to execute the works in an off-hand, stream-of-consciousness manner. His dislike of too much planning, his refusal to keep earlier works at the studio, and the speed with which he works are all intended to encourage impulse in his work. Spontaneous visual associations are generated by the artist, such as those made between different roles of women in *Score XXIV (Off Kilter Keys)*. Casual remarks during conversation will often set the artist on a new direction, and stylistic decisions are made with even greater immediacy. The strength of Rauschenberg's working method is his ability to capture the surface of life in its constantly changing, faceted character. At the same time, Rauschenberg refuses to plumb the depths of thought, to engage in processes of elimination, and to make fine distinctions. He does not seek to hypothesize and synthesize in order to reach conclusions, and he is not interested in ordering information so as to categorize it. The artist's world-view is one of openness to change, uncertainty, and complexity, and his work is meant to foster this sensibility.

In a recent interview, Rauschenberg commented on the state of mind with which he approaches his work:

> There's nothing in my mind before I start to work. There is no pre-conception, there's no sense of something having to be of a certain quality. That's my adventure; moving into some unknown territory so I can surprise myself.

> It's not really specific or consciously done. I make a situation have as many possibilities as I can and things grow out of it.

> I'm after total involvement which includes all those things. I want to positively be a distraction, and remind people that there isn't really anything that should be avoided.[22]

*　　*　　*

Given this description of Rauschenberg's studio practices, it is appropriate to investigate general modes of invention parallel to his manner of thinking about his works. One further way to understand Rauschenberg's creative approach is to compare it to the concept of lateral thinking. The manner in which Rauschenberg encourages intuition in his studio practices is analogous to the type of thinking today labeled as lateral, which may provide a paradigm with which to grasp better Rauschenberg's art. Since the 1950s, lateral thinking, also called divergent thinking, has been accepted as an important way of generating new and unexpected hypotheses. Theories of lateral thinking were developed in the post-World War II education boom. They received additional emphasis during the early years of the space race. In that period, it was feared that America was falling behind the Soviet Union in education and in the development of new ideas for technology. The advancement of lateral thinking is thus coincident with Rauschenberg's own early development as an artist. The psychologist Edward de Bono has elaborated many of the concepts associated with lateral thinking and has been a prime advocate for this approach to thought process.[23] He has summarized the differences between lateral and vertical thinking:

> Rightness is what matters in vertical thinking. Richness is what matters in lateral thinking. Vertical thinking selects a pathway by eliminating other pathways. With vertical thinking one selects the most promising approach to a problem, the best way of looking at a situation. With lateral thinking one generates as many alternative approaches as one can.[24]

This initial description of lateral thinking is surprisingly close to Rauschenberg's modes of thought as exemplified in his works. The purpose is not to propose that Rauschenberg self-consciously uses lateral thinking – he does not. Rather, I am suggesting that the creative practices that Rauschenberg has developed instinctively might be better understood through reference to the concept of lateral thinking.

As evident in the above quotation, lateral thinking provides methods for generating options, making discoveries, using information in new ways, suggesting unusual associations and patterns of ideas, and opening new avenues of exploration. Lateral thinking proponents set it in contrast to vertical thinking which they contend is the primary type of thinking individuals are trained to accomplish in modern Western society. For them, vertical thinking is the result of an emphasis on the reasoned discourse that dominates the Western intellectual tradition. Vertical thinking attempts to assimilate new information into existing patterns and has a strong tendency to discount information that does not fit into those patterns. Vertical thinking is linear in structure, working from one assumption or fact to the next, and it is used to argue by negation, thus eliminating hypotheses that are viewed as inappropriate to a single solution.

Advocates of lateral thinking argue that this type of mental activity is difficult to assimilate because the mind is more easily adapted to vertical thinking than to lateral. They believe that individuals are more naturally inclined to refine concepts than to generate new ideas. For them, vertical thinking is characterized by the desire for strong patterning. Edward de Bono provides the most succinct list of patterning characteristics of vertical thinking, the opposite tendency to Rauschenberg's thought patterns. These begin with the notion of centering. In this process, successive strands of information are placed in fixed patterns. The next step in vertical thinking is assimilation. Through assimilation, new patterns of information are made to fit with existing paradigms. The third phase is fixation, through which patterns of concepts are used to reinforce rather than to alter existing ideas. Fixation is followed by linkage. In linkage, connections are sought between all patterns of thought. Wholeness is an essential component of vertical thinking, and parts of intellectual configurations are viewed as representations of a larger whole. Lastly, vertical thinking depends on sequencing. Patterns of thought are placed in temporal order.

The advantage of vertical thinking is that it allows the individual easily to assimilate new information. New facts and novel ideas are placed in the context of already existing exemplars. Information that does not merge easily into those configurations is often discounted as eccentric and not worthy of continued attention. Thus a strong and constant existing order is present which allows people readily to deal with the flood of new information which bombards them on a daily basis. The limitations of vertical thinking, however, are significant. The units and patterns of thought become rigid over time. There is a natural tendency for the thought configurations to become so strong that we alter new information to fit them rather than new information changing the patterns. In these situations, organizing models can become self-perpetuating myths, and we can fail to make any new observations except those that support existing ideas. In vertical thinking, time sequence can easily become too important. Information that is absorbed first automatically becomes the fundamental and most important data into which later intellectual events must be assimilated. In this case, it is difficult for all but the most persistent and startling new facts to have significance equal to early discoveries. Vertical thinking imposes order, but the order is likely to be traditional and even artificial rather than based on the most recent input of information.

Proponents of lateral thinking believe that, despite the tendency of most people to be vertical thinkers, all individuals have some ability and sympathy for lateral-type thinking. Two indicators of this tendency are our interest in the notions of insight and humor. On occasions, most people have felt excited when a tedious way of doing something suddenly gives away to a simple, elegant solution or when a vexing problem is suddenly solved by taking a new approach to it. The common response is "Why didn't I think of that before?" Humor is also a sign of lateral thinking tendencies. Humor involves a different way of looking at a problem. It is based on surprising "illogical" solutions to situations and dilemmas. The pleasure that humor provides, like the good feelings from insights, is that of a sudden and fortuitous discovery. Insight and humor, however, are considered haphazard by lateral thinking advocates, who attempt to provide a new methodology for intellectual invention. As is already clear from my discussion of Rauschenberg's studio procedures, insight is an essential part of his art, and humor is also an important component. In fact, over the years Rauschenberg has developed innately creative methods that allow inspiration to dominate his work to an extensive degree. The power of his art comes from his ever-changing responses to events and materials. In his art, Rauschenberg has emphasized invention, newness, surprise, and unfettered creativity.

Lateral thinking ought to be differentiated from its cousins "free association" and "automatism," which were cultivated as creative methods first by the Surrealists and then by the Abstract Expressionists. While Rauschenberg owes a profound and oft-noted debt to Abstract Expressionism, the difference between lateral thinking and free association tells us of the important differences between his mode of thought and that of his artistic predecessors. Free association is inextricably linked to psychoanalysis. The term became popular when Sigmund Freud claimed in his *The Interpretation of Dreams* that unforced remarks made by patients during treatment unwittingly revealed their wishes and motives. Free association was also used by Carl Jung in conjunction with his notion of archetypal images.[25]

In Abstract Expressionism, free association resulted in the creation of powerful symbolic forms that were repeated almost obsessively with only slight variation. One thinks of Mark Rothko's color fields, Jackson Pollock's dripped webs, Robert Motherwell's black and white Elegies to the Spanish Republic, and Willem de Kooning's *Women*. By contrast, Rauschenberg's lateral thinking is based on variety, change, and inclusiveness, which are among the leitmotifs of his art. His works attempt to capture what vision and thought apprehend on the surface of things rather than explore the depths of personality.

Rauschenberg has spoken adamantly about his attempts to negate personal psychology in his work. As an example, when discussing his Black Paintings of 1951 he commented:

> Lots of critics shared with the public a certain reaction: they couldn't see the black as pigment. They moved immediately into association with "burned out," "tearing," "nihilism and "destruction." That began to bother me. I'm never sure what the impulse is psychologically; I don't mess around with my subconscious. I try to keep wide-awake. If I see any superficial subconscious relationships that I'm familiar with – clichés of associations – I change the picture. I always have a good reason for taking something out but never a good one for putting something in. I don't want that because it means that the picture is pre-digested."[26]

In a manner similar to Rauschenberg's desire to avoid a pre-digested picture, lateral thinking is involved with rearranging available information so that it is snapped out of established patterns of thought. Lateral thinking counteracts the selective process of vertical thinking and deliberately brings about arrangements and juxtapositions of information that might not otherwise have occurred. Such deliberate variety is similar to that sought in Rauschenberg's art. Some general principles informing lateral thinking that are agreed upon by a number of writers follow.

Lateral thinking should generate as many alternative possibilities as feasible. While vertical thinking chooses between two alternatives, lateral thinking creates multiple options. Non-sequentiality is also an essential aspect of lateral thinking. The usual process of thinking is to move forward step by step. In lateral thinking, instead, one jumps into a problem at a different point or at several points and waits for them to suggest a linkage. In lateral thinking, one should attempt frequently to change the frame of reference. For the lateral thinker, it is often better to do something and then afterwards to understand what one has done. Lateral thinking should be concerned with undoing the selection process. In logical thinking, each step must be justified, otherwise it is blocked as a negative element. Lateral thinking does not seek justification; it breaks down patterns of selection. Lateral thinking also depends on rotation of attention. The lateral thinker changes the focus of his/her attention frequently and thus disrupts the sequential flow of thoughts. Methods include focusing on a seemingly trivial detail or refusing to focus consciously on any particular aspect of the problem. Another way for the lateral thinker to rotate his/her attention is through random input of information. For the lateral thinker, deliberate exposure to chance events or ideas from outside of the immediate problem disturbs existing patterns of thought and encourages new ideas and discoveries. The lateral thinker may also use reversals. In lateral thinking, a search for the polar opposite of an idea or problem can lead to new discoveries. Finally, cross-fertilization is an important concept for the lateral thinker. The lateral thinker seeks information from individuals and from fields of learning different from his/her own in order to spark new ideas.

These categories systematize procedures that Rauschenberg employs naturally in his art. Over years of working, Rauschenberg has developed approaches to his art that parallel those that the writers on lateral thinking have outlined in a more systematic fashion. In one of a number of statements about his creative methods, Rauschenberg has talked in a down-to-earth manner about some of the "tricks" he uses to foster surprise in his art:

> I have various tricks to actually reach that solitary point of creativity. One of them is pretending I have an idea. But that trick doesn't survive very long because I don't really trust ideas – especially good ones. Rather, I put my trust in the materials that confront me, because they put me in touch with the unknown. It is then that I begin to work . . . when I don't have the comfort of sureness and certainty. Sometimes Jack Daniel's helps too. Another good trick is fatigue. I like to start working when it is almost too late . . . when nothing else helps . . . when my sense of efficiency is exhausted. It is then that I find myself in another state, quite outside myself, and when that happens there's so much joy! It's an incredible high and things just start flowing and you have no idea of the source.[27]

Rauschenberg's studio practices, as I reviewed them in the creation of the *Scores*, exemplify the ideas of lateral thinking. He uses a wide variety of unusual materials, and his silkscreen images allow an extensive range of choices in imagery and style as well as speed of execution. In the *Scores*, aluminum construction allowed him to invent a variety of new shapes. The silkscreen procedures gave him immediate access to hundreds of images and the transferral of those images to the painted surface was nearly immediate. His new studio has been entirely designed to suit such speed and flexibility. Rauschenberg works in a non-sequential fashion around generalized themes rather than executing pre-determined ideas. The techniques that he has developed do not require him to work on the individual art works in any particular sequence and permit him to switch rapidly from work to work. As seen in *Score XXIV (Off Kilter Keys)*, the linkages that Rauschenberg employs are not linear but rotate around sweeping concepts. There, the dancer-like shapes of the panels led to notions of female beauty in the cement Venus, which in turn became associated with ideas of female roles in Eastern and Western cultures. These thoughts led full circle to associations with Trisha Brown. Rauschenberg does not censor or reason out such connections but accepts them as serendipitous events to be incorporated in the works. In fact, the artist cultivates the types of distractions that might lead to such new patterns of thought, and he tries to remain open to surprising discoveries. In the *Scores*, for instance, he was surprised both by his choices of individual motifs and by the overall look of the series after he had finally left so many of the surfaces white.

His decision to contrast the empty and image-filled surfaces of the *Scores* is an example of the artist working by opposites, as he often does, and it parallels the concept of reversals proposed by theorists of lateral thinking. Rauschenberg encourages random input that distracts his attention and introduces new and unplanned techniques into his work. Thus, the many assistants present while he works with their banter and even the television in his studio are necessary elements in Rauschenberg's creative activities. The fall of light on a work, a comment from an assistant, or something that appears on the television news can change the direction of a work. Rauschenberg deliberately cultivates these events; it is his way of letting the world into his works. In the studio, Rauschenberg alternates between intense attention and seemingly arbitrary changes in focus as suggested by lateral thinkers. In addition, throughout his career, Rauschenberg has connected his art to other disciplines. In the *Scores*, ideas from architecture, dance, social customs of other countries, and technology are explored. The manufacture of the *Score* panels themselves exemplifies Rauschenberg reaching out to other technical disciplines. Variations on the creative practices I discussed with the *Scores* can be found throughout Rauschenberg's career, and they inform his entire working method. Rauschenberg is a brilliant lateral thinker. His ability to generate alternatives, to arrive at unusual and surprising modes of expression, to be inclusive in style and content, is central to his art.

*   *   *

Rauschenberg's mode of creative thinking has been described as a procedure that is deliberately cultivated in his studio practices. It is probable that his creative method is also influenced by an innate physiological characteristic – dyslexia. Although his dyslexia is relatively common knowledge, it has never been discussed in detail in the literature on his work. If indeed dyslexia is an important factor in Rauschenberg's perception of his environment, it will provide a new baseline from which his art should be examined. In an interview during which Rauschenberg discussed printmaking, he commented:

> Well, that's what happens when you are working with a dyslexic, I already see things backwards! You see in printmaking everything comes out backwards so printing is an absolute natural for me. It is difficult for a lot of artists to do prints because they draw one way and can't imagine it another way. I always had trouble reading as a child. Every few minutes my mind would shift and I would pick out all the O's then all the letter A's on the page. I still have a struggle reading and so I don't read much . . . Probably the only reason that I'm a painter is because I couldn't read yet I love to write, but when I'm writing, I know what I'm writing;

when I'm reading I can't see it because it goes from all sides of the page at once, but that's very good for printmaking.[28]

One of the most interesting first-hand discussions of Rauschenberg's distinctive way of seeing the world is given by the dancer Steve Paxton, who was Rauschenberg's closest companion from about 1960 until 1970. It is worth quoting at some length:

> In 1961 in the bus as we traveled around [on the Merce Cunningham Dance Company's American tour], Rauschenberg said of himself, "I tend to see everything." This gnomic appraisal stuck in my mind. How would it actually work? In his paintings, he not only saw a lot of images, but he positioned them with passages of paint, which contextualized both, much as light, the weather, and the sky over a painted landscape interplays with the scene below . . . Seeing everything is different from the way we normally see. Our consciousness is usually focused on one thing after another. In reading, for instance, we focus on one section of words at a time. Seeing-everything reading, according to Rauschenberg, is to associate words with words all around them, instead of just the words on the same line. When I read linearly, I feel like a tape is passing by my focus. When I try to see everything, each paragraph becomes a shifting gestalt . . . Rauschenberg stretched us between an array of visual images and their multiple interpretations: so many kinds of invention occurring at once in this bus, as the culture rolled by, rather slowly.[29]

Dyslexia is a complicated condition, existing in many variations, and is still not fully understood by scientists. Most research on dyslexia concentrates on exercises to correct the condition rather than investigations of the manners in which a dyslexic person perceives the world. Despite the need for further research, a number of basic characteristics of the condition may be isolated, but first some common misconceptions should be addressed. While dyslexia is usually associated with reading difficulties, it also affects image perception and the perception of all representational systems, not just the written word.[30] Dyslexia is most evident in reading and writing because our written system requires a set of graphic signs whose rules do not allow them to be altered in orientation or position. In the rest of the visual environment, the dyslexic person usually learns to cope with visual disorientation much more easily.

At the outset, one should also note that, according to the most recent research, it is incorrect to think of dyslexia as a handicap. It is better thought of as an alternative mode of perception. It has been observed that if modern Western society had not developed its emphasis on writing, which involves placing graphic signs in a particular order, dyslexia might not be noticed and would certainly not require treatment. Some researchers have even suggested – and this idea is particularly germane to Rauschenberg – that in another type of society, dyslexic individuals would be highly valued. Their alternative modes of perception would allow them to see the world differently from other people, and thus they would be able to accomplish tasks that other members of the society could not execute.[31]

Experientially, if not scientifically, dyslexia has been connected with lateral thinking. In 1990, Priscilla Vail, one of the leading educators of dyslexic children, spoke at a national conference about the traits she found in such children.[32] Vail identified great curiosity as common among dyslexic children and stated that the curiosity often sprang from three-dimensional, hands-on experience. She noted that the same children may not be excited at all by verbal abstractions or analysis. Vail observed that, contrary to popular opinion, dyslexic individuals have great concentration upon tasks that interest them, but this concentration may be at odds with traditional schedules that allow limited and set-time periods for assignments. She stated: "Many dyslexics have a weak or absent sense of time; they may be literally atemporal when immersed in thought." Thirdly, Vail observed that numerous dyslexics have exceptional memories for experiential and emotional events while their memory for abstract rules, such as spelling or multiplication tables, may be very weak.

Vail found that dyslexics often display a "rapid grasp of concepts. They are able to find the solutions to certain types of problems so quickly that it often appears that the knowledge lies inside waiting to be awakened simply by being mentioned." At the same time, she noted, such a person may not be able to analyze how that insight was obtained. Vail's conclusion was that dyslexics are often divergent (lateral) thinkers. She said:

> Divergent thinkers who enjoy open-ended questions can tolerate the ambiguity of seeing things from several different points of view, and are happiest exploring questions that have no verifiable answers . . . Divergent thinking is the fountainhead, or wellspring, of barrier breaking questions and concepts. The dyslexic may abound in them but gets into trouble because of them.

Priscilla Vail speaks in the inspirational language of a dedicated teacher, yet her observations are based on decades of experience. Her comments form a parallel to observations of Rauschenberg at work in his studio and to an analysis of the resulting art. In the studio, Rauschenberg alternates between rapid movement from project to project and intense concentration on a particular work. His long work hours, which often run completely through the night, are indicative of his atemporal sensibility. Rauschenberg has a remarkable memory for specific images and a grasp of solutions to particular problems without an interest in underlying systems. His art relies on the capacity for sudden insights without investigations of how he arrived at these discoveries. In fact, Rauschenberg believes that such investigations would destroy the freshness of his art. Over his long career, Rauschenberg has developed creative techniques and an environment that support his physiological mode of perception. The success of Rauschenberg's solutions are noteworthy because Vail's positive observations are balanced by a number of studies on dyslexia and autobiographies by dyslexics themselves that describe in poignant detail their attempts to cope with a world that seems more disorienting to them than it does to other people. A well-known example, *Susan's Story*, begins, "One day I will take two right turns instead of left and become hopelessly lost for hours . . ."[33]

Rauschenberg also suffered psychologically as a child because of his dyslexia, which was not diagnosed until he was an adult. He told one interviewer, "I grew up being reassured everyday that I was inferior because of my dyslexia."[34] Rauschenberg was informed by his teachers and parents that his hardships in school were due to a lack of intelligence. But the artist also believes, in his own words, that his most creative work "may come out of my constructive insecurity. If you have nothing to lose, you can bring courage to your work naturally." Rauschenberg is unusual because he not only learned to cope with his dyslexia but turned it into a creative strategy. He developed his studio practices and the resulting art in such a manner that his dyslexia is related to his creative inventiveness. In addition, he uses his dyslexia to express the character of a confusing, volatile modern world. For all of us, modern life is marked by speed, sudden change, and complexity; we are bombarded by more information from more divergent sources than at any time in history. Rauschenberg has embraced these characteristics, which are highlighted by his dyslexia, and created from them art works that express a distinct characteristic of modern life.

The emerging scientific analysis of the visual world of dyslexics is beginning to confirm the experiential data of Vail and others. In an article on developmental dyslexia – Rauschenberg's type of dyslexia – Professor John Stein of Oxford University has written:

> The detailed studies of sensory and perceptual skills of dyslexics described earlier have really confirmed what many teachers and dyslexics have long suspected, namely that their perception is subtly different from the rest of us. When asked about perceptual aberrations many reveal strikingly more vibrant experiences than normal. Not only does the world seem to move around for many, but objects seem to dilate and shrink, sounds vary in loudness and tone and hands and feet may suddenly appear extraordinarily large or small.[35]

In 1966, the United States Department of Health and Education listing of the symptomology for dyslexia included: impaired discrimination of size, impaired discrimination of figure and ground, impaired discrimination of part and whole, impaired spatial orientation, and impaired orientation in time.[36] More recent studies have concluded that the effects of dyslexia may consist of spatial confusion, especially the orientation of oneself in relation to objects, the inability to rotate objects and easily recognize them, the inability to separate easily a central object from surrounding objects, and inability to judge accurately the position of moving objects.[37]

As to the causes of these visual effects, some of the most recent studies on dyslexia suggest that they are a result of difficulties in early visual processing. Tests on dyslexics seem to indicate that ocular motor control is compromised. Researchers have concentrated on the magnocellular division of the visual system, the division that controls eye movements. Difficulties with these motor controls prevent the dyslexic viewer from "fixating" on visual targets for a sufficient amount of time. The results are binocular instability when the eyes converge for tracking movements. This instability is particularly noticeable with objects in motion, complex visual environments, and complicated patterns like written letters.[38] One article concluded, "Objects would appear unclear and jumbled at least for the duration of the persisting image from the last fixation control."[39]

There are a number of specific features in Rauschenberg's art works that relate to the visual conditions of dyslexia. One of these is image reversal and rotation. Rauschenberg spoke of this effect in his statement about printmaking cited earlier, and the viewer need not look far among the artist's works to see how many images are altered in this manner, sometimes appearing in several different positions within the same painting. As examples, one might cite images of John F. Kennedy, right side up and upside down, as well as the parachute on its side in *Untitled* (1964, private collection). Other examples include the upside-down space capsule, statues of George Washington, and New York rooftops in *Skyway* (1964; see fig. 41), as well as the eagle on its side in the same work. Related to these rotations is the notion of image retention and identification. For all of us, these reorientations – as well as other changes, such as those in scale and color – make images look different. This is part of the visual excitement of a work by Rauschenberg, where a familiar object suddenly looks fresh and novel. The ability to identify objects when such changes as rotation, scale, and color occur is much more difficult for the dyslexic person.[40] Thus, these rudimentary changes would make each image appear just that much more unusual and thus more exciting to Rauschenberg. He has spoken about this effect when discussing his silkscreen paintings of the early 1960s:

> There's the same quality of surprise and freshness [in the silkscreen paintings] that I have when using objects. When I get the screens back from the manufacturer, the images look different from the way they did in the original photographs, because of the change in scale, so that's one surprise right there. Then, they look different again when I transfer them to the canvas, so there's another surprise. And they keep on suggesting different things when they're juxtaposed with other images on the canvas, so there's the same kind of interaction that goes on in the Combines, and the same possibilities of collaboration and discovery.[41]

At the same time that Rauschenberg clearly courts such visual variety in his works, he also employs designs so that their intricacy does not become overwhelming. In many of Rauschenberg's compositions the rotated images and objects are organized in a grid. Dyslexic individuals are typically taught to use horizontal and vertical axes as orientation devices to help them better organize information.

Another common perceptual condition of dyslexia is difficulty in figure–ground discrimination. One of the basic properties of vision is the easy ability to separate an object from its surrounding background. Such distinctions are much harder for some dyslexic people to make. In Rauschenberg's works figures and backgrounds are frequently allowed to merge. In his Combines, Rauschenberg either frequently over-lapped several objects or painted over and around objects attached to the surface of the canvas so that it is difficult to separate them from their surroundings. In silkscreens, multiple screens painted in different colors were overlapped so that their images merged. Sometimes the same image was printed many times, each in a slightly different position. These multiple registers both embed the images in each other and suggest movement that is confusing and uncertain in direction. The manner in which the newspaper advertisements and art reproductions are painted over in *Collection* (1952; see fig. 20) is an example of Rauschenberg's proclivity for embedded images. The mirror attached to the surface of *Collection* – Rauschenberg has included mirrors and reflective surfaces in many of his works – increases the spatial confusion. In *Trapeze* (1964, private collection), the multiple images of the parachuting astronauts suggest both dynamic and uncertain motion. It might also be noted that, spatially, one of the most difficult forms for the dyslexic person to resolve is the Necker Cube, a common illusional cube formed from twelve lines. Variations on Necker Cubes appear frequently throughout Rauschenberg's work, as pointed out in *Score XVIII (Off Kilter Keys)*, and another example is the four tumbling blocks in the upper right section of *Skyway*.

The dyslexic person often sees things in fragments. He/she has difficulty with what is called "selective attention"; peripheral stimuli are not easily separated from central stimuli. The great number of Rauschenberg's works that include dozens of images or objects within a single composition relate to this condition. Similarly, in Rauschenberg's works visual hierarchy is avoided. Most objects and images seem to vie with each other for the viewer's attention. Such a sense of complexity and confusion in the visual environment is part of the dyslexic person's experience. Also, a short attention span is common among dyslexic individuals, often coupled with its opposite – obsessive attention to particular details. My observations of Rauschenberg's studio practices, as well as earlier records of him in the studio, indicated the speed with which he executes works and his uncanny ability to have several works in progress at the same time, switching attention from piece to piece.[42] As an opposite response also common to dyslexics, the artist often loses track of time, becoming highly focused and lavishing attention on the smallest details of a work.

There is strong evidence that Rauschenberg's dyslexia has an important effect on his art. Essential aspects in the appearance of his art and his studio practices parallel both the experiential and scientific discussions of dyslexia. While most dyslexic individuals have struggled with their condition as they have attempted to assimilate themselves into a society that has little tolerance for such a state, Rauschenberg seems to have turned his dyslexia to his advantage. If the connections suggested by educators, like Priscilla Vail, between dyslexia and lateral thinking are correct, Rauschenberg displays the gifts of a lateral (divergent) thinker. He has the curiosity to pursue open-ended questions and the ability to present a wide variety of creative responses, and his art is expansive rather than limiting. The other side of dyslexia, the inability to read well, some confusion in the visual environment, and difficulty in cases where systematic order is required, should prove a detriment. But the artist seems to have turned these aspects to his advantage. Not only has he pursued a profession where reading skills are less important but he has also created a studio environment where the negative effects of dyslexia are minimized. Even more significantly, Rauschenberg has communicated the disorientation that results from his dyslexia as a sign of the intricacies of contemporary life.

This preliminary discussion of Rauschenberg's studio procedures and the suggestions about his modes of thought provide some guidelines for interpreting the artist's works. Rauschenberg's art works revolve around general themes and subjects. These themes are loosely conceived and often modified in the process of creating the work. Not every item in a given work fits with an overall idea, and his works are full of free-flowing and overlapping references that interrupt one another. The images in his work are not random, but neither is there a deeply worked out, complex and/or hidden iconography. Rauschenberg's greatest strengths are his instinctual responses to images, materials, and formal structures as well as his ability to absorb the complex surface of life. His works are best seen in the context of the exterior events that surround him, something the literature on him does not sufficiently emphasize. As a whole, Rauschenberg has aimed at a public, not private, language. He may use a personal incident as the beginning point for a work, but his intent is not to reveal his intimate history in a personal or expressionist manner. His desire is to provide information that connects to our everyday experiences. The images that Rauschenberg paints are mostly common, and their commonality makes them powerful because they lead us to rethink familiar visual experiences and to question long-held assumptions.

The procedures that Rauschenberg follows in his studio provide information about how the artist approaches his works and the type of mental and physical procedures that he goes through in creating them. Lateral thinking contributes a model that has useful parallels to the way that Rauschenberg works, and it allows us to conceptualize his process. Rauschenberg's dyslexia may provide one essential clue to the way his mind works. Yet the artist has communicated his personal condition in a universal manner that informs, to some extent, the way that all of us view the world. A next step in understanding Rauschenberg is to place him and his art in a specific environment; the milieu is New York City during the 1950s and early 1960s. That locale is an essential factor in understanding the formation of Rauschenberg's art.

two urban experiences

An extremely complex random order that cannot be described as accidental.[1]

Robert Rauschenberg is an artist whose work is conditioned by his immediate surroundings, and the single greatest influence on his works during the 1950s and early 1960s was the chaotic, culturally diverse, and volatile urban atmosphere of Lower Manhattan, where the artist lived during most of those years. From 1953 through 1960, Rauschenberg occupied three nearby addresses adjacent to and in the South Street area of Lower Manhattan, and in 1960 he moved to 809 Broadway just below 12th Street.[2] The visually agglomerated South Street environment encouraged Rauschenberg's inherent view that modern experience existed in conditions of constant change and led him to view downtown New York City as a paradigm of the heterogeneity present in twentieth-century life (fig. 14).

During the 1950s, the South Street area underwent a series of urban crises, to which Rauschenberg's art responded. At that time, Lower Manhattan had only 4,000 residents while its daytime working population swelled to 40,000, and the older South Street neighborhood was surrounded by Wall Street skyscrapers that threatened to overwhelm it. By the mid-1950s, many of the residential buildings had already been taken over under the provisions of the Title I Housing Development Act and were slated for destruction, as was Rauschenberg's second studio on Pearl Street. By 1960 the Lower Manhattan Development Association, headed by David Rockefeller, had published plans to eradicate the entire area and replace it with high-rise office buildings, residential towers, and open plazas. In fact, the original location for the World Trade Center was proposed for the South Street area, practically on top of Rauschenberg's early studios.

Rauschenberg's art evolved in this urban context. The works follow three periods that coordinate with the changes in the city environment around him. From 1953 to 1958 the early Combines, like *Collection*, *Curfew*, and *Monogram*, show the excitement of his discovery of the downtown cityscape. Then from 1959 to 1962 his works were cooler and more structural. As new building near the South Street area accelerated, Rauschenberg's art featured a sort of technological realism. In works such as *Studio Painting*, *Wall Street*, and *First Landing Jump*, allusions to myth, narrative, autobiography, and feelings found in his earliest urban works were replaced by concerns with time, space, transformative states, and new materials. In contrast, Rauschenberg's silkscreen paintings, created between 1962 and 1964, are retrospective works. They present a vision of recent urban history in Lower Manhattan, as Rauschenberg had experienced it, after he had left the area. These works advocate variety in the downtown urban environment that Rauschenberg saw rapidly disappearing, and they parallel the campaign for neighborhood preservation that was being launched in New York during those years. Rauschenberg's direct response to his city surroundings may be clearly seen when the history of the area is reviewed, and his art is examined closely in that context.

The Rauschenberg literature occasionally has connected him with modern urbanism in a generalized fashion. The best discussion of his urban roots is found in Brian O'Doherty's "Rauschenberg and the Vernacular Glance" of 1973.[3] O'Doherty contends that Rauschenberg's art is conditioned by what he calls "the city dweller's rapid scan," a disinterested, momentary attention to the passing scene. He contends that, lacking a particular focus, the urban citizen's gaze jumps from object to object:

14   *Fulton Street and Dutch Street*, New York City. Milstein Division of United States History, Local History, and Genealogy, The New York Public Library, Astor, Lenox and Tilden Foundations.

The vernacular glance does not recognize categories of beautiful and ugly. It's just interested in what's there . . . It dispenses with hierarchies of importance, since they are constantly changing according to where you are and what you need. The vernacular glance sees the world as a supermarket."[4]

The artist's own statements confirm a sensibility in keeping with O'Doherty's discussion. Rauschenberg has said, "New York is a maze of unorganized experiences peopled by the unexpected – change is unavoidable."[5] There are, however, two short-comings to O'Doherty's thesis. First, it supposes Rauschenberg's art to be entirely random, simply a chance accumulation of visual instances. This is a common misinterpretation of Rauschenberg's art, but as I have already said in Chapter 1 of such works as the Scores (Off Kilter Keys) – and will be seen in many more instances – Rauschenberg's art combines chance procedures with clearly defined themes, ideas, interests, and procedures. His art embodies what he has called "random order."

Second, O'Doherty does not take into sufficient account the specific urban milieu in which Rauschenberg found himself during the 1950s and 1960s. Rauschenberg's response to his environment would have been very different if he had been living on 59th Street, Upper Manhattan, the Village, in another metropolis, or outside of a city setting. Through understanding Rauschenberg's particular environment and through a more careful analysis of the art works, we will be better able to understand the motivations behind his significant discoveries and to be clearer about the artist's intent when he states that he thinks of painting "as reporting, as a vehicle that will report what you did and what happened to you."[6]

In March 1953, after Rauschenberg returned from his sojourn in Italy and North Africa with the artist Cy Twombly, he moved into a loft at 61 Fulton Street. In 1955 he transferred to another loft space around the corner on 278 Pearl Street. His space on the top floor was directly above that of his friend Jasper Johns. Rauschenberg was evicted from that building when it was scheduled for demolition, and he moved two blocks closer to the water on 128 Front Street at the corner of John Street. In 1961 he finally moved out of the South Street neighborhood to 809 Broadway where he remained until purchasing the building that he still owns on Lafayette Street. Rauschenberg's first three locations involved him deeply with an extremely complex urban area in transition – South Street. After he moved to Broadway and created his early silkscreen paintings, he continued to look back consciously to that neighborhood as his generative urban experience.

Of the places in the city that Rauschenberg might have chosen to live in the early 1950s, the most obvious would have been the 10th Street area. This locale had been colonized by the Abstract Expressionist artists during the late 1940s. Harold Rosenberg has tellingly described 10th Street before the Abstract Expressionists moved there as a totally nondescript row of low brick buildings populated by workers and "winos."[7] But by the 1950s, 10th Street had become the center of avant-garde art in New York, and it was already attracting a second generation of Abstract Expressionist painters as well as various hangers-on. Nearby were the Cedar Tavern where the artists talked and drank in the late evenings and the Club, founded by

15 *Fulton Street and Nassau Street*, New York City. Milstein Division of United States History, Local History, and Genealogy, The New York Public Library, Astor, Lenox and Tilden Foundations.

the Abstract Expressionists in 1948 on 8th Street. The critic and art historian Dore Ashton, who was part of that group, has described the Club:

> From its commencement the Club functioned, as all its members agreed, as a surrogate Parisian café. It was where they went to have a drink or coffee, to bring a woman, and to reassure themselves that someone else was there, in the same situation as they were . . . The impetus to storm the gates of American culture was inherent in large gatherings of artists and their fellow travelers during those hectic years. The overflow into the studio quarter and into such meeting places as the Cedar Tavern became legendary. Many a youthful provincial heard about the Club or the Cedar, and came to New York to have a chance to drink with the big boys, to call out "Hi, Jack," or "Hi, Bill," or "Hi, Franz," and to feel part of something that was not yet defined that was happening in the arts.[8]

It was precisely this atmosphere that Rauschenberg avoided. He chose instead to live in an environment of small merchants, dock workers, cargo handlers, fishermen, and the out of work, all of whom influenced his art and view of urban life. Certainly, finances played a role in Rauschenberg's choice of the South Street area. The rents in 10th Street were already increasing due to the success of the artists. In contrast, South Street was an undesirable and inexpensive place to live. Rauschenberg paid ten dollars per month for his first loft on Fulton Street; the landlord asked fifteen dollars, but the artist talked him down. Rauschenberg was one of the first artists of his generation to live this far downtown. He was followed in 1955 by Johns and a number of other painters, including Ellsworth Kelly, Agnes Martin, Robert Indiana, and James Rosenquist, who set up studios in Coenties Slip. Except for Johns, Rauschenberg saw relatively little of these individuals.[9] While Rauschenberg had an increasing presence in the avant-garde art scene, which was fostered by such events as his 1951 first one-person exhibition at the Betty Parsons Gallery, his inclusion in the first 9th Street Gallery show, his joint exhibition with Cy Twombly at the Stable Gallery, and his early designs of sets and costumes for the Merce Cunningham Dance Company, it was to the South Street area, with its unique combination of early history, working-class vitality, and decrepitude, that Rauschenberg returned. There he found the objects and images to be included in his works, and there his ideas about modern city life were formed (fig. 15).

The urban environment surrounding Rauschenberg was complex and multi-faceted – both invigorating and decaying: Rauschenberg's first loft at the corner of Fulton and Cliff Streets was four blocks from the East River, the Fulton Fish Market, and the decrepit docks. Historically, this waterside area was one of the most interesting in New York City, and it included wooden and brick buildings that went back to the time of Herman Melville. Schermerhorn Row contained the only group of Federal Period commercial buildings remaining in the city, yet none of the area was preserved as it is today. Rather it was simply a working neighborhood dominated by warehouses, bars, ship chandlers, and cheap restaurants. The buildings were mostly run-down; some were used for storage, many were abandoned. On the water, barges, tug boats, and flat boats could be seen moving up and down the river and using the

East Side docks. An essential aspect of South Street was that, unlike so many other areas of New York, it was not an ethnic neighborhood. Rather, since the eighteenth century, it had contained a mixture of races and social classes, all drawn there by the promise of commerce and trade. The social heterogeneity of this area encouraged ideas about the value of urban diversity that are essential to Rauschenberg's artistic viewpoint. The WPA Guide to New York City, although written in 1939, captures a feeling for this area still applicable in the 1950s:

> The rumble of speeding trucks, the blasts from nearby steam shovels, the intermittent whistles from passing river traffic join in crescendos of dissonance. Sailors in pea jackets and dungarees, workmen in overalls, neat office clerks and shabby drifters throng the highway. On mild sunny days the drifters sit along the docks with their "junk bags," share cigarette butts, and stare endlessly into the water.[10]

Rauschenberg was especially sensitive to the nautical environment. He once commented that he had always lived near the sea – in Port Arthur, Texas where he was born, in New York, and presently in Captiva, Florida. For him, city ports represent commerce, travel, and exoticism. They remind him of the constant changes in the world around him. As he has noted, the South Street area during the 1950s was one of the few places in New York where the city's "origins as a seaport were apparent."[11]

During the 1950s, the docks near Rauschenberg's studio had deteriorated but were still partly viable. The advent of container shipping during World War II had already diverted the majority of such commerce to New Jersey ports where there was enough space for the larger ships and dockside storage for their cargo containers. The East River docks that were not abandoned were used for smaller specialty products that were distributed directly into the city. Nearest Rauschenberg's studio, Docks 14, 15, and 16 were employed respectively by Standard Fruit and Steamship Company, Caribbean Lines, and Lawes Shipping Company.[12] Fruits, coffees, and exotic Caribbean food were the primary imports. The three docks directly below these were abandoned. This environment intrigued Rauschenberg: contemporary commerce interacted with the history of small-scale shipping; refurbished ships and transport equipment existed beside discarded materials and tools; the vibrancy of the active piers played against the lonely stillness of those abandoned.

The Fulton Fish Market was one of the most active enterprises in the neighborhood. The market was the arrival and distribution point for the majority of fish eaten in New York and surrounding areas. Much of the truck traffic that rumbled across Fulton Street and many of the workers in that immediate area came from the fish market. The laborers were rough, hardworking individuals. The spirit of the market is captured in Barbara Mensch's *Last Waterfront*, a series of interviews with laborers at the fish market. A figure identified as "Local Resident" recalled:

> My first reaction [to the market] was based on what I heard. What I heard was that there was a great deal of subliminal violence, or intimated violence, secrecy, mystique, heavy mob influence . . . Underneath that face – when I first started to work there, with these guys – they were very simple, almost childlike.[13]

16 Rauschenberg with *White Painting* [seven panels] and *Untitled* [large black painting] (1953), Fulton Street studio, New York City, c. 1953, photo by Robert Rauschenberg.

Rauschenberg was interested in the market atmosphere, and he included newspaper clippings about the docks in several works of the period including *Charlene* and *Collection*.

In these early years, Rauschenberg's own struggles to survive allowed him to iden- tify with such laborers. His loft at 61 Fulton Street was a big attic space with twenty- foot ceilings (fig. 16). As mentioned earlier, the rent was ten dollars per month. The loft had neither heat nor running water, and Rauschenberg at first used a bucket and a hose in the backyard as his basin. When possible, he bathed at the apartments of friends and eventually made a tub out of a tarred crate. When he first moved to the loft, he slept on fish crates. His food budget was fifteen cents per day – most of which he spent at Rikers, a workers' cafeteria nearby. He supplemented this diet by bruised fruit picked up from the Standard Fruit and Steamship Company dock. Although these were clearly difficult circumstances, he remembers those years as among the most interesting of his career.[14]

Fulton Street itself provided a contrast to the exotic but decaying docks. It was one of the busiest streets in the city – more so during the 1950s than today, since the city had yet to complete the East Side Highway.[15] As a result, Fulton Street was one of the major cross-routes in Lower Manhattan. It was filled with the shops of small merchants that provided both the physical materials for Rauschenberg's early Combines and the models for urban diversity that interested the artist. The wide street with its continuous, congested, and disorganized traffic flow further inspired the artist's ideas of movement, change, and chaos as essential ingredients of modern life. Rauschenberg used the cobblestones removed from Fulton Street in his early Elemental Sculptures (1953), and his important *Automobile Tire Print* (1953) consists of the imprint of a car tire driven along Fulton Street, thus providing a model for movement through the city.[16]

The buildings along the eastern end of Fulton Street were low structures, typically four or five stories in height, built of brick and dating to the nineteenth century. In fact, as late as 1958, fifty-two percent of the buildings in Lower Manhattan were more than one hundred years old.[17] These buildings were constructed for local merchants, storage, and small manufacture. They contained little architectural ornament; the brick work on their facades was rough; and doors and windows featured simply carved frames. By the mid-twentieth century, the buildings were not well kept, and the paint applied to both their woodwork and brick facades was peeling. Metalwork details such as railings were rusty, and repairs to joints between the woodwork and brick were often done with tar, which was left dripping down the building walls. Abandoned buildings near South Street were the most dilapidated, while those inland were in somewhat better condition.

The look of these building can be seen in contemporary photographs, and the gritty character of their facades profoundly influenced Rauschenberg's Combines, whose rough surfaces with splattered paint have these structures as a major source.[18] In addition, the rectilinear shape of Rauschenberg's Combines and the rectilinear organization of elements on their surfaces was inspired by, and is meant to remind us of, the irregular grids of windows and doorways. In these buildings, Rauschenberg found embodiments of the simultaneous vitality and decay that characterized his world. In fact, the Combines may be thought of as building facades recreated by the artist.

The Lower Manhattan buildings were also remarkable for the number of objects attached to their facades (fig. 17). In these utilitarian structures, fire escapes often projected from the fronts, and the documentary photographs show that electrical conduits leading to naked light bulbs were sometimes run along the buildings' surfaces, as were metal heating pipes. The manner in which objects were attached to the fronts of these buildings was an immediate basis for Rauschenberg's attachment of metal and wood objects to the surface of his Combines, as well as the exposed electrical wires and bulbs appended to the surfaces of such works as *First Landing Jump* (1958; see fig. 34).

The most frequent objects placed on the Fulton Street buildings were commercial signs. Contemporary photographs show that the buildings were awash with advertising graphics. The signs came in all sizes but were frequently quite large. They were painted on the buildings, screwed flat to them, placed in windows, and projected from the buildings on metal armatures. The proliferation of advertising images was a result of the radical growth in consumer goods of the post-war years. There were

17 *Pearl Street at Hanover Square,* New York City. Milstein Division of United States History, Local History, and Genealogy, The New York Public Library, Astor, Lenox and Tilden Foundations.

no sign codes in New York City at that time so that the merchants tended to cover their workplaces with the names of practically every product they carried. The advertising slogans were so plentiful that they overlapped one another as one stared down the street, creating a confusing jumble of letters and image fragments.

For the advertising industry, the 1950s was a transitional period. According to articles in *Printer's Ink*, the most authoritative journal of commercial design business, the profession had moved in the late 1940s away from modes that featured explanatory text to large-scale graphic images with simple logos.[19] The success of the Coca-Cola label was a prime example. The distinctive and straightforward advertising designs of the 1950s suited Rauschenberg and complemented the energetic configurations in his works. The Coca-Cola sign, for instance, appears in such works as *Dylaby* (1962, Sonnabend Collection), and fragments of lettering from street billboards can be found in dozens of his works from this period. Rauschenberg favored such placards as representations of the dynamism of urban society. In this spirit, he wrote about advertising signs attached to the sides of trucks, "With sound scale and insistency trucks mobilize words, and broadsides by a combination of law and local motivation which produces an extremely complex random order that cannot be described as accidental."[20]

For Rauschenberg, another essential feature of the Lower Manhattan environment resulted from the discarded and worn-out materials and objects that were often thrown into alleys and left at curbsides for disposal. As with the Combines, Rauschenberg later spoke of assembling materials for one of his performance pieces, *Map Room*:

> I began that piece by getting some materials to work with – again we have that business of limitations and possibilities. I just got a bunch of tires, not because I'm crazy about tires but because they're so available around here in New York, even on the street. If I were working in Europe, that wouldn't be the material.[21]

Early photographs of the area around Rauschenberg's studio show the apparently prolonged periods during which refuse was left on the streets. Contemporary newspaper articles indicate that slow garbage collection was an issue along such commercial streets as Fulton and Nassau. Nearer to South Street, worn-out objects and packing crates were allowed to litter the sidewalks until they decayed or were scavenged. On a city-wide scale, it is notable that New York's largest product during the 1950s was garbage. Such a fact impelled Gay Talese to write *New York: A Serendipiter's Journey* in 1961, an ironic tale partly concerning the role of refuse in the history of New York City.[22]

The worn-out objects were signs of human use and history for Rauschenberg, and it was precisely these objects that provided the material for his early works. On one hand, his use of such discarded items is a documentation of his environment. On the other, his choices clearly express a world-view. Rauschenberg's works show that the impersonal character of machine-made things can be modified by human use. Through wear and patchwork alterations, the objects take on the personal character that interests the artist. Each becomes an expression of individual history in which the human being has interacted with and altered a potentially impersonal item.

Such objects differ radically from those used by the Pop artists, who were partly influenced by Rauschenberg, and the contrast highlights the distinctive nature of his vision. The Pop artists invariably chose newly manufactured products, thus suggesting an idealized manufacturing and commercial system based on clean and unmarred objects. Their art and world-vision are impersonal rather than individual, and it visualizes a utopian permanence rather than constant change. Rauschenberg's aged objects are certainly not utopian but they do have an optimistic character. They express a belief that cast-offs, the things rejected by society, can be re-used. Society's debris was revived by the artist and found a new purpose in his work. Thus, Rauschenberg expressed an essential optimism about human inventiveness and creativity. Objects that had been cleverly modified by others but that eventually wore out and were thrown away, were provided yet another life in Rauschenberg's Combines, and the artist's works became an additional link in a chain of human ingenuity.

Rauschenberg's identification with downtown Manhattan entailed not only his works' resemblance to building facades but also extended to the social structure behind those appearances. The artist identified with the independent merchants and manufacturers who surrounded him. The heart of the New York City economy through the 1950s was small industry, as well as wholesale and retail commerce. In 1956, Manhattan contained 440,000 shopkeepers, and two-thirds of the industries there had fewer than twenty employees. 63 percent of the region's industry served local consumers and sixty-two percent of all wholesale businesses for the metropolitan region was located in Manhattan.[23] The keynotes for these enterprises were individualism, new ideas and new materials, flexibility in design, and speedy communication with the consumer. Such businesses were responsive to acquiring materials on short notice, suddenly changing a labor force, and altering loft spaces according to production needs. They created and sold small-scale and unusual items which were adaptable to rapidly changing markets.

Such industries and merchants resembled the individuality, flexibility, resourcefulness, and creativity of Rauschenberg's artistic methods. Like the merchants and manufacturers, Rauschenberg viewed art as a kind of home industry. He took materials that surrounded him and re-assembled them in exciting new forms. His works were constructed by combining parts as one might redesign a machine needed for some new task or regroup items in a shop window. Rauschenberg has always emphasized the role materials played in his art and has even suggested that his pieces are based on discovering the nature of their particular materials.[24] With this attitude, he consciously rejected the metaphysics of the Abstract Expressionists for a more physical and pragmatic approach to his art, an attitude closer to the concerns of the working people who surrounded him.

I am able to be more specific about the types of commercial ventures that surrounded Rauschenberg. New York City's Reverse Telephone Directories, which list telephone subscribers by address, give an idea of the types of businesses that were adjacent to Rauschenberg's studios during the 1950s.[25] On Fulton Street in the block between Gold and Cliff Streets, where Rauschenberg lived in 1953–55, there were nearly fifty businesses. The most frequent types were dedicated to precisely the materials that Rauschenberg came to use in his Combines. The block was dominated by printers, electricians and electrical supply outlets, tool and dye distributors, and cloth merchants. Names include Morton Press and Eland Press at 55 Fulton, Merchant's Electrical Supply and Repair at 77 Fulton, and Standard Metal and Stencil Company and Stafford Manufacturing (for commercial signs) next to Rauschenberg's building at 59 Fulton. The Pearl Street studio, which Rauschenberg occupied in 1955–58, was on a much less densely populated street, but one that contained similar businesses to those on Fulton. There were about forty businesses over a three-block area, and they included printers, electrical suppliers, chemical suppliers, importer/exporters, and cloth wholesalers. These industries and distributors disposed of some of their unwanted products by leaving them for pick up on the street corners where the artist often discovered them and took them back to his studio for re-use in his works.

One of the materials that dominates Rauschenberg's Combines beginning in the 1950s is cloth. Key early paintings like *Charlene* (1954) and *Hymnal* (1955; see fig. 23) are notable for their use of different types of cloth, and works throughout Rauschenberg's career feature a wide variety of textiles. The Jammers (1975–76) and the Hoarfrosts (begun 1974) are particularly notable in this regard. The artist has indicated that his interest in cloth may be traced to his youth when his mother created handmade shirts for him.[26] In that early context, the shirts represented his mother's frugality and skilled work through her ability to create usable clothing out of remnants that would otherwise have been discarded. Rauschenberg has recalled that the resulting patchwork shirts were somewhat embarrassing to him as a young boy but that they also marked his individuality and made him feel special. This combination of frugality, skill, and individuality is germane to Rauschenberg's attitude to his art.

Certainly, Rauschenberg's early interest in cloth must have been revived by the wide range of cloth distributors and garment manufacturers near his Lower Manhattan studios. While the center of the garment industry was split between 14th Street and the upper thirties on the West Side, records show that there were six garment distributors alone on Rauschenberg's block of Fulton Street. This density was not surprising on an important commercial street, because over eighty percent of New York's regional garment industry was centered in Manhattan. The garment industry was the characteristic small independent business that thrived in Manhattan. Its constantly changing products captured the spirit of the times.[27] Rauschenberg certainly realized that cloth is one of the most common elements in our daily existence; it is both an expression of personal taste and defines much of the surface character of life because it literally covers our bodies. Textile patterns and clothing are tangible records of the fashion at moments in history, and the use of cloth became for Rauschenberg an essential record of daily life.

Even more than garments, the communications industry was an expression of the fast-paced and momentary character of modern urban life. After the Cubists, Rauschenberg is one of the artists most responsible for the inclusion of material from the print media within art works. His interest in newspaper and magazine texts and photographs, as expressions of contemporary existence, is so great that it should be regarded as one of the central aspects of his oeuvre. Rauschenberg's use began with collage fragments on such early paintings as *Should Love Come First* (c. 1951, repainted). Newspapers are embedded in the surfaces of the Black Paintings (1951–53), and newspaper text and illustrations appear throughout the Combines. Newspaper and magazine illustrations are the basis of the transfer drawings of the 1950s, the early lithographs of the 1960s, and then the Silkscreen Paintings (1962–64). The Currents of 1969–70 are entirely composed of contemporary newspaper fragments. From the Silkscreen Paintings through recent works, Rauschenberg's art continues to rely heavily on newspapers and magazines.

Rauschenberg's intense interest in this form of communication began in New York. Manhattan was the core of New York's regional communications industry and one of the world centers for news media. Seventy-five percent of the area's communication employees and seventy-four percent of the printing employees were located in Manhattan during the 1950s. New York City had two communications centers, one in 42nd Street and the other, older location in the area just below City Hall and a short distance north of Rauschenberg's Fulton Street studio.

One chronicler of American journalism has summarized the varied character of New York newspapers:

> Because of the large concentration of population in the metropolitan area, experiments in journalism could be, and have been tried. A large and sufficient market could be found to support any type of journalism which might be evolved. Extensive groups of people in every class – the low economic, the industrial workers, the middle class and upper high-bracket class – lived in the area. All levels wanted news and the features that journalism provided for entertainment. The heavy, informative *New York Times* and the breezy, entertaining tabloid, the *New York Daily News*, have succeeded.[28]

The sheer quantity and variety of newspapers were hallmarks of New York City during the 1950s. The *New York Times* was complemented by the *New York Tribune*, *New York Herald*, *The Sun*, the *Evening Post*, and *The Journal*. Clippings from almost all of these newspapers were included at one time or another in Rauschenberg's Combines. Another growth area in the New York newspapers during the 1950s was the special section – labor, science, sports, politics, urbanism, and so on. This diversity appealed to the artist's wide-ranging curiosity. The dyslexic Rauschenberg was certainly not an in-depth reader of the news, but he responded instinctively to a large assortment of odd and interesting by-lines that caught his attention. They represented to him the sheer multiplicity of human conditions and events in the city.

A major issue that affected journalism of the 1950s was censorship of the press.[29] During the early Cold War in 1951, President Truman issued an order restricting the release of governmental news from both civilian and military agencies. The restrictions were misused during the Joseph McCarthy years as a way of controlling the press, and as a result issues of censorship were widely discussed in the press itself.

In fact, one of the campaign promises made by John F. Kennedy when he ran for president in 1960 was that he would end excessive government secrecy and that he would take the country into his confidence.[30] Rauschenberg's use of the news media throughout his works might also be seen as a deliberate assertion of freedom of information in the face of such restrictions.

The tabloids were another type of daily publication which thrived during the 1950s and were of interest to Rauschenberg. The *New York Daily News* had a special fascination for the artist, who employed clippings from it in numerous works. The character of the *Daily News* appealed to his interest in popular culture. During the 1950s, the paper greatly increased the number of its provocative editorials, which provided exciting commentaries on local and national events – exactly the kind of stimulating coverage Rauschenberg loved. The *Daily News* was also widely known for its photographs, which naturally attracted Rauschenberg and which he included in many of his works. In addition, the *Daily News* featured "funny pages," and it was almost the exclusive source for the comic strips that Rauschenberg has used in his art.

News magazines also proliferated in the 1950s. By mid-century fifteen American magazines had circulations of more than two million. Of all the news magazines, Rauschenberg utilized *Life*, the picture magazine, most frequently. I shall show, for instance in Chapter 3, that the great majority of his photographs of the NASA space program were taken from this publication. Parallel to Rauschenberg's interest, *Life* had enormous appeal to an increasingly photograph-minded America. By 1968, the magazine had 7,400,000 home subscribers and newsstand purchasers. *Life* was squarely aimed at the mass market, which suited the populist character of Rauschenberg's works, and its owner Henry Luce stated that "*Life*'s purpose is to see life and to see it whole, to eyewitness great events . . . to watch the faces of the poor and proud . . . to see and be amazed."[31] This goal is not so distant from that of Rauschenberg's art.

As a whole, newspapers and news magazines embodied New York's stamina and its thirst for information. The New York dailies provided more information than one could possibly use or even remember concerning every aspect of life. They were the ultimate expression of the historical present. The newspapers captured the constant flux of urban life in all of its multiplicity and confusion. Newspapers are products without standardization: like Rauschenberg's art, the content of each edition is new. They also embodied the glut of information in the modern age. The stories in a newspaper are presented with little hierarchy and there is often no relationship between one story and those adjoining it. From one point of view, newspapers are the best representatives of the fragmentary and transitory character of information at mid-century. This sensibility is germane to Rauschenberg's understanding of the world. Most of today's news will be of very little concern tomorrow, and newspapers proclaim that it is the present moment that matters. John Cage adroitly captured the conceptual relationship between Rauschenberg's art and newspapers when he observed, "There is no more subject to a Rauschenberg *combine* than there is in a page from a newspaper. Each thing that is there is subject. It is a situation involving multiplicity."[32]

Rauschenberg's use of newspapers is certainly also related to the Cubists' pioneering manipulation of newspaper collage early in the twentieth century. Like Rauschenberg, Georges Braque and Pablo Picasso lived in an age of information explosion. The utilization of newspaper collage elements in their works partly reflects the vast and confusing quantity of information with which they were bombarded in early twentieth-century Paris. The Cubists, however, were primarily concerned with the paper fragments as metaphors. They transformed them either into representations of whole newspapers or into other still-life objects. In contrast, Rauschenberg's newspaper fragments retain their material integrity. They are nothing more than the samples that he has collected from the newsstands and streets around him. In this way, Rauschenberg remains in close contact with everyday reality. Among his earliest works that contained newspaper clippings were his Black Paintings.

*   *   *

In 1953, the first paintings that Rauschenberg completed in his new Fulton Street studio were the Black Paintings.[33] These were works that he had begun during the summer of 1952 at Black Mountain College, North Carolina, where he had been in residence from fall to spring 1948–49 and during the summers of 1951 and 1952. The last and most extensive group of the Black Paintings had been stored in New York while Rauschenberg traveled in Europe during the fall and winter of 1952. When Rauschenberg returned to the city and set up his studio on Fulton Street, he felt an urgency to repaint and modify these works in accordance with his new vision of the life in Lower Manhattan.

To understand Rauschenberg's intent, it is necessary to discuss briefly the works done at Black Mountain. By 1951 Black Mountain College had become one of the centers of avant-garde study in America.[34] In addition to visual artists, it attracted dancers, composers, poets, writers, and musicians. Such individuals as Buckminster Fuller, Franz Kline, Willem de Kooning, Charles Olson, Robert Motherwell, and Jack Tworkov had been involved in its programs. Significantly for Rauschenberg, John Cage and Merce Cunningham also spent the summers of 1951 and 1952 at Black Mountain.

An important exchange of ideas between Cage and Rauschenberg took place at the college, one which led to their life-long friendship. Cage arrived at Black Mountain having already achieved considerable stature for his innovative musical compositions of the 1940s. At the college, he continued to investigate ideas of Zen Buddhism that had interested him for several years. Change, randomness, and receptivity were concepts that concerned him deeply. Cage had become profoundly committed to the suppression of individual artistic ego. In the context of his interaction with Cage, Rauschenberg created his most radical paintings to date, the White Paintings of 1951. These are a series of modular canvases with pure and uninflected white surfaces. The rectangular white canvases were pre-conceived by the artist to be grouped in arrangements from one to seven panels. Negating personal touch and thus artistic ego, the paintings were made with complete neutrality. In fact, Rauschenberg later indicated that, if they deteriorated, the White Paintings might be restored or completely recreated by others. As a result of their unmarked surfaces, these paintings depict literally nowhere.

Incidents within the White Paintings and their very appearance depend entirely on their environment. It is the play of reflected light and shadow over their surfaces and the shadows of passing viewers that provide the determining factors in their constantly but subtly changing appearance. Cage understood the meaning of their neutral receptivity perfectly when he called them "landing strips" for dust motes, light, and shadow.[35] The importance of the White Paintings as receptors for their environment and as works which literally reflect viewer interaction has remained with Rauschenberg over the decades. At first, it seems that the White Paintings and the Combines are exact opposites – the former concerned with how little the artist can do on the canvas surface, the latter showing a great deal of artistic activity. As distant stylistically as his New York Combines are from the White Paintings, the interest in exterior surroundings as related to the art work provides a conceptual affinity. A direct example of the long heritage of the White Paintings is that they were, much later, among the major inspirations for Rauschenberg's *Scores (Off Kilter Keys)*. Closer to the time of their creation, Rauschenberg's White Paintings were also the primary inspiration for Cage's seminal 1953 musical score *4'33"*, in which the composer investigated the significance of silence and chance noises. As mentioned earlier, the original title of Rauschenberg's *Scores* is, of course, partly a homage to Cage.

Rauschenberg's Black Paintings of 1952 began as an extension of the ideas found in the White Paintings, and the first example of the Black Paintings was a matt black triptych. Although this work was an interesting exploration in opposition to the earlier series, Rauschenberg executed only one of these highly reductive black works, not a series as was the case with the White Paintings. The reason may have been that the subtle reflections which provided the environment for the White Paintings proved impossible on the light-absorbing black surface, but the artist solved this problem with his next series of black works. These were executed in more reflective, high-gloss, black enamel paint. In addition, Rauschenberg built up the canvas surface with layers of newspaper placed irregularly across it before applying the pigment. As the enamel dried, it contracted. Thus, where the enamel was painted over newspaper, it puckered the surface, creating a noticeable texture.

The visual effect of this group of Black Paintings, despite the activation of their surfaces, is still related to the White Paintings. The textured areas of glossy black paint do not function as individual incidents that may be read. Rather, they act to increase the play of light over the skin of the paintings. Shadows do not have the same important role they did in the White Paintings, but reflected light on the enamel and textured surface creates a myriad visual effects. An installation photograph of the largest of these works, consisting of five panels and shown at the Third Annual Stable Gallery exhibition, demonstrates that Rauschenberg lit it with high, very bright spotlights so as to emphasize the reflective character of the surface. Like the White Paintings, these works are responsive to their environment.

In the next group of Black Paintings – ones still completely executed in North Carolina – Rauschenberg included sheets of newspaper that had not been over-painted. This addition changed the nature of the works because the newspapers became containers for information in addition to being receptors for light and reflections from the outside world. This group of Black Paintings marked the most extensive use thus far of newspapers in Rauschenberg's oeuvre. Unlike his earlier Black Paintings, Rauschenberg's newspaper pages anchor these works in time and location because the viewer is able to read the dates and the publication locales of the papers. These later works are more connected to particular historical moments, and the newspapers suggest that Rauschenberg was thinking of urban events, to which the news was connected. Three different newspapers were used in these paintings. In addition to the expected local paper, the *Ashville Citizen*, Rauschenberg included clippings from the *New York Times* and the *New York Daily News*. As the end of the summer neared, in the company of artists like Cage and Franz Kline, Rauschenberg's thoughts must have turned from the rural isolation of North Carolina to New York City.

Despite the textured surfaces and readable newspaper fragment in the last of the Black Paintings done in North Carolina, these works still have a clean, uncluttered appearance. In contrast, the examples that Rauschenberg re-worked in New York have a different character: their density and ruggedness suit the urban situation in which Rauschenberg found himself. They have architectonic, deliberately craggy, surfaces that recall the old and worn buildings around the artist, and the amount of painterly activity in them suggests the constant change that is central to big city life. Rauschenberg said of these works, "I wanted to see how much I could include without saying anything particular."[36]

Untitled [black painting with portal form] (1952; fig. 18) is an example of the later Black Paintings. Here the tonal range is much richer. The brown color of weathered newspaper is set off against varying densities of black, and there are spots of white throughout, as well as small touches of gold. The surface is extremely rough, like the battered wall of a dilapidated building; its texture has the solidity of jagged masonry especially in areas where the heavy pigment has cracked as it dried. The torn newspaper fragments attached irregularly in layers throughout the surface might suggest broadsides, which present the news of the city, pasted to a building wall. The black rectangular area at the center is like a doorway, although its surface, which is both raised and glossy, does not permit reading it as recessional space. Finally, the material ruggedness of the entire work is enhanced by the manner in which the canvas is attached to the frame.[37] As opposed to being stretched around the framing bars as is the traditional practice, it is stapled to the outer face of the wooden stretcher with the frayed canvas edges visible. The effect is one of crude solidity, and the character of the painting as a roughly constructed physical object is emphasized.

To highlight the relationship between these works and the architectural environment, Rauschenberg photographed several of them set against the rough walls, and he placed others within doorways in nearby old buildings. Rauschenberg framed these photographs with the camera lens so that the paintings are deliberately compared to their architectural environment. For the artist, these roughly constructed

18 *Untitled* [black painting with portal form],
1952, oil and newspaper on canvas, 51 $\frac{1}{8}$ × 54 $\frac{1}{4}$",
Mr. and Mrs. Peter Haas.

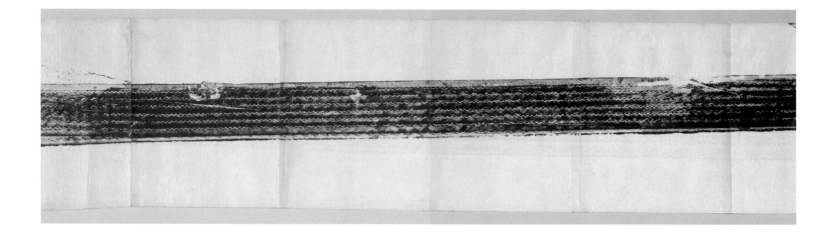

19　*Automobile Tire Print*, 1953, monoprint: house paint on twenty sheets of paper, mounted on fabric, 16 $^1/_2$ × 264 $^1/_2$", collection of the San Francisco Museum of Modern Art, purchased through a gift of Phyllis Wattis.

and decaying buildings, each of which carried a history of its use on its surface, had already made a powerful impression – one that was reinforced and expanded in later works.

In New York, Rauschenberg began to experiment with radically different modes of expression, yet the new works were connected by his strong interest in his new city environment. *Automobile Tire Print* (fig. 19), made immediately after his arrival in New York in 1953, is one of Rauschenberg's best-known early pieces. To prepare for it, he glued together twenty sheets of drawing paper forming a continuous strip approximately twenty-three feet long. On a Sunday morning, he rolled out the adjoined sheets on Fulton Street, immediately outside of his studio, and directed John Cage to drive slowly over them in Cage's Model A Ford while Rauschenberg applied black paint to the rear tire. This elongated work on paper has been maintained as a rolled scroll ever since, and more recently it has been mounted on a fabric backing for preservation.

While *Automobile Tire Print* has been considered in the Rauschenberg literature as either a new formal design or as a predecessor to conceptual art, its expression is profoundly connected to Rauschenberg's image of the city. In this work, he literally took his art out of the studio and onto the street; Rauschenberg enfranchised the street by making it the means for his creation. *Automobile Tire Print* epitomized ideas of movement, change, and dynamism which were the central experiences of Fulton Street. As described earlier, this major east–west route through Lower Manhattan was dominated by the cars and trucks that constantly transported people and goods across the city. Fulton Street embodied the social and commercial mobility that were essential to the New York experience. A view down the long straight street gave the city a visual scale that was balanced against the different appearance of individual buildings.

When unrolling *Automobile Tire Print*, the two dominant impressions are its extreme length and its variety. Progressively revealing the work is akin to the experience of unrolling a Chinese scroll in which a varied landscape, rather than cityscape, appears. Beginning with *Automobile Tire Print*, the tire, as a sign of mobility, became a central motif in Rauschenberg's art. It plays a key role in *Monogram* (1955–59; see fig. 28) and *First Landing Jump* (1961; see fig. 34), both to be discussed below, and Rauschenberg's idea of the literal span of an art work as revealing the ongoing and unfolding process of life reaches its apotheosis in *The 1/4 Mile or Two Furlong Piece* (1981–present, collection of the artist), an art work that is currently over one-quarter mile long. Both ideas – mobility and extension – were also featured in Rauschenberg's Combines. Because of differences in the street pavement and variations in the evenness with which Rauschenberg was able to apply paint to the tire, the *Automobile Tire Print* looks different in each section. This character of variety within seeming uniformity and of art's extensiveness, rather than confinement or isolation, is central to Rauschenberg's aesthetic and to his view of urban life, one that informs his Combine paintings.

*   *   *

The Combines primarily occupied Rauschenberg between 1953 and 1962. He named the group of work ostensibly because they combined painting and sculpture, but the combination is far greater. The works integrate the widest range of both materials and experiences in Rauschenberg's early career, and they became a model for his inclusive attitude – his feeling that art should open itself as completely as possible to the surrounding environment. *Collection* (1954; fig. 20) is one of the first of Rauschenberg's works fully to celebrate the variety of feelings he connected with the city, and it is one of two monumental Red Paintings that he created between 1953 and 1954; the other is *Charlene* (1954, Stedelijk Museum, Amsterdam). Because of the variety of elements added to the surfaces of these two works, they mark the transition to Rauschenberg's Combine paintings. *Collection* captures the city's multiple experiences. In it, the artist attempts to gather many aspects of the multivalent urban environment. The painting deliberately takes a position of multiplicity and theatricality, and it reflects Rauschenberg's feelings of excitement in New York. In the literature, it has been asserted that *Collection* refers to art collections alone. Certainly, art collections are part of the meaning but the references are more broadly based and cover the entire urban situation.[38]

The work measures 79 × 95 inches – it is environmental in scale – and consists of three vertical panels. The first overall impression of *Collection* is one of confusion and messiness. Like the environment in which Rauschenberg lived, something is happening everywhere on the surface, and all objects in the work seem worn and patched together. Paper, cloth, oil paint, and metal appear to have been thrown onto the surface with the seeming disorder found in Rauschenberg's gritty urban world. The Combine was untitled until Rauschenberg gave it the title *Collection* in 1976. He must have recognized in looking over the work at this later date the manner in which it collected together the many types of experiences.

Only after some time do the connections between Rauschenberg's artistic decisions in *Collection* become apparent. Although all three panels are dominated by red, the center is accented with yellow and the right with blue. The painting thus contains the triad of colors on which all others are based, and its hues are in keeping

with the work's overall theme of inclusiveness. The bright, primary colors found in *Collection* are those of the made environment like a playground, amusement park, or colorful street filled with signs; *Collection* does not feature the more muted hues of the natural world. When Rauschenberg discussed his use of red, not long after completing the Red Paintings, he said, "I picked what was for me the most difficult color at the time to work with – the one I considered the most aggressive."[39] The red color of *Collection* mirrors the vitality and aggressiveness of the Lower Manhattan environment. The dates on several of the newspapers attached to the surface indicate that much of the painting was executed during the summer of 1953 when, according to contemporary newspaper accounts, there was a heat wave in New York, and the city was red hot.

In creating *Collection*, Rauschenberg explored the wide variety of materials that
he could attach to the surface of the painting. Objects on it include newspaper pages,
sections of comics, fragments of wood, a scarf with art reproductions, and a mirror
(fig. 21). All of these elements are surrounded by and painted over in pigment applied
in a variety of spontaneous ways that range from surfaces encrusted with heavy
impasto to drips and rills. The congested and jumbled appearance of the work is
entirely consistent with the images of shop fronts in Lower Manhattan during this
same period as seen in contemporary photographs. In the left-hand panel, some of
the largest print type in the work is the single vertically placed word "CITY," clipped
from a *New York Sunday News* headline. Next to this word is one of the few clearly
readable dates in the work, August 22, 1954, so that *Collection* is set in location and
time.

Beneath the casual appearance of *Collection*, the organizing principle is the
rectilinear grid, the favored method of urban organization. The streets around
Rauschenberg were ordered as a grid, and the buildings themselves featured a
roughly grid-like design of their architectural elements. In fact, the vertical organization of *Collection*'s three panels, which are like abutting building facades, are distinctly architectural. The bottom of each panel utilizes paint and attached fabric in
three planes of red, yellow, and blue, and the simplicity of these three planes allows
them visually to support the Combine like the structural foundation of a building.
On the next level, the most active paint and collage activity takes place; this is similar
to the body of a building. At the top of *Collection*, Rauschenberg has placed pieces
of wood in a cornice-like arrangement, completing the allusions to architecture.[40]

The pieces of wood at the top of *Collection* also emphasize the city's ethnic diversity. One portion has a cigar tin (the P. F. Umberto brand) attached to it. It reminds
the viewer that the Hispanic population was then one of the most quickly growing
immigrant groups in the city. The center pieces of wood are cut in elaborate patterns
which resemble Chinese letters. They look like the particularly colorful and exotic
signs hanging outside of Chinese stores and restaurants. There was a Chinese
restaurant with such a sign at 57 Fulton Street, next to Rauschenberg's studio, and
Chinatown was not far away.

Reproductions of art works dominated the central panel of *Collection*. Part
of the experience of New York was the proliferation of art, both in its museums
and in reproductions through widely available publications. Most of the art works
in *Collection* are reproductions cut out from a scarf that was produced by the
Metropolitan Museum of Art in the early 1950s titled "Great Works of Art through
the Ages." On the scarf, sixteen art works were reproduced from photographs and
silkscreened onto red cloth. While the scarf reflects the commercialization of art,
there is nothing in *Collection* to suggest that Rauschenberg takes a negative view of
such advertisements. Rather, for him, such reproductions allow these remote masterpieces to become part of everyday experience.

The reproductions that Rauschenberg chose from the scarf are marked by their
variety and in most cases the deliberate lack of relationship to his immediate
artistic concerns. They include a geometric period Greek amphora, Velázquez's

equestrian portrait of Philip IV, Van Gogh's *Vase with Fourteen Sunflowers*, and Renoir's *Girl with a Watering Can*. With the possible exception of the painterly Van Gogh, none of these works was immediately applicable to Rauschenberg's current artistic concerns, and a figure such as Renoir was generally out of favor with the avant-garde. Instead, the chosen reproductions represent a variety of possibilities available to the artist, and they condemn the idea of the isolated masterpiece. Reproductions of the art works allow dissemination, just as inclusion in Rauschenberg's *Collection* further distributes them. For Rauschenberg, art is one part of a continuous and interwoven information network. To this end, the art-work reproductions are surrounded by and partly over-painted with thick layers of red pigment so that they are not allowed to be visually separate but are part of an integrated environment. Another significant element in the center panel is a small round mirror. We see ourselves when looking at *Collection*. The mirror undermines the permanence normally associated with works of art because the viewer's momentary image joins it. The mirror also emphasizes viewer participation in the work – an idea at the center of Rauschenberg's oeuvre.

The left and right panels in *Collection* are dominated by newspaper clippings and comic strips that look like leaflets glued onto building walls. Rauschenberg's choices of these items reveal the sort of loosely connected chains of association discussed in Chapter 1, and they are examples of his lateral-type thinking. The advertisements and comics emphasize the variety of experiences in the city. There are advertisements for a Macy's furniture sale and a dandruff cure, which resemble those advertisements Rauschenberg would have seen in nearby store windows. Rauschenberg further highlighted the commercialism which surrounded him by placing a comic strip directly below these advertisements whose punch line is "If you'll loan me a dollar, I'll pay you back." While the reference is clearly humorous, it may have also struck a personal chord with the artist, who was then extremely poor.

The "funny papers" also feature several strips of the popular character Moons Mulligan flirting at the beach. Rauschenberg frequently took the nearby Staten Island ferry to the beach on hot summer days. There, beach-combing, he would find wood and metal debris to incorporate in his works. The "funny papers" highlight slapstick, lowbrow humor that Rauschenberg found just as essential to his urban experience as "high" art. The "funnies" are one of the most simplistic forms of visual communication to be found in modern life. Their naïveté was far greater than that of the more sophisticated visual designs of comic books later favored by the Pop artists. It is significant that Rauschenberg, who has used the "funnies" throughout his career, deliberately chose this low form of visual communication to include in his works. It demonstrated that nothing was beneath his attention and that he found all experiences viable for inclusion in his work.

In contrast to the slapstick humor of the "funnies," Rauschenberg did not shy away from the discord that was also part of urban life. One of the largest newspaper clippings that Rauschenberg attached to *Collection*'s right panel is an upside down photograph of an individual identified as Richard C. Patterson, accompanied by the headline "It's Money He Wants" (fig. 22). While the headline seems to complement

22 Detail of fig. 20.

the humorous spirit of the commercial advertisements near it, the content is more serious, and most New Yorkers of 1953 would have quickly recognized Patterson's name.[41] Patterson was Mayor Robert Wagner's new appointment as Commerce Commissioner. His office was assigned responsibility for finding sites for small businesses displaced by the city planner Robert Moses's ambitious schemes to demolish and then rebuild areas in the city that he personally deemed "slums."[42] Patterson's department had no office and no budget, and his ineffectiveness, along with allegations that he was taking bribes from contractors, marked the first signs of an uprising against Moses's policies. Rauschenberg's choice of this article is fortuitous because his South Street neighborhood was soon threatened by Moses's policies, and, as shall be seen, a good portion of the artist's views on urbanism were either directly or indirectly influenced by the battle for New York neighborhoods that took place during the 1950s.

A number of the newspaper selections in *Collection* also focus on urban violence. There, as well as in a number of other Combines and later silkscreen paintings, Rauschenberg acknowledges and confronts the violence of city life as an inherent aspect of the urban experience. In *Collection* these references are for the most part gathered in the left-hand panel, and many are centered on Rauschenberg's own neighborhood. The clippings include "Six tearful gang boys . . . in shooting," "16, He Breaks in Just to Sit at Caddy Wheel," "Thugs Rob Store," and "in Stickup." An article about Budget Director Abraham D. Beame's efforts to raise money for more police is also included. Among the other articles chosen are those concerning attempts to deal with dock violence – a subject particularly relevant to Rauschenberg given his proximity to the docks.

As a whole, *Collection* attempts to capture the full variety of Rauschenberg's New York experience from the Metropolitan Museum of Art to the docks, and from Fulton Street to Jones Beach. The Combine features the variety and energy of the city. *Collection* is casual and good-humored, thoughtful and sophisticated, seedy and unkempt, like the world in which Rauschenberg lived. But Rauschenberg's openness – his assertion of freedom to depict anything and everything that he sees around him – was ultimately a serious contention at this time in American history. *Collection* was created during the McCarthy years and the national scandal created by the investigations of the House Committee on Un-American Activities. At the very center of *Collection* is a front page from the *New York Herald Tribune* in which the text reads "Plot Is Evident" and to the left of this statement "Red Ban Believed." Rauschenberg's red painting *Collection* asserts that the artist will not be banned from his freedom of experience and of expression. During the spring of 1954, at the time *Collection* was being created, McCarthy had begun to fall from power after it was revealed that members of his committee had threatened army officials, and the highly publicized and televised investigations of McCarthy's committee eventually led to his censure by the Senate. In the context of these events, Rauschenberg's pun on the color red took on a serious meaning for the artist because his belief in receptivity to all life's experiences and freedom of creative expression was the core of his developing world-view.

The Combine *Hymnal* (1955; fig. 23) expresses a different sense of the city – an almost religious reverence for the urban environment. Near the center of the work, a Manhattan telephone directory is placed in a carefully constructed rectangular recess. For Rauschenberg, the telephone directory documents the density and variety of New York's population. It includes all types of people in a non-hierarchial format and thus is a model for inclusiveness. The manner in which the telephone book is centrally placed in its niche resembles the way a religious icon might be located in the wall of a church. Of course, the title of the Combine is that of a church song-book. There is a religious undercurrent to a number of Rauschenberg's works that has been largely overlooked in the literature on him. During his childhood, Rauschenberg had wanted to be a preacher, and he continued to attend church during his early years in New York. Religious titles were used for several of his earliest paintings, including *Mother of God* (c. 1950, San Francisco Museum of Modern Art) that shows a brilliant white orb painted over a collage of American city maps. *Odalisque* (1955–58, Museum Ludwig, Cologne) contains a church donations envelope and a reproduction of a painting depicting Christ in a "noli me tangere" scene, and *Co-Existence* (1961, Virginia Museum of Fine Arts) features an actual reliquary case, with a tooth in it, that Rauschenberg had found. As one later example, Christian religious imagery plays an important role in Rauschenberg's ROCI/Chile works to be discussed in Chapter 6. In *Hymnal*, the religious references are a way of indicating the mysterious and awe-inspiring character that the city holds for the artist. The evocative spirit of *Hymnal* is enhanced by the Paisley fabric covering most of the surface. Its dark colors seem ineffable and the spiraling organic pattern which is centered on the telephone directory resembles the elaborate decorative reliquaries of the early Christian tradition. Of course, Paisley patterns are actually of foreign origin so that, in the spirit of New York's diversity, varied cultural traditions are being mixed. Five additional pieces of cloth are attached to the surface of *Hymnal* in order to emphasize such diversity, and I have already discussed Rauschenberg's career-long fascination with fabrics. The fabrics, which vary from velvets to a simple scrap of white linen, also give the Combine an antique patched together look, as if the viewer had discovered some early artifact of urban culture.

Toward the bottom of *Hymnal*, Rauschenberg attached three printed images: they include a photograph of two children swimming, a murder victim lying face down on a city street, and an FBI "wanted poster". The images have visual similarities that lead us to compare them – the faces of the two children parallel the two, frontal and profile, photographs in the FBI poster, and the body position of the dead man resembles the pose of one swimming child. As in *Collection*, Rauschenberg does not avoid the violence present in the urban world, rather images of violence, criminality, and childhood innocence are deliberately juxtaposed. Yet, in this case, the photographs are placed behind pieces of translucent tissue paper, intimating that they are seen through the veil of memory. Set between the photographs is a graphically powerful black arrow on a white ground. It is abutted by a black brushstroke extending in the same direction, one of the relatively few brushmarks made by the artist in *Hymnal*. Both the arrow and the paint strokes point outside of the work, insinuating that the viewer should now look beyond the confines of *Hymnal* to the city itself.

23 *Hymnal*, 1955, Combine painting: oil, paper, fabric, printed paper, printed reproductions, and wood on fabric, plus section of telephone directory with metal bolt on string, 64 × 49 $^1/_4$ × 7 $^1/_4$", Sonnabend Collection.

Directly below the telephone book in *Hymnal* is a rectangular board with graffiti carved onto it. The board is attached to the surface of the Combine and protrudes from it, thus providing a counterpoint to the recessed telephone book. As the telephone directory is treated like an icon, so the board partly resembles the type of small wood panel used in traditional religious painting. Because of the worn character of the board and the crude carving, it appears simultaneously as an ancient artifact and contemporary debris picked up from the street. Historically, the debris of one generation becomes the archaeological find of another, as Rauschenberg was well aware from his travels in Italy with Cy Twombly.

The graffiti found in *Hymnal* also appear in a number of later Rauschenberg works, and he was among the first artists of his generation to recognize the characteristics of graffiti as a naive art form, document of human history, and sometimes a record of intimate relationships. Found primarily in urban contexts, graffiti personalizes otherwise anonymous objects, just as the worn and rebuilt tools are signs of the individual in other Rauschenberg works. Earlier, Willem de Kooning had re-created elements of graffiti in an abstract manner in his Black Paintings of 1947, and starting in 1960 Cy Twombly made graffiti-like scrawls on the surface of his canvases a centerpiece of his art. During the late 1970s, the so-called Graffiti Artists emerged in New York and created their own synthesis of graffiti and modern painting. In these contexts, Rauschenberg is distinctive in that he does not recreate the graffiti but appropriates it de facto. Thus, his graffiti function less as an artistic trope and remains more a document of a particular time and place in history.

The particular graffiti in *Hymnal* contain a number of names scratched within heart-shaped configurations but by far the most prominent name carved vertically along the face of the board, is "JOHAN." Rauschenberg may have chosen this particular board because the name scrawled on it reminded him of his close relationship with Jasper Johns.

Between 1954 and 1961, Rauschenberg and Jasper Johns were involved in a significant personal and artistic relationship (fig. 24). The two were confidants and lovers, but most importantly they shared ideas about their developing art. Regarding their relationship, Rauschenberg once said:

> Jasper and I literally traded ideas. He would say, "I've got an idea for you," and then I'd have to find one for him. Ours were two very different sensibilities, and being so close to each other's work kept any incident of similarity from occurring.[43]

The artistic interaction between these two individuals is extremely complex and a full discussion is well beyond the confines of this chapter, but something of their interchange might be suggested. Rauschenberg's statement, quoted above, incisively sets forth the artistic connection. While shared motifs and forms can be found, these devices are often used in deliberately opposite manners. The relationship between the works of these two artists is most often one of assimilation and then negation, as one artist answers the other through reversing his original intent. As Rauschenberg

24 Rauschenberg and Jasper Johns in Rauschenberg's Pearl Street studio (c. 1955), photo by Rachel Rosenthal.

stated, he and Johns have "two very different sensibilities," and paradoxically, as he pointed out, it was their acute awareness of each other's works that kept them from similarity. In this regard, the dynamic between the two artists differs from more common situations of mutual support that lead to common inventions, like Braque and Picasso's joint creation of Cubism.

Johns and Rauschenberg met during the winter of 1954 on 57th Street, introduced to each other by Rauschenberg's friend the art critic Suzi Gablik, as Johns was walking home from a temporary night job that he had taken at the Marboro bookstore. The meeting was not one between artists of equal experience. Rauschenberg was six years older and, while he was still very much in his formative years, his artistic background, which included his travels in Europe, encounters at Black Mountain College, and setting up a studio loft on Fulton Street, was well beyond that of Johns. Like Rauschenberg, Johns was a Southerner, born in Augusta, Georgia, and the common heritage was probably an initial attraction. Johns had come from a difficult family situation, but he had been interested in art ever since childhood. He had attended the University of South Carolina but dropped out in his second year and came to New York to commercial art school. Johns soon left that school and was drafted into the army where he spent six months in Japan, beginning a career-long interest in Japanese art and culture that he shares with Rauschenberg. Returning to New York, Johns entered City College on the GI Bill, but finding the classes confusing and uninteresting left after a single day, taking a job at the Marboro bookstore. At that time, Johns was only making some watercolors and drawings and knew almost no one in New York. Under these circumstances, the first influence was clearly to be Rauschenberg's, and Johns has been candid about the initial role model that Rauschenberg provided, saying, "Bob was the first person I met who was a devoted painter, whose life was geared to painting. I had never met anyone like that."[44]

Rauschenberg soon persuaded Johns to quit his job to devote more time to his art, and under Rauschenberg's influence Johns became acquainted with Lower

25   Rauschenberg working in Pearl Street studio, New York (c. February 1958), works shown are *Charlene* (1954), *Untitled* (c. 1954), and *Monogram* (second state) (c. 1956; partial rear view), photo by Dan Budnik.

Manhattan. When an opportunity came during the fall of 1954 to move to the South Street area, Johns did so. While Rauschenberg was living on Fulton Street, a mutual friend, the artist Rachel Rosenthal, found the building on Pearl Street just around the corner from Rauschenberg's loft. It was a dilapidated but solid structure in an area slated for eventual demolition under the Title I Act, but there were no plans for its immediate destruction. Johns took the loft of the fourth floor and Rosenthal the fifth floor space. Given the nearby studios, Johns and Rauschenberg began to see each other on a daily basis. In September 1955, when Rosenthal took a teaching position in California, Rauschenberg took over the fifth floor loft (fig. 25).

The earliest works by Johns reflect the clear influence of Rauschenberg because of their reliance on found objects and on active viewer involvement. For instance, *Construction with Toy Piano* (1954; fig. 26) consists of a child's miniature piano that has been mounted flat on the wall so that its numbered keys run along the top edge. The surface of the piano has been covered with collage papers, some of which belonged

26 Jasper Johns, *Construction with Toy Piano*, 1954, graphite and collage with toy piano, 11 $^9/_{16}$ × 9 $^1/_8$ × 2 $^3/_{16}$, Offentliche Kunstsammlung Basel, Kunstmuseum. © Jasper Johns/Licensed by VAGA, New York, N.Y.

to Rauschenberg. The papers identify contemporary history and geography much as similar collage items had in Rauschenberg's *Collection*, a significant difference being that Johns seems to have chosen more exotic news items mostly involving locations other than New York City. The notion that the viewer might play the piano keys is in keeping with Rauschenberg's idea of viewer interaction with the art works, but there are important distinctions. Johns's work is intimate and his careful placement of the collage elements stands in contrast to the bravado of Rauschenberg's works which mimic the messiness of urban life around him. The numbers on the piano keyboard already indicate Johns's interest in the underlying systems and abstract structures by which we order information, concerns that are opposite to Rauschenberg's fascination with variety. The particular spectator interaction with *Construction with Toy Piano* results in music – it is an art work that concerns making art. In this aspect, Johns's piece diverges from Rauschenberg's interest in the relationship between art and everyday activities. On the whole, Johns's earliest works are difficult to study because late in 1954 he destroyed all pre-*Flag* paintings and constructions that were in his possession. (Only the few he had given to friends, like *Construction with Toy Piano*, survived.) Such self-editing is typical of Johns's critical view of his own work as opposed to Rauschenberg's tendency to preserve nearly everything that he has made, which is the same impulse that leads Rauschenberg to embrace all aspects of his environment. Johns has suggested that the destruction of the earliest works was internally motivated, resulting from his decision to no longer "become" an artist but to "be" one. It may well be, however, that the primary reason was that Johns's works, distinctions above not withstanding, were too derivative of Rauschenberg's art.

Since its creation, Johns's *Flag* (1954, The Museum of Modern Art, New York) has been the subject of artistic celebrity and extensive critical discussion. In these analyses, the painting has not been viewed as an answer to Rauschenberg's art and as Johns's deliberate assertion of the distinctive character of his own ideas as separate from Rauschenberg's. The oppositions between *Flag* and Rauschenberg's contemporary Combines are notable. While the single most important feature of the Rauschenberg Combines is multiplicity of materials and visual experiences, *Flag* is initially read as a single indivisible image. In the Combines, the collage elements may be used to locate the works in place and time and to connect them to Rauschenberg's varied urban experiences. Johns began *Flag* with similar collage material, but the papers are so fully buried beneath layers of encaustic mixed with pigment that they are all but impossible to read. For Johns, concealment rather than disclosure is a primary artistic motivation. Several years ago, Joan Carpenter, an art historian, arranged for infra-red photographs to be made of *Flag* and was able to demonstrate that many of Johns's collage fragments had personal significance for the artist, in a mode similar to Rauschenberg's. So it seems that Johns began *Flag* with a reference to Rauschenberg's artistic attitude and then took the work in exactly the opposite direction by deliberately submerging such references. While Rauschenberg's Combines, like *Collection*, were frequently executed in multiple panels that are clearly distinguished from one another, *Flag* consists of three attached panels, but these are so carefully concealed beneath the overall design that one can view the painting on several occasions before realizing that it consists of more than one piece of canvas. Even Johns's newly developed use of encaustic, which looks spontaneous but must be applied very carefully in small areas before the wax hardens, is the polar opposite of Rauschenberg's spontaneous and dashing brushwork.

While Rauschenberg is often given some credit for influencing Johns's interest in such common objects as a flag, Johns's impetus in choosing this image is actually antithetical to Rauschenberg's concerns. The American flag is a universally recognized design, identifiable anywhere in the world. For Johns, the flag was not connected to the social situation or politics of America at a particular time in history but rather functioned like a philosophical proposition because it allowed him to investigate complicated underlying assumptions. These assumptions had to do with the ubiquitous properties of sight, thought, and picture making. Johns has used *Flag* and other such motifs to speculate that seeing actively involves such intellectual processes as selection, correction, association, analysis, and problem solving. When Johns said, referring to *Flag*, that he wanted to paint something "the mind already knows," he was speaking of such underlying and broad questions about how the eye and mind interact.[45] Further, Johns's well-known assertion that the flag came to him as the result of a dream, gives the image the character of a deep mental compulsion and further separates it from the sort of specific urban situations that inspired Rauschenberg.[46] In fact, it could be easily argued that Johns's works of the 1950s, including *Flag*, did not need to be executed in New York. Johns's perceptual and philosophical investigations could be developed irrespective of locale, whereas Rauschenberg's artistic discoveries were totally bound to the particular environment of New York City. This is a major distinction between the two artists, and it establishes the differing trajectories of their early careers.

As regards the urban milieu, Rauschenberg's *Curfew* (1958; fig. 27) suggests one type of Lower Manhattan experience that had a direct impact on the artist – night in that part of the city. The somberness and isolation expressed in this work was a significant aspect of the area in which Rauschenberg lived. Lower Manhattan had a large active population by day (40,000 people) but was nearly deserted (4,000 people) by night. Rauschenberg has always been a night-worker. During the 1950s, he would wander the streets at night looking for objects to include in his works. At night, the abandoned character of Lower Manhattan, which had been filled with human activity during the day, interested the artist. While a curfew is a regulation governing the withdrawal of people from the streets, the artist breaks that "regulation" in order to experience that world and to make his art. The black tonality of *Curfew*, broken by streaks of white, recalls the dark streets with spots of illumination from electric lights. A major aspect of the work consists of four Coca-Cola bottles set within a niche, resembling that used for the telephone directory in *Hymnal*. Coca-Cola imagery appears with some frequency in Rauschenberg's work. For instance, the bottles are the central feature of *Coca-Cola Plan* (1958, The Museum of Contemporary Art, Los Angeles, The Panza Collection) and the Coca-Cola sign is an important element in *Dylaby*.

Coca-Cola was indeed a constant feature of everyday life during the 1950s and 1960s. In 1950, *Time* magazine did a cover story on Coke; it was the first devoted to a product rather than a personality. The article stated that because Coca-Cola franchising plants were run overseas by American business systems the product was having a global effect in terms of spreading American ideas. By 1961, Coca-Cola was sold in 115 countries, and 1,700 plants provided 65 million servings each day. The *Time* article emphasized the pervasiveness of Coca-Cola and the efficiency of the company's management. When the Pop artists began using Coca-Cola imagery in the 1960s, they concentrated these aspects of the product through their clean, assembly-line images.

Rauschenberg used his Coke bottles with a different and more complicated intent than the Pop painters. On one hand, the four Coke bottles in *Curfew* comment on the ubiquity of the product. The fact that they are placed in a niche sets them apart almost like religious icons but, on the other hand, Rauschenberg's bottles are debris

27 *Curfew*, 1958, Combine painting: oil, fabric, wood, engraving, printed paper on canvas and wood, with four Coca-Cola bottles, bottle cap, and unidentified debris, 56 $^1/_2$ × 39 $^1/_2$ × 2 $^5/_8$", David Geffen, Los Angeles.

recovered from the street. These used and battered bottles placed in the context of a dark and rather dirty looking painting comment on the debris in the urban landscape. Both abundance and wastefulness are parts of our consumer society. Here one thinks of J. K. Galbraith's *The Affluent Society*, also of 1958.[47] In that book, Galbraith argues that the surface richness of our society covers private squalor. He asserts that over-production and over-consumption divert society from socially beneficial acts. While Rauschenberg did not read Galbraith's treatise, ideas of urban consumption and decay were prevalent during this period, and the artist had only to look around himself at the trash heaps to see this aspect of society.

Unlike Galbraith, Rauschenberg does not condemn the debris but rather recovers and re-uses it. The old Coke bottles play a proud and prominent role in his Combine. He records manufacture, use, and discard as part of modern industrial society. Through the use of worn bottles that are slightly different due to their manufacture in different plants, the artist also expresses the consumption of Coca-Cola as a simple pleasure shared by a diverse population, young and old, black and white, rich and poor. In Rauschenberg's work the commercial icon is brought down to earth and given commonality. The same sensibility inhabits the battered Coca-Cola sign of *Dylaby* and the photograph of a common man next to a Coca-Cola sign in the silkscreen *Harbor* (1964), discussed at the end of this chapter.

Next to the Coke bottles in *Curfew* hangs a charred piece of wood suspended by a wire. Images of construction and destruction are called forth, and one thinks of the simple urban materials – blocks of concrete, metal spikes, and pieces of wood – that dominated the artist's environment. Such materials intimate that Rauschenberg had been on a type of archaeological dig in his urban surroundings. A photograph of an Egyptian cat sculpture from the Metropolitan Museum of Art occupies the upper-right quadrant, reinforcing the theme of artist as archaeologist of recent urban artifacts. Cats were the most prominent presences as Rauschenberg wandered the night streets, and there were frequent discussions in contemporary newspapers of the "cat problem" in Lower Manhattan.[48] But for the artist, they mirrored his own will to survive through scavenging in the tough urban environment.

At the center of *Curfew* is a reproduction of a nineteenth-century engraving by the English artist Edward Landseer showing dogs attacking a stag, but Rauschenberg has cut off the upper part of the stag's head including the antlers so that two dogs appear to be fighting with each other. Rauschenberg's modification of this image to give it new meaning is typical of the manner in which he alters found materials. Illegal dog fights, held for sport, were a problem discussed in Manhattan newspapers of the period, and they often took place at night.[49] Rauschenberg's image adds to the menacing character of the work, especially because the artist since his youth has been a great lover of animals, particularly dogs. The dog fight theme recurs in the artist's Night Shades of the 1980s, a series of works that also concerns urban menace. Several of these works, which were done in black on metal sheets, feature a fighting dog that Rauschenberg rescued during his trip to Chile for the ROCI/Chile project. All of this imagery, together with the very tattered pieces of cloth attached to the surface of *Curfew*, emphasize the other side of the urban experience from that shown in *Col-*

lection. Curfew concerns the loneliness, melancholy, and even danger that were part of Rauschenberg's urban world.

In *Monogram* (1955–59; fig. 28) which features a stuffed Angora goat, Rauschenberg explored yet another impression of the city – its exoticism. He has said that his aim was "to see if the goat could be related to anything else."[50] *Monogram* has become one of Rauschenberg's best-known and most frequently illustrated works and has come to symbolize for the public the artist's willingness and ability to incorporate nearly any object in his art. It is also unusual in his oeuvre in that it took him nearly five years to arrive at the final composition. The work has several drawings which accompany it, and it existed in two previous states, all uncommon features for Rauschenberg's art, which is usually generated with less planning and less revision. In 1955, Rauschenberg discovered the stuffed goat in a pawnshop several blocks from his studio and fell in love with its strangeness. After passing it in the store window for several weeks, he offered the shop owner a down-payment and promised to return with the rest of the money – something he forgot to do. The goat became one of the very few objects in the early Combines that Rauschenberg purchased rather than found. In the first state of *Monogram* (1955), he placed the goat on a platform projecting from the surface of a vertically oriented painting. The appearance of this work was certainly dramatic, with the goat hanging well above the viewer's head on a shelf set against a colorful background of collage fabrics, cut-out photographs, and a tie. The goat's head, which had been damaged, was repaired by Rauschenberg using paints. In this first version, the head dramatically extends beyond the edge of the platform. Yet, despite the powerful presence of the goat, there is still a sense in this version that it has been (literally) elevated into the world of art and that it is isolated from its everyday origins.

In the second and in the final versions of *Monogram*, Rauschenberg put the goat "back on the street," where he found it.[51] In these versions the goat is placed on a horizontal platform. In the second, the goat stands on a narrow panel with an equally narrow Combine painting extending vertically behind it (see fig. 25). The goat is more part of our environment, but is still connected visually to the rear panel. Rauschenberg abandoned this version because it appeared to him that the goat "was pulling the painting."[52] In fact, a drawing for this version shows the artist's intention had been to put the piece on wheels. This arrangement was partly inspired by the moving dollies used by workers to transport items from store to store along the Lower Manhattan city streets. In the second version of *Monogram*, Rauschenberg encircled the goat with an automobile tire. The tire, placed around the goat's middle, functions as one of the most memorable contrasts in Rauschenberg's works because its sheer improbability excites the mind. The tire and the goat function as polar opposites; one industrially manufactured and the other formerly a living creature, one geometric and the other irregular and organic, one black and the other white, one relatively smooth and the other textured, and so forth. Both tires and animals had already appeared in Rauschenberg's works separately, but the contrast of the two sharpens the distinctive identity of each.

While the goat certainly struck Rauschenberg as an exotic discovery on the streets of New York, it was a creature with which the artist also had some familiarity because

28 *Monogram*, 1955–59, freestanding Combine: oil, paper, fabric, printed paper, printed reproductions, metal, wood, rubber shoe heel, and tennis ball on canvas, with oil on angora goat on rubber tire, on wood platform mounted on four casters, 42 × 63 ¹/₄ × 64 ¹/₂", Moderna Museet, Stockholm.

he had owned a pet goat as a child in Texas. From this experience, Rauschenberg knew that goats are survivors; they eat almost anything and can subsist on land unusable by nearly any other creature. Like Rauschenberg himself, who was able to live and create art out of the left-overs from the streets of New York, the goat is a scavenger. But the particular stuffed goat that Rauschenberg had acquired was an angora goat. The angora was also the most valuable commercial breed because its long silky hair is the source for fine mohair wool used in clothing. Texas is particularly famous for its angora goats and yields most of the mohair used in America. So this angora goat, with Texan origins, is at once an animal that can survive anywhere and a valuable, special creature. It is likely that the artist found an analogy for himself

29 *Sketch for Monogram*, 1959, Watercolor, pencil, fabric, and crayon on paper, 19 ¹/₈ × 11 ³/₈", collection of the artist.

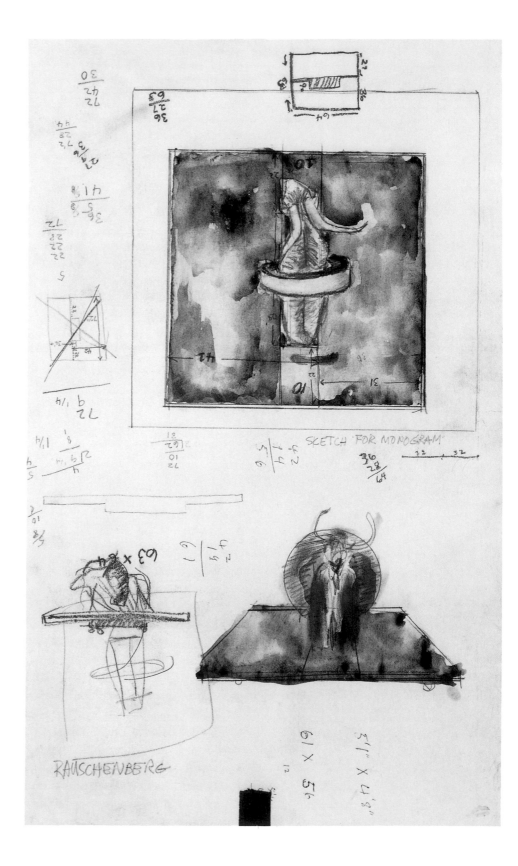

in the goat, a supposition that is supported by Rauschenberg's application of paint to the animal's face. While Rauschenberg has described this action as a way of repairing the damaged head, painters never quite get all the pigment off themselves after working in the studio. One other feature inherent in goats is their sure-footedness. Wild goats are nomadic and are legendary for their ability to climb and maneuver through difficult terrain. Instinctively, Rauschenberg may have found a parallel between the mobility and the tire, a sign of technological movement which he placed around the goat's waist, and the goat's own inherent agility.

Automobile tires represent for Rauschenberg movement and change in the modern world. They have played a role as such in *Automobile Tire Print* (1953) and works like *First Landing Jump* (1961), in which the canvas is placed above a tire so that it appears that the canvas might roll away. Rauschenberg does not see technology and nature as contradictory forces. This seeming dichotomy has proven an intellectual stumbling block for many artists. But for Rauschenberg nature and technology can be complementary factors. The theme underlies many of his works including the NASA projects, to be discussed below, where for instance Florida pelicans standing on their long legs are compared to the gantry supporting a rocket. The title of the work, "monogram," reflects the interweaving of the goat and the tire as the letters in a monogram are interlaced.[53] More significantly, the interweaving might suggest the close relationship between nature and technology in Rauschenberg's art.

In the final version of *Monogram*, the goat and tire are placed on a rolling platform with no vertical elements. The wheels, derived from workers' dollies, are retained. These wheels also imply that the work can easily change locations in the gallery; for Rauschenberg movement is an essential feature in contemporary life. The platform on which the goat stands resembles a city street with debris spread on it, and the goat is placed directly in this urban environment. A Rauschenberg drawing of 1959 (fig. 29) depicts a view of *Monogram* from directly above and thus emphasizes the importance of looking down on the work as one might see it rolling by on the street. On the platform of *Monogram*, Rauschenberg has attached a broken street barricade, a man's shirtsleeves as if tossed on the pavement from a garment truck, and a signboard with letters on it. In addition, there is a shoe heel, a photograph of figures looking across the floor of a building interior, four ink footprints, and directly behind the goat a tennis ball which has been painted brown to resemble excrement left by the animal. Obviously, things that lie on the ground or fall to it dominate. Rauschenberg legitimizes the urban street and the mementos of society that are found on it, and thus provides the context in which this exotic scavenger exists.

*   *   *

Rauschenberg's early Combines like *Collection*, *Curfew*, and *Monogram* are based on his response to his new surroundings. Their objective nature is balanced by the artist's felt responses to his environment. His emotions, reflected in the fun-house excitement of *Collection*, the dark mystery of *Curfew*, and the exoticism of *Monogram*, are as significant as the materials of his new urban environment. Between

1959 and 1962, Rauschenberg's works became less involved with feelings. Works from the end of the decade do not embody emotions as much as states and conditions of materials. The urban environment is seen less as a carrier of personal responses and more as an embodiment of things and of changing circumstances viewed in an objective manner. The works are less focused on personal experiences and more on the facts of the environment surrounding the artist. There is a coolness and intellectual distance. These Combines include *Third Time Painting*, *Studio Painting*, *Winter Pool*, *Broadcast*, *Black Market*, and *Empire*. During this period, Rauschenberg commented:

> When I go out on the street, I'm fascinated to see how much higher they've built a new building, or how much deeper they've dug a hole. Or I notice the construction workers' hats are silver instead of orange. New York is so exciting because the edges haven't got knocked off it. In Europe there's always a different feeling, smoother, with a kind of patina over everything. Here you can never predict what you are going to see when you go out on the street. I don't think New York is a melting pot at all. Nothing melts here, it all just stands out like a sore thumb.[54]

The cool factual tenor that one finds in Rauschenberg's works from this time is a response to changes in his urban environment.

In March 1958, Rauschenberg moved from Pearl Street to a building on Front Street near the corner of Pine. Rauschenberg took a studio on the second floor and Jasper Johns moved onto the third floor. As opposed to the small merchants and retailers who dominated both Fulton Street and Pearl Street, Front Street was dominated by crafts people and small machine shops. On Rauschenberg's block, there were five electrical contractors and three companies devoted to the repair of electric motors. These businesses left their used materials in the street where the artist discovered them, and one thinks of the dominant use of electrical items in Rauschenberg's works of the late 1950s. In addition, there were two plumbing repair firms on the block and two construction companies. Three more nearby individuals are listed in the telephone directory as machinists.[55] This milieu led Rauschenberg toward the more constructed character of his late 1950s works, which may also show some increased influence of Johns's art on Rauschenberg. While Rauschenberg's use of varied material and the specific urban character of his works remain distinctive, the Combines from the late 1950s use fewer items, and composition order is more readily apparent. The viewer is confronted with a few powerfully articulated objects rather than many things. Again, Rauschenberg sometimes relied primarily on value changes rather than dramatic colors. In these aspects, Johns's reductive sensibility, rather than Rauschenberg's instinctively additive nature, may be detected.

Around 1958, construction in Rauschenberg's immediate vicinity was dominated by the South Street Elevated Highway. This one and one-half miles of elevated roadway was an immense project being completed virtually outside of Rauschenberg's studio. Placed between South Street and the piers, the steel and concrete structure was the most expensive undertaking – eleven million dollars in cost – ever managed by the Manhattan Borough Presidents.[56] The project required the assembly of 300 tons of steel beams, and at the height of the activity more than two hundred construction workers were on the job. Rauschenberg included a photograph of this elevated highway in a number of his Silkscreen Paintings, which are discussed below. Initially, the response of the South Street area businesses was positive because the highway promised more efficient means of moving goods in and out of Lower Manhattan. The use of construction materials and devices in Rauschenberg's works of the late 1950s and early 1960s reflects his own excitement over these building projects. The artist likened his use of new materials and structural inventions to the fabrication of the highway and the nearby skyscrapers.

During the 1950s, the South Street area was also ringed by skyscraper construction that emanated from Wall Street. For Rauschenberg, the construction was not yet intrusive; rather it provided an interesting contrast to the older buildings and smaller businesses near the water, and such contrasts epitomized to the artist the vigor of contemporary life. Some of the larger buildings that were erected in the immediate area include: in 1952, the twenty-one-story International Style building on 161 Williams Street; in 1953, the renovation of the Seaman's Bank Building at 30 Wall Street; in 1955, two buildings purchased and demolished at 20 Broad Street to be replaced by twenty-seven-story buildings erected for the New York Stock Exchange; in 1956, the twelve-story International Style building at 156 Williams Street and the twenty-six-floor building by Roth and Sons at 123 Williams Street.

An even more dramatic event for this area of Lower Manhattan was the November 1955 decision by David Rockefeller to build the new Chase Manhattan Bank in the area bordered by Nassau, Pine, Williams, and Wall Streets. Previously Rockefeller had indicated that Chase Manhattan might leave the area, but he changed his mind and decided to promote this location. The Chase building was planned as an immense, eighty-story, building which, together with its extensive pedestrian plaza, took up nearly four city blocks. The anonymous-looking International Style structure was built by Skidmore, Owings & Merrill and cost 75 million dollars. Construction began in January 1958, and the project was completed in 1960. Chase eventually moved 8,700 employees from nine locations around the city to the new building. The excitement of the construction thrilled Rauschenberg as a sign of the modern world and as a counterpoint to life near South Street.

Shortly after announcement of the Chase Manhattan plans, the Downtown-Lower Manhattan Association was formed. This group of fifty-five businessmen, headed by the president of the Seaman's Bank with David Rockefeller as chair of the executive committee, issued a forty-eight-page report that called for the revitalization of the Lower East Side of Manhattan.[57] The plan would directly affect the area in which Rauschenberg lived, yet initially the plan seemed to support the type of diversity that so interested the artist. The report pointed out that fifty-two percent of the downtown buildings were over one hundred years old and that generally housing was inadequate. It stated that the piers could be utilized more fully and that transportation systems must be improved. The questions of relocating the fish market and widening roads were raised. But it was promised that any changes would be respectful of neighborhood interests. The area below Fulton Street was designated as commercial. The report assured that historic buildings would be saved and that small merchants would be protected. Housing would be upgraded and prices would be reasonable.

The initial responses to the report were enthusiastic. The Mayor accepted the document and directed it to be studied by the Redevelopment Authority and the Borough President's Office. A *New York Times* editorial hailed it as "a manifestation of tremendous vitality" and praised the intelligent re-zoning and redesign of the streets and the modernization of the waterfront.[58] Despite all the positive publicity, there were a few skeptics. In his *New York Times* column "About New York," Meyer Berger, for instance, lamented the loss of neighborhoods and the displacement of hardworking merchants. This disillusionment with the plan grew dramatically in the early 1960s. But for the moment the mood was one of ebullience over revitalization of the area. It was in the spirit of such enthusiasm that Rauschenberg's works from 1959 to 1962 were created. In 1960 Rauschenberg told a reviewer that some of his earlier works had "a souvenir quality, which I am now trying to kill. Nostalgia tends to eliminate some of the directness. Immediacy is the only thing you can trust."[59]

Different materials entered Rauschenberg's new works. He began more frequently to use electrical devices, industrial hardware, and other large, physically assertive objects. The new Combines tended toward fewer and larger attached elements. Animals that had associations with the natural world and that were often exotic in an urban context were eliminated in favor of more mechanized and industrial items. Objects such as street barricades, auto tires, ladders, chairs, and wheels of various sizes were favored. Rauschenberg also included electric lights more frequently as well as clocks, fans, and other electrical components. Many of these devices actually worked and were plugged into wall sockets by means of exposed cords. Physical space, passing time, and the potential of the works to change states became major themes for the artist.

Studio Painting (1961; fig. 30) is an example of Rauschenberg's more structural work; the Combine consists of two abutting, equal panels (overall dimensions $72^1/_2 \times 34$ inches) that are pressed together by a rope running horizontally across them. The rope is fixed to one panel, and the other has a pulley attached to its center. The rope passes through the pulley and is weighted by a sandbag attached to its end, thus forcing one panel against the other. This system of tension and compression demonstrates the basic forces that apply to much of our physical environment. The laws of opposing forces, gravity, and friction are made obvious in *Studio Painting*. These physical laws are particularly important for construction, and the engineering connection is made explicit by a photograph of the steel lattice work of a radio transmission tower that Rauschenberg included in the upper-left quadrant of *Studio Painting*. The photograph also sets out a contrast between its illusory character and the physical reality of the sandbag.

The two canvases of *Studio Painting* feature some of Rauschenberg's most gestural painting of the period, and the paint areas are clearly applied against a white ground. The left one is executed primarily in grisaille while the right contains areas of different hues. Thus the two components of color, value and hue, are delineated and one aspect of an artist's work, applying pigment, is emphasized. Paint is dripped

30   *Studio Painting*, 1961, Combine painting: oil,
fabric, paper, rope, metal pulley and clasps, stuffed
canvas bag, and charcoal on canvas, 72 $^1/_2$ × 72",
Private Collection.

extensively throughout the surface and, therefore, the physical activity of paint application as well as the effects of gravity on pigment are highlighted. The appearance of Rauschenberg's paint handling resembles that of Hans Hofmann who developed a more palpable and tangible interpretation of Abstract Expressionism through his famous theory of the "push and pull" application of pigment, an idea related to the concreteness of *Studio Painting*.[60] Pieces of clothing are also attached to the surface of *Studio Painting*, as Rauschenberg had done in his earlier Combines. The fabric here is not the exotic and unusual materials often found in those earlier works; but, rather, it is simple worker's clothing. It seems that Rauschenberg is emphasizing himself as a worker and accentuating the material aspects of his profession.

Similarly, *Magician* (1959; fig. 31) stresses the tangibility of the artistic process. Here the emphasis seems to be on the characteristics of sight. Attached to the surface are four pieces of signboard containing fragments of boldface roman lettering. These are the types of signs that Rauschenberg found hanging on the shops that surrounded him in Lower Manhattan, and such sign fragments appear in numerous works of this period. In the case of *Magician*, the letters contained on three of his fragmented signs are SEE, SE, and C. It seems clear that Rauschenberg is urging the viewer to "see." The fourth fragment contains the letter A, leaving open the question, "to 'see a' what?" In a mode common with the artist, Rauschenberg opens his work to viewer interpretation and completion.

In addition to the lettered panels, *Magician* has a commercial color chart, of the type given out in paint stores, attached to it. The color chart suggests a systematic investigation of the role that color plays in the visual process. Most of the pigment applied by the artist consists of shades of gray, focusing, like one panel of *Studio Painting*, on the role of value changes in vision. A rusted light reflector is hung from the surface of *Magician* and reminds one that the painting is a type of light reflector. To emphasize both the physical and illusional character of painting, the reflector's real shadow is contrasted with a painted shadow below it. Rauschenberg nailed a crumpled piece of polished metal to the bottom section of the Combine. This metal sheet absorbs more light than it reflects and distorts images; thus, it highlights other types of visual experiences. In an irregularly framed box to the right of *Magician*, the viewer sees through to the wall, so that the perspective illusionism of painting in the Renaissance tradition is replaced by real space and the physical presence of both the painting surface and the wall on which it is hung. The counterweight suspended below this box similarly emphasizes real projection from the surface of the Combine as well as the forces of gravity, like those demonstrated in *Studio Painting*, which affect every physical object. Rauschenberg seems to be telling us that the magic of *Magician* consists of visually understanding our material world.

One element that *Magician* does not include is sound. Rauschenberg made sound a major component of *Broadcast* (1959; collection of Kimiko Powers). The painting contains three radios that are located behind the canvas surface. Two knobs project through the surface of the Combine – one is volume and the other is station frequency – so that one radio may be tuned by the viewer. The work was fabricated so that the viewer can never clearly listen to a single station, and the noise from the

31 *Magician*, 1959, Combine painting: oil, fabric, wood, printed paper, printed reproductions, and metal on canvas with fabric pouch and string, 65 $^3/_4$ × 38 $^1/_2$ × 16 $^1/_4$", Sonnabend Collection.

radios adjusted to different channels runs parallel to the constant variety and change that the artist strove for visually in contemporary works. Rauschenberg has commented on the genesis of the ideas for *Broadcast*:

> The previous summer I had been involved in a theater project which would have used them [the radios] as part of the costumes; it didn't materialize, but I kept on thinking of the effects of using radios. In *Broadcast* I was interested, academically, in the relationship that sound would have to looking . . .[61]

Here Rauschenberg is interested in the cacophony that the three radios might produce, and this dissonance is like that encountered in a city environment. The artist is absorbed by the concept of time and related memory, specifically the inability of memory to retain a multitude of subtly varied information either through the auditory or visual senses.[62] The more analytical nature of Rauschenberg's questions are in keeping with the works of these years. Yet his concern with the absence of clarity in modern experience is a motif of his work that recurs in many forms throughout his oeuvre.

In *Reservoir* (1961; fig. 32), Rauschenberg focused on the passage of time as a theme. The painting has two clocks imbedded in its surface. The clock on the upper left was set at the time of the day when the artist began the work, and the one in the lower left was set at the time when he finished the painting. Both clocks were allowed to run once the work was completed, and they both run whenever it is exhibited. At first, this system seems to record in a straightforward manner the duration of *Reservoir*'s creation. The time period of its making was saved by the clocks in the manner that a reservoir preserves such materials as water. Yet, unlike the materials in a reservoir, time cannot be retrieved.

When the viewer contemplates Rauschenberg's "system" in *Reservoir* more questions are asked than answers supplied. Because of the twelve-hour cycle, we cannot be certain how long it took the artist to complete the work. In addition, just observing the clocks cannot help answer a variety of more complex questions. They include: how long ago was the Combine made, how often are the clocks run, what else was happening, and what was the artist's state of mind at the time *Reservoir* was executed? Historical time is revealed by *Reservoir* to be fluid and inexact rather than stable.

Contemporary time, however, is more immediate and understandable. The clocks tick away the seconds and minutes as we contemplate the work. Although they do not tell us the correct time of day, they record the passage of these moments. The notion of momentary change is presented throughout the Combine because two wheels are attached to its surface. Not only is the wheel a longstanding sign of movement for Rauschenberg but also these examples can be spun by the viewer – in a more permissive environment than that of the museum – thus putting the work in actual motion for a specific and limited period of time. Of course, the wheels with their spokes also resemble the divided circular configuration of the clocks as well as being reminiscent of Marcel Duchamp's 1913 assisted readymade *Bicycle Wheel and Stool* (The Museum of Modern Art, New York).

32 *Reservoir*, 1961, Combine painting: oil, metal, fabric, wood, string, and wheels on canvas with two electric clocks, 85 $\frac{1}{2}$ × 62 $\frac{1}{2}$ × 14 $\frac{3}{4}$", National Museum of American Art, Washington, D.C.

Paint application in *Reservoir* is particularly spontaneous with a thin layer of white pigment and drips of dark paint as records of the artist's activity. A can is precariously suspended from a piece of cloth, so that apparently it might fall at any moment. On the right side of the painting an empty shelf has been attached. In most earlier works such shelves had been filled by the artist; this vacant one suggests that it is waiting to be supplied with items, perhaps by the viewer.

The fluidity of time has been an essential concern in the twentieth century, an interest inspired by Einstein's Special Theory of Relativity in which time and space were shown to be less stable than previously thought. Cubism's view of the universe was influenced by relativity, and Marcel Duchamp also had a special concern with theories of time. He described the *Large Glass* as "delay in time." Time, as recorded by clocks, is especially important in the urban context. In the country, time is measured by the length of daylight and by the seasons; it thus may seem to pass more slowly. In the city, we are everywhere surrounded by clocks, and we are at the mercy of multiple and sometimes conflicting schedules measured often by the minute. Time is essential to fast-paced city experiences. For Rauschenberg, the present moment is life's primary reality. In his view, time is a series of instants, and his art is a response to those moments. Rauschenberg tries to live in the continuous present, and this attitude is one manner in which he attempts to preserve the continual freshness of his work. *Reservoir* conspires to convince the viewer of the importance of the moment and of the more slippery nature of historical time.

The 1961 *Wall Street* (fig. 33), of course, was named after the street that is the center of New York's financial district, just six blocks from Rauschenberg's Front Street studio. During the 1950s and early 1960s, Wall Street was the center of building activity that was taking place all around Rauschenberg. In 1961, for instance, seven major construction projects were being completed on Wall Street. Also, street improvements were being undertaken on Wall, Nassau, Pine, and Pearl Streets during that year. The title Wall Street not only suggests Rauschenberg's involvement with street life but is also a pun on the placement of the painting; it was inspired by the street and ends up on the wall.

The major element in *Wall Street* is the street barricade which runs across the center of the canvas and extends beyond its edges. Such barricades were prominent in Lower Manhattan during the 1960s. They were evidence of the rapid changes taking place and were objects easily retrieved by the artist. In everyday life, the street barricade prohibits entry but in *Wall Street* it functions in the opposite manner, because the barricade provides a connecting link between the various elements in the Combine. The black and white striped pattern of the barricade inspired Rauschenberg's black and white paint application on the canvas, and a yellow block of wood nailed to the barricade accounts for the yellow patch of paint to the far left of the canvas. Similarly, the blue can nailed to the upper-right corner of the painting's stretcher is paralleled by the nearly identically colored blue area of paint below it.

In *Wall Street*, the street barricade extends beyond the canvas to the viewer's right side, and a piece of tire is attached to it. While the tire picks up the black color of

33 *Wall Street*, 1961, Combine painting: oil on canvas with paper, zinc sheet, fabric, string, wooden plank, rubber, and fire hose, 72 × 89", Museum Ludwig, Cologne, Ludwig Donation.

the barricade as a motif, it is soft and curved as opposed to the rigidity of the barricade. In turn, the flexible tire is connected to a fire hose which hangs down the wall and is coiled on the floor. The Combine thus reaches out into the viewer's space. *Wall Street* is a model for Rauschenberg's belief in creating a complex environment through connecting disparate objects. Not only does pigment relate to objects outside of traditional art space as represented by the canvas, but also to objects that are hard and soft, ones that are made of wood, rubber, and cloth, ones that extend, hang, and coil can all be related to one another.

The Combine *First Landing Jump* (1961; fig. 34) sums up this materially oriented, constructed period of Rauschenberg's work. Strong contrasts of black and white again dominate this Combine. The surface is partly rough unprimed canvas and partly a black cloth tarpaulin. The artist's canvas is no more significant or interesting than the worker's tarpaulin, and the tarpaulin's stitching and grommet patterns are of equal interest to the paint marks made on the canvas by Rauschenberg. Judging by its tattered appearance the black cloth had fallen into disuse and had been re-employed as a worker's drop-cloth before Rauschenberg recovered it; thus it carries the clues to its history on its surface. A shirt is glued to the lower section of the Combine, and like the other shirts used during this period, it is a worker's shirt rather than one consisting of decorative material, as Rauschenberg had used in earlier Combines.

Above the shirt in *First Landing Jump*, Rauschenberg attached a rusted automobile license plate. The rusted plate suggests both the dominance of the automobile in modern society and the decay of the industrial environment in which throw-away products became increasingly commonplace. Next to the license plate hangs a tin can with a blue electric light bulb inside; the exposed electric cord which provides power hangs below the canvas. *First Landing Jump* has been at various times exhibited with the electric cord hidden, and the artist has objected rigorously to this mode of display. For him, the appearance of the functional electrical cord is an essential part of the work's meaning. The bare hanging bulb in *First Landing Jump* is reminiscent of those found in older unkept buildings and on construction sites. The bulb also suggests an active relationship between the Combine and its environment. Rather than simply being lit by that environment, the work of art provides its own illumination which alters the room around it. This device is one of many used by Rauschenberg to activate his works so that they engage the surrounding world. When asked about his most important inventions, Rauschenberg once mused, "I don't know – screwing light bulbs into paintings maybe. Trying to make the light come from the painting. Adding luminosity from the painting to match the environment. That is the first evidence that I had wanted the work to *be* the room itself."[63]

In *First Landing Jump*, another street barricade is employed as an element of extension beyond the canvas. Here the barricade provides a vertical connection between the canvas and a tire. On one hand, the tire visually supports the Combine, connecting it to the floor and undermining the traditional notion of the art work as object hanging on a wall. On the other hand, the tire suggests mobility; like a truck loaded with its cargo, the work might roll away at any moment. The circularity of

the black tire is complemented by the white metal light-reflector at the top of the Combine. These two objects – black and white, rubber and metal, stationary and potentially moving in their everyday function – set up the creative dichotomies on which Rauschenberg's art relies. The light-reflector is the type of mundane object also found in the old buildings of the artist's neighborhood. Its battered appearance suggests the wear and tear that is part of the modern urban world.

The white light-reflector with its fluted edges also resembles the circular shape of a parachute that has been deployed. This relationship partly accounts for the title of the painting. Parachuting is a frequent motif in Rauschenberg's art. *First Landing Jump* is one of the first direct indications of this theme whose indirect predecessors are umbrellas, like that used in *Charlene*. Rauschenberg has used cloth in the shape of parachutes in numerous works; a small parachute was included in *Untitled* (c. 1955, Stephen T. Edlis Collection); and he actually skated with a parachute attached to his back in *Pelican* (1963, 1965; see fig. 76), the performance of which is discussed in Chapter 4. Images of parachutists have appeared throughout his career, and space capsules parachuting to earth, as will be discussed in Chapter 3, are among the most frequent of his space flight images. The attraction of parachuting for the artist is the combination of high adventure with a sense of limited control. As the parachutist floats to earth, she/he is partially at the mercy of the winds which determine the direction of drift. Here, the artist finds an analogy to his art. In his work, Rauschenberg sets up situations which, in theory, allow him to be only partly in conscious control. Outside events, materials at hand, and unexpected mental associations all create welcome surprises in his art works. In *First Landing Jump*, Rauschenberg is asserting that he is aesthetically skydiving into new artistic territory.

*   *   *

At about the time Rauschenberg was completing *First Landing Jump*, the perception of urban development was changing nationwide and this change, particularly evident in New York, is reflected in Rauschenberg's art. A largely unrealized crisis that reached its height in 1962 had been brewing in New York since the end of World War II. The post-war economic boom had hidden some of its effects, but the warning signs emerged in the late 1950s. Since the war, Manhattan had been experiencing an increasing percentage of failures among small businesses. Growth industries which required large parcels of land were also leaving the city. Simultaneously the middle class was abandoning New York for the promise of suburban life, and the rate of poverty in the city was rising. New York was becoming increasingly dominated by the wealthy and the destitute. The public also became more aware of high levels of government corruption, which worked against the average citizen.

New York City's problems were highlighted by three publications of 1959. The first was Edgar M. Hoover and Raymond Vernon's *Anatomy of a Metropolis*, the initial volume of a nine-volume study conducted under the aegis of Harvard University. The authors warned, based on their statistical analysis, that New York City faced "an eventual loss of population, industry, trade, and jobs." They argued that such a decline would occur because housing, transportation, and streets were largely outmoded. They observed that there was no space for growth in the inner core of the region and that the outer rings would grow instead, as the core deteriorated. The authors predicted that many neighborhoods would become blighted and that New York City would become home to the "very rich and the very poor."[64]

The Hoover/Vernon study made front pages in newspapers throughout the city and metropolitan region. One month after the book was published, in July 1959 *Newsweek* magazine did a special report, "Metropolis Is a Mess." Written in a sensationalist style, it emphasized the flight of the middle class from the city as well as the proliferation of slums, crime, and racial tension. In the following issue, Mayor Robert Wagner published a response that did little, however, to counteract the changing attitude about New York.[65]

In October of 1959, the *Nation* published an issue titled "The Shame of New York" by two award-winning reporters Fred J. Cook and Gene Gleason.[66] Their essays set out to expose corruption in city government and focused on the Title I slum clearance programs. They showed that under cover of these laws developers bought condemned buildings, not to tear them down and provide better housing, but to let them decay while collecting high rents. The developers, who were allowed to buy the properties at bargain rates, paid neither taxes nor interest to the city, and they frequently sold the properties to other developers for further gain.

Cook and Gleason laid most of the blame on Robert Moses, who then held the position of city planning commissioner. In the section of their essay titled "Moses the Mighty," they depicted Moses as a power broker who had never been elected to public office and who had absolutely no empathy for the people of the city. The essay reported on the 1954 scandal involving kickbacks to developers in the area surrounding the New York Colosseum. Although Moses was never directly connected with this scandal, his involvement had long been assumed. The authors described uprooted families who had been moved six times with the promise of better, affordable housing never fulfilled, and they blamed Moses and his policies for their despair and anger.[67]

The troubling legacy of Robert Moses touched Rauschenberg's life as it did every New Yorker of the period. The Downtown-Lower Manhattan Association's proposals, that threatened to change Rauschenberg's neighborhood, were only subdivisions of Moses's overall vision. Beginning in 1924 when appointed president of the New York State Parks System, Moses had wielded enormous power in New York. By 1930, he was designing 9,700 acres of parks on Long Island, including the lido at Jones Beach, and miles of suburban parkways. Eventually, Moses simultaneously held twelve city and state offices. By the late 1930s, he had already turned his sights toward New York City housing. In 1941, Mayor La Guardia named him head of the New York City Housing Authority, and in 1949 Mayor William O'Dwyer named him chair of the Mayor's Committee on Slum Clearance.

Moses envisioned a city cleared of lower-class housing and dominated by uniformly constructed high-rise, rent cooperative skyscrapers. In fact, by 1959, Moses had redeveloped 345 acres with towers that contained 28,000 living units. In this plan, he was the inheritor of the schemes for utopian urban life that had been developed, but already undermined by severe criticism, in Europe between the world wars by Le Corbusier, Mies van der Rohe, and at the Bauhaus and other locations.

To enact changes in New York's urban fabric Moses's weapon was Title I of the Federal Housing Act of 1949. While the act was intended to facilitate the improvement of inner-city housing, Title I was open to abuses. It allowed city officials to condemn large tracts of land and to parcel these out to individual developers for a write-down cost based on the difference between the market value of the condemned land and an appraisal made by the developer that included the costs of clearance and site preparation. This difference was then paid directly to the developer, two-thirds coming in the form of a one-time Federal grant. Obviously, the potential for undervaluation by the developer was enormous unless city officials acted as watchdogs. In Moses's case, the desire to raze whole neighborhoods and rebuild the city as quickly as possible was so strong that he abdicated this responsibility and was later accused of "reckless abandonment of public oversight of private redevelopment."[68] In 1958, Rauschenberg had been evicted from his Pearl Street studio under the ordinances of Title I and his Front Street studio was in a building also slated for demolition. As the 1960s approached, Rauschenberg became increasingly aware of the encroachment of new buildings on the old Lower Manhattan neighborhoods and began to think that the working neighborhoods might not be allowed to co-exist with new development schemes directed by Moses in the manner that the artist had previously hoped.

To those with an interest in urban life, the antithesis of Moses was Jane Jacobs, the newly emerged hero of the inner-city neighborhood and of the common urban dweller. Formerly, Jacobs had written essays for *Architectural Forum* criticizing International Style buildings and showing an interest in city planning and the structure of city government. In 1961 her book *The Death and Life of Great American Cities* was published. It had an immediate and profound effect on the perception of cities. Jacobs called for decentralized neighborhood-based planning, and she celebrated urban density and the variety of life on the streets. She praised the "seeming disorder of the old city" as a "complex order . . . all composed of movement and change." She concluded, "We call this the art of the city."[69] It is remarkable how close Jacobs's ideas of urban vitality are to contemporary concepts that Rauschenberg expressed in his art works. Like Rauschenberg, Jacobs celebrated public contact, news that spread on the street, the debris of urban existence, high-density living conditions, small manufacturers, and the variety of urban life. Her notion that the seeming disorder of the city was actually a complicated order parallels Rauschenberg's early statement that urban experience "produces an extremely complex random order that can not be described as accidental."[70]

The shifts in urban thinking that centered on New York City during this period related specifically to the area in which Rauschenberg lived. By 1960 the full implications of the Downtown-Lower Manhattan Association's plans had become clear, and the revisions were published in the *New York Times*. These plans included: 1. "razing" all outmoded structures; 2. closing most of the narrow streets in the area; 3. forming an interior traffic loop, and 4. replacing the piers with a heliport and marina. The association revealed that it saw the South Street area as a center for business offices, banks, hotels, clubs, and department stores. Their plans, if followed through, would have resulted in the destruction of the entire neighborhood.

In 1961, the Downtown-Lower Manhattan Association expanded its proposal by designating the South Street area as the site of a "World Trade Center." The center was to be a combination: a 50–70-story hotel with a six-story international trade mart. The entire complex would stand on a three story podium occupied by shops. The structure would occupy 13½ acres bounded by Old Slip, Fulton, Water, and South Streets, and the association hoped that the New York Stock Exchange would also eventually move into the buildings. The complex would be built directly over the area where Rauschenberg had lived since 1953. The plan also had provisions for high-rise housing units for 2,100 people to be built between Fulton Street and the Brooklyn Bridge. David Rockefeller wrote in a letter to the *New York Times* that the project was the "the hottest thing that I'm involved in at the moment." He added that he viewed the East River as a commercial slum "right next to the greatest concentration of real estate values in the city," concluding that "the existence of these slums provides a great opportunity, because they pose a minimum problem of relocation."[71]

At this point, the comprehensive plan of the Downtown-Lower Manhattan Association for the East River area was brought to a dramatic halt. The first stage of the plan would have been the widening of Fulton Street, which would have shut down the businesses of the merchants on that street for a prolonged period and forced many to relocate. The outcry by those store owners forced the cancellation of the project.[72] Subsequently, city newspapers featured a large number of editorials questioning the association's plan. On November 17, 1960, the New York City Planning Commission rejected the proposal for the East River waterfront, with Moses being the only dissenting voice. In 1962 after much debate and pressure from local merchants and neighborhood activist groups, the Port Authority rejected the World Trade Center plan. In 1963, the new proposal for the complex on the western side of Lower Manhattan was made and accepted, where it was built and remained until the terrorist attack of 2001 destroyed it.

Despite the rejection of the association's plans, South Street remained a designated Title I area, and a large number of its buildings were eventually torn down. As mentioned earlier, one of the structures slated for removal was Rauschenberg's studio on Front Street, just as the artist had been evicted from his Pearl Street studio through Title I statutes. Although Rauschenberg was not officially evicted from Front Street, the event seemed imminent in 1961, and under this pressure he decided to move from the area to a new studio at 809 Broadway just below 12th Street. It was in this new studio that Rauschenberg began his Silkscreen Paintings in 1962 (fig. 35). Rauschenberg's loft on Broadway was undoubtedly the best working space that he had yet occupied. The neighborhood, however, held little interest for him. When Rauschenberg began his Silkscreen Paintings, one of their major themes was urbanism, but the urban environment that he depicted was not that of Broadway. Instead, his subject continued to be the South Street area, the images of which include the harbor, dockside markets, the historic Battery Maritime Building, small

35 Rauschenberg working on lower panel of *Skyway* (1964) in Broadway studio, New York (1964), photo by Hans Namuth.

retail stores, earlier downtown buildings, the South Street Elevated Expressway, and street signs from Lower Manhattan.

Rauschenberg's use of silkscreen images has, by its nature, a retrospective character. Taken from newspapers and magazines, the silkscreens picture the recent past. In these works, Rauschenberg did not take objects from the actual environment as he had in the Combines, but viewed his world through the eyes of the media. One aspect of these paintings is certainly a commentary on the ubiquitous character of newspaper photography, pictorial news magazines, and increasingly television. Another consideration was Rauschenberg's desire to explore different aesthetic territory. He has stated that he was feeling too "comfortable" with the Combines and wanted to investigate new areas. But, for an artist who had been so thoroughly involved in the actual stuff of everyday life, there is a significant degree of removal in the Silkscreen Paintings. They concern previously captured images rather than the physical things of his immediate milieu.

He was no longer living in the type of urban environment he wished to depict. Further, his relationship with Jasper Johns had also disintegrated, encouraging a more reflective view of his past in that area. There were strong indications that such varied urban landscapes were in danger of being extinguished. Rauschenberg's Silkscreen Paintings suggest his desire to depict an urban fabric in the South Street area that seemed doomed to extinction by the uniform and anonymous living environment that the Downtown-Lower Manhattan Association had proposed. At the same time, the silkscreens, because of both their subject matter and their style, which is assertively handmade and individual, plead for a continuation of the type of social, economic, and architectural diversity that made Lower Manhattan interesting to Rauschenberg.

The artist's 809 Broadway loft was on the fourth floor of a five-story cast iron building. The loft was a continuous space about 80 by 30 feet broken only by iron supporting columns. It had nine-foot ceilings and three large windows facing onto

Broadway. With low walls, the artist divided off a small sleeping and eating alcove and the remainder of the space could be used for his work. On the floors of this loft, the Silkscreen Paintings were planned and executed with additional painting taking place once they were hung on the walls. Yet, the area around Rauschenberg's new loft was less exciting than its interior. Nearby 10th Street had been the location of many of the Abstract Expressionists' studios, and Rauschenberg's familiarity with the area came from occasional visits during the 1950s. By 1960 the group had scattered, and the art scene on 10th Street had dissipated as artists moved to other locations, including ones outside of the city. Neither Washington Square to the south nor Union Square to the north particularly interested Rauschenberg. Greenwich Village was too traditionally bohemian for him, although that nearby area was the center of Jane Jacobs's neighborhood preservation battle.

On Broadway, the area immediately surrounding Rauschenberg's studio was dominated by large-scale clothing and sportswear companies.[73] There were also shoe, handbag, and glove distributors. A number of plastic novelty item distributors were nearby, and within the block there were twelve lawyers and ten insurance agents. Some of the artists who remained in the area listed themselves in the telephone directory in a commercial manner as artist, sculptor, designer, and so forth. In this section of Broadway, the environment was largely based on professional service providers and larger scale merchandise distributors that conducted office business with sales representatives. It held little sense of dynamic change and the feelings of decay and renewal that characterized the physical working environment of South Street. The products of the Broadway area were anonymous and pristine, as opposed to those in Lower Manhattan that invariably appeared hand-manufactured and marred by hard use, carrying the history of human interaction on their surfaces. The streets in this area were cleaned regularly, and the debris that proved so essential to Rauschenberg's Combines was not to be found. Neither did the Broadway neighborhood contain the same dynamic mix of social classes and ethnic groups found in Lower Manhattan. As a result of these factors, Rauschenberg's Silkscreen Paintings contain memories of his earlier milieu, not experiences of the one on Broadway in which he then resided.

For Rauschenberg, the silkscreen process began with his selection of illustrations from magazines, newspapers, and from his own photographs. He then sent the photographs to a commercial screen-maker with instructions as to scale and the number of colors to be used in each image. When placed on a canvas, or any other flat surface, the artist was able to re-create those photographic images by pressing paint through the weave of the screen, which is left blank in those areas unexposed in the photographic original. To provide imagery for his Silkscreen Paintings between 1962 and 1964, Rauschenberg eventually had about one hundred different screens made. Before his involvement with the silkscreening process, it had been used almost exclusively in commercial printing, primarily for billboards, posters, and product labels. Rauschenberg and Andy Warhol, who were friends, discovered silkscreening at the same time. They used the same technicians to produce their screens, but their uses of the media were actually diametrically opposed. While Warhol stressed the flat, hard-edge, and repetitive character of silkscreen in keeping with its commercial origins, Rauschenberg's silkscreens featured complex, blurred, and overlapping images, and their paint handling was free and individual.

Within his own oeuvre, the immediate sources for Rauschenberg's Silkscreen Paintings were his transfer drawings, begun in 1958, and his first lithographs of 1962. In the transfer drawings, he moistened a newspaper or magazine illustration with a solvent, usually turpentine or lighter fluid. He then placed the drawing face down on a piece of paper and rubbed the verso to impress the image on the paper surface. These drawings are intimate in scale and contain pale ghostlike imagery. Their small size and subtle appearance do not translate well to painting because the transfer images are limited to the size of the original illustration and their insubstantial visual presence can be easily overwhelmed by the more assertive colors and textures of oil paint.

Another source for the Silkscreen Paintings was the artist's early lithographs. In 1960 Tatyana Grosman, founder of Universal Limited Art Editions, had approached Rauschenberg about making lithographic prints. Rauschenberg's immediate response was that the "second-half of the twentieth century was no time to start drawing on rocks."[74] By 1962 he had relented. Sources for Rauschenberg's first lithographic images point directly to his urban concerns as well as his interest in newspapers as carriers of modern information, and therefore they lead directly to his Silkscreen Paintings. For the lithographs, Rauschenberg persuaded his friend Brian O'Doherty, art critic for the *New York Times*, to take him to the *Times*'s picture morgue. There he collected a number of the lead and zinc-cut blocks used for the newspaper's illustrations. Rauschenberg subsequently inked these and recombined them in his prints where they were juxtaposed with his own free marks, made with lithographic touche, on the stone. The lithographs' contemporary subject matter, complex intermingling of images, bold contrasts of white paper against black printer's ink, and their reproducible character – each plate could be re-used in different works – are all direct predecessors for the Silkscreen Paintings.

The Silkscreen Paintings are also tied to the increasing popularity of television during the 1950s and 1960s. The hazy images in the silkscreens are like the slightly blurred early television pictures, and the artist's decision to begin the Silkscreen Paintings in black and white may further signal this early relationship to television, which was then broadcast only in black and white. In addition, the juxtaposition of several images on the screen was a favorite device of early television broadcasting. By the 1960s, such "insets" were frequently used in both television commercials and news broadcasts. These decades were ones of enormous growth for television. Between 1950 and 1967 the number of homes with television sets jumped from 4.2 million to 66.4 million, and the number of commercial stations in America increased from 104 to 608.[75] The levels of sophistication and excitement in the visual imagery also increased dramatically as camera equipment became more portable, and camera crews grew more mobile and creative in their coverage.[76] The medium that had featured reporters drawing on chalk boards before World War II later provided live coverage of such events as General Douglas McArthur's triumphant return from the Far East, the Civil Rights riots, the Kennedy election and assassination, as well as the rocket launches and capsule recoveries from the developing space exploration program.[77]

Rauschenberg was sensitive to this new and popular form of visual communication. In his view, television provided yet another way to combine art and life. Powerful and varied visual images of world events as well as those from everyday existence were brought directly into the home, effects not unrelated to those he sought in his art. This popular medium provided significant parallels to his work, and since the 1960s Rauschenberg himself has watched television avidly. As mentioned in Chapter 1, Rauschenberg has large-screen televisions in his home and studio, and he is seldom in a room, even when working in the studio, without a televison being turned on. He has commented that they provide "a way of bringing the world into the studio."[78]

*   *   *

Different themes feature in the Silkscreen Paintings: space flight, technology, militarism, media, eroticism, and sports are common. Among these subjects, urbanism is one of the most frequent and interesting. In terms of content, the 1962–64 Silkscreen Paintings divide into three brief periods. The earliest examples are a mixture of subjects, as if the artist were experimenting with all possible thematic combinations. They are also executed mostly in black, white, and gray tones. By 1963, Rauschenberg was concentrating primarily on urban subjects, particularly those images that related to his impressions of the South Street area. By 1964, national themes tended to dominate his work. At that time, Rauschenberg began to view his art in a less regional, more national context.

The silkscreen *Tadpole* (1963; fig. 36) is one of the few early paintings with objects attached to it, and thus marks a transition from the Combine paintings. *Tadpole* concerns the importance of the old harbor and shipping to the city, and it reminds us of the maritime roots of Manhattan at a time when plans to turn the working harbor on the East Side into an upper-class recreation area were being debated. The silkscreen image in the lower half of the painting depicts the Battery Maritime Building on South Street at the foot of Manhattan where Whitehall Street ends. The elaborate facade on this aging ferry slip, that provided a service to Governor's Island, consists of forty-foot sheet metal columns, which are painted green to mimic bronze. The 1906 building is characteristic of the variety and the quirky individualism that marked the endangered historic architecture of Lower Manhattan. The gray-blue paint that Rauschenberg smeared over part of this scene suggests that such structures might soon disappear.

Attached to the upper half of *Tadpole* is two-thirds of an automobile inner tube and a strip of aluminum. These elements come across as both factual and romantic. Metal and rubber are two of the basic materials of industrialized society and are among the materials frequently shipped in and out of Lower Manhattan. In addition, the inner tube implies another mode of transportation, the automobile, and metal refers to the structure of ships, cars, and such city structures as the Maritime Building. Like the ferry boats, Battery Maritime Building, and other old buildings

36   *Tadpole*, 1963, oil and silkscreen ink on canvas with objects, 48 × 30 $^1/_4$", collection of Barbara and Richard S. Lane, New York.

depicted in *Tadpole*, these objects are worn but durable – the inner tube has several patches and the aluminum is bent. Yet for Rauschenberg there is a romance in the everyday working city. The inner tube might be used to float in the river – a form of simple child's play in which the process of freely drifting while the imagination wanders resembles Rauschenberg's interest in parachuting. Such a simple activity is opposed to the elaborate entertainment facilities planned for this area. The title "tadpole" suggests a creature of the natural world, as well as ideas of growth and childlike activities. The open area at the center of the inner tube might also be read as a moon shining down upon the city during a hazy night, another romantic image of the urban condition. *Tadpole* makes the old working city a nostalgic and suggestive environment.

The 1964 *Harbor* (fig. 37), which is richly colored as are most of the silkscreens of that year, picks up the theme of the Manhattan harbor. The vibrancy of the hues is accompanied by an exciting composition. The primary subject of the silkscreen painting is the bustle of market activity near the harbor. The watery location is set forth by rivers of blue pigment which dominate the center of the work. Silkscreened photographs of fruit appear in the upper and lower sections of the painting, and, although these images are derived from the same screen, the variations in hue and cropping of the pictures seem to show all different types of produce.

In the upper-right section of *Harbor*, the Statue of Liberty identifies the location as the New York City harbors. The buildings that appear in the lower half of the painting are typical of the low-rise architecture near South Street, and the image to the right shows the decay that is also an important part of Rauschenberg's urbanism. A prominently placed thermometer reminds us that weather is an important factor for the outdoor workers and for the shipping and storage of produce. Toward the bottom of the silkscreen, an army helicopter is seen in flight and a space capsule floats after splashdown. Along with the Statue of Liberty, they are part of the more national-based themes that find their way into Rauschenberg's art in 1964. In this context, however, they function more as humorous asides to the local subjects. The artist playfully intimates that the helicopter is delivering fruit and that the space capsule is floating in the harbor.

Along with such works as *Overdrive*, *Windward*, and *Bait*, *Estate* (1963; fig. 38) epitomizes the domination of urban content in Rauschenberg's silkscreens of 1963. Its overall composition mimics the ordered chaos which was part of downtown life. The underlying grid arrangement of the silkscreen photographs and their dominant rectilinear design are pitted against freely brushed passages and the sheer proliferation of scenes. Images that lean at precarious angles and that are multiplied, reversed, and overlaid with each other abound in *Estate*.

A microcosm for the totality of *Estate* might be the signpost that dominates the upper portion of the painting. This signpost is the very model of multiplicity in the city. It communicates vital information, but the information is confusing and seemingly contradictory. This particular signpost tells us to go in two different "One Way" directions and to "Stop"; an air raid shelter sign points in yet another path. This accumulation of opposing routes would be confusing to anyone, but to a dyslexic it would

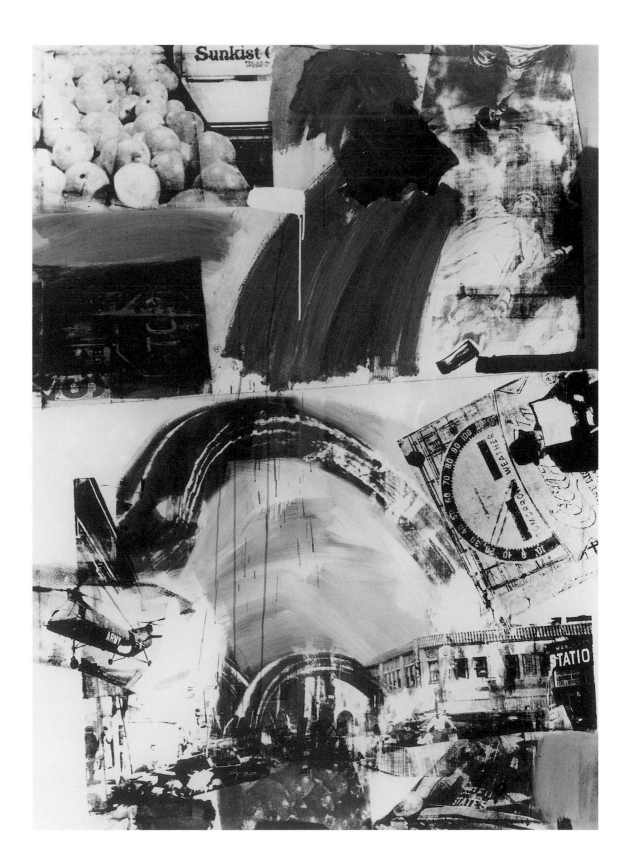

37   *Harbor*, 1964, oil and silkscreen ink on canvas, 84 × 60", Private Collection.

be particularly perplexing because of his/her frequently reduced ability to orient him/herself in terms of left and right directions. The signpost that Rauschenberg shows in *Estate* was located at the corner of Nassau and Pine Streets. Those streets were re-directed as one-way avenues for the construction of the Chase Manhattan Bank complex. By the time Rauschenberg made *Estate*, the street sign had been taken down to be replaced by a new, more efficient model at the corner of the bank building. The signpost is a reminder of the interesting complexity and variety of that area, which the artist feared might be eliminated.

Buildings dominate *Estate*, but most of them derive from a single photograph that has been silkscreened throughout the work. It is clearest in the upper left-hand corner and has been repeated four more times (including once under the image of the Sistine Chapel). Because of its placement and the way it is cropped, the photograph almost seems to be a different locale in each reincarnation. The building shown in it is a six-story warehouse dating to the 1940s that existed at 123 Front Street, and to the upper left, one can see the East River behind it. In the center of the canvas, Rauschenberg contrasts this everyday modern building, which displays a straightforward functionality, with a section of the decorative cornice from the upper floor of a nineteenth-century edifice. In Rauschenberg's view, the old and the new easily co-exist. A more startling contrast is made between such architecture and a photograph of the Sistine Chapel. Here Rauschenberg combines one of the most revered monuments of Western art with an everyday structure and shows his predilection to mix past and present events, high and low culture, lofty and mundane experiences; or, better, his aim of denying that these distinctions even exist. In the photograph, the Sistine Chapel is filled with people, and Michelangelo's frescos, which appear to be a jumble because they are seen at a distance, bear similarities to the clutter of city life. Rauschenberg has literally merged the Sistine Chapel with modern life by printing its image over that of contemporary buildings and by adding the clock over the *Last Judgment* in the chapel. The idea that Christian time has run out is made humorously literal, and Rauschenberg has connected *Estate* to his fascination with the passage of time as seen in such works as *Reservoir*. When Rauschenberg added the clock, he quipped that he was "making a modern painting" out of the Michelangelo.[79]

In addition to the architecture shown in *Estate*, Rauschenberg included a photograph of the elevated South Street Elevated Highway that he had watched being built on a daily basis between 1953 and 1958. For him, the highway represented exciting progress that was nevertheless still compatible with the existing milieu of the old working city. In addition, *Estate* contains aspects of the natural world in the urban environment. At the bottom of the painting, three water glasses on the floor are references to rain falling and being gathered. Water is a natural element that in the context of the city is regulated by being captured in reservoirs and stored temporarily in the building-top water towers that Rauschenberg depicted in many of his works. As such, the collection of rainwater is a model for the interaction of nature and technology in the urban environment.

Other aspects of the outdoors are represented by the three birds on the left of *Estate*. They are mixed with some of the most lavish paint handling in the composition, and their sideways position suggests their mobility. Birds, of course, are among the few wild creatures that exist in the city, and like the parachutists and children floating on the water, their flight stands for freedom of the imagination. The birds' freedom is not constrained by the urban surroundings. In fact, it is perhaps more exciting to see them soar in that context. In the Silkscreen Paintings with city subjects like *Estate*, Rauschenberg tries to re-create the feeling of a varied cityscape, one that can accommodate the widest range of human incidents. These paintings support a type of urban situation that is organic and neighborhood-based – one that accommodates diversity. By implication, they oppose the standardized urban planning schemes represented in New York by the ideas of Robert Moses and members of the Downtown-Lower Manhattan Association. In *Estate*, Rauschenberg is suggesting that the ability of the modern city to accommodate variety is one of the great legacies of modern experience. The title obviously refers to real estate, but in a broader context it is an inheritance or a legacy.[80]

As mentioned earlier, Rauschenberg's silkscreens of 1964 partly switch from urban and regional themes to national concerns. In the works of 1964, the image of President John F. Kennedy first appeared and subsequently became the most frequently used likeness in Rauschenberg's work of that year. The American bald eagle was also used, which Rauschenberg identified with "authority."[81] Depictions of one of the nation's most celebrated causes, the space race, are found with increasing frequency during 1964, and Rauschenberg's particular interest in the space race will be discussed in the next chapter. For the moment, I note that these changes in the artist's interests coincide with his increasing national and international prominence. In 1963 Rauschenberg had a major retrospective exhibition at the Jewish Museum, New York. He also choreographed and performed *Pelican* at the POP Festival, Washington, D.C., and he won first prize for his print *Accident* at the Fifth International Exhibition of Prints in Yugoslavia. In 1964 he performed with the Judson Theater Group at the Moderna Museet in Stockholm, began a world tour with the Merce Cunningham Dance Company, and won the Grand Prize at the Thirty-Second Venice Biennale, becoming the first American painter to do so. It seems likely that Rauschenberg's increased prominence prompted his interest in national themes. He began to relate himself and his work to events outside of his immediate urban environment. The media orientation of the Silkscreen Paintings certainly encouraged this tendency by providing a wide range of American subjects from which the artist might draw. In his later career, it will be seen that Rauschenberg's more nationally oriented goals were supplanted in turn by his interest in establishing an international context for himself. This later tendency is most exemplified by his Rauschenberg Overseas Culture Interchange (ROCI) of 1984 to 1991.

Simultaneously, Rauschenberg's depictions of the urban scene became much less positive. *Choke* (1964; fig. 39) is dominated by a silkscreen photograph of the debris from a building that has been torn down. The destruction is so complete that there is no hope here for the type of creative re-use of materials that had engaged Rauschenberg in the Combines. The remainder of the picture surface is so dense with overlapping and indistinct images that it can hardly be read. The title of the silkscreen articulates such visual congestion as well as the idea of a dangerous lack

40 (*right*) *Prowler*, 1965, solvent transfer with silkscreen, collage, tape, and watercolor on paper, 51 × 61", Mr. and Mrs. William Hack.

41 (*facing page*) *Skyway*, 1964, oil and silkscreen ink on canvas on masonite, 216 × 192" overall (two parts), Dallas Museum of Art.

of air in the painting. The city has become the locale of needless destruction, and its density is now pictured not as creative diversity but as unmanageable chaos. Directly above the rubble at the center of *Choke*, a swath of red paint with a "One Way" sign and arrow imbedded in it directs the viewer aloft and out of the painting, as does the helicopter lifting off on the upper-right side; the need for escape seems paramount. At the bottom of *Choke*, another red arrow, upside down, points to a sign for "Public Shelter." *Choke* is a prime indicator of Rauschenberg's changing view of the urban world and *Prowler* (1965; fig. 40), a transfer drawing with silkscreen, delivers a similar message. There, the silkscreen photograph used in *Choke* is expanded to show the whole scene of the working-class neighborhood with a construction crane destroying buildings at its core. Near the debris are ink fingerprints, like those that might be found at a crime scene. To one side of the crane, Rauschenberg has executed a transfer drawing of a danger sign and on the other side a drawing of an automobile wheel. In this context, the wheel as indicator of constant change does not seem to have the constructive connotations found in works such as *First Landing Jump*. The title, *Prowler*, reinforces the feeling of the illicit and unwelcome activities found throughout the drawing.

Rauschenberg's changing view of his role in relation to the city and his search for a broader context for his art are exemplified in *Skyway* (1964; fig. 41). Except for *Barge*, *Skyway* (216 × 192 inches) is the largest of the Silkscreen Paintings of the 1960s, and it achieved national prominence due to having been created for exhibition in the New York State Pavilion at the 1964 New York World's Fair. *Skyway* is dominated by images of John F. Kennedy, the bald eagle, and particularly the space race. These subjects suggest Rauschenberg's dominant concern with the future of the country as

linked to science and space exploration. (Shortly afterwards, Rauschenberg began to work with a number of scientists and engineers on joint projects that eventually resulted in the foundation of E.A.T., Experiments in Art and Technology.) The city scenes that do appear toward the center of *Skyway* are two versions of a crane destroying buildings, as found in *Choke* and *Prowler*, and two photographs of an isolated single individual, his back to the viewer, striding toward a nearly empty background. The only element in his environment is a signpost with a stop light and a "One Way" sign that points to a blank area of the canvas. Even this signpost contrasts with its more information-filled relative in *Estate*. The urban images that Rauschenberg selected for *Skyway* imply the desolation and isolation of city life as opposed to the excitement and energy of space exploration. They coordinate with a nationwide dismay about urban possibilities in the mid-1960s.

In cities throughout America, scenarios close to that of New York's occurred – even if lacking the intensity of Robert Moses's crusade. Slum clearance reduced the supply of low-rent housing, dislocated thousands of poor families, increased rents, and condemned many individuals to live in anonymous high-rise structures cut off from their neighborhood roots. Despite President Johnson's announcement in his 1964 "state of the union" message of "an unconditional war on poverty," the frustrations in the inner cities continued to grow. It rapidly became clear that Johnson's program would never live up to its expectations, partly because the rhetoric used to express the goals was so inflated and partly because the South Asian conflict distracted the nation's attention from urban problems. On August 11, 1965 rioting broke out in the Watts section of Los Angeles. As millions of Americans watched news reports on television, the conflagration grew over five days, eventually leaving 35 people dead, more than 4,000 people under arrest, and 200,000,000 dollars in property damage. The remainder of the decade witnessed so many instances of urban violence that city officials came to dread the approach of each new "long hot summer."[82] Rauschenberg's scenes of urban destruction in *Choke* and *Prowler*, as well as the scene in the lower-right corner of the silkscreen *Die Hard* (1963; see fig. 46) – where the artist shows his favorite early image of New York water towers, but now printed flame red and overlaid with an image of firemen rushing to the scene – are strangely prescient of the urban chaos that lay just around the corner.

In *Skyway*, however, Rauschenberg contrasted depictions of urban collapse with the heavens and clearly indicated that his attention was now focused on that realm. The upper section of *Skyway* is dominated by a diagram of the planned trajectory for an American spacecraft landing on the Moon. Accompanying the diagram are silkscreen photographs of a newly designed radio telescope employed to listen for signs of life from deep space, an astronaut practicing a para-balloon descent, and the Gemini 2 space capsule at splashdown. The title of Rauschenberg's work, *Skyway*, appropriated from the term used for large raised city highways, indicates the artist's belief that the world's future lay in travel through space rather than on the American roads. The monumental *Skyway*, unveiled at the New York World's Fair, is a predecessor to Rauschenberg's deep interest in space exploration that developed during the 1960s and that will be explored in the following chapter.

three   space exploration works

Art is social.[1]

One of the most prominent questions in Rauschenberg's works is how to determine meaning. What do the works tell us, and how do they connect with their historical periods? I have shown that Rauschenberg relies on spontaneity and intuition as working methods. Yet within his intuitive approach, areas of focus are apparent. My discussion of his urban-based works of the 1950s and 1960s indicates something of his procedures. There are recurring themes in Rauschenberg's works; his selections and deletions have significance; his accumulation of information, while deliberately varied, is not random. A further methodology is needed with which to analyze such works and through which to create a context for Rauschenberg's art.

The best approach to interpreting Rauschenberg's art is to study a theme rather than an isolated work. The analysis of a group of related pieces by the artist allows one to examine Rauschenberg's ideas over a period of time and through a number of permutations. In this manner, one can separate recurring motifs, the ones whose repetition seems to indicate that they have significance for the artist, from ideas that might be added to works but are not central to their overall content. While isolated works by Rauschenberg have been occasionally examined in some detail, rarely has a thematic group by the artist been given sufficient attention.[2] This chapter investigates a series of related works by Rauschenberg in more depth than has been attempted in the literature.

As a starting point, the best theme would be one that includes numerous works executed over a relatively condensed period of time. In this way, the examination of a body of related works allows us to assess similarities and variations of the individual motifs used within it. Since Rauschenberg largely takes his materials from sources in popular culture, his selection of images and things should be examined in the context of the wide variety of options available to him. The topics of his various series should be placed in the context of his own internal development and in the framework of the time and environment in which the artist worked.

The sorts of questions that might be asked are: how and why did Rauschenberg become involved with the given subject; why did he choose certain images and objects and reject others; how did he alter the source material; why did he combine certain images and seek particular relationships; what technical innovations were made during the series and how do they relate to the overall meaning; and finally why did Rauschenberg abandon the theme or lose central interest in it? The art works themselves should be analyzed from the point of view of a thorough knowledge of the particular period. Individuals with whom Rauschenberg worked on the project and who might be experts in the particular subject should be consulted. Because of Rauschenberg's belief in collaboration, he often works with teams of individuals on a given project. Any additional documents or statements by those involved in the project should be consulted. From all of this information, Rauschenberg's outlook about the given theme should be compared with popular perceptions and those of the experts in the field to determine if a particular attitude is evident and, if so, what it is. While much of this sounds like basic historical research, such research has rarely been done on Rauschenberg's works.

A good theme with which to utilize the methods just discussed and also an important and interesting subject in Rauschenberg's oeuvre is space exploration. This topic marked the transition of Rauschenberg's self-image during the 1960s from that of a regionally based artist in New York to an artist with a national and international perspective. Space exploration images appear in approximately eighty of Rauschenberg's works (fig. 42), most prominently in those created between 1962 and 1970. This number of works provides a significant sample and many permutations. The time period is neither too narrow nor too broad. The subject of space exploration and the American "space race" has its own complex and wide-ranging history to which Rauschenberg's attitude can be compared. If the method used here to examine a Rauschenberg series proves informative, it may be employed to interpret other groups of works, either condensed projects like individual ROCI venues, more broadly related groups like the *Venetian* series of the 1970s or the *Kabal American Zephyr* series of the 1980s, or a single extended work like *The 1/4 Mile or 2 Furlong Piece* (1981–present).

Robert Rauschenberg's intense interest in space exploration places him in the context of a line of modern artists who have been fascinated by flight, and it connects him to one of his greatest heroes, Leonardo da Vinci, who speculated extensively about flying machines. For many of the early twentieth-century artists, flight became a symbol of all that was positive in the modern era and of the soaring character of artistic imagination. The last decades of the nineteenth century were marked by a stream of marvelous inventions including the railway, telegraph, telephone, electric light, skyscraper, automobile, photography, and the cinema. Yet the most sensational invention, flight, remained elusive until the first decade of the twentieth century. When the Wright Brothers achieved their first powered flight from Kitty Hawk, North Carolina on December 17, 1903, international headlines were made. At a demonstration of their airplane in Hanaudières, France during the next summer, one witness was heard to exclaim in wonder, "We are all the children of the Wrights."[3]

On several occasions Rauschenberg has indicated that the Wright Brothers were among his most admired heroes. He dedicated his first choreographed dance *Pelican* (1963, 1965; see fig. 76), which will be discussed in the next chapter, to Wilbur and Orville Wright. In that work, as mentioned before, Rauschenberg and his partner danced on roller skates with open parachutes attached to their backs. Thus they mimicked the flight of the great gliders that the Wright Brothers first used. In *Trust Zone* (1969; fig. 43) one of Rauschenberg's space exploration works from the *Stoned Moon Series*, a giant schematic rendering of the Apollo program space suit is matched by a photographic image of the Wright Brothers during their first powered flight. In 1990, Rauschenberg created *Rocket/ROCI USA*, which consists of a bicycle outlined in neon tubes. The bicycle is suspended off the ground and the neon outline makes it seem to fly; the work, thus, connects the Wright Brothers as bicycle makers with rocket flight. To signal the importance of this connection, Rauschenberg used *Rocket/ROCI USA* as the entrance piece at the Solomon R. Guggenheim Museum, New York for his 1997–98 retrospective.

Rauschenberg recognized that the Wright Brothers, who worked in Dayton, Ohio, were outsiders amid the sophisticated European-centered flight community, just as the young man from Port Arthur, Texas was an outsider to the New York art community. Further, the Wright Brothers were pragmatic American tinkers. They learned through doing, not through aeronautic theory. Wilbur firmly believed that the solution to flight lay in the wing control of their plane and that these practical problems could be solved only through repeated experimentation and logging time in the air. Similarly, Rauschenberg is a pragmatist who creates through practical experiments and physical contact with materials. On the whole, the idea of the Wright Brothers, who were American self-taught inventors, appealed highly to Rauschenberg.

The early modern artists who act as predecessors for Rauschenberg's fascination with flight include Robert Delaunay. In 1909 Delaunay had followed day by day the preparation of the great French aviator Louis Blériot for his flight across the English Channel. Afterwards he and Sonia Delaunay attended the parade to welcome the aviator home, and Robert even wrote Blériot a letter of congratulation. Then in 1913 Delaunay painted his *L'Hommage à Blériot*. In it the sun disks that he had created in works of the previous year are combined with images of spinning propellers and landing wheels, the Eiffel Tower, earlier planes that include a Wright Brothers-like biplane and a flying machine that resembles Leonardo's imaginings. The figures shown in Delaunay's painting are ground crew preparing planes, not heroic pilots. Delaunay suggests that flight is the culmination of a grand collective effort including the artist's imaginative creation. This idea is very much in the spirit of Rauschenberg's space exploration works that also emphasize history, understandable technology, and collective effort.

The Russian artist Kasimir Malevich had also been inspired by airplane flight and acknowledged that his development of Suprematist painting was indebted to flying

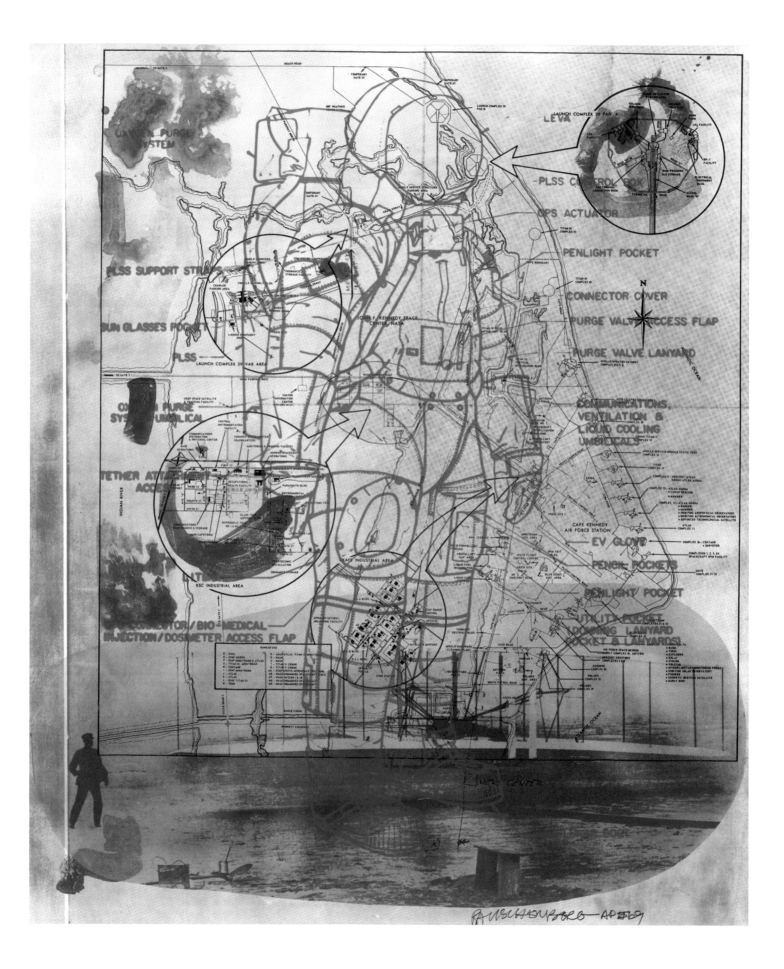

RAUSCHENBERG—APR69

machines, titling one of his paintings *Suprematist Painting: Airplane Flying* (1915).[4]
The series of photographs that Malevich chose to illustrate an environment that
stimulates Suprematist painting, and which he planned to show to accompany
lectures at the Bauhaus in Germany, comprise aerial photographs and images
of airplanes and dirigibles. Malevich saw flight as a spiritual experience, in his
words "Everything was striving to leave the globe, and to make its way further in
space . . ."[5] While Rauschenberg, in contrast, views space exploration as an achievement based on human aspirations, there is a spiritual component to the works. It
will be seen that he finds the soaring character of the artist's imagination an equivalent for space flight. Rauschenberg also was aware of the fascination that Picasso
and Braque had with flight. During the years that they invented Cubism, they used
Wilbur and Orville as nicknames, and one of Picasso's famous Cubist works contains the phrase "Notre Avenir est dans l'Air."[6]

In the context of Rauschenberg space imagery and his dedication to the peaceful
use of space exploration, it is worth noting that the image of aviation for artists
changed drastically in the years leading up to World War II. The bombing of the
Basque town of Guernica on April 26, 1937 marked the first use of aircraft deliberately to destroy a civilian target in order to demoralize the enemy. Subsequently, this
type of bombing was used by both the Fascists and the Allies during World War II.
After the bombing of Guernica, the airplane took on new sinister meaning for artists,
one very different from the adulation of the air war "ace" of World War I. Although
Picasso did not include aircraft in his anti-war *Guernica* in order to universalize the
theme and to focus on the human suffering, the machines that caused that suffering were on the minds of everyone who saw the work.

After Picasso's *Guernica*, other artists picked up the idea of terror from the sky.
For instance, David Smith created *Bombing of Civilian Populations* as one of his
Medals for Dishonor in 1939, showing a stork-like creature dropping eggs of death
onto helpless women and children. Later Smith welded a series of steel sculptures of
fearsome primal birds, such as *Jurassic Bird* (1945) and *The Royal Bird* (1947–48). These
predators, resembling pterodactyls, were harbingers of destruction from the air.
Their skeletal shapes remind us of the superstructure of aircraft, and they are fero-
ciously against aerial technology, suggesting that the world was going to bomb itself
back into a prehistoric age. Their meanings are made more powerful by contrast with
the traditional religious association of the sky as heaven containing flying angels.
During the war years, such artists as Jackson Pollock, Seymour Lipton, Max Ernst,
and Jacques Lipchitz developed similar imagery. The twentieth-century art history
of aerial subject matter which runs the gamut from utopian belief to fearsome terror
forms a general background for Rauschenberg's space exploration works.

Aerial imagery began to appear in Rauschenberg's art in the mid-1950s. The form
that it initially took was parachutes, umbrellas that are parachute-like, birds, and
occasionally airplanes. Rauschenberg's *Untitled* (1954, Museum of Contemporary
Art, Los Angeles) is one of his seminal early Combines. Notably the work contains
a stuffed Plymouth Rock hen, a photograph of a dashing young man in a white suit
that has been taken for a symbolic self-portrait, and a pair of white shoes. *Untitled*

also contains photographs of Rauschenberg's mother and sister as well as other photographs of mothers and children. *Untitled* is about flight from home: the artist has left his provincial home to work in New York. Appropriately, the Combine contains images of flight. Rauschenberg's first use of a photograph of a parachutist appears in this work as well as his first image of an airplane. For Rauschenberg, birds are also symbolic of flight. Here the stuffed bird, freed from its confinement, might be seen as an illusion to the artist's rural background, suggesting that the bird has flown the coop.

Of Rauschenberg's early flight images, the parachute is the most common. It is noteworthy that many of his depictions of space exploration are also those of capsules parachuting to earth or of a parachuting astronaut. An umbrella that first appears in *Charlene* and umbrellas in many works afterwards are parachute-like.[7] In *First Landing Jump* the round metal light-reflector implied a parachute shape and led the artist to title the work alluding to a parachute jump into new artistic territory. In *Untitled* (c. 1955, Stephan T. Edlis Collection), two prominent items included on a nearly empty canvas are a parachute and a sock, symbols of an artist imaginatively floating through the sky and materially grounded on the earth. It is noteworthy that in all of these works Rauschenberg avoids military parachutists, and the space exploration works scrupulously avoid militaristic imagery.

Parachutes were of great interest to Rauschenberg in his early works because those transportation devices are only partly controlled by the user; they are also at the mercy of the unseen forces of the wind. In parachuting, one drifts through the sky with a breathtaking overview of the world. Rauschenberg found in parachuting an analogy for one aspect of his works, the one opposite to his materiality. It comprises flights of fantasy, imaginative associations, and the chance discoveries that allow him to create surprises in his work. To him, this manner of dreaming up images and techniques seems like the free drift of a parachutist.

The loose collection of aerial imagery in Rauschenberg's earlier work was superseded by his intense concentration from 1962 until 1970 on the subject of space exploration in a large number of his Silkscreen Paintings and in his *Stoned Moon Book* and his *Stoned Moon Series* of prints. It is a subject that has also appeared with some frequency in his work after that date. His interest parallels the growth of popular interest in outer space after the Soviet Union launched Sputnik and America announced that putting a man on the moon was a national priority. Between 1962 and 1964, nineteen of Rauschenberg's seventy-nine silkscreen paintings feature space exploration imagery, making it the most frequent theme outside of the urban environment. The subject of space exploration appeared sporadically in Rauschenberg's art from 1965 through 1969, partly because he was primarily involved in performance and technology pieces. The technology works, however, had a profound influence on the particular ideas that Rauschenberg expressed in his space exploration works.

In 1969 along with several other artists Rauschenberg was invited to the launch of the Apollo 11 flight to the moon. He was given extraordinary access to Cape Canaveral, and he spent four or five days there before the blast-off on July 16, 1969. Rauschenberg was also allowed access to hundreds of diagrams and photographic images relating to the space shot. From these, he created the *Stoned Moon Book*, a nineteen-page journal with collaged photographs. The book has not been published and until now remains undiscussed in the Rauschenberg literature.

In early August 1969, Rauschenberg traveled to the Gemini G.E.L. print shop in Los Angeles and, using the hundreds of images given to him by NASA, made the *Stoned Moon Series*. The series contains thirty-three lithographs that Rauschenberg and the printers at Gemini created in thirty-four days, often working fourteen to sixteen hours a day. Among those lithographs are *Sky Garden* and *Waves*, the largest lithographs (each measuring 7′5″ in height) made until then on a hand-operated lithography press.

Not only have the space exploration works received short shrift in the Rauschenberg literature, but they have also been for the most part negatively viewed. The contention is that they show Rauschenberg's unthinking homage to the NASA program and reveal him as a pawn, intentionally or not, of the government, military, and business establishment. Closer investigation will demonstrate, in fact, that Rauschenberg's support of the space program is much more thoughtful and judgmental than has been previously believed. In the catalogue for Rauschenberg's 1970 print exhibition at the Institute of Contemporary Art, University of Pennsylvania, Lawrence Alloway paid the space exploration works the backhanded compliment of comparing them to Rubens's *Medici Cycle* (1621–21). Although Alloway cites the "wit and fidelity" of Rubens's paintings as the basis of his comparison, other implications are clear.[8] The Rubens cycle uses fantastic images to glorify, without qualification, a troubled member of the European royalty. In it Rubens employs his erudition and artistic energy to the service of a rather simple-minded political statement.

An even more damaging critique of the space exploration works was dealt by Max Kozloff in 1973 in a seminal article, "American Painting During the Cold War," which discusses the political implications of mid-century modern art. Generally speaking, Kozloff portrayed Pop art as supportive, rather than ironically critical, of the governmental and commercial status quo during the socially and politically troubled 1960s and early 1970s. (This is an overall view that now may be called into question.) Kozloff concluded, "The Pop artists became sporadically active on the fringes of dissent . . . Rauschenberg secretly financed much of the Artists' Peace Tower against the war in Los Angeles in 1965. But he also celebrated the triumph of American space flight technology, the trip to the moon, for NASA in 1969."[9] While Kozloff's comments on Rauschenberg are brief, his article has become required reading for nearly every scholar and student interested in the political implications of American modern art. Not only does Kozloff suggest that Rauschenberg was shortsighted and politically naive in his space exploration works, but also the phrase "celebrated . . . for . . ." suggests that he was working for NASA in some sort of collusion, and that he did not have the courage to make his "secret" financial support of the peace movement public through his art. In fact, Rauschenberg was not working for NASA, and his space exploration works are intimately tied to his particular vision of world peace.

The most extensive treatment of Rauschenberg's space exploration works appeared more recently in the writings of Christin Mamiya. She first discussed

Rauschenberg in 1992 in her book *Pop Art and Consumer Culture* and then expanded that discussion in 1993 in the article "We the People: The Art of Robert Rauschenberg and the Construction of National Identity."[10] In her article, Mamiya makes a number of connections between Rauschenberg and American popular culture. Her central thesis is that Rauschenberg's art can best be understood through the development of America's self-image in the years following World War II. Mamiya's broad historical approach to Rauschenberg's art is laudable, and the present book emphasizes research in much the same direction. Regarding the specifics of her arguments, however, Mamiya often reaches conclusions that are too hasty, and this is the case with her interpretation of Rauschenberg's NASA works.

Mamiya errs in insufficient analysis of Rauschenberg's works which leads her to incorrect conclusions about the artist's intentions. She describes NASA's goal as using art to make their scientific and technological endeavor more understandable to the public. Indeed the public relations motive was certainly an important component of the NASA Art Program. Mamiya then concludes that Rauschenberg simply fulfilled their "commission." In this conclusion, she does not venture beyond the opinions expressed by Alloway and Kozloff. Her assertion is that Rauschenberg's thoughts were entirely controlled by the goals of the NASA program, stating, "Rauschenberg's art succeeded in conveying an appropriate message about the U.S. space program and American national strength."[11] Mamiya's error in treating Rauschenberg's NASA works as a commission was then repeated by Mary Lynn Kotz in her biographical study of Rauschenberg, where she states that NASA contacted Rauschenberg in an effort to improve its reputation.[12]

It is incorrect to treat Rauschenberg's NASA works as a commission with the presumption, as in the case of traditional art commissions, that the artist was fulfilling the ideals of his patron. During the late 1960s, NASA had very little need to improve its reputation. The agency was at the height of its popular appeal and on the threshold of "winning" the "space race." Counter to the suggestions of Mamiya and Kotz, the higher officials at NASA did not follow the arts with any specificity. The NASA Art Program was a very small division of the space efforts. Lacking much interest in modern art, the high-level officials at NASA did not, for the most part, even know who Rauschenberg was.[13] The honorarium promised Rauschenberg for coming to NASA to witness the Apollo 11 launch was a mere 800 dollars intended to cover his travel and material expenses, and Rauschenberg never even bothered to collect it.[14] Clearly, he was not involved in any sort of traditional commission. While the artist certainly chose a subject that had enormous public appeal at the time, his works are the result of his own deep interest in space exploration, and it will be seen that they express his particular ideas about the directions that space voyages should take.

In the article on Rauschenberg, Mamiya supports her conclusions by analyzing only a single work, *Trust Zone* (1969; fig. 43) from the *Stoned Moon Series*, and she misinterprets it. The print *Trust Zone* features a large-scale diagram of an astronaut's suit overlaying a map of Cape Kennedy. At the bottom of the work is a shadowy image of a small figure looking off into the distance. Mamiya concludes that the space suit presents a de-humanized image because of its technological complexity and that the small isolated figure below represents the average individual dwarfed by the space program. According to her, Rauschenberg's message is to assure us that "the average American citizen cannot possibly expect to understand it [the space program] but should trust in those in a position of authority – engineers, scientists and government officials."

In fact, Rauschenberg's message in *Trust Zone* is exactly the opposite of that proposed by Mamiya. The figure below is not simply an "individual citizen" – he is Orville Wright watching his brother Wilbur in the historic first powered flight of their airplane in December 1903. The soaring biplane can be clearly seen in the lower center of Rauschenberg's print. Rauschenberg's message is the historical connectedness of the space flight stemming from early planes created by these two amateur inventors and pilots. In fact, Rauschenberg has aligned the images in *Trust Zone* so that the space suit appears to be standing in the desert at Kitty Hawk, where the Wright Brothers made their first flight, and the desertscape resembles the moonscape. The diagrammatic space suit that dominates *Trust Zone* is not indecipherable, as Mamiya claims, but quite clear. It is taken from a NASA drawing intended to brief lay people on the space program. In the NASA archives from which Rauschenberg acquired this photograph, he could have chosen any number of complex engineering diagrams but he deliberately avoided them. The suit is also depicted in sky-colored, blue inks that make it an appealing image. The centrality of the space suit in *Trust Zone* is meant to remind us of Rauschenberg's largest print to that date, and the largest print pulled up to that time on a hand lithographic press, *Booster* (1967; see fig. 57), a work that will be discussed below. *Booster* is dominated by an x-ray photograph of Rauschenberg's own skeleton. In *Trust Zone*, the artist compares the mechanics of the space suit to his idea of the body as structural machine in *Booster*.

Similar to the diagrammatic clarity of the space suit in *Trust Zone* is the map of Cape Canaveral over which it is placed. The map lays out the location of the space launch site and supporting facilities just as the suit is labeled with its component parts. One of the many connecting features between the space suit and the map is the placement of the circular enlargement of the launch pad so that it is directly in front of the circular face-shield on the astronaut's helmet. In fact, the map Rauschenberg used in *Trust Zone* is the one that was given to him when he came to witness the Apollo 11 launch, and it contains his personal hand-written notations. So, the map clarified the NASA complex for the artist and marked his personal connection to the momentous historical event of the moon launch.

Trust Zone is a celebration of wide-ranging human inventiveness and of Rauschenberg's belief in the participation of all citizens in adventures of space exploration. In accordance with this meaning, a "trust zone" is a work area at NASA in which outside personnel, who are not part of the NASA staff, have been introduced because of their varying expertise. On the whole, Rauschenberg's space exploration works do not simply follow the purposes of the NASA program but, while supporting the goal of space exploration, they explore specific ideas peculiar to Rauschenberg's own interpretations of those events.

Further examination of the history of the American space effort, public sentiments about space exploration, and the sources that were accessible to Rauschenberg make clear which images he chose and which he rejected. Thus, one can determine with more confidence the meanings of his selection and re-organization of that material. In America, popular awareness of space exploration began with the Soviet Union's launch of Sputnik on October 4, 1957. That launch was followed one month later by the Russians placing the first living creature in space, the dog Laika.

The Eisenhower administration took a position of "calm conservatism" regarding the Soviet rocket successes. The president commented at a press conference that he could not see what all the fuss was about because the "Russians have only put one small ball in the air."[15] Eisenhower refused to approve any "manned" space programs beyond Gemini and even considered disbanding the Space Council, the overseeing body for space exploration before NASA was formed in 1958, because it had accomplished so little.

In contrast to Eisenhower's attitude, the public was incensed and scared by Sputnik. The American people had been unprepared for its success, and contemporary newspaper and magazine articles capitalized on the fear of Russian missiles from space. American newspapers noted that the Russians were using the successes of Sputnik to show the superiority of Soviet technology and the socialist system. It is noteworthy that Rauschenberg never engaged in this mood of paranoia. In fact, a number of his *Stoned Moon* prints highlight the Soviet space program, a fact that has not been discussed in the literature on these works.

John F. Kennedy came to office with little knowledge of or interest in the American space program. A series of surprising events led to Kennedy's May 25, 1961 declaration that putting a man on the moon before 1970 would be a national priority. The most direct cause of Kennedy's declaration was Yuri Gagarin's successful single orbit of the earth on April 12, 1961. This event made national and international headlines in a way that the previous space flights had not. The headlines in the *New York Times* read "Soviet Feat Caps Intense Effort," "A New Era In War May Be Opened, with Space Ships Used in Battle" (an article complete with drawing and dire warnings about combat in space), and "Space Flight Tied to Man's Advance" (a series of quotations from public figures and intellectuals pointing to space flight as a crowning human achievement). The publicity on all fronts ranging from military threat to human accomplishment was overwhelming.

Other events that drove Kennedy to focus on what the newspapers soon labeled the "space race" included a slow economy, the failed Bay of Pigs fiasco, and indecision about what military commitment to make in Southeast Asia. The confrontation between the military and NASA for control of a space initiative made the issue effectively a presidential decision. Vice-President Lyndon Johnson did have an interest in the space program, and Kennedy placed him in charge of a hasty investigation of whether it was possible to put humans on the moon before the Russians. In short, the seemingly overwhelming popular support for the program and the need to improve his image in the early days of his administration motivated Kennedy.

In a speech of May 25 titled "Urgent National Needs" and billed as a second "state of the union" address, Kennedy spelled out the financial and human commitment needed for the moon landing and, in effect, asked Congress and the American people for a mandate of support. The House approved the authorization and Kennedy's budget on July 20 by a vote of 354 to 59. There was virtually no dissent.

The popular press provided Rauschenberg with information about the country's new priority. While Rauschenberg was certainly enthusiastic about the idea of putting a man on the moon, as was most of the nation, it is interesting to compare Rauschenberg's overall attitude with that dominant in the press. The press coined the term "space race" in 1958 and used it continually in the literature thereafter. Fueled by the Cold War fear of the Soviet Union, articles about space exploration in the news had a decidedly anti-Russian twist. A *Washington Post* editorial stated, "The fact that the Soviet space feat must be faced for what it is, a psychological victory of the first magnitude for the Soviet Union . . ."[16] Rauschenberg did not participate in this jingoism. Although some of his works do display the American flag and the eagle, they are not anti-Soviet. They contain no images of Soviet military threat and, in fact, three of the *Stoned Moon Series*, including *Arena II*, feature Soviet astronauts and space equipment. Rauschenberg's approach falls more into the category of space exploration "for the good of mankind" that was emphasized by leaders like Martin Luther King.

Public statements by NASA emphasized the perfection of the program and discussed virtually none of its flaws. The popular press picked up on the theme of NASA's flawlessness. Magazines repeatedly recorded statements like this one found in a 1962 issue of *Newsweek* from which Rauschenberg took many photographs that he made into silkscreens for his space exploration images: "Without question, the scientists and engineers for the Apollo Project will succeed."[17] Today we know, through the research of historians of the era, that the NASA program committed numerous errors and misjudgments.[18] Rauschenberg could not have known about these, but he does show that humor, awkwardness, and tragedy were part of the program. As one example, *Ape* (1969; see fig. 62) shows the astronauts engaging in playful activities during training. The deliberately chaotic and hazy design of *Air Pocket* (1969) suggests the baffling speed and sometimes confusion with which NASA worked. The government seal that dominates *Banner* (1969; see fig. 63) indicates the dominance of the program by bureaucracy, an issue that Rauschenberg also discussed in his *Stoned Moon Book*.

Rauschenberg playfully animated the space machinery in works such as his 1968 print *Booster*, which, as noted before, likens his own full-scale skeleton to a booster rocket. Also, Rauschenberg did not shy away from the most significant early tragedy of the American space program. His print *Brake* (1969; see fig. 65) depicts the astronauts killed in the 1967 Apollo fire. Prophetically for Rauschenberg who believes in omens, the lithographic stone broke during printing.[19] Thus the print's title refers simultaneously to the break in the stone, the ending of these lives, and the widely speculated notion that this accident would put the "brakes" on the space program. In all, Rauschenberg approached the space program with references to human frailties and errors that were largely absent from the popular press.

In the magazines and newspapers of the period, the military uses of outer space were frequently emphasized. Articles often featured illustrations of missile stations in space and other such battle hardware.[20] These images of futuristic space weapons never appear in Rauschenberg's works. He was aware of the military presence in the space program, as he stated in *Stoned Moon Book*, but in his art he emphasized the civilian effort and scientific discoveries.

The popular press also accentuated the heroism of the individual astronauts; the press made them the folk heroes of the age, as when *Life* magazine commissioned biographies of all the Apollo astronauts. In contrast, Rauschenberg usually depicted the astronauts anonymously, and frequently he chose to portray the average workers who constructed and assembled equipment rather than the astronauts, thus emphasizing the team effort and broad-based commitment to space exploration. In the press, space exploration was often discussed as a unique condition in human history, and futuristic space colonies were illustrated to indicate a total change in the manner that humans would live in the future. In contrast, Rauschenberg emphasized the historical connections of space exploration. His works depict the space program not as an unique enterprise but as a stage of a continuous human drive to learn and to explore the unknown. Rauschenberg accomplishes this goal through such direct historical connections as showing Charles Lindbergh in *Banner* and the Wright Brothers in *Trust Zone*. More generally, he uses visual associations like placing the image of a space capsule near that of New York City water towers in the Silkscreen Painting *Overcast I*, thus playing on their similar shapes against the sky and commenting on old and new technology.

As indicated earlier, Rauschenberg's space exploration imagery comes in two stages, first in his 1962–64 Silkscreen Paintings then in the *Stoned Moon Series*. In the former, Rauschenberg relied on imagery from popular magazines. The process of having the images turned into screens from which Rauschenberg could paint was expensive, and once a screen was made Rauschenberg would use it in multiple works. Thus, one can reasonably assume that he took some care with his choices. By finding the sources for Rauschenberg's images and also examining available photographs that he chose not to use, one can better understand Rauschenberg's ideas and motives.

Rauschenberg had nine different screens depicting space imagery made which he used in nineteen of his seventy-two Silkscreen Paintings. From the special issue of *Newsweek* (October 8, 1962) titled "The Space Age," Rauschenberg took a photograph of engineers simulating a future docking procedure between a Gemini capsule and an Agenda D space vehicle. A drawing of an early design for an awkward-looking Lunar Bug was taken from this same issue as well as a drawing comparing three types of rockets: Atlas, Titan, and Saturn. Three photographs were taken from *Life* magazine (October 26, 1962) of Wally Schirra's six orbits of the earth for the penultimate launch of the Mercury Program. (*Life* claimed that they were the best yet done of the space program.) One photograph represents Schirra's capsule floating in a safety ring attended by divers. A sequential strip shows the capsule landing in the water, and a final photograph depicts the blast-off of Schirra's Atlas rocket.

From the September 27, 1963 issue of *Life* Rauschenberg utilized a photograph of an astronaut, seen from above, floating down to earth in a balloon/parachute (ballute). This device was intended to allow the Gemini astronauts to rescue themselves if forced to bail out during a launch. The exotic-looking balloon would allow them to float to earth after their ejection seats had fallen away. From the same issue, Rauschenberg also took a diagram of trajectory and orbital paths from the earth to the moon, and a photograph of the large spidery shape of a satellite tracking dish.

The images from these magazines that Rauschenberg rejected tell us as much about his ideas as those that he selected. The magazines from which Rauschenberg chose his photographs contained many dramatic pictures of rockets taking off. Rauschenberg used only one of these and in only a single Silkscreen Painting, *Untitled* (1963), where it is so blurred as to be almost unrecognizable. The artist used none of the wealth of photographs of individual astronauts like those featured in *Life* magazine's (September 1963) extensive photo-survey of their professional and family lives.

A number of simulations of the capsules in space, both interior and exterior views, were among those that Rauschenberg did not select. Perhaps the most dramatic new images in the magazines were the photographs from space; Rauschenberg used none of these. He also paid little notice to the technical equipment and diagrams that appeared in these articles, although he made extensive use of such diagrams later in his *Stoned Moon Series*. Finally Rauschenberg was uninterested in the futuristic renditions of space colonies that dominated several of the magazine essays.

The images that Rauschenberg chose for his Silkscreen Paintings were those that emphasized space exploration as a collective endeavor. They are neither overly technical nor futuristic but show space exploration as part of a continuing human search for knowledge and adventure. Instead of emphasizing particular heroes, Rauschenberg's paintings concentrate on the collective work of a variety of individuals. The images do not shy away from awkward situations and even employ sexual puns in order to relate the space race to the "common man." As a whole, Rauschenberg sought to humanize space exploration and relate it more closely to the average person.

Overcast I (1962; fig. 44) is one of the early black and white Silkscreen Paintings to be dominated by space imagery. The work emphasizes the collective energy that it takes to reach the dramatic moment of a space launch. The title of the work refers simultaneously to the relationship between the rich variety of grays in this early work and to an overcast day. Throughout the painting, Rauschenberg has brushed and rubbed the surface with thin skeins of grey paint. The effect is that of clouds, light fog, and the richness of such atmospheric phenomena. Overcast days provided dramatic moments in space launches because decisions had to be made as to whether to conduct thms. In the early days of the space program a scrubbed launch could mean weeks of re-preparing equipment and waiting for the right rotational position of the earth to allow a correct ocean landing for the capsule.

In *Overcast I*, the photograph of the NASA workers simulating the docking of a Gemini capsule is used four times. The photo looks as if the capsule is being assembled for launch, and the four overlapping images from upper left to lower right give a sense of sequential events, movement, and passage of time in the painting. The last of the screened photographs is rotated vertically so it appears that the capsule is ready to shoot into space. The sequence not only emphasizes the passage of time but also highlights the amount of labor that is required to make the launch possible. As a

44 *Overcast I*, 1962, oil and silkscreen ink on canvas, 97 $^1/_2$ × 72", Barbara and Richard S. Lane.

whole, Rauschenberg has modified the usual vertical and horizontal arrangement of his imagery so that it rotates slightly in a clockwise direction. This formal arrangement communicates activity and process.

To the left of center and at the lower edge Rauschenberg included two images of baseball players. Such depictions had dominated slightly earlier silkscreens like *Brace* (1962, Robert and Jane Meyerhoff Collection). In *Overcast I*, Rauschenberg seems to suggest a parallel between the baseball players, who were national heroes, and the anonymous workers for the space program. He posits perhaps that our new national pastime should be space exploration.[21] Rauschenberg may also be drawing a parallel – which continues throughout the entire series of space exploration works

– between himself and those involved in launching space craft. As we have seen in Rauschenberg's working methods, the artist employed a great deal of planning to allow him to make sudden dramatic decisions on the canvas surface. In the artist's mind, there was an analogy between preparation followed by a dramatic, seemingly effortless, launch of a rocket and the artist's own creative methods.[22] In the *Stoned Moon Series*, discussed below, Rauschenberg made explicit the direct connections between the work of the rocket engineers and his creative process.

In the lower-right quadrant of *Overcast I*, Rauschenberg placed a photograph of water towers on top of New York City buildings – an image that was important to him. This photograph was taken by him from the window of his first New York City loft of Fulton Street and eventually became one of his most frequently used silkscreen photographs.[23] Here, he compares the water towers, set against the sky, to the rocket directly above. Old and new technology, Rauschenberg's love of urbanism, and his new fascination with space exploration are set side by side in this pairing. At the lower center of *Overcast I*, Rauschenberg screened two photographs. One shows Manhattan seen from the air – a space-age view of the city. The other depicts the sea with the word "sea" printed on the photograph. The combination of these pictures with those of the rockets allows Rauschenberg to include the triad of earth, air, and water, basic elements that are a frequent motif in his work. Also the sea refers to the successful conclusion of the space mission when the capsule lands in the water. Next to the sea, Rauschenberg screened an image of the Lunar Bug, partly covered in white paint so that it looks as though it is "splashing down." The pivotal image in *Overcast I*, however, is that of two hands, one taking the pulse of the other. Rauschenberg seems to be saying that space exploration is taking the pulse of the nation or even that of the modern world.

The 1963 *Trellis* (fig. 45) is one of Rauschenberg's multi-color silkscreens that dominated the years 1963 and 1964. As has been noted in the Rauschenberg literature, the artist's creation of color silkscreen paintings, which required the use of multiple screens, was the result of his increasing familiarization with the medium. The color silkscreens are simultaneously much more assertive and aggressive-looking works. Their forceful character is related to Rauschenberg's increasing self-confidence and vision of himself as a national artist and as a spokesperson for the country. This attitude and the color silkscreens arose after his first retrospective, held from March to May of 1963 at the Jewish Museum, New York. The retrospective was also the first that the museum had given to a post-World War II artist, and it led to a major critical reconsideration of Rauschenberg's art.

As opposed to the more regional view of the Combines or urban silkscreens, *Trellis* suggests a world-view. The formal motif is circularity, like the shape of the world. The circles have been placed over and dominate a grid formed by images of building construction and of the skyscrapers of New York City. These can barely be seen to the lower and upper center of *Trellis*. The only dominant rectangular shape in the works is the Necker Cube spinning in the upper-left corner. As discussed earlier, the Necker Cube is a particularly ambiguous and exciting form for someone with dyslexia. As opposed to the anchored grids of the buildings, the cube floats magically in space like a vessel from another planet. It provides spatial illusion, and its

45 *Trellis*, 1963, oil on silkscreen ink on canvas, 56 × 50", collection of the Doris and Alan Freedman Family.

frequent appearance in the space exploration works may be a visual pun on the artist's new passion for outer space.

In *Trellis*, there are three overlapping circular configurations. The first is a global map and the second is a round temperature gauge. (One of the touted advantages of space exploration during these years was the fact that satellites would allow us better to predict the weather.) The third circle is that of the satellite tracking dish taken from *Life* magazine of September 1962. As mentioned earlier, the dish shows anonymous workers climbing on it. Satellite dishes appear in numerous Rauschenberg works after this date. As an artist who tries to see everything around him, Rauschenberg was clearly fascinated by devices that hear minute noises in distant space.

The circular configurations give the painting a sense of baroque energy. This design is complemented by rich sensuous coloration and by active paint handling: the work is full of drips and rills of white pigment that run across its surface. The overall sensibility of *Trellis* is that Rauschenberg has taken a global view and is excited by that perspective. The title was inspired by the woven pattern of the satellite dish, but the common use of a trellis is a structure on which plants grow. Rauschenberg's optimistic hope of growth through space technology is evident throughout the work, and it will be seen that the relationship between technology and nature is a constant

46 *Die Hard*, 1963, oil and silkscreen ink on canvas, 72 × 144″, Private Collection.

theme in his space exploration works. At the top of *Trellis* is a figure, a photograph of Rauschenberg's close friend and collaborator Merce Cunningham spinning in the midst of a dance move. Clearly, Rauschenberg is suggesting that avant-garde artistic energy is part of a whirling universe of modern discovery.

The silkscreen work *Die Hard* (1963; fig. 46) is a large-scale (72 × 144 inches) painting that provides an early summary of Rauschenberg's ideas about space exploration. The title was popular slang for never giving up and was used in reference to the dedication of workers in the space program in several of the magazines from which Rauschenberg took his imagery. The scale of the painting and its images speak of Rauschenberg's new ambitions as a national commentator. The work's proportions, as well as its overall red, white, and blue colors, are reminiscent of the American flag, and it is dominated by celebratory space imagery.[24]

The upper tiers of *Die Hard* depict a pair of silkscreened film strips of Wally Shirra's Mercury capsule parachuting into the ocean at the end of its successful mission. The landing sequence connects to Rauschenberg's interest in parachuting, for in parachuting, technology and nature, control and chance, seemed to meet most dramatically. In the early days of the space program, the capsule landings were sensational. Contact with the astronaut was lost during re-entry and sometimes the capsule would land miles off course. The rescue ship launched helicopters with divers to attend to the capsule, and one capsule was even lost by sinking when its hatch was prematurely opened. At the bottom of *Die Hard*, Rauschenberg shows the successful resolution of the space mission by including a silkscreen of Schirra's capsule with the divers having successfully attached flotation rings to it. Next to this image, the army helicopter, which had appeared as a threatening military image in other silkscreen paintings, takes on the role of rescue vehicle.

In *Die Hard*, the actual flight of the space rocket is suggested by the cloud-like white paint on the left of the painting. In the center of that area is a red and orange oval. It is actually a detail of fruit that appears in other Rauschenberg paintings.[25] But here in its fragmented form, it looks like either the glow of rocket engines seen from below or a starry nebula above, an example of types of visual associations and transformations that Rauschenberg makes. Below this area, a piece of cloth is both related to Rauschenberg's longtime use of fabrics in his work and reminds us of the striped parachute cloth seen in the photographs of Schirra's capsule. It also resembles the stripes of the American flag. Near this area Rauschenberg screened two photographs, one of Jean-Antoine Houdon's famous marble sculpture *George Washington* (1791, Virginia State House, Richmond). Washington, silhouetted in an arch of gray paint, looks on with approval at the capsule landing. Nearby, the Statue of Liberty lies on its side so that its torch both points to space and in the direction of the capsule landing.

Urban subject matter that had been one of Rauschenberg's primary themes up to this time plays a different role in *Die Hard*. As discussed in the previous chapter the early 1960s were a troubling time for those who sought humanistic change in the urban environment. In New York, particularly, the press focused attention on the destruction of neighborhoods and the corruption of both political officials and urban planners, especially Robert Moses. Four images of the city are shown in *Die Hard*. In the lower right-hand corner, Rauschenberg depicted the water towers that had been compared favorably to rockets in *Overcast I*. But now the city is shown red as if aflame, and Rauschenberg silkscreened representations of firemen over it.

At the upper corner of the city/fire photograph is a destitute-looking scene, shown in black and white, of buildings being torn down. To the left side of the painting is another red representation of the city; it is a nearly deserted urban play-lot with two children isolated from each other. Next to the children some sort of ovoid object, surrounded by a halo of white paint, seems to have magically appeared. While the object in question is actually a football, it appears otherworldly and may suggest a space vessel, which adds mystery to the otherwise desolate scene.[26] The final representation of the city is in the upper-right corner. It is a distant and raised view, looking across the Hudson River, that makes the gritty urban environment seem more exotic. In this representation, the city flies on its side and is overlaid with the Necker Cube. The arrow adjoining that cube points toward the landing space capsule as if to suggest the solution to our urban problems might also be linked to the discoveries of space flight.

The attitude expressed in *Die Hard* that urban difficulties may be aided by the developing space program is closest to that found in a 1962 special issue of *Newsweek* magazine.[27] The magazine summarized the sentiments of the liberal press during the period, ones with which Rauschenberg was in sympathy. Rauschenberg took three silkscreen images from this issue for his paintings, so despite his difficulty in reading, there is a chance that he glanced over the text. In the introduction, the editors emphasized the relationship between the space program and solving social issues in the world. They ranged from the broad perspective of discussing space flight as a form of self-knowledge to specific social issues. They quoted from Dr. Hugh Dryden, Deputy Administrator of the National Aeronautics and Space Administration, who described the national space effort as "an instrument of social change in many areas . . ."[28] New jobs and service industries were discussed, as was a strengthened economy that had resulted from the aeronautics industry.

The *Newsweek* editors expressed their belief that racial prejudice would be reduced by the common goal and by such practical features as moving sophisticated research and manufacturing centers with their international communities of scientists and technicians into the south. They cited the George C. Marshall Space Flight Center in Huntsville, Alabama that brought with it 130 German scientists and contributed to the founding of a fifty-five piece symphony orchestra in that city. Although the editors' claims proved far too optimistic, their beliefs provided a context for similar liberal social thinking connected to the space program as exhibited by Rauschenberg during the same period.

Faced with the urban decay and isolation that he felt keenly, Rauschenberg looked to space exploration, to technology, and to national pride, as it was proposed by the Kennedy administration, as a solution to some of the country's crises. With the assassination of Kennedy, whose charismatic leadership was embodied in a number of other Rauschenberg silkscreens, it became even more imperative in Rauschenberg's view to arrive at public solutions to the nation's dilemmas. In 1963 and 1964, Rauschenberg increasingly saw the persuasive public possibilities of art and saw himself in an influential role. His 1963 retrospective and such public projects as the debut of his first choreographed dance *Pelican* (see fig. 76), related to space flight, encouraged this attitude. The viewpoint was solidified by Rauschenberg's winning the International Grand Prize in Painting at the Venice Biennale in June 1964.

In retrospect, it is not surprising after these successes that Rauschenberg should have turned to public performance and to his technology projects as a major emphasis for the next six years. His focus on these endeavors is often explained by the artist's legendary restlessness and his desire not to be caught in one type of activity, an explanation that was encouraged by Rauschenberg himself. But his belief in group effort and peaceful uses of technology, as is evident in his early space exploration works, also led him along this course. It was his interest in communal forms of creativity that mixed art with technology to the benefit of both disciplines that drove Rauschenberg toward his performance pieces and most importantly toward the co-founding of Experiments in Art and Technology (E.A.T.).

The founding of E.A.T. resulted from the interaction between Rauschenberg and Billy Klüver, an engineer who worked with Bell Laboratories in New Jersey. Rauschenberg and Klüver first met in 1960 for the opening of Jean Tinguely's *Homage à New-York*, which according to Tinguely's plan self-destructed at the Museum of Modern Art sculpture garden. Klüver had helped Tinguely with its engineering and Rauschenberg contributed a subsidiary piece to it that he called "Money Thrower." As Tinguely's piece devolved, *Money Thrower*, consisting of a metal box rigged with a spring to which were attached silver dollars and a small explosive charge, tossed coins in the air in mock homage to Tinguely's construction. Klüver has noted that the idea for a collaboration came from Rauschenberg, who went to the engineer and said "What can we do together?"[29] Between 1962 and 1965, Klüver and Rauschenberg

47 Rauschenberg and Lucinda Childs discussing the capabilities of the theater electronic environmental modulator for "9 Evenings" with (from left to right) Herb Schneider, L. J. Robinson, Per Biorn, and Billy Klüver (1966).

did indeed work on *Oracle* (1965, Collection Musée National d'Art Moderne, Centre Georges Pompidou, Paris), a complicated sound sculpture made from urban debris and equipped with five radios whose volume and speed of channel sequencing could be altered by the viewer; thus the viewer could play the sculpture like an orchestra of popular culture sounds.

Even more significant for Rauschenberg's overall ideas about technology was the organization of "9 Evenings: Theatre and Engineering" and the founding of E.A.T. The pieces consisted of a series of ten different performances each created through the collaboration of an artist and engineer. Among those involved were John Cage, the dancers Lucinda Childs and Yvonne Rainer, and Rauschenberg himself. The performances were almost all designed at Rauschenberg's new home/studio on Lafayette Street during late evenings and through the nights over the course of nine months from January through October 1966 (fig. 47). This preparation gave Rauschenberg extensive contact with engineers. He had an opportunity to witness some of the latest ideas in modern technology, to see how engineers work, and to appreciate the fruitful collaboration between the areas of science and art. Klüver recalls Rauschenberg saying that art has "no direction" or "all directions" while engineers think in a linear fashion. Klüver concluded that the challenge for the engineers was to make the artist's vision come through.[30] The "9 Evenings" were staged October 13–23 at the 69th Regimental Armory Building in New York City and, despite mixed reviews by the critics, showed the creative possibilities of such interactions (fig. 48).

Immediately after the "9 Evenings" Rauschenberg and Klüver together with the artist Robert Whitman and the engineer Fred Waldauer founded E.A.T., which was intended to be a service organization and a clearing house for matching artists with engineers so that they could work together on projects. At E.A.T.'s first meeting in November 1966, three hundred artists signed up for help from engineers. During E.A.T.'s first year, Klüver and Rauschenberg enlisted the support of the labor mediator Theodore Kheel and received corporate support from such companies as AT&T,

48 Poster for "9 Evenings: Theatre & Engineering" presented at the 69th Regimental Armory, New York (1966), poster designed by Rauschenberg.

IBM, and Atlantic Richfield. In November 1967, E.A.T. announced a competition for the best work produced in collaboration between an artist and an engineer, with the prize going to the engineer. Some of the works from that competition were exhibited in the 1968 Museum of Modern Art exhibition "The Machine," and all of them were included in a Brooklyn Museum show "Some More Beginnings." By the spring of 1968, E.A.T. had forty chapters in America and abroad and its members numbered three thousand artists and engineers.

For Rauschenberg and Klüver, E.A.T. was not simply a practical way to bring artists and engineers together. It embodied a plan for a better world and a moral imperative in an otherwise troubled planet. Because of its moral and social basis, E.A.T. has a historical relationship to the technological interests of the Russian Constructivists, the Bauhaus, and the de Stijl movement. Rauschenberg came to believe as he stated that technology was "contemporary nature" and that human interaction with machines would define the modern era.[31] He concluded that the problems with the environment and with the military and industrial complex could not be solved by a return to some simpler form of life but rather by active and responsible involvement of people in the technological world.

The E.A.T. publications, which have been largely ignored in the Rauschenberg literature, emphasize this message of accountability. Its March 1968 newsletter states, "E.A.T. is concerned with the process of making art and not with the work of art as a final product. Our main concern is to facilitate contact between the individual and the new technology and promote experimental application of new technology in the human environment."[32] The same issue gives the credo of E.A.T. Billy Klüver has identified the first two sentences of this statement as written by Rauschenberg and the third by himself. He has also noted that Rauschenberg subsequently called it one of his most important statements. It reads:

MAINTAIN A CONSTRUCTIVE CLIMATE FOR THE RECOGNITION OF THE NEW TECHNOLOGY AND THE ARTS BY A CIVILIZED COLLABORATION BETWEEN GROUPS UNREALISTICALLY DEVELOPING IN ISOLATION. ELIMINATE THE SEPARATION OF THE INDIVIDUAL FROM TECHNOLOGICAL CHANGE AND EXPAND AND ENRICH TECHNOLOGY TO GIVE THE INDIVIDUAL VARIETY, PLEASURE AND AVENUES FOR EXPLORATION AND INVOLVEMENT IN CONTEMPORARY LIFE. ENCOURAGE INDUSTRIAL INITIATIVE IN GENERATING ORIGINAL FORETHOUGHT, INSTEAD OF A COMPROMISE IN THE AFTERMATH, AND PRECIPITATE A MUTUAL AGREEMENT IN ORDER TO AVOID THE WASTE OF A CULTURAL REVOLUTION.[33]

Rauschenberg's emphasis on the constructive use of technology was echoed in the autobiographical text that he included in his major print of 1969, *Autobiography*. He ends that text, which is the most extensive written statement the artist has ever provided about his life, "The beginning of E.A.T., experiments in art & technology to function as a catalyst for the inevitable fusing of specializations creating a responsible man working in the present." Major Rauschenberg themes are featured in this statement. They include collaboration, focus on the present, and above all working with responsibility to the world. It was in this spirit, rather than in a mode of thoughtless support of the military–industrial environment, as has been suggested in writings on Rauschenberg, that the artist threw himself into the *Stoned Moon Series*.

*   *   *

Before looking at the *Stoned Moon Series* itself, NASA's motives for inviting artists to witness the space launches should be briefly examined. The NASA Art Program was instituted in 1962, and it paralleled the Kennedy administration's efforts to assure widespread public support for the space program. The idea for the art program was conceived by the NASA administrator James E. Webb, who sought the advise of Dr. H. Lester Cooke, curator of painting at the National Gallery of Art, who became the principle art advisor to NASA until his death in 1973.[34] The NASA Art Program was directed by James Dean, who had been trained as an artist and worked in design development for the government. Beginning in 1963 letters of invitation were sent to the artists to witness the last Mercury orbital flight. Since then, sixty-three artists have participated in the program. Artists were invited to witness launches, Mission Control activities, recoveries, and even to watch astronauts suit-up. The program requested that each artist donate at least one work to the NASA archive. The works from this archive have been organized in exhibitions, including a significant early one at the National Gallery of Art in 1965, that have traveled around the country. A second exhibition was held at the National Gallery in 1969 that comprised works related to the Apollo project, including Rauschenberg's *Sky Garden*.

Clearly NASA hoped that favorable and exciting views of their program would result from these invitations. It would be naive to think that the NASA officials did not desire positive publicity. At the same time, the literature concerning Rauschenberg's participation in the program has been incorrect, as mentioned earlier, in portraying that involvement as a commission whose content was controlled by the NASA authorities. The records indicate that the artists were never told what to represent, and they were left free to interpret the subject matter as they saw fit. If there was a control, it resulted from the invitations issued. For instance, it is hard to imagine an extremely confrontational artist like Hans Haacke being invited to participate in the program. Yet James Dean expressed the relatively open attitude of the program: "We should invite artists to come and see what is going on and to respond to it. Don't tell them what to paint or how to do it."[35] His statement indicates that there were no efforts to control the artists' works. It is also worth reiterating that the honorarium provided the artists was so small as to be inconsequential, and it certainly did not allow their works to be considered NASA "commissions." All of this is relevant to Rauschenberg because the artist's NASA-related works were not a commission that was manipulated by NASA officials; he was not working "for" NASA, as has been claimed.[36] Rauschenberg certainly supported the space program, but he emphasized the particular aspects of the program that suited his world-view. The issues that concerned him and the manner in which he revealed them in his art becomes clearer in a study of his *Stoned Moon Series*.

In 1969, Rauschenberg was one of seven artists invited to witness the launch of the Apollo 11 space craft for its journey to the moon – as noted before. James

Dean commented, "I knew Apollo 11 would be really special, and I thought that this would be the one for Bob Rauschenberg."[37] Dean also recalls that he had to explain to a lot of people at NASA who Rauschenberg was. When offered the invitation, Rauschenberg did "not hesitate an instant in accepting" – an indicator of his enthusiasm for the project. On the first afternoon of his arrival, Rauschenberg was taken immediately to the hillside near the launch pad, a location beyond the press area, where the immensity of the rocket was fully apparent. Although no one was allowed in this area during an actual launch – if the rocket exploded anyone this close would be killed by flying debris – it is from this vantage point that Rauschenberg visualized the Apollo 11 lift-off in several works from the *Stone Moon Series*.

Rauschenberg and Dean returned to the same site that night, and saw the rocket dramatically lighted by spotlights and covered with ice during its final fueling. At that time, Dean recalls Rauschenberg's special interest in hearing the frogs and bellowing alligators as a contrast to the awesome technological spectacle of the rocket. In between these events, Rauschenberg toured the huge Vehicle Assembly Building, a 500-foot-tall single interior space. Taking the glass elevator to the roof, he could view the entire Cape Canaveral area. He then visited the old launch sites from the Mercury and Gemini periods. Rauschenberg was particularly interested in the rusting gantries with sea birds nesting in them and weeds coming up through the pad. (He later asked for access to the Cape Canaveral refuse area for materials but was denied permission.) Rauschenberg also toured the launch control room. Before daylight on the next day, he went with Dean and other guests to the press site for the launch. All the events of these four or five days play an important role in the *Stoned Moon Series*.

Immediately after the launch Rauschenberg decided to create a major and extensive series of works based on Apollo 11. He took no photographs during his two days at Cape Canaveral, but absorbed the event and sights. Approximately one week after the launch, he returned to NASA and went through their archives selecting the documentary photographs he would use in the *Stoned Moon Series*. Two weeks later he traveled to Washington, D.C. where he similarly sorted through the NASA photographic archives, and his selection reveals his intentions in the *Stoned Moon* series.

As a result of his Apollo 11 experience, Rauschenberg created his most complex and extensive series of prints to that date. He remained at Gemini G.E.L. print studio in Los Angeles for the month of August to make his space exploration series. A way to approach these works is through a much less known project. While Rauschenberg worked on the series at Gemini, he simultaneously assembled photographic images that he had collected from NASA with notes that he had written while witnessing the Apollo 11 launch into a journal, the *Stoned Moon Book*, that has been neither published nor discussed.

The *Stoned Moon Book* gives a unique insight into the artist's working ideas as he was beginning his print series. It consists of a cover page, seven unnumbered pages with images alone, and eleven numbered pages with both images and text. All of the images have been either cut and pasted onto the page or applied by means of transfer drawing, and the text has been cut from typewritten sheets and glued to those

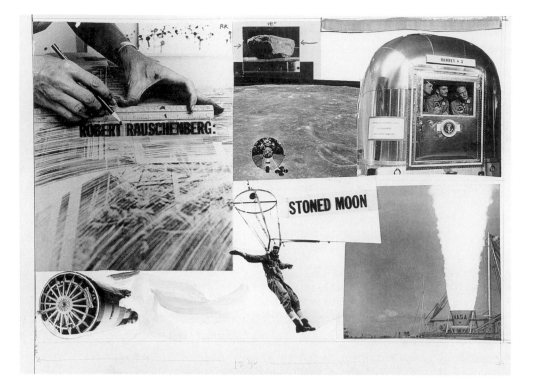

49   Cover page, *Stoned Moon Book*, photo collage with watercolor, press type, acetate, graphite, and blue line pencil on illustration board, 16 × 20 ¹/₈", collection of the artist.

pages. On most of the pages there are two types of text: the passages that are all in upper-case letters are by Rauschenberg. Those in upper and lower case were contributed, at Rauschenberg's request, by Henry Hopkins, then curator of the San Francisco Museum of Modern Art. In its text and its imagery the *Stoned Moon Book* reveals the range of ideas that Rauschenberg had about the NASA program. The book maintains a sense of immediacy and freshness as Rauschenberg attempted to express and resolve differing viewpoints. The overall appearance of the *Stoned Moon Book* is one of spontaneity and variety; some pages are nearly empty while others are filled with text and pictures. While the originality of Rauschenberg's approach is noteworthy, his freedom of design has historical antecedents in the graphic inventions of the Dada and Russian Constructivist movements, with which Rauschenberg was familiar. Nevertheless the fragmented photographs and the cut-up strips of text suggest that the artist is literally piecing together a vast wealth of information and conflicting ideas before our eyes. In contrast Hopkins's textual contribution is much more carefully composed. It appears in longer segments and is self-consciously historical.

Even the title *Stoned Moon* reveals the varied manner with which Rauschenberg saw space exploration. On one level, it refers to the moon rocks that were brought back by the astronauts. Physical material from the moon returning to earth with the astronauts was extremely exciting at the time. The cover to the *Stoned Moon Book* (fig. 49) contains the image of one of those rocks. In fact, Rauschenberg wrote a letter to James Dean, the leader of the NASA Art Program, asking if he could acquire a moon rock to use in one of his art works.[38] Rauschenberg also employed rocks to make his space exploration prints, the lithographic stones at Gemini G.E.L. print shop. He actively sought parallels between his making art and the process of the space journey, so the rocks were an appropriate metaphor for him. Also, in the age of the Counter Culture, Rauschenberg's reference to being "stoned" can hardly be missed.

50 Drawing for *Stoned Moon Book*, photo collage with watercolor, blue line pencil, graphite, and paper collage on paper, 16 × 20 ¼", collection of the artist.

The artist sympathized with many aspects of 1960s youth culture, including its environmental and anti-war positions and its playful sensibility. He certainly would not have agreed with the sentiment expressed by newsman Walter Cronkrite that reaching the moon "would put the hippies and dissidents in their place."[39] Instead, the title of Rauschenberg's series suggests that space exploration could also be seen in the creative spirit of the "generation of love."

The unnumbered page that Rauschenberg intended as the frontispiece for the *Stoned Moon Book* (fig. 50) sets out the themes that the book explores. One of these is the relationship between artistic activity and the historic event of the space launch. This page features Rauschenberg, in the lower right corner, seen from the rear, overlooking the launch site. Directly above this scene is a close-up photograph of a swimmer. Rauschenberg has frequently used the swimmer in his art as a symbol of "human struggle to cope with an ever-changing, ever-expanding world."[40] As an extension of the swimmer's stroke, Rauschenberg's hand applies liquid ink to a lithographic stone. To the left side of the launch-site photo, the artist has placed a picture of the print-drying racks at the Gemini studio; the racks look like the gantry supporting the rocket prior to launch, and beside this image the studio clock suggests a countdown is taking place. Further left, the dramatic splash-down of a space capsule is shown, and directly below it is a comic-book depiction of a space ship with a flying dog beside it, an image taken from an illustrated edition of Jules Verne's *Journey to the Moon*. Rauschenberg compares Verne's fantasy to his role as imaginative artist, a position complementary to that of historical witness at the actual space flight.

The first numbered page of the *Stoned Moon Book* (fig. 51) shifts to the artist's personal experience. Rauschenberg revealed that his dog Laika had just given birth to pups. By discussing this event, he personalized the enormity of the space launch, and in the pages that followed the artist drew several parallels between the launch and a

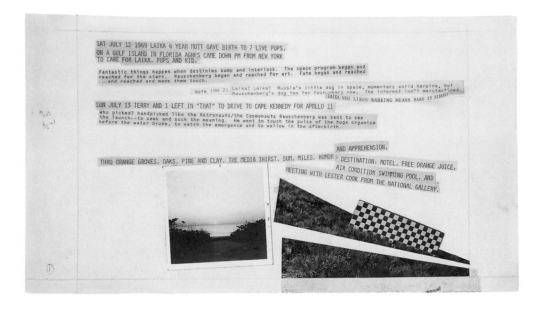

birth. The page also contains Rauschenberg's observations about the trip from his Captiva studio to Cape Canaveral during which nature dominated his experiences – "ORANGE GROVES, OAKS, PINE AND CLAY." The theme of nature and technology is central to the *Stoned Moon Series,* and such individual prints in the series as *Sky Garden* (see fig. 66) and *Marsh* focus on this issue. The photographs chosen for this page complement the text. They include a polaroid snapshot of a sunset seen from Rauschenberg's studio and details of foliage – one of which features a checkerboard road sign – that have been cut in diagonal strips so that they suggest spatial perspective and movement. In the last section of text, Rauschenberg reiterates mundane events to humanize the historical one. "DESTINATION: MOTEL, FREE ORANGE JUICE, AIR CONDITION SWIMMING POOL . . ."

On page two , Rauschenberg abruptly changes mood by exploring the potentially violent conflict between nature and technology, symbolizing the space launch as a savage birth. Initially some beautiful photographs of marsh grasses and the sky are accompanied by the words "LIVE AUDUBON FLAT MARSH WET SMELL." Directly below he writes:

DEVELOPMENT CRACKING THE WALLS OF CONTROL.

CAVES SHIELD AGAINST AN INVITED THREAT.

Rauschenberg is an ardent environmentalist. At the same time, he believes in the essential role of technology in the modern world. The artist has often been faulted for his too-easy reconciliation of these forces, but here he reveals that he understands the danger of unharnessed technology and the need for responsible use of its forces.

On page three Rauschenberg highlights another troubling aspect of the NASA program, its relationship to the military–industrial complex. The text reads "MEMORIES OF WAR AND WEATHER INSTANT AGGRESSION ATMOSPHERIC AUTOPSIES, MILITARY AFFLUENCE. RETIRED POWER. LIFE IN THE EMPTY COKE MACHINE." In the statement, Rauschenberg makes the exploration of space into a military assault that is also related to commerce, recalling the popular phrase "the conquest of space."

While the artist does not present a solution to the military and commercial exploitation of space, he is able to suggest in the lower section of the page that his

52 *Stoned Moon Book,* page 7, collage on illustration board, 9 ³/₈ × 16", collection of the artist.

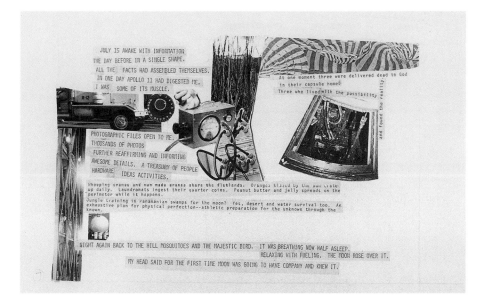

preferred direction is the balance between technology and humanist concerns. For Rauschenberg the key idea here is responsibility for one's actions and an attempt to assure that technological inventions benefit humanity. He wrote,

LAUNCHING CONTROL TWO IDEOLOGIES MAN

TECHNOLOGY CO-EXISTING, RESPONSIVE RESPONSIBLE. COMPETING ACTIVITIES.

CONTROL COUNTERCONTROL . . . HABITING A CRITICAL ARENA WHERE ALL IS PER-

FORMANCE.

After the questions and misgivings just presented about NASA in the early pages, Rauschenberg admits to being totally caught up in the drama of the event. The text of page seven (fig. 52) states that the artist feels physically and mentally absorbed by the launch:

JULY 15 AWAKE WITH INFORMATION THE DAY BEFORE IN A SINGLE SHAPE. ALL THE FACTS HAD ASSEMBLED THEMSELVES. IN ONE DAY APOLLO 11 HAD DIGESTED ME. I WAS SOME OF ITS MUSCLE. PHOTOGRAPHIC FILES OPEN TO ME. THOUSANDS OF PHOTOS FURTHER REAFFIRMING AND INFORMING AWESOME DETAILS. A TREASURY OF PEOPLE HARDWARE IDEAS ACTIVITIES.

This page contains a dramatic array of imagery similar to that found in the *Stoned Moon Series* prints. To the upper right, Rauschenberg has attached a photograph of striped parachutes like those used to float the lunar command module safely down to the ocean. Such parachute imagery is central to the largest print of the series, *Sky Garden.* The center area of the page contains the measuring device with its complex network of wires that is also featured in the print *Ape* (see fig. 62), and the right side depicts a NASA support vehicle and the steel-grid wall of the rocket assembly building found in *Waves* (see fig. 61). Despite Rauschenberg's unbridled enthusiasm, he refuses to dismiss the dangers of space exploration. The photo prominently displayed on the right side of page seven, below the blossoming parachutes, shows the burnt capsule in which astronauts Virgil Grissom, Ed White, and Roger Chaffee were killed in a fire during countdown practice on January 21, 1967. This event became the subject for the print *Brake* (see fig. 65), discussed below.

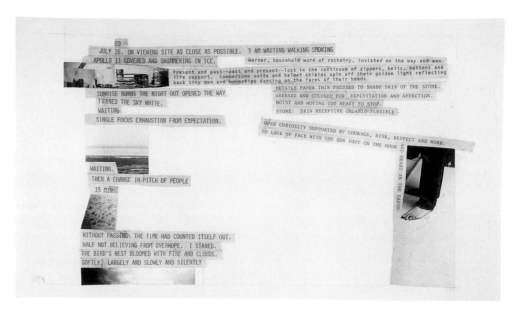

At the end of page seven in the *Stoned Moon Book,* Rauschenberg indicates that he has returned during the night to the launch site. The idea of the rocket as a living creature occurs to him again as a way of connecting it to the natural world and to other types of human experiences. He mentions mosquitos, among the smallest flying creatures, and the majestic "bird," the slang NASA engineers used for the rocket, and adds that it was "breathing half-asleep," a reference to the escaping vapors during the final fueling process. Rauschenberg ended this page with a powerful affirmation, "MY HEAD SAID FOR THE FIRST TIME THAT THE MOON WAS GOING TO HAVE COMPANY AND KNEW IT."

On pages nine and ten (figs. 53 and 54), the artist records the actual launch with a poetic energy that recalls Walt Whitman's *Leaves of Grass* (1855). Rauschenberg wrote:

> APOLLO 11 COVERED AND SHIMMERING IN ICE
> SUNRISE BURNT THE NIGHT OUT OPENED THE WAY
> TURNED THE SKY WHITE.
> WAITING
> SINGLE FOCUS EXHAUSTION FROM EXPECTATION
> . . . .
> WITHOUT PASSING THE TIME HAD COUNTED ITSELF OUT.
> HALF NOT BELIEVING FROM OVERHOPE I STARED.
> THE BIRD'S NEST BLOOMED WITH FIRE AND CLOUDS.
> SOFTLY. LARGELY AND SLOWLY AND SILENTLY
>
> APOLLO 11 STARTED TO MOVE UP.
> THEN IT ROSE BEING LIFTED ON LIGHT.
> STANDING IN MID-AIR 11 BEGAN TO SING HAPPILY
>   LOUD.

54 *Stoned Moon Book,* page 10, collage on illustration board, 9 $^3/_8$ × 16", collection of the artist.

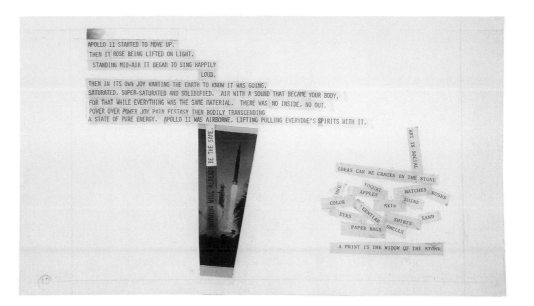

THEN IN ITS OWN JOY WANTING THE EARTH TO KNOW IT WAS GOING,

SATURATED, SUPER-SATURATED AND SOLIDIFIED.

AIR WITH A SOUND THAT BECAME YOUR BODY.

FOR THAT WHILE EVERYTHING WAS THE SAME MATERIAL.

THERE WAS NO INSIDE, NO OUT.

POWER OVER POWER JOY PAIN ECSTACY THEN BODILY TRANSCENDING.

A STATE OF PURE ENERGY. APOLLO 11 WAS AIRBORNE,

LIFTING PULLING EVERYONE'S SPIRITS WITH IT.

NOTHING WILL ALREADY BE THE SAME.

With this powerful ode to the rocket, Rauschenberg included a single photograph of Apollo 11 breaking free from the gantry and lifting off. It is the only color photograph in the book, and next to the ascending rocket he aligned the statement, "NOTHING WILL ALREDY BE THE SAME," an affirmation of the importance of this event and the artist's overall belief in the power of the moment. On the right side of this page, a jumble of single word like "eyes," "skin," "color," "roses," and "mud" suggest an attempt to reconcile everyday sensations with the drama of the launch. Amid this jumble of everyday impressions, Rauschenberg suggests that the connecting link is art. He wrote, "IDEAS CAN BE CRACKS IN THE STONE." The reference is to chance occurrences and varied ideas that the artist compiles in his work and specifically to Rauschenberg's most famous early lithograph *Accident* (1963) that resulted from an accidental break in the lithographic stone. Rauschenberg highlighted these thoughts on art with a phrase that summarizes his overall message in the *Stoned Moon Book*, "ART IS SOCIAL."

On the eleventh page of the *Stoned Moon Book* (fig. 55), Rauschenberg recorded his return to the studio and to artist's work but recognized a world changed by the

55 *Stoned Moon Book,* page 11, collage on illustration board, 9 ³/₈ × 16", collection of the artist.

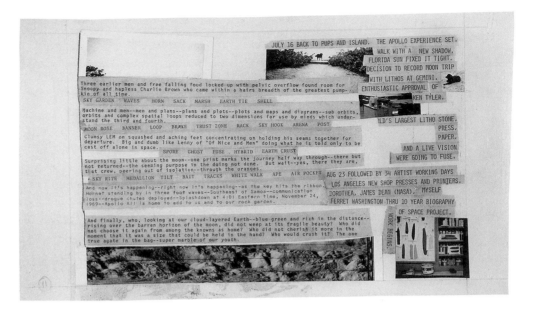

55 *Stoned Moon Book,* page 11, collage on illustration board, 9 ³/₈ × 16", collection of the artist.

moon landing. On this page, he selected one of the famous photographs of human footprints in lunar dust, clearly relating it to the photograph of his bare feet in the studio and of the beach shown two pages earlier. Coupled with that historic image are two photos of his dog Laika and another of color charts on the wall of his studio. A portion of the text reads:

JULY 16 BACK TO PUPS AND ISLAND. APOLLO EXPERIENCE
SET.
WALK WITH A NEW SHADOW.
FLORIDA SUN FIXED TIGHT.
DECISION TO RECORD MOON TRIP WITH LITHOS AT GEMINI. ENTHUSIASTIC
    APPROVAL OF KEN TYLER.
WORLD'S LARGEST LITHO STONE,
PRESS,
PAPER AND LIVE VISION.
WERE GOING TO FUSE.

AUG 23 FOLLOWED BY 34 ARTIST WORKING DAYS
LOS ANGELES NEW SHOP PRESSES AND PRINTERS.
DOROTHEA. JAMES DEAN (NASA), MYSELF.
FERRET WASHINGTON THRU 10 YEAR BIOGRAPHY OF
SPACE PROJECT.
WORK BEGINS.

Here, Rauschenberg is enthusiastically outlining the parameters of his print series at Gemini. The page also contains the titles of all the *Stoned Moon* prints made at Gemini. The *Stoned Moon Book* does not end, however, on this strictly enthusiastic note. An end page (fig. 56) brings the viewer back to the world crises occurring simultaneously with the moon landing. A central photograph of the sky is surrounded by transfer drawings containing some of the more brutal events of the late 1960s. The expressionistic rub marks and the indistinct character of the transfer images give the work a haunting quality.

To the lower-left corner American soldiers are standing over a pile of dead Vietnamese. To the upper-right side there appears a wounded American soldier with a bandage over his eye – denial of vision. In another photographic grouping, a black combat soldier is shown near an image of three lynched black men. At the upper center a large square-fronted truck seems about to run over all of these figures. The photograph of the heavens at the center of this page seems faraway and dream-like compared to the brutality on earth. Rauschenberg shows that his vision of peace through space exploration stands in contrast to, and may be overwhelmed by, the brutalities dominating other aspects of contemporary life.

Despite, or perhaps because of, the rather grim message in the last page of the *Stoned Moon Book*, Rauschenberg decided to express his ideas about the peaceful and productive use of technology through creating a major series of works about space exploration. Because of Rauschenberg's interest in spreading his ideas to a wide segment of the population, he chose print as the medium for this project. Two years earlier, Rauschenberg had been contacted by a new Los Angeles print atelier, Gemini G.E.L. Gemini had been founded by three partners, Sidney B. Felsen, Stanley Grinstein, and Kenneth Tyler. The birth of the atelier was one reflection of the growth of the Los Angeles art scene during the 1960s. Felsen and Grinstein both had connections to the business and collecting community. The former was a certified public accountant who had gone to art school during the late 1950s and early 1960s. Grin-

56 Drawing for *Stoned Moon Book*, solvent transfer with photograph, graphite, and watercolor on illustration board, 10 × 14 ⁷/₈", collection of the artist.

stein owned a forklift business and had become a collector. Ken Tyler had been the technical director at the ground-breaking Tamarind Lithography Workshop in Los Angeles. In 1965, Tyler had left Tamarind to open his own print contract shop, Gemini Ltd. Having developed an interest in publishing prints and in working on a long-term basis with the artists, he joined with Felsen and Grinstein in 1966.

Before Rauschenberg's work with Gemini, the print house had been involved in relatively modest projects. The most notable had been a pair of *White Line Square* prints by Joseph Albers. In 1967, Rauschenberg came to Gemini with the desire to stretch the print medium and to test the potential of the atelier beyond what could have been anticipated. The result was the creation of *Booster* (fig. 57), as noted the largest print ever pulled from a hand lithographic press. The print was essential to demonstrate that printmaking could establish a visual drama in terms of large-scale depictions that rivaled that of modern painting at mid-century. The central image in *Booster* is a life-size skeletal image of Rauschenberg made from a composite of five x-ray prints of his body.

Sidney Felsen recalls the genesis of Rauschenberg's idea to use his skeleton as the core of *Booster*. According to Felsen, he picked Rauschenberg up at the airport and asked him about ideas for the print he intended to make at Gemini. Rauschenberg responded, as if he had not yet thought about the issue, that he wanted to "make a self-portrait," and he asked Felsen to find him a doctor to make an x-ray of his body. Felsen's distinct impression was a spur-of-the-moment decision on Rauschenberg's part. Yet Rauschenberg's intuitive response related to his long interest in photography – among his first art works had been his 1951 life-size solarized images of the human body – and particularly to his recent passion for science and technology. The x-ray of his own body is also characteristic because on one level it is highly personal – it is his skeleton – but on another it remains impersonal, a depiction of the body as structure relevant to the artist and every viewer.

Booster also incorporates themes of space exploration that Rauschenberg later expanded in his second project with Gemini, the *Stoned Moon Series*. The term "booster" was the slang word frequently used during this period for the rockets that were launching capsules into space.[42] Rauschenberg's upright skeletal image looks remarkably like the profile of a rocket with gantry beside it, ready for launch. He made this connection abundantly clear in the largest of his *Stoned Moon* prints, two years later, *Sky Garden*. There the rocket occupies the same central position as the skeleton in *Booster*. Through his skeleton, Rauschenberg explores the idea of the body as a machine. He depicts its structural core and, through his analogy to the powerful booster rocket, suggests the human potential to perform extraordinary tasks. The jumping basketball player to the lower right highlights this point in terms of physical activities. In addition to the body's ability to perform complex activities, it is admirable for its functional simplicity. Rauschenberg makes this clear by the comparison to the elegantly simple chair shown in the upper-left corner of *Booster*.[43]

Rauschenberg's notion of the body as structural machine has many sources, including ones that extend back to the beginning of his career. An immediate stimulation, however, was the 1963 issue of *Life* magazine from which he took the

57   *Booster*, 1967, color lithograph and silkscreen on paper, 72 × 35 ¹/₂", published by Gemini G.E.L., Los Angeles, edition of 38.

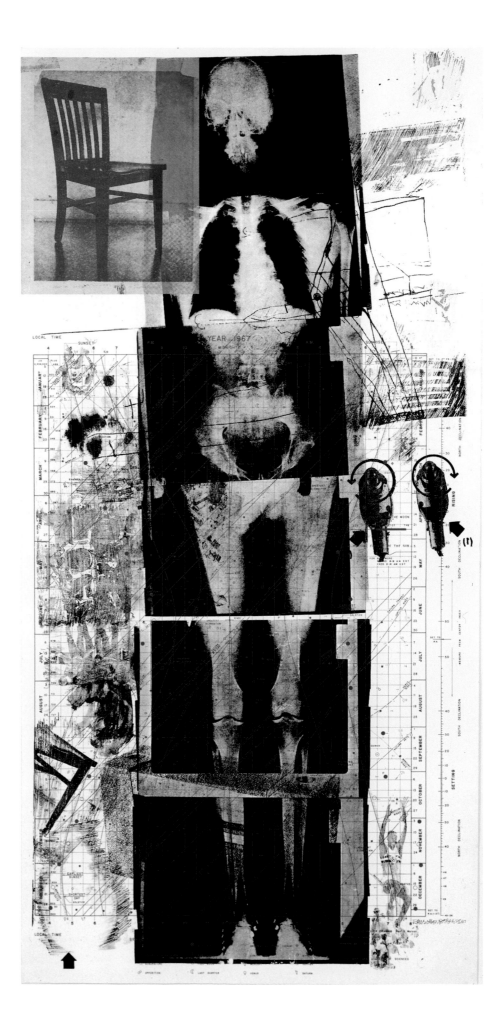

photographs of Wally Schirra's space capsule.[44] That issue also featured "The Workings of the Human Body." The pictorial article depicted stop-action photographs of dancers in motion along with diagrams of skeletal structures. These, in turn, were visually compared to such engineering devices as the struts of a bridge, a hinge, the rigging of a ship, and a crane. Rauschenberg had a silkscreen made of one of the stop-action photographs from this article of a nude female going down stairs, which resembles Marcel Duchamp's celebrated painting *Nude Descending a Staircase* (1912, Philadelphia Museum of Art), and used it in *Express* (1963; see fig. 73), a painting all about motion. In terms of Rauschenberg's use of the skeleton, as noted earlier one of his greatest heroes is Leonardo da Vinci, artist, scientist, and inventor, who studied the human body.[45] Rauschenberg's ideas about the mechanics of movement will be further explored in Chapter 4, which analyzes his dance collaborations.

A small photograph of the Cape Canaveral launch pad on the upper-right side of *Booster* further relates it to space exploration; the skeleton is overlaid with a celestial chart of the planetary movements for the year 1967. So, the skeleton on earth – the body's most basic form – is connected with the movement of the planets in the universe. In Rauschenberg's view, it is the exploration of space that will make our connections to the cosmos most direct.

The other dominant image in *Booster* is the pair of electric drills to the right center of the print. These refer to man as worker and manipulator of tools. Without our ability to make tools, the advances that eventually led to space exploration would be impossible, and arrows around the drills indicate the circular motion of the drill bits. This motion, a microcosm, coordinates with the circular rotation of the planets in the solar system and relates to the planetary chart shown next to the drills.

The placement of the two drills next to the pelvic area of the skeleton is also undeniably sexual, and their shapes pun on the male sexual organ. The *Stoned Moon* prints contain a number of sexual puns. Rauschenberg is clearly aware of the rocket as a phallic image, an interpretation that is also found in the popular imagery of the period. This analogy results not only from its shape but also its action as a force penetrating space. For most of his career, Rauschenberg's imagery has included sexual innuendos. Particularly notable among the space exploration works is that of workers inserting a Gemini space capsule in the Agenda D docking station, a photograph that Rauschenberg took from *Newsweek* magazine and used in *Overcast I* as well as other works.

Recently, there has been much discussion in the Rauschenberg literature of homosexual themes in his art. These interpretations have remained highly speculative and often problematic. In the view of one author, the majority of Rauschenberg's circular configurations are anal. In another highly speculative text, Rauschenberg's Dante's *Inferno* drawings have as their major source gay bath houses.[46] In fact, Rauschenberg's views on sexuality as expressed in his art are more traditional and more circumspect than these authors suggest. Rauschenberg was not involved with the camp gay community that surrounded Andy Warhol during the 1960s. Sexually, he was more reserved and private. This attitude is reflected in his art. His sexual references tend to be indirect rather than direct. They take the form of visual puns rather than gay manifestos. His imagery is not exclusively male; erotic females such as the images of the Venus taken from Velázquez and Titian play a substantial role. Maternal figures also appear with some frequency in the works. In fact, Rauschenberg's images of men and women, despite his sexual orientation, remain quite conventional in the spirit of popular culture during the 1950s. His males are muscular, athletically fit adventurers and his females are sensual, often self-admiring, and less active. Rauschenberg's sexual content is not explicitly pro-gay but rather explores sex as a life force. Generally, it seems that for Rauschenberg sex is not a political cause but rather a sign of energy and vitality. In a conversation with Walter Hopps in 1992, Rauschenberg made it clear that he did not wish to be labeled as homosexual but rather "pan-sexual."[47] As such, the sexual urge in all its variations becomes, for Rauschenberg, a symbol for creative energy.

Sexuality is just one of many subjects that appears in the *Stone Moon Series*. The development of the space exploration themes that had occurred in the Silkscreen Paintings and the *Stoned Moon Book* came to the forefront in the series. The launch itself inspired Rauschenberg, in his words, to "make a major artistic statement." Consumed by this vision and working with the printmakers at Gemini, Rauschenberg created thirty-four prints in thirty-three days. Almost certainly, neither Gemini nor any other modern print atelier up to that time had experienced such an intense schedule. Rauschenberg often worked fourteen-hour days. Since there were eight printers, they would work in shifts with Rauschenberg, and sometimes the exhausted printers slept on the printing presses so as to awake the next day ready for work. Sidney Felsen recalls several days during which Rauschenberg worked twenty-four straight hours on the project.[48] Ken Tyler remembers that the print studio had never before or after had such an experience: "I think it was Bob's spirit and the mood surrounding Apollo 11. He was quite simply the most charismatic person around at the time, and he was able to seduce people around him to work that way."[49]

The *Stoned Moon Series* began with the smaller works in the series and developed toward the larger more complex pieces such as *Banner*, *Wave*, and *Sky Garden*. Forty different stones were used in the series as well as many more plates for color; typically all four presses at Gemini were operating simultaneously. The techniques for creating the series were so complicated that they led Rauschenberg to compare his working at Gemini to the labor of the technicians at NASA. The basic procedure may be described as follows. Rauschenberg came to Gemini with the NASA photographs in hand. First, he sorted out the ones he wished to use and decided on the sizes for each.[50] They were then sent to a photographer. The images returned as positive and negative sheets. Rauschenberg began at that point to cut the sheets and pin them together in a collage-like manner (fig. 58). The collaged images were then reproduced on photographic plates. The photographic plates were in turn chemically reproduced on transfer paper (fig. 59). Rauschenberg would often do additional drawing on the transfer paper. The transfer paper was then placed over the lithographic stones and Rauschenberg rubbed on the paper, providing the variety of expressionist strokes (fig. 60). Often tuche washes were laid over the images and on the naked stone. Tyler worked the stones with the "rub-up" technique that he had

58 Rauschenberg working with source material and proofs for the *Stoned Moon Series* at Gemini G.E.L., Los Angeles (1969), photo by Malcolm Lubliner.

59 Rauschenberg checking transfer sheet for *Trust Zone (Stoned Moon Series)* at Gemini G.E. L., Los Angeles (1969), photo by Malcolm Lubliner.

60 Rauschenberg drawing on the lithograph *Sky Garden (Stoned Moon Series)* at Gemini G.E.L., Los Angeles (1969), photo by Malcolm Lubliner.

developed. This produces a slight relief on the surfaces of the stones, and both provides more detail in the printed images and permits the stones to be worked over many times without loss of previously made marks.

During his days at Gemini, Rauschenberg would work on a large number of stones at one time, and Tyler and his assistants also worked on multiples stones. Transfer papers that Rauschenberg used to draw onto the stones were being produced simultaneously; Tyler estimates that the individual *Stoned Moon* prints took Rauschenberg anywhere from one hour to a day. Tyler recalls that the team of Gemini printers were at their best during the *Stoned Moon* project. In his words, "They realized that this was a golden moment and they weren't going to let us down."[51] Amid the hectic, diverse, and fast-paced activity of creating the series, Tyler particularly remembers Rauschenberg's control over the project:

> Nothing was random. It is very, very much intuitive, but also his hands-on ability to work with imagery is uncanny. Everything is so fluid and concentrated in Bob's hands. The way he cuts a piece of paper, the way he lays a thing down, the way he chooses the next image. When you are working side by side with a man like that you are always suspicious that he will make an error. With trembling hands working at one o'clock in the morning after fourteen hours of labor, reaching for a stylus and putting down just the right amount of information. Nothing is thrown away. It is uncanny. But that is where he is at his best; that is his world. In my experience, the visual interplay that he is capable of on such a fast level is unique.[52]

Each one of the prints from the *Stoned Moon Series* epitomizes a different thematic idea about space exploration. Some of these ideas were introduced in the Silkscreen Paintings, but they reached their fruition in this series. It demonstrates how Rauschenberg uses his art works to express his concerns about a particular subject. Since Rauschenberg worked back and forth between the prints, keeping several going at once, there is not necessarily a progression of his ideas as the series continued. Rather the prints present alternative and multivalent readings of the artist's thoughts about space exploration at the dramatic moment when humankind first set foot on the moon.

Together with *Sky Garden*, *Waves* (89 × 42 inches; fig. 61) is the largest print of the *Stoned Moon Series* and, having exceeded the dimensions of *Booster*, became the largest print that had ever been pulled on a hand lithographic press. In fact the print was created on two stones that were laid end to end so that they would print on a single piece of paper. The stones were laminated together using materials that had been developed for the space program. This was one of many facts that led Rauschenberg to compare his work at Gemini with that done by NASA scientists. Because of the complexity involved in the scale of *Waves*, the printing was overseen by Ken Tyler with five assistants. *Waves* concerns the sheer drama of the Apollo 11 events and its size promotes such a dramatic presentation. The verticality of the print suggests the rocket soaring skyward. Unlike *Sky Garden*, which utilized, in addition to the two lithographic stones, four aluminum plates and a silkscreen for the printing, *Waves* is pure lithography and was printed only in black and white. While

61 *Waves (Stoned Moon Series)*, 1969, lithograph on paper, 89 × 42 $^{1}/_{8}$", published by Gemini G.E.L., Los Angeles, edition of 27.

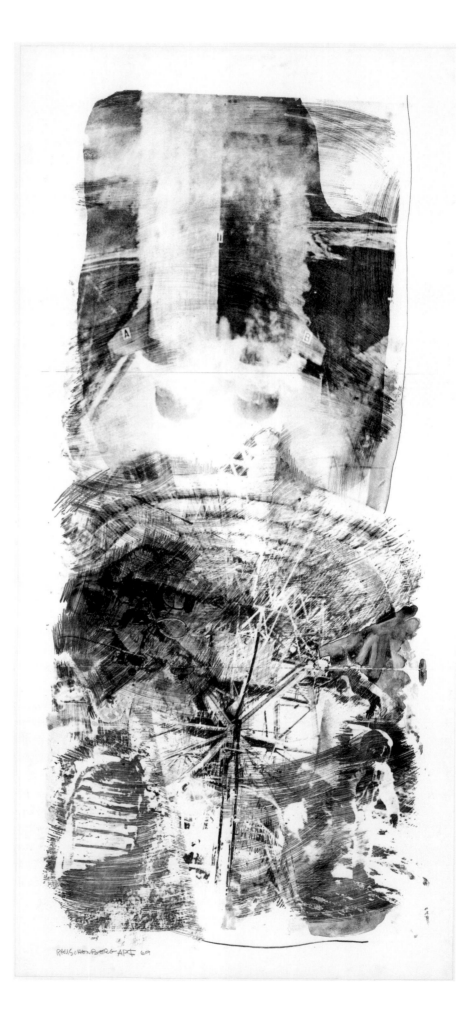

the colors of *Sky Garden* lend it a rich sensuality that will be discussed below, the sharp contrasts of *Waves* emphasized the raw power of the images. The black and white tonalities also remind us that those images were transmitted around the world as black and white photographs of the launch and most dramatically in the live film footage taken on the moon.

The entire upper zone of *Waves* is occupied by a dramatic photograph of the Apollo 11 rocket lifting off. The photograph was cropped so as to include just the lower section of the Saturn 5 booster and the exhaust from its engines. The image focuses on the enormous force of the thrusters, and the lithographic ink has been deliberately applied in a loose fashion that complements the smokey effect of the vapors. For the lay person, the lift-off of a Saturn rocket may be the most sensational aspect of the entire enterprise; the Saturn 5 rocket generated 7.5 million pounds of thrust at take-off. The cropped photo suggests that the rocket is shooting right off the surface of the print. This image of the rocket recalls pages nine and ten of the *Stoned Moon Book* and Rauschenberg's unbridled poetic enthusiasm as he saw Apollo 11 soaring skyward. Previously, Rauschenberg had avoided such highly charged depictions in favor of more circumspect images of space exploration. But here he clearly felt that the event warranted a highly emotional response. The "wave" referred to in the title is the sound waves caused by the rocket but also the waves of excitement that rolled over all who experienced the event. The effect of the sound waves during lift-off is a fascinating component of the event – one that captured Rauschenberg's imagination as he watched the launch. When witnessing a lift-off from a nearby position, as Rauschenberg did, one first sees the rocket begin to rise before hearing anything. One then sees the grass in the field between the viewer and the rocket begin to waver, then the water in a pond near the launch area starts rippling, finally one hears the explosive noise of the rocket and simultaneously one's clothing vibrates from the sound waves.[53] James Dean remembers that Rauschenberg was especially amazed by this aspect of his experience during the Apollo 11 lift-off.

In *Waves*, the rocket above is balanced by the large image of a tracking dish below it. The dish recalls a similar photograph used in such silkscreen paintings as *Trellis*. In fact, Rauschenberg had long been fascinated by the combination of intricacy and delicacy in these satellite dishes, as well as the fact that they provided one of our most important links with the universe before space travel. Rauschenberg's first image of the satellite dishes may be a photograph at the center of his Combine painting *Dam* (1959, Hirshhorn Museum and Sculpture Garden, Washington, D.C.).[54]

In *Waves*, the complexity of the latticework of steel girders in the dish contrasts with the plume of rocket exhaust above; the circular shape of its radiating grid of lines also makes it look like a hemispherical projection of the earth with latitude and longitude markings on it. The dish points skyward toward the disappearing rocket, and it reflects the polarities of the Apollo 11 experience: earth and sky, those who actually experience outer space and those who await information about the adventure. A photograph of Rauschenberg working in the Gemini studios shows enlargements of the two photographs, rocket launch and satellite dish, placed prominently on the wall beside him as inspiration.

The bottom of *Wave* takes us full circle to the ultimate purpose of the rocket's launch. At the base of the print are depicted two of the most celebrated photographs of the Apollo 11 mission. To the right is Neil Armstrong walking on the moon and to the left is a footprint – in this case the footprint is Buzz Aldrin's – on the lunar surface. These images represent Rauschenberg's belief that space exploration is one of the ultimate human adventures, and they combine two themes that run throughout his work – movement along the ground and flight through the air.

Another print in the *Stoned Moon Series*, *Ape* (fig. 62), exhibits a very different aspect of the space program from the high drama of *Waves*. This work emphasizes the more everyday character of the training program and the astronauts' sense of humor. The title of the work comes from its central image depicting three of the astronauts, from left to right, Ed White, James McDivitt, and Neil Armstrong, during an airplane training session for weightlessness. The three sit crossed-legged floating in the air one each covering either his mouth, ears, or eyes in imitation of the children's game "monkey speak no evil, hear no evil, see no evil." Rauschenberg's view of the astronauts contrasts with the popular press depictions. In the press, the astronauts were mostly treated with unbridled adulation. The stresses and strains of their jobs were emphasized. They were the folk heroes of the age, and in addition to their exploits in space, their other successes, rise through the military ranks, personal values, and family lives were almost uniformly praised. There was a much smaller counter-current of criticism of the astronauts. John Glenn was early regarded in some press articles as "too famous." There was additional criticism about greed when each of the original seven astronauts was said to have signed a fifty-thousand-dollar contract with *Life* magazine for his life story.[55] (The "speak no evil . . ." pose may have been a playful commentary on this negative press.)

Rauschenberg avoids both of these positions and instead shows the astronauts as human beings, who are playful, humorous, and who enjoy their job. The viewpoint reflects the artist's attitude about the often fun-filled character of his own work. His depiction humanizes the astronauts and is in keeping with his overall goal of showing the space program as an endeavor with which the ordinary person could easily identify.

The other features of *Ape* create an almost carnival atmosphere. It was printed using two stones and one aluminum plate in colors of rust, red, and orange – all bright and vibrant tones. The manner in which the images are cropped with their curving edges and thin washes playfully resembles hanging fabric and makes us think of Rauschenberg's career-long involvement with textiles. The dial to the upper left is an astrolabe, an ancient navigational instrument used before the invention of the sextant to chart the altitude of the sun and stars. Its presence provides a reference to the history of celestial navigation and is part of Rauschenberg's aim to connect the space program with historical sources. In the carnival spirit of *Ape*, the astrolabe looks, to the average person, like the wheel of fortune or some other fun-house device.

Another image in *Ape* is of an unidentified astronaut strapped into a harness to simulate weightlessness, coordinating with Rauschenberg's long interest in parachutists. As discussed earlier, he finds the free-floating aspect of parachute flight analogous to imaginative freedom. This particular astronaut has a smile on his face.

62   *Ape (Stoned Moon Series)*, 1970, color lithograph on paper, 46 × 33", published by Gemini G.E.L., Los Angeles, edition of 46.

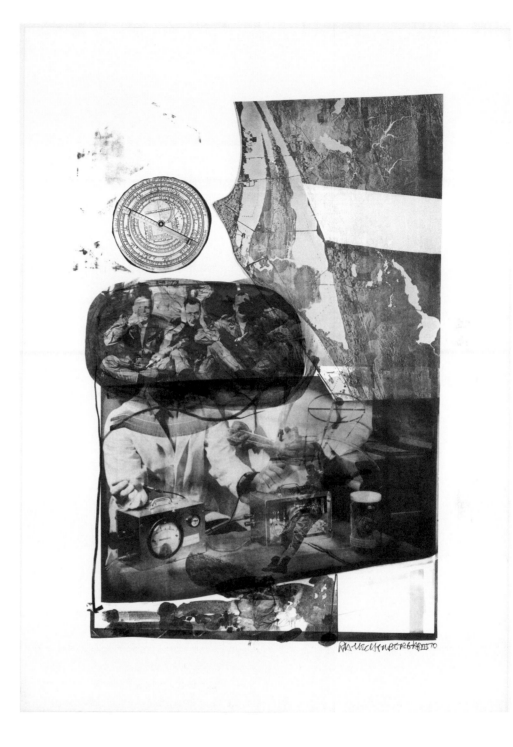

Like the playful trio of astronauts above, he looks somewhat silly hanging in the air, and he is clearly enjoying his training.

At the top of *Ape* is an aerial view of Cape Canaveral upside down – as if it also is weightless – and apparently seen from the vantage point of a spacecraft. To the bottom center of the print are some scientists producing experiments. They emphasize the army of unknown workers involved in the space program; collaboration is a theme that appears frequently in Rauschenberg's space exploration works. They also hint at another aspect of the space program that was played down in the popular press at that time. The astronauts were human guinea pigs, and one of their most

63   *Banner (Stoned Moon Series)*, 1969, color lithograph on paper, 54 $^1/_2$ × 36", published by Gemini G.E.L., Los Angeles, edition of 40.

important purposes was to test the effects of space travel on the human body. All of these elements of *Ape* support an interest in the human aspect of space exploration.[56]

In contrast to the playfulness of *Ape*, a strong sense of the scientific and governmental control over the astronauts is portrayed in *Banner* (fig. 63). Initially, *Banner* seems to represent the Apollo 11 astronauts at their moment of triumph. A brief history of their flight is presented: the rocket taking off is shown to the right side of the print and the space capsule falling to earth is depicted on the left border. At the bottom of the print is the well-known photograph of Buzz Aldrin, Neil Armstrong, and Michael Collins at the end of their space mission. They were picked up in the Pacific Ocean in their ship the *Columbia* by the carrier the U.S.S. *Hornet* on July 24, 1969. As seen on the right side of Rauschenberg's print, the small sign above the chamber reads "Hornet + 3," indicating that the three astronauts are on board.

Yet the image of the astronauts in *Banner* is quite small relative to the overall scale of the print; and because their depictions, made from the lithographic stone, are so hazy compared to those of oranges shown at the center of the work, the astronauts clearly remain secondary figures. The three astronauts stare out from the confinement of their silver isolation van, where they had to remain for several weeks for tests because some scientists feared biological contamination brought back from the moon. One recalls from the press coverage of the event that there was a strong sense of anti-climax because the astronauts could not emerge to talk freely with the public. One author commented:

> It was feared that the lunar spacemen could pick up germs from the moon, bring them back to earth and let them loose on an unprotected population of earthlings. So when Neil Armstrong, Michael Collins and Edwin Aldrin came back from the moon they were unceremoniously bundled in blue overalls and gas masks and locked in a sealed caravan for three weeks.[57]

In *Banner*, more outstanding than the faces of the trio of astronauts is the presidential seal below them. President Nixon was on the Hornet to greet them, and the original photograph contains Nixon, before Rauschenberg eliminated him from the scene. Nevertheless, it looks as though the three astronauts have been wrapped up as a political prize. This message is reinforced by the dominant forms at the center of the print. They are a representation of Florida oranges in bright colors sealed in a box with the Florida state seal on it. The relationship between the boxed oranges and the contained astronauts with the presidential seal is unmistakable. The fact that the Florida seal shows a scene of colonization with a lone native American in the foreground and the European ship behind her adds irony to the comparison. (Rauschenberg probably also liked the analogy between that ship and the modern rescue ship for the astronauts.) The seal bears formal and official language, "The Great Seal of Florida" and "In God We Trust."[58] Colonization and national control of space were hot issues of the day. On the left side of the print is a photograph of the lunar command module in space. In other works it can represent the adventure of space flight, but in the context of *Banner* it is another container in which the astronauts had been sealed, and its shape resembles that of the circular oranges.

The controlled packaging of the astronauts is completed by the two verbal phrases shown in the print – "Do not hoist" and "prep complete" – both of which are regulating commands. The orange and blue colors of the work are bright like those of a flag. While the word "banner" signals joyful triumph, its strict definition is "a piece of cloth attached to a pole and used by a monarch or leader as a rallying point." Rauschenberg was aware of the variety of governmental forces involved in space exploration. He was cognizant of the controlling presence of the federal government and of the military interest in the space race. In the *Stoned Moon Book* he expressed some of these misgivings, and *Banner* deals with similar issues.

It has been claimed by critics that Rauschenberg was solely interested in the American space effort. He did not, however, absent the Russian cosmonauts from his works. In six of the *Stoned Moon* prints, there are representations of the Russians. *Arena II* (fig. 64) features a large-scale and heroic image of the cosmonaut Adrian Nikolayev.[59] After Yuri Gagarin, Nikolayev was one of the best-known Soviet cosmonauts. In 1962 he flew the third Soviet manned space mission in Vostok 3, which to the surprise of the Western world was followed by the launch of Vostok 4, so that two Soviet cosmonauts were simultaneously in space.[60] Nikolayev also piloted the first of the Soyuz space shots in 1969, at a time when Soviet plans to put a man on the moon first were still intact. While Nikolayev was known as the "Iron Man" by his colleagues, the figure that Rauschenberg presents is a more peaceful, visionary one.

In his helmet, looking skyward, Nikolayev is the most dramatic portrait of a space traveler in Rauschenberg's body of work. The large trapezoidal area below the head of the cosmonaut looks like a plinth on which a sculptural bust might stand. (It is actually the flame deflector placed below rockets during lift-off.) Nikolayev looks up toward six circular shapes. While they are actually three pairs of wheels traversing rough terrain in order to test a lunar vehicle prototype, they resemble planets arrayed in the sky at which the cosmonaut is staring. It is revealing that Rauschenberg reserved such a depiction for a cosmonaut: his intent to internationalize space exploration is demonstrated here. *Arena* exists in two states. In state two, Rauschenberg heavily reworked the area around the cosmonaut by drawing onto transfer paper over the original lithographic image and rubbing it heavily to make his image more outstanding. *Arena II* was then printed in a more celestial blue ink.

The large image of Nikolayev in *Arena II* is matched by a small one of Charles Lindbergh at the top of the print. Thus a chief representative of the American history of flight and one of the country's heroes is paired with a modern Russian hero, suggesting the common nature of great human accomplishments. The third figure in *Arena II*, a sailor, appears in a small photograph on the left edge of the print. He stands for the ordinary person who plays an important role in Rauschenberg's interpretation of history. It is perhaps relevant that his own military service was as an enlisted man in the navy, and the artist thus may be identifying himself as one of the everyday people affected by space exploration. Rauschenberg's message of internationalism in *Arena II* is complemented by the print *Medallion*. In that work the central image is a global map shown from the perspective of the North Pole. From that viewpoint America and the Soviet Union seem very close together – almost appearing as united land masses.

64　*Arena II State II (Stoned Moon Series)*, 1969, lithograph on paper, 47 × 32″, published by Gemini G.E.L., Los Angeles, edition of 50.

In the *Stoned Moon Series*, Rauschenberg also included the tragedies of the space program. *Brake* (fig. 65) is a memorial work that depicts the events surrounding what had been called, in the years before the Challanger disaster, the "gloomiest period [of the NASA Program], a time of self-doubt and near paralysis."[61] The first manned flight for the Apollo program had been scheduled for February 1967. As mentioned before, on January 27, during a countdown rehearsal, a fire broke out inside the spacecraft cabin and spread rapidly in the concentrated oxygen environment. Three

65 *Brake (Stoned Moon Series)*, 1969, lithograph on paper, 42 × 29", published by Gemini G.E.L., Los Angeles, edition of 60.

astronauts were killed in the fire: Virgil ("Gus") Grissom, a veteran of the Mercury and Gemini programs; Ed White, the first man to walk in space; and Roger Chaffee. In their analysis of the accident investigators found "many deficiencies in design and engineering, manufacture and quality control" in the NASA program.[62]

The accident and subsequent report became a rallying point for critics of space exploration. They objected that such talent and money could be better used to solve more down-to-earth problems like slums, poverty, racism, and the Vietnam War. The scientific community largely rallied to the support of NASA, and in a spirit that is similar to Rauschenberg's beliefs, the anthropologist Margaret Mead stated that the critics were "shrinking away from the future." She forcefully declared, "A society that no longer moves forward does not merely stagnate, it begins to die."[63] At NASA, the engineers and scientists slowly began to regroup after the Apollo disaster, rebuilding the spacecraft and subjecting it to more rigorous tests. It was not until November 1967 that the next launch took place, when a Saturn 5 rocket placed an unmanned Apollo spacecraft in orbit.

Brake is one of the few works in the *Stoned Moon Series* done in black and white; its tonalities fit the elegiac mood of the print. In handling the medium, Rauschenberg also made it one of the most expressionistic in the series, scribbling heavily over nearly all the images with the lithographic crayon on transfer paper and dripping rivulets of lithographic ink, like tears, on the surface. The upper portion of the stone has then been scraped, and there appears to be an image of scaffolding beneath these marks, but the violence of the scraping has all but obliterated the technology. The effect of the upper portion of the print is one of overbearing darkness, perhaps a visual equivalent of the lethal smoke that filled the space capsule. At the center of the print, scribbled marks reveal a confused bundle of wires; it was an arcing spark from such wires that started the deadly fire.

The most haunting image in *Brake* is that of the command module to the lower-left side, a burnt shell depicted in black lithographic ink. Beneath the heavy working of the stone in the upper portion are three photographs of Mission Control, rotated at different angles. In the choice of these images, Rauschenberg may be emphasizing the shared blame that the entire NASA operation felt, and the rotated positions of these images suggest the disarray into which the whole program temporarily fell.

Yet Rauschenberg does not allow *Brake* to become mired in despair. In the lower right-hand corner of the print, the three astronauts are shown before the accident. They appear in their space suits, smiling. So the final tone of the print is conditioned by a remembrance of their sacrifice rather than a mood of total loss. The stone for *Brake* cracked in the lower section while proofing the edition. Rauschenberg decided to print the edition using the broken stone, because he considered the break related to the emotions of the work.[64] The title of the print refers to that fissure as well as the "brakes" that were put on the space program by the loss of astronauts' lives.

Contemporary historians investigating the early years of the NASA program have turned up numerous close calls and near disasters, and many have been critical of the speed with which the program proceeded, which in their opinion led to accompanying safety risks.[65] These issues were certainly not known to the general public, and not even to many insiders, during the years that they occurred. While Rauschenberg remained supportive of the space program, it is noteworthy that he chose its greatest disaster to that date as one of the themes of the *Stoned Moon Series*.

The summary print for the series was *Sky Garden* (fig. 66). In keeping with Rauschenberg's interest in process and change, *Sky Garden* was not executed at the end of the series but conceived at its beginning and evolved while the other prints

66 *Sky Garden (Stoned Moon Series)*, 1969, color lithograph and screenprint on paper, 89 $^{1}/_{4}$ × 42", published by Gemini G.E.L., Los Angeles, edition of 35.

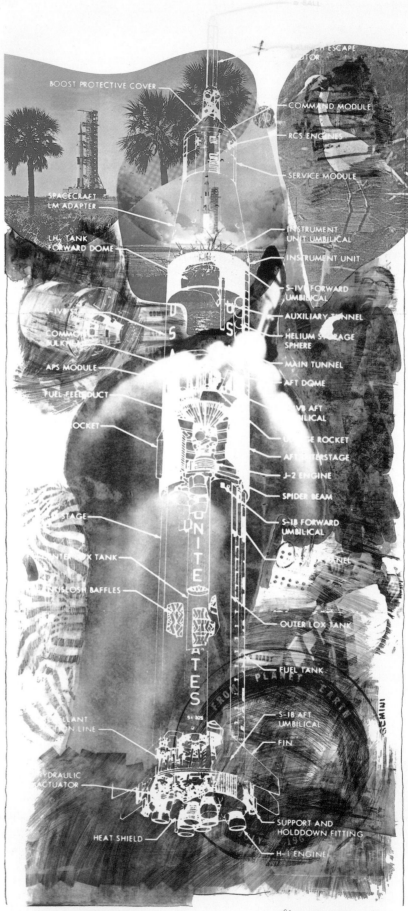

were developed. The scale of *Sky Garden* and its complicated printing techniques were conceived by Rauschenberg to stretch the limits of technology at Gemini G. E. L., and the artist has often stated that he discovers new ideas through the innovative use of materials and techniques. In this particular case, the scale of the print suited its public and historic intent and, in the artist's mind, coordinated with the huge technological accomplishments of the NASA program. As mentioned earlier, Rauschenberg likened his working process with the printmakers at Gemini to the cooperative endeavors of the scientists at NASA.

Rauschenberg worked on *Sky Garden* throughout the month of August, and proofing and printing continued through October. The master printers Ken Tyler and Charles Ritt both oversaw the procedure assisted by no fewer than six printmakers. Printing for the edition of *Sky Garden* required two stones, four aluminum plates, and a silkscreen. Beyond its regular edition, six different types of trial proofs were pulled. Several trial proofs experimented with different color combinations and contained additional manipulation of the imagery by the artist. Also, two special six-color proofs were printed – one of which was given to the NASA archives – on which Rauschenberg executed additional drawing.

Sky Garden encompasses many of the themes that are central to the *Stoned Moon Series* and those ideas that Rauschenberg wished to emphasize as his viewpoint about space exploration. Dominating *Sky Garden* is a labeled diagram of the Saturn rocket with an Apollo spacecraft atop it. The rocket is a grand and powerful machine; and, as discussed earlier, its location in the print clearly links it to the human body as machine. The labels on the rocket are of the sort that make it understandable to the general public, as did those on the related diagram of the space suit in *Trust Zone*.[66] As with *Trust Zone*, Rauschenberg could have chosen any number of complex engineering diagrams that were also available to him in the NASA archives. Instead he picked one that would reveal information to the average citizen because his object was clarification. When thinking of labeled objects in the history of late modern art, one is reminded of the designated body parts by Larry Rivers in such works as *Parts of the Body, English Vocabulary Lesson* (1963, private collection) and the words accompanying objects in such Jasper Johns paintings as *Fool's House* (1962, Collection of Jean Christophe Castelli). Rauschenberg's diagram neither has the punning irony of Rivers nor does it encompass the sophisticated philosophical puzzles of Johns. In contrast to these works, Rauschenberg's diagram presents information as directly as possible.

The rocket that is shown in the diagram is actually a Saturn 1B, not the one used in the moon launch but an Apollo 7 rocket. The rocket thus connects with the history of the space program, and it may have interested Rauschenberg that this was also the booster used to send Wally Schirra aloft in the Gemini launch, the events of which provided photographs for Rauschenberg's Silkscreen Paintings of 1962–64. The coolly factual rocket diagram is lithographed over a dramatic image of the Saturn Five rocket during the Apollo 11 lift-off. Its explosive power, seen close up, is communicated by the rapid and fluid application of the lithographic ink that Rauschenberg used throughout this area. It seems as if the entire bottom two-thirds of the print

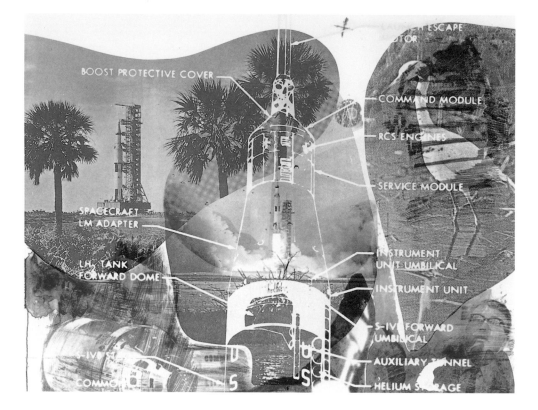

is a combination of fire and steam. One can see the layers of ice, built up on the rocket skin from the super-cool liquid fuel within it, falling away as it soars into space. Rauschenberg thus establishes a dialogue between emotional and intellectual responses to the event.

To the upper-left side of the Saturn 5 rocket is the command module, seen in outer space, and below this a portion of the three parachutes deploying as it splashed down in the ocean. (The billowing parachutes are visually analogous to the steam from take-off.) So in this portion of *Sky Garden* the entire lunar mission from lift-off to arrival at the moon to landing is summarized. In the upper area of *Sky Garden* (fig. 67), the cool blue color contrasts with the red below. Here Rauschenberg shows a more remote view of the lift off and a related image of the Saturn Five rocket being wheeled onto the launch pad. Both are seen at a distance through palm trees. This is the viewpoint from which Rauschenberg first saw the rocket. The blue color beneath the rocket makes it look as if it is floating on the water. There was a small lake between Rauschenberg and the launch site, and the blue color recreates its effect. The shapes of the blue areas themselves are like water droplets. Rauschenberg's colors further suggest that sea, air, and sky are mixed together.

An idea that Rauschenberg is promoting in this part of the print is the interaction between nature and technology. That notion is further supported by the blue-tinted image of a Florida egret on the upper-right edge of *Sky Garden*. The egret's long tubular body and its spindly legs bear a surprising visual similarity to the rocket. In fact, the red striations that appear over the bird's body are actually Buzz Aldrin's footprint on the moon, shown here as if he were exploring the Florida marshes not the lunar landscape.

In the third page of *Stoned Moon Book*, Rauschenberg speculated through images and words on the potentially violent disruption of nature by technology, and he concluded that humankind was accountable for the responsible use of technology. A number of the *Stoned Moon* prints deal with the theme of nature and technology.[67] *Hybrid* compares the rocket with Florida palm trees and birds, and *Tilt* shows an astronaut in a space suit engaging in a simulated moon walk next to an ecologist doing an environmental study in the Everglades. *Marsh* depicts rockets colored in verdant green and overlaid by photographs of marsh grasses, as if the rockets themselves are growing in the marshes.

When Rauschenberg visited Cape Canaveral, he was told that environmentalists were initially concerned that the rocket center would drive away wildlife, but it appeared that the ecology had adapted, and wild creatures had remained in the marshy areas surrounding the launch pads and facilities buildings. Vultures had even begun to use the crumbling scaffolding from the Gemini project as a nesting area. Rauschenberg was interested in these stories and thought of them as a sign that nature and technology could co-exist.[68] In *Sky Garden*, the relationship between nature and technology, even at the moment of the dramatic launch, is harmonious. In this summary work, Rauschenberg took a global view that earth and space, water and air, humans and their creations, technology and nature are part of a great unified force. In fact, the colors and images of *Sky Garden* suggest the four primal elements: air, earth, fire, and water.

While Rauschenberg's beliefs about nature and technology are perhaps idealistic, he was not alone in this viewpoint. In the face of criticism that the space program ignored problems on the earth, one of the major positions taken by scientists and NASA officials was to predict the positive effect that space exploration would have on understanding the earth. NASA publications stressed better comprehension of the origins of the planet and the ecological systems of the earth, of improved weather tracking, of advanced warning for natural disasters, of the understanding of global changes in the environment, and other benefits to the earth that would come from space. In *Sky Garden*, Rauschenberg echoed these hopes.

In addition to the rocket and the space module in the lower section of *Sky Garden*, Rauschenberg chose two images of the people involved in the space program: one of the most famous scientists involved in the American space effort is seen in the upper right photograph, the rocket engineer Wernher von Braun. With a visionary expression on his face, von Braun is looking skyward as a launch is taking place. Directly below him is an anonymous figure from the mission launch room.[69] This figure is similarly looking up from his control board, thus also emphasizing the dramatic moment of the launch. (Generally, the only time that the control room personnel would allow their eyes to leave the instruments was in the last seconds before launch because the countdown had become automated.) Taken together, these two figures highlight the theme of cooperation and broad involvement in the space program, and in effect they enfranchise the viewer as part of space exploration.

Dominating the lower-right section of *Sky Garden* is the official insignia of the NASA moon program, legible on it the words "From Planet Earth" and the date "July 1969." Interestingly, Rauschenberg obliterated from the seal the NASA symbol. In this manner the seal is generalized and thus relates to one of Rauschenberg's most dearly held beliefs, the internationalism of space exploration and its character as an overall human quest. At the same time, Rauschenberg signed his own name in this area of the print, asserting his intimate identification with space exploration. (He also wrote "Gemini" to identify the print atelier. Rauschenberg certainly found it a fortuitous sign that his print atelier had the same name as a star configuration and as the second stage of the NASA program.)

The *Stoned Moon Series* was executed during some of the most difficult years for America in the post-World War II era. Martin Luther King and Robert Kennedy were assassinated in 1968. These two horrifying events were accompanied by the violent beatings of demonstrators at the Democratic National Convention in Chicago, riots in the urban ghettos, and massive demonstrations against United States involvement in the Vietnam War. Rauschenberg was committed to the protests against government policies during those years. He contributed the solvent transfer drawing *Political Folly* to a Chicago exhibition to protest against the brutality meted out to anti-war demonstrators at the Democratic National Convention, and he gave money to the *Artists' Tower* (Against the Vietnam War), designed by the sculptor Mark di Suvero. Rauschenberg donated works to the Art For Peace Program, an auction the proceeds from which were used to help elect anti-war candidates to Congress, and he was one of the artists to withdraw works from the 1970 Venice Biennale to protest about U.S. government sponsorship of that event.[70]

In the context of these occurrences, the space program was one of the few government-sponsored endeavors that Rauschenberg felt he could support. Rauschenberg recalled of the Apollo 11 launch, "The whole project seemed one of the only things at the time that was not concerned with war and destruction."[71] Clearly, he supported the space program and admired its accomplishments, as did most Americans. Analysis of the works has shown that Rauschenberg was aware simultaneously of the conflicting interest groups, especially the military involvement, in the program. Rauschenberg had a particular set of ideas about the aspects of the space program that were most praiseworthy, and he deliberately set out to support and advocate those values. As is characteristic of Rauschenberg, he did so not by attacking the faults of the program but by optimistically emphasizing those features he viewed as its strong points.

The values that Rauschenberg emphasized in the *Stoned Moon Series* included non-military objectives, through his pointed exclusion of any military imagery. In the prints, internationalism plays an important role. Despite Rauschenberg's pride in American accomplishments, the Soviet Union is represented and the notion of a "space race" or an "us against them" mentality does not appear. In the *Stoned Moon Series*, the possible cooperative relationship between technology and the environment is a major theme, and it subsequently became a career-long issue for the artist. His call for the responsible use of technology underlies the entire series, and he saw his cooperative work with the Gemini printers as an example of such a responsible activity. In the *Stoned Moon* prints, space exploration is connected to the general history of the human search for knowledge, and he attempted to de-mystify the complex machinery and to encourage the involvement of the lay person. Through his representation of unnamed workers, he highlighted broad involvement in the space program. The large scale of *Sky Garden* and *Waves* particularly announced that these works were meant for the public arena as the artist attempted to spread his ideas among the general populace. This is the reason that Rauschenberg chose to create the *Stoned Moon Series* in the print medium, with its possibility of multiples and its venerable history of social and political education, rather than to make silk-screen paintings. Ken Tyler recalled, "It was our idea to make all of this as public as possible."[72]

Rauschenberg wished to distribute his ideas widely through the *Stoned Moon* project. At the same time, the complexity of these prints, their rich colors, the actively worked surface, and often their scale made them rivals for the public character of paintings. As Tyler has said, "It was almost as if landing on the moon was one heroic act and this was going to be another."[73] The size of the edition of each print, averaging in the low fifties, was reasonably large for such complicated prints and one of the series, *Sub-Total*, was printed in an edition of five hundred to create a wide public for the series.

The *Stoned Moon Series* was shown in two parts at Gemini's studios in Los Angeles during the winter and spring of 1970. It was also exhibited during November 1969 at Leo Castelli, New York, at the Museum Haus Lange in Krefeld, Germany, at the Fendrick Gallery in Washington, D.C., and at the New York Cultural Center. There were, however, relatively few reviews. The conservative critic for the *New York Times*, John Canaday, after writing of "How wonderfully [Rauschenberg] combines celestial diagrams, photographs of Cape Kennedy, navigation charts, x-rays of the human body, and a whole category of related data from the space program . . ." concluded bitingly that the works would make "good porch decorations."[74] A more positive review in the *Washington Post* focused on the fact that Rauschenberg saw no contradiction between his withdrawal of works from the 1970 Venice Biennale as a protest against American foreign policy and his support of the space program.[75] The review did not specifically discuss individual works of the series.

Two other short reviews of the *Stoned Moon Series* took up the issue of the contemporaneity of Rauschenberg's subject matter. In his discussion of Rauschenberg's prints, Donald Karshan wrote that the power of the series resulted from Rauschenberg's personal experience of the Apollo 11 launch and the subsequent individual character of his interpretation.

> What is most extraordinary about the accomplishment is that the subject matter – for there is plenty of it – is inextricably bound to the artist's experiences and perceptual illumination. Rather than being a "commemorative" of the Apollo moon launch, as one critic has called them, the prints, although inspired and drawn from actual events and their documentary residue, are profoundly experienced points of departure for intuitive perception.[76]

For Karshan, Rauschenberg's "intuitive perception" was based upon his ability to dissolve the paper surface through his complicated graphic techniques and to create a new sense of spatial ambiguity. The implication is that such spatial concerns were particularly appropriate for the theme of the series. In his review of the Los Angeles exhibition of the series, Joseph E. Young formed the opposite opinion. He found the topicality of the subject matter limiting: "The history of art indicates, among other things, that in pictorial art, imagery which is too topical, too firmly fixed at one point in time, faces the distinct possibility of becoming a nostalgic curio in short order." Young concluded, however, that "Rauschenberg is capable of sur-mounting the limitations of topical imagery as his *Booster* and *Banner* lithographs amply indicate."[77]

These short reviews show that Rauschenberg had been able to focus some critical attention on the manner in which his art presented a significant event in contempo-rary history. But the attention was limited and did not extend to specific discussions of the artist's ideas in the series. So, in the short term, the *Stoned Moon Series* could not be judged to have influenced public opinion as Rauschenberg hoped it might.

* * *

National exhilaration over the moon landing and Rauschenberg's own thoughts about space exploration were cut short by his awareness of increasing social unrest. Anti-war demonstrations grew harsher after the revelation of the secret U.S. inva-sion of Laos and the disclosure that American troops had murdered several hundred Vietnamese civilians at the village of My Lai. Rauschenberg was overwhelmed by this news. It suddenly seemed to him that positive social and political commitment was useless. In the face of these circumstances, he decided to escape to Malibu, California to make works inspired by nature. Instead, he found that he could not get away from the force of contemporary occurrences, and he created *Currents* (fig. 68).

In this series, Rauschenberg clipped headlines, news stories, and photographs from the January and February 1970 editions of the *New York Times*, the *New York Daily News*, and the *Los Angeles Times*. With virtually no editing, he arranged the clippings into thirty-six collages, each thirty inches square and called them "Currents." In order to reach a larger audience, he then had them printed. When shown together the col-lected collage filled a large room. Rauschenberg described the project as "the most serious journalism I had ever attempted."[78] Yet in *Currents* he actually abrogated the power of selection and organization that had allowed him to express his views on space exploration in the *Stoned Moon Series*. Here he yielded to the overwhelming character of world events and expressed the emotion of being overcome by them. *Currents* is in fact nearly as far from art making as Rauschenberg has ever moved. The series is based on the artist's refusal, as far as is possible, to avoid conscious selec-tion and manipulation of information. One of the most interesting exhibitions that Rauschenberg held was a simultaneous showing of the *Stoned Moon Series* and the *Currents* at the New York Cultural Center during July and August of 1970. There Rauschenberg's opposing approaches to dealing with contemporary life were sharply contrasted. Unfortunately, there was no critical discussion of this exhibition.

After the *Currents*, Rauschenberg moved to his newly established studio in Captiva Island, Florida, again seeking serenity. But on October 4, 1970 he learned that his

68 Opening of *Currents* exhibition at Dayton 12 (1970).

friend Janice Joplin – they had both escaped the stifling conformity of childhoods spent in Port Arthur, Texas – had died of a drug overdose. As a summary work to the exciting and troubled decade of the 1960s, Rauschenberg created the screenprint *Signs*. The print joined together some of the most powerful images of the decade including photographs of wounded American soldiers in Vietnam, portraits of John F. and Robert Kennedy, a photograph of Joplin during a concert, and one of Martin Luther King in his casket. But the largest of the images is that to the lower right, of Buzz Aldrin in his space suit on the moon. His visor reflects the moon's surface, the lunar module, and Armstrong walking on the moon. Directly below this image Rauschenberg initialed the print, and it is this gesture that indicates his continued identification with space exploration as well as his hope for the future amid the disasters that marked much of the decade.

Rauschenberg has not focused again on space exploration with the intensity found in the *Stoned Moon Series*, but his interest in the subject is a recurring theme in his art. Dozens of his works contain space exploration imagery. In 1971, he created *Star Quarters I–IV*, four works that feature screenprinting done on mirrored plexiglass so that the viewer's reflection becomes part of the work. These panels, produced in an edition of forty-five, contain a profusion of space technology images combined with symbols taken from astrological charts. In them, Rauschenberg combined his interest in the science and the mythology as ways that humans have tried to understand the heavens.

Rauschenberg returned to Cape Kennedy on April 12, 1981 for the first launch of the space shuttle Columbia as one of eight artists invited by NASA to witness the launch.[79] The shuttle marked another highpoint of enthusiasm for the NASA program, one that almost rivaled the moon shot. NASA had been plagued for years by negative reports about the expense of manned flight and the public's perception of a lack of direct material gains from the lunar program. The space shuttle, ideas for which had been under research since 1971, provided a cost-effective manner to continue to send humans into space. By reducing the size of the launch vehicle and creating re-usable exterior fuel tanks as well as partially re-usable solid-fuel boosters, launches were far less expensive. The space shuttle itself was re-usable and was for the public the most exciting aspect of the new design. Its huge cargo bay with mechanical arm allowed it to be utilized for a wide variety of scientific projects as well as commercial ventures for which the shuttle could be rented. The fact that the winged shuttle could glide to an earth landing after its mission added to the visual drama of the new system. Because of the increasing demands of the scientific and commercial communities for operations in space, NASA's Space Transportation System, with the shuttle as its prime component, became the center of NASA operations. With the advent of the space shuttle, it seemed that Rauschenberg's dream of a continuous human presence in space was closer to reality.

As a result of Rauschenberg's witnessing the shuttle launch, he created the monumental print *Hot Shot* (fig. 69). In the view of Robert Schulman, the second director of the NASA Art Program, Rauschenberg's print epitomized the high level of enthusiasm of the early shuttle years.[80] Indeed, *Hot Shot* is filled with excitement, and even the title, which uses the World War II slang for fighter plane aces, captures the aggressive confidence of the space program at that moment. The title is also a play on Roy Lichtenstein's famous Pop art painting *Okay, Hot-Shot* (1963, David Geffen Collection).

The vertical print reminds us of the monumental character of *Sky Garden* and of *Waves*, and its dominant blue colors are those of the sky. Rauschenberg combined aerial and earthbound images, high and low culture, humor and adventure. The upper half of *Hot Shot* is dominated by powerful images of the space shuttle. Framed to either side of the print are two close-up views of the shuttle ready for launch. These shadowy depictions feature the shuttle's dramatically new silhouette. The left image is a silkscreen taken from positive film, and it is covered by a chart of planetary movements for the year, as was the skeletal x-ray of *Booster* in 1967. To the right, a negative print – like an x-ray – of the shuttle was employed, giving it the appearance of disappearing in the atmosphere. At the top center the shuttle soars through the sky to its landing. At the base of these images a technician prepares the shuttle, continuing the Rauschenberg theme of homage to anonymous workers.

The bottom half of *Hot Shot* is more playful and involved with popular culture. It is also multicolored and contains more detail than the strikingly simple shapes at the top of the print. At the bottom the shuttle is being towed to the launch site. With crowds gathered around, the event looks like a festive holiday parade, and one thinks of frequent parade images used in Rauschenberg's silkscreen paintings. Next to the shuttle parade are the popular billboards put up at local motels wishing the shuttle well. They include the invented word "Shuttlemania," next to which Rauschenberg has placed an arrow pointing to the photographs of the shuttle at the top of the print and to the heavens. Rauschenberg's ability to capture a historical moment in its completeness, including high and low culture, is a leitmotif of his work. Next to the

69   *Hot Shot*, 1983, color lithograph with collage on paper, 81 × 42", published by Universal Limited Art Editions, edition of 29.

rudimentary rectangular shapes of the billboards is a photograph of the Columbia control panel in all its technological complexity.

At the lower center of *Hot Shot*, Rauschenberg chose an image of a plant growth experiment. The fragile plants contrast with the massiveness of the shuttle, but the juxtaposition embodies Rauschenberg's dearly held hope that technology and nature would be co-dependent. Set across from and overlapping the plants is the shuttle's huge mechanical cargo-bay arm, but here it jokingly looks like a hose nozzle that will water those plants. Below the arm is another playful image of an astronaut. He is actually standing next to a weather balloon, but its proximity to the plants suggests that the balloon is some sort of giant round vegetable. Jubilant and enthusiastic humor are hallmarks of *Hot Shot*. On the whole, the print captures what Robert Schulman called the "go-go attitude" of the early shuttle era.[81]

In 1990 Rauschenberg made the space shuttle the focus of one of his fourteen *ROCI/USA* compositions. After traveling around the world to eleven countries to make art over a seven-year period for the Rauschenberg Overseas Culture Interchange, *ROCI/USA* was a homecoming for the artist, and the *ROCI/USA* works comprise the last pieces that he did in the series. All of the works were executed on large-scale mirrored aluminum panels. The imagery was transferred to the panels via fire wax, a new technique just invented by Donald Saff, printmaker, Rauschenberg's long-time technical collaborator, and the project coordinator for the overseas ROCI ventures.

Initially Rauschenberg's use of aluminum panels for *ROCI/USA* seems odd. Many of the other ROCI works are object-oriented and concern specific materials that Rauschenberg discovered in those countries. The shimmering reflective surfaces of the *ROCI/USA* works are by contrast elusive. But, in retrospect, the aluminum is appropriate. It is a modern material that suits the technological drives of the country. At the same time its surface yields wavy unclear reflections that have a dream-like character. The material reality and the visionary character of inventions are simultaneously present. The aluminum panels can also be easily crumpled and torn, and many of the works are shown in this state so that this high-tech material is depicted not as infallible but subject to wear, a state that communicates the artist's interest in history and mutability. Finally, the aluminum vibrantly reflects the lights around it and, most importantly, reflects us. We see indistinct images of ourselves as part of the works, and Rauschenberg thus suggests that he is telling our history.

One of the fourteen *ROCI/USA* works, *Shuttle Buttle* (fig. 70), features the space program. Composed of three vertically stacked aluminum panels, the monumentally scaled (72$^1/_4$ × 144$^3/_4$ inches) painting contains two images to its right side of the space shuttle prior to take-off. On the left, there is energetic brush painting in blue and red. This brushwork covers a silkscreen image of a sign that Rauschenberg had discovered. It shows a pointing hand with a text above it that reads "Bob's hand." Above this area, a piece of aluminum mesh with a reflective grid of woven metal is attached to the surface. It was originally used for heat insulation in high-tech industry. At first *Shuttle Buttle* seems purely effervescent because of the images of the shuttle at rest, the energetic paint application, and the playful reference to the hand of the artist.

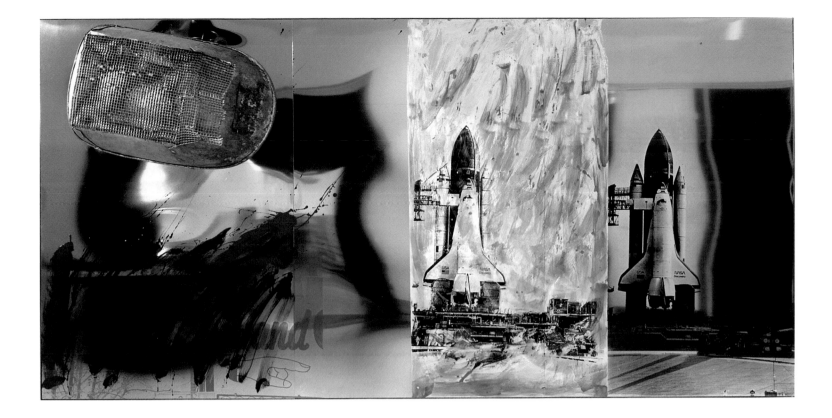

Slowly one notices the expressionistic character of the brushwork, which threatens to obliterate "Bob's hand" and covers part of the shuttle, while the other image of the shuttle is darkly painted. This more troubled mood is confirmed by the fact that the picture of the space shuttle is the well-known photograph taken of the Discovery just before its first launch after the Challenger disaster. The photograph was reproduced in the September 29, 1988 *New York Times* and numerous other locations.

The explosion of the space shuttle Challenger occurred on January 29, 1986, and all seven astronauts on board were killed. The disaster was seen on national and international television during live coverage of the launch, and American viewers particularly focused on the death of Christa McAuliffe, a schoolteacher and the first civilian taken on a spacecraft. For the space program, she was a symbol of the importance of educating future generations about space exploration. The nation was traumatized, and the space program came to a near halt for two years as the accident was investigated. This tragedy may have had special meaning for Rauschenberg because he was one of the individuals, along with such figures as Walter Cronkite, who applied to fly on the space shuttle as the first civilian in space. Although NASA quickly decided on a teacher as the profession of the first civilian spokesperson to go into space, Rauschenberg was featured in a *Life* magazine article of October 1984 as one of the candidates. The article shows the print *Hot Shot* comprising part of a plexiglass triptych. Through the center panel, the viewer sees the space shuttle on its launch pad and Rauschenberg busy painting the right panel. The photograph is a precursor to the design of *Shuttle Buttle*.

The Challenger disaster, however, changed the whole complexion of the American space program. Although the technical problem that caused the disaster was traced specifically to sealing rings in the solid-fuel booster rocket, there were widespread recriminations over quality control at NASA, and the haste, without deference to some safety considerations, with which the program had proceeded. The damage done to the image of reliability that NASA had cultivated was far greater than that arising after the 1967 launch-pad fire that killed three astronauts and inspired Rauschenberg's print *Brake*.

It was not until nearly three years after the Challenger accident that NASA was ready for another manned launch of the shuttle. Despite the clear measures that had been taken to correct the booster flaws, the nation watched in anxiety. The morning after the flight, the nervous state of the country was recorded in the *New York Times's* coverage of the event:

> The space shuttle Discovery, picking up the baton from the fallen Challenger, raced into orbit Thursday carrying five experienced astronauts and the nation's hopes for revival of its civilian space program.

> The successful launching ended 32 months of gloom, self-doubt and redesign following the worst disaster in the history of space flight.

> With dark memories of the Challenger explosion shadowing their every step, space agency officials pressed ahead with the tense and frequently interrupted countdown. They wrung their hands over wind conditions aloft, but after hours of analysis and deliberation, they finally gave the "go" command for the planned four-day mission, waiving a rule against launching in unfavorable wind conditions in their determination to return to space.[82]

Although created in 1990, when shuttle launches had again become more commonplace, *Shuttle Buttle* reflects the tension that marked the return of the manned space program. Its mood is very different from the all-out confidence exhibited in *Hot Shot*. In *Shuttle Buttle*, the Discovery waits expectantly on the ground, and the anticipation that was felt by everyone involved in the program and by all Americans with an interest in manned space flight is evident. On the right-hand side, the black and white image of the shuttle is precise but somewhat foreboding. On the left side of the painting, the shuttle is buffeted by blue paint strokes that perhaps recall the wind conditions that delayed the launch. The light reflecting off the aluminum surface speaks of the engineering sophistication of the shuttle, but its constantly changing patterns also make the image somewhat fragile and elusive.

The left side of *Shuttle Buttle* contains opposing visual areas. At the bottom of the work, the words "Bob's Hand" make a humorous pun but also express Rauschenberg's continued deep identification with the space program through his art. The text "Bob's hand," as mentioned above, is nearly eradicated by the brushwork over it. Yet the hand itself emerges from the paint and points toward the shuttle. The artist is creating a visual metaphor for the energy and drive that propelled the space program forward after its disaster. Above this expressionistic brushwork is the aluminum insulating mesh. This area contains closed shapes unlike the open paint strokes below, and it consists of attached objects rather than paint on the surface. Although these objects might be debris from some engineering or science project, perhaps even debris from a space failure, they comprise the most beautiful and ethereal area of *Shuttle Buttle*. With its sparkling woven surface, the oval shape floats above almost like a magic wing. In it, the forces of decay and disintegration have been turned by the artist into a graceful and fantastic form.

For Rauschenberg, there is a spiritual as well as intellectual component to the continued quest for space. In his art, flight is a recurring metaphor for invention and a soaring imagination. Yet he simultaneously keeps one foot firmly on the ground. His art always returns us to the earthbound world of chance encounters, everyday things, and contemporary events. Through his creative interpretations of the space program, and through other such themes, Rauschenberg seeks to encourage the responsible use of new technology, to open avenues for the exploration of new ideas, and to encourage involvement in contemporary life.

The variety of ideas behind *Shuttle Buttle*, like Rauschenberg's other space exploration works, benefits from increased knowledge of the space program and the artist's relationship to it. Such information puts Rauschenberg more firmly in the context of his time and allows more interpretative depth for his works. As a whole, the study of Rauschenberg's art would benefit from more detailed analyses that consider the historical circumstances related to particular series and that consider the individual pieces in those series in the context of related thematic concerns. Rauschenberg's use of source material and his collaborative projects make such methodology especially appealing.

four   dancing on the edge

The dances, the dancers, the collaboration, the responsibilities and trust which are essential in cooperative art because the most important & satisfying element in my life worked positively with the privateness and loneliness of painting.[1]

Collaboration is a sleight of hand located in the mind where both participants remain vigilant to their separate disciplines as they both cantilever their expectations in suspense of result.[2]

Until recently, Rauschenberg's involvement in dance has been treated as a peripheral issue in his oeuvre, yet his work in choreography, set design, costume, and lighting is powerfully related to fundamental aspects of his art-making.[3] At its core, Rauschenberg's art is performance-based; he finds the process of creation as important as the resulting art object. His works are often made so that, like theatrical events, they change over time, create their own environments, or alter appearance according to their physical relationship to the viewer. For the artist, audience engagement and response are of extreme importance, and he attempts to captivate the viewer through the different visual possibilities that the works offer. It has been seen that Rauschenberg's studio process, resembling a sort of spontaneous choreography, is oriented toward intuitive and quick-paced actions. His dedication to the immediate surroundings and objects of his Lower Manhattan environment during the 1950s, which resulted in works that had some of the characteristics of stage sets, and his attempts to capture contemporary history in the NASA works of the 1960s are but two subjects that demonstrate his focus on living events, an interest that informs his deep commitment to the dance world.

Rauschenberg has often spoken of the parallels he finds between his paintings and the world of theater and dance, stating "I've always been interested [in theater], even back in high school. I like the liveliness of it – that awful feeling of being on the spot, having to assume responsibility for the moment, for actions that happen at a particular time . . . I don't find theater very different from painting." When asked about his creative process, the artist noted, "Activity is the thing almost as if the painting is a by-product of this."[4] On another occasion when questioned about the relationship between his art and performances, Rauschenberg commented, "My work has always been environmental, more or less. Sometimes it gets quite flat, other times it turns into sculpture. I've always attempted to bring art into real time – where it will change because of someone's presence. That probably was the lead in."[5]

This chapter will focus on twenty years of collaborations with the choreographer and dancer Trisha Brown and Rauschenberg's stage, lighting, and costume design for five of Brown's dances.[6] The modes of collaboration will be examined, and each of the dances will be analyzed in detail. I shall also look into the performance backgrounds of Brown and Rauschenberg, charting common influences and differences. They both trace their heritages to the Judson Dance Theater, the now legendary proving ground for post-modern dance. Both had been involved with Merce Cunningham, although Rauschenberg's activities with Cunningham were much more extensive, and both learned from but ultimately reacted against the Cunningham method. Brown once summarized her artistic approach versus Rauschenberg's: "I make order out of chaos, he makes chaos out of order." But she then elaborated, suggesting more fully their crucial importance to each other in terms of experimental development: "Not a lot of people have a habit for discussing choreography, so we choreographers are pretty much on our own. But Bob always talks about it, so we are both out on our own limbs. And that comes out of ideas, challenge, courage. There is, in our relationship, a great trust that we can experiment with each other."[7] In fact, the collaborations between Brown and Rauschenberg have had a profound

71 *Minutiae*, 1954, Combine painting: oil, paper, fabric, newspaper, wood, metal, plastic, with mirror on string, on wood structure, 84 $\frac{1}{2}$ × 81 × 30 $\frac{1}{2}$", collection of the artist.

influence on both their arts; each has responded to the other and changed through the mutual contact.

Before looking into the initial connections between Brown and Rauschenberg, it is worth summarizing Rauschenberg's extensive involvement in theater as a lighting, costume, and set designer, and as a choreographer and performer. Already, at Jefferson High School in Port Arthur during the early 1940s, Rauschenberg had created costume and set designs for the school theater, and at the Kansas City Art Institute, which he briefly attended in 1947, one of the odd jobs that he held was fabricating movie sets. Rauschenberg's real introduction to avant-garde dance and performance began at Black Mountain College where he studied with John Cage and Merce Cunningham during the summer of 1952. Significantly, he participated in the now famous *Theater Piece #1*, which because of its use of everyday activities and chance procedures in determining some of the events, as well as its multi-disciplinary aspect, is considered a wellspring for late modern dance.

When Rauschenberg moved to Fulton Street in 1953, Cage and Cunningham lived nearby, and in 1954 Rauschenberg designed his first stage set for Cunningham. The dance was *Minutiae* (fig. 71), and the set that Rauschenberg created was a small free-standing structure in the style of his current Red Paintings. The set was a playful miniature (approximately 7′ × 6′9″ × 2′6″) of a proscenium stage. It contained a backdrop, wings, and a frontal plane like a curtain. Constructed of canvas, cloth, newspaper, gauze, and wood, it allowed the dancers to move through it, partially concealing them. Rauschenberg carried such ideas of tearing apart and re-creating the traditional proscenium through to his collaborations with Trisha Brown twenty-five years later. In 1954 he also met Paul Taylor, who had recently left Cunningham's dancers to form his own dance company. Over the next four years, Rauschenberg was involved in nine of Taylor's dances. For the first, *Jack and the Beanstalk*, the set included beanstalks suspended by gas balloons. During this same period, Rauschenberg executed sets, lighting, and costumes for six Merce Cunningham dances. These included *Nocturne*, of which substantial portions were danced in total darkness, and *Antic Meet*, in which Rauschenberg contrived to have Cunningham dance with a chair strapped to his back.

From 1960 to 1962, Rauschenberg attended dance composition classes taught by Robert Dunn, a composer who had studied with John Cage. At these classes he met the individuals, including Trisha Brown, who formed the Judson Dance Theater. During these classes, ideas of non-dance movements, unfixed choreography, and everyday objects as props were explored. At this time, Rauschenberg also became involved with Steve Paxton, who was dancing with the Cunningham company, attending the Dunn classes, and beginning to develop ideas that led to his radical development of Contact Improvisation. Rauschenberg's eight-year relationship with Paxton profoundly affected his ideas about modern dance.

In 1961, Rauschenberg began to make Combine paintings that included such items as electric fans and clocks. While these works were partly related to the urban environment around him, as discussed earlier, they also reflect an increased interest in motion and real time. The works "perform" and have a theatrical dimension. In the spring of 1961, Rauschenberg traveled to Paris to participate in *Homage to David Tudor*. His contribution to the event was *First Time Painting* (1961, private collection), which was created on stage with the back of the painting facing the audience and contact microphones attached to its surface in order to amplify the sound of its making. When an alarm clock attached to the painting rang, Rauschenberg wrapped the work and had it taken off stage without the audience ever seeing its front. In this work, one of several that he created on stage during his early career, his painting and performance entered a symbiotic relationship.

From 1961 until 1964, Rauschenberg became the official lighting director and stage manager for the Merce Cunningham Dance Company. He taught himself in these fields and became an indispensable member of the company. The radical sets that Rauschenberg designed for Cunningham during these years included *Aeon* in which elaborate smoke and flare effects were used, and *Winterbranch* in which the lighting scheme was regulated by chance, which often left the stage in complete darkness. In 1963, Rauschenberg also acted as lighting designer for the first performance of the Judson Dance Theater, "An Evening of Dance." Between June and November 1964 he traveled with the Cunningham Dance Company as lighting, set and costume designer, and stage manager for a world tour of thirty cities in Europe and Asia.

The most important event for Rauschenberg during these years, however, was the development of his own choreographed works. The first was *Pelican* (1963, 1965; see fig. 76) in which, as noted before, Rauschenberg and a fellow dancer performed on roller skates with parachutes attached to their backs. In 1964 he premiered *Shot Put* featuring a solo with him dancing in the dark, a flashlight attached to his leg, so that he appeared to be drawing with light.

The story of Rauschenberg's world tour with Cunningham has been told several times.[8] Toward the end of the tour, the company performed in Venice just as Rauschenberg, whose works were being exhibited in the Biennale, won the International Grand Prize in Painting. There was a dramatic break between Cunningham and Rauschenberg at that time, and after the tour the two did not work together for another thirteen years. That break has been attributed throughout the Cunningham and Rauschenberg literature to personal relationships, and it has been said that Cunningham felt upstaged by Rauschenberg's success in Venice.[9] Although personal feelings may have been a factor, the separation was primarily due to creative differences. Rauschenberg's ideas of intuitive dance procedures and response to physical situations created on the stage were at odds with the more classical control that Cunningham favored in his dances.

During the Cunningham world tour, the radical and improvisatory character of Rauschenberg's performances demonstrated the growing creative distance between Cunningham and Rauschenberg. On the tour, Rauschenberg gave the only performance of his choreographed work *Elgin Tie* (fig. 72), a piece that consisted of him lowering himself onto the stage through a skylight by means of climbing down a rope; donning clothes tied to the rope as he descended; and ending up in a barrel of water placed on top of a hand-pulled flatbed. During the performance, a cow was also led onto stage. While in Japan, Rauschenberg had responded to requests from

72 Rauschenberg performing *Elgin Tie* (1964),
photo by Hans Malmberg.

Japanese television for an interview by creating an art work on stage over a four-hour period. The Combine, *Gold Standard*, consisted of painting on and attaching objects to a traditional Japanese gold screen. Rauschenberg was interested in the contrast between traditional Japanese culture and the assimilation of Western culture, a fascination later elaborated in ROCI/Japan (1986).

Toward the end of the world tour, the Cunningham company performed *Story*. The dance represented Cunningham's attempt to absorb elements of Rauschenberg's freer creative method. The dancers were allowed more latitude to invent some of the phrases on stage than Cunningham had permitted before or since. The freedom of *Story* departed too radically from the control that Cunningham wished to exercise, and, after the world tour, Cunningham has rarely allowed *Story* to be performed. Upon returning to New York, Rauschenberg, together with Paxton, Alex and Deborah Hay and several others, left the Cunningham Dance Company. Between late 1964 and 1966, Rauschenberg centered his attention on the Judson Dance Theater. While performing in and helping with dances designed by Brown, Alex and Deborah Hay, Paxton, Yvonne Rainer, and others, Rauschenberg also continued to create new works including *Map Room II* performed by Brown, Hay, Paxton, and Rauschenberg himself. The piece began with blindfolded performers lined up and holding cards each with a single word on it, thus creating nonsensical phrases. White placards were hung on the backs of audience members, and movie footage from a travelogue was projected onto them. Rauschenberg revived the use of projected images during his first works with Trisha Brown. Automobile tires, symbols of movement and dynamism in Rauschenberg's art, were also used extensively in *Map Room II*. Trisha Brown rolled onto stage curled up entirely within one, and Paxton walked across stage with each leg inserted in a tire. In the piece, Deborah Hay appeared in a wire-cage dress with three live doves in it, and as the finale, Rauschenberg walked across stage with his shoes imbedded in twenty-pound blocks of clear resin, created by the artist Arman, and carried a neon tube in each hand. The electrical connections for the neon were made through the artist's body thus lighting the tubes. There was speculation that if Rauschenberg touched the floor, not being insulated by the resin shoes, that the electrical shock would kill him.

In 1965 Rauschenberg also participated in the First New York Theater Rally organized by Paxton and Alan Solomon, former director of the Jewish Museum, who had overseen Rauschenberg's 1963 retrospective. At the rally, Rauschenberg revived *Pelican* and premiered *Spring Training* (see fig. 78), a dance including forty turtles with flashlights strapped to their backs and a shopping cart full of alarm clocks that sounded during the event. Rauschenberg walked on stilts and poured water into a can of dry ice suspended from his waist. Slides of the New York skyline were projected onto the back of Trisha Brown as she danced.

By 1966, the Judson Dance Theater had begun to break up and, as seen earlier, Rauschenberg and several engineers formed Experiments in Art and Technology (E.A.T.). But the idea of performance art, now with a technological basis, remained foremost in his mind. His overall notion was that the discoveries of engineers and the creativity of artists could be brought together in a public arena and thus

171

positively influence the growth of modern society. The first planned event was "9 Evenings: Theatre and Engineering," which took place in October 1966 at the 69th Regimental Armory. Performers included Cage, Lucinda Childs, Öyvind Fahlström, Alex Hay, Deborah Hay, Paxton, Yvonne Rainer, Rauschenberg, David Tudor, and Robert Whitman. For this event Rauschenberg designed *Open Score*. The piece featured a tennis match between Frank Stella and a local pro, Mimi Kanarek. Their rackets had been wired with transistors so that the sound of hitting the ball was amplified throughout the auditorium, and every time the ball was hit a light in the auditorium was turned off. When the armory was completely dark, a closed-circuit infra-red television, a recently invented device, revealed ghostly heat images of five hundred people who had quietly assembled on stage. *Open Score* summarized several of Rauschenberg's performance ideas of the period, including use of new technologies, chance events, non-dance movements, and the effects of contrasting minimal and maximal visual experiences.

Between 1970 and 1977, Rauschenberg had little involvement with theater. Having moved his major studio to Captiva, Florida, he worked primarily on new painting and printmaking projects. By 1974, he had also developed a desire to experience art in cultures around the world that eventually led to ROCI. In 1977, he returned to modern dance by designing the sets and costumes for Merce Cunningham's *Travelogue*. The next year Rauschenberg became Chairman of the Board of the Trisha Brown Dance Company, which Brown had founded in 1970. Over the subsequent twenty years, Rauschenberg's dance activities were focused almost exclusively on his relationship with Brown. The set designs, lighting, and costumes for Brown's dances that will be explored in detail in this chapter include those of *Glacial Decoy* (1979), *Set and Reset* (1983), *Astral Convertible* (1989), *Astral Converted* (1991), and *If You Couldn't See Me* (1994).

The first contact between Brown and Rauschenberg came during activities centered around Merce Cunningham and through Cunningham's relationship to John Cage. Brown came to New York in 1960. In 1959, she had attended a dance workshop at Connecticut College; there she worked briefly with Cunningham, and more importantly, to her mind, heard John Cage's lecture "Indeterminacy." In New York, Brown was studying on a scholarship at the Cunningham studio four days a week. As part of the scholarship she answered the telephones at the studio and recalled, "This man called Bob Rauschenberg used to call, and I had the greatest conversations with him."[10] At the Cunningham studio, Brown became friends with Steve Paxton. Paxton, who had moved into Rauschenberg's loft, rented his own apartment to Brown. Thus she and Rauschenberg began to know each other. By this time, Rauschenberg had already worked with Cage and Cunningham, so it is appropriate to begin with the influence that Cunningham exerted on the dance world in which Brown and Rauschenberg lived.

By 1960 Merce Cunningham was a significant figure in mid-century dance, having already choreographed seventy dances. He had begun his career with the Martha Graham Company and became the company's principal male dancer. In 1939, he met Cage while teaching at Bennington College. By the mid-1940s, Cunningham had started collaborating with Cage and had formed his own dance company. Cunningham's style of dance grew out of early modern dance, and his pieces were a clear departure from conflict and resolution, or the cause and effect structure that still dominated modern dance. His dances did not have a narrative structure, and he incorporated everyday movements into his phrases. Cunningham shared with Cage a fascination with chance and, using the *I Ching* (Chinese *Book of Changes*), introduced the concept of randomness into his artistic procedures. For Cunningham movement was no longer dependent on the rhythm of the music. Each element of the choreographed piece – lighting, stage set, costume, music, and movement – could be independent of the others. All of these aspects had enormous influence on the younger avant-garde artists with whom Cunningham came in contact.

While the literature on Cunningham rightly emphasizes these ground-breaking aspects, there were limitations in Cunningham's willingness to experiment. In his chorcography, Cunningham made departures but with technical and contextual restraints. His particular vocabulary of movements was specialized and difficult to learn, and he developed a style that was just as rigorous as that of early modern dance. Although sections of his dances could be performed in different orders, those sections were completely set as self-contained units. For Cunningham, elements may have been set by chance procedures, but once determined they were rigorously rehearsed so as to be exactly repeatable. Cunningham's strict use of timing in his pieces was a method of absolute choreographic control over the unfolding dance. Humor, intuition, and playfulness had relatively little role in his works.

It has not been emphasized in the Cunningham literature but the rigors of his formal methods had a relationship to the procedures in abstract art that appeared during the inter-war years, particularly in the context of the Bauhaus. His exacting separation of dance components – movement from music and visual presentation – resembles the segregation of different media by their inherent characteristics that one finds in abstract art theory between the wars. Modernist notions of perfection and accuracy underlie these ideas. This sensibility was revived with Minimal art during the 1970s, partly influenced by Cunningham's example, where each medium strove to define its essence. In many ways, Cunningham may be seen as a culmination of modernism, rather than as a choreographer who breaks from modernism into a post-modern expression.

The rigor of Cunningham's underlying structure perhaps made it inevitable that he and Rauschenberg, who was more informal in his artistic attitude, would eventually part company. It was Cunningham's strictness against which members of the Judson Dance Theater group, such as Brown, Paxton, and Rainer, rebelled. And it may have been inevitable that the visual artist who has been the longest and closest supporter of Cunningham has been Jasper Johns, an artist whose works are based on a similar intellectual rigor.

Cunningham's *Aeon*, 1961, is an example of the strict design that underlies his seeming freedom and of the differing attitude that Rauschenberg took in his dramatic and radical visual presentation for the dance. Cunningham noted of the dance:

In that piece – I wasn't playing a trick – I decided to try something. I put a perfectly clear and concise theme and variations near the end – absolutely clear, with
six variations, its what the dancers call the "horror phrase." Nobody saw this. I
knew they wouldn't, because you have to be told that there's a theme and variations, then you look for it. But it's an absolutely clear theme which is stated, and
then variations come along.[11]

The title *Aeon* suggests the length and complexity of the piece as well as its epic
theme. In the relationship between the male and female dancers, *Aeon* seems to be
about man and woman in a primal setting outside of historical time. One can trace
the strict patterns of Cunningham's design. The dance opens with all the dancers on
stage. One man begins to move, then that movement is picked up by two women
then by two more men, then all the dancers move in place. A brief duet has one man
carrying a woman from place to place. All the women run in a circle and then are
joined by all the men. Slightly later, the dancers form into two trios of a man and
two women in each; first one group falls to the floor then the other. Finally, they collapse onto the floor together. All of the women leave as a third man enters. Three
men walk across the stage pausing three times to clasp a foot. This brief description
shows Cunningham's mastery in patterning the dancers and in inventing exits and
entrances. While it is always difficult to predict his next move, once the patterns are
seen they can be clearly understood.

The dramatic visual presentation that Rauschenberg contrived for *Aeon* departed
somewhat from the coolness of Cunningham's dance. As the curtain rose, three
small magnesium explosions took place at the footlights, the ascending smoke from
which gradually cleared during the first few minutes of the performance. During one
leaping phrase, the dancers were intended to trigger small flash bulbs attached to
their wrists. In another sequence, the dancers unwound and passed a fire hose among
themselves. During one of the periods when the dancers collapsed to the floor, a
"machine" was moved across the stage over their heads by means of a rope and
pulleys. Like one of Rauschenberg's Combines, it was made of the frame of an
umbrella, scrap metal, and a dented aluminum water pitcher. A hurricane lantern
hung below it and the pitcher contained dry ice which poured out vapor. The crossing of this nonsensical machine seemed to add a note of humor and fallibility to
Cunningham's cooler interpretation of life's journey, just as the explosions added
overt drama. On the whole, Rauschenberg's interpretation was more eccentric and
experimental than Cunningham's.

Two years after the premier of *Aeon*, Rauschenberg made the silkscreen painting
Express (1963; fig. 73). At its upper center, *Express* features a photograph of the
Cunningham dancers performing *Aeon* and another single image of Merce
Cunningham leading a rehearsal. *Express* is a painting about motion, and on one
level it is a homage to Cunningham. On another it expresses Rauschenberg's idea
that there are many more types of motion than Cunningham was investigating. To
the left-hand side, there are four overlapping images – so we see them in a blur – of
a horse and rider jumping gates. To the lower center, army troops belay over a cliff,

and to the right are sequential photographs of a nude female descending a staircase. These latter photographs are Rauschenberg's reference to Marcel Duchamp, the most iconoclastic of early modern artists and one whose ideas ranged across multiple disciplines. Duchamp's famous *Nude Descending A Staircase* (1913, Philadelphia Museum of Art) was his early study of motion as a way of communicating real time in painting.

To compound Rauschenberg's references, the actual photograph of the naked woman descending stairs that he used in *Express* came from a *Life* magazine edition on movement. This segment made comparisons between the body in motion and that of a wide variety of machines. In *Express*, silkscreen images of gears are shown directly below the nude. In the lower-right corner, is a historical photograph of Generals Robert E. Lee and Ulysses S. Grant staring across a table at each other after signing accords at the end of the Civil War. Although no one is moving, the unfolding of history is another definition of motion. Throughout *Express*, Rauschenberg has used all sorts of active paint handling that includes both free brushwork and splashed pigment. Even the dynamic red bar at the top of *Express* activates the painting. Thus *Express* both celebrates Cunningham's discoveries and shows Rauschenberg's goal of extending beyond them to other, more varied, sources for movement.[12]

Rauschenberg's awareness of Cunningham's differing approach is also found in a comment he made about Cunningham's dance *Story*. In addition to the stage sets that were made from found materials, Rauschenberg's costumes for that dance consisted of garments that he scavenged every night just before the performance. The clothing was put in a pile and the dancers were allowed to choose whatever they wished to wear. In response to the suggestion that this procedure would make the dancers uncomfortable, Rauschenberg later said:

> They loved it! Because Merce was an incredible disciplinarian, his choreography – unless he does one of those free things – is incredibly rigid, and there's no beat. The beat is the whole piece itself. If you're in the wrong place, there isn't anything that's going to help you get there. For them it was a kind of revenge.[13]

Story marked a breaking point between the performance approaches of Cunningham and Rauschenberg. As indicated, it represents Cunningham's reaction to Rauschenberg and to the early performances at the Judson Dance Theater. The dance seems to have made Cunningham extremely uncomfortable because of the degree of control that he was forced to relinquish. It was also said that the dancers disliked the piece because the seeming freedom that he gave them was actually limited since many restrictions were built into the choreography. The Cunningham Company archivist David Vaughan wrote, "They felt that Cunningham had solos, duets with his primary female dancers Carolyn Brown and Viola Farber, and trios with both of them and that the other dancers became secondary like a traditional 'corps de ballet.'"[14]

The dance was performed twenty-nine times during the world tour and rarely performed after Rauschenberg and other dancers left the company at the end of the tour. It consisted of a series of sections that could freely lead into one another so that their order could be changed. Within each section the movements given a particular dancer could change in time taken to perform them, space in which performed, and order of the actions. From Cunningham's point of view *Story*'s greatest benefit, due to its flexibility, was that it could be performed in a wide variety of spaces, ranging from proscenium stages to gymnasia. The sections were given names for identification, such as "Object," "Floor," and "Entrance." For instance, "Object" referred to an object that varied with each performance, which was carried around the stage by the dancer. "Floor" indicated a piece done by two dancers that could start anywhere on or off stage. The dancers walked slowly around emphasizing contact with the floor.[15] The variables that were changed at each performance included length of the whole, length of each section, and placement of the sections. A performance order, with the timings of various sections, was posted in the wings before each presentation of *Story*.

Rauschenberg's stage sets for *Story* were even more varied than Cunningham's choreography. The artist relied on materials found at the site of each performance, so that the sets were different every time *Story* was danced. The two most celebrated, and for Cunningham difficult to accept, consisted of Rauschenberg creating a painting, *Story* (1964, Art Gallery of Ontario, Toronto) on stage, and his activities as "live decor." In a performance at Dartington Hall, Devon, when Rauschenberg was unable to find any interesting objects in the immediate vicinity, the set consisted of him and Alex Hay ironing their shirts at the rear of the stage. Here, seemingly mundane actions were so fascinating for the audience that apparently "the dancers felt somewhat upstaged."[16] This set design embodied, more than any of Rauschenberg's others for Cunningham, his ideas about isolating certain everyday activities, "art and life," and providing the audience with true choices concerning the stage events on which they would focus their attention. These concepts reappeared later in Rauschenberg's set designs for such Trisha Brown dances as *Glacial Decoy* and *Set and Reset*.

Decades later, Cunningham's memory of *Story* reflects not his interest in the piece's freedom but his discomfort at the lack of choreographic control, which he even equated with a degree of physical danger:

> As we toured more it got harder and harder on everybody, because by the time you get someplace you're so tired, you can bring yourself physically together, but in performance while you're trying to keep your energy together, you also have your head jumping around, it's very hard, and there's a great tendency toward accidents . . .

> It's all right if you know exactly what you're to do, to bring it together and do it. One of the reasons we did *Story* everywhere was that it could be done in different spaces.[17]

In contrast to Cunningham's memory, Steve Paxton recalled the general philosophical divergence between Cunningham and Rauschenberg: "We were always being represented by John Cage's philosophy, but the truth was that John's philosophy did not coincide with what either John or Merce did in practice. They're both very formal at heart, and incredibly disciplined. Bob Rauschenberg was not."[18] Toward the end of the world tour Rauschenberg and Paxton, Alex and Deborah Hay, and the dancer William Davis informed Cunningham that they were leaving the company.

*   *   *

While Rauschenberg absorbed and subsequently rejected the Cunningham tradition, Trisha Brown's contact with Cunningham was more indirect. She carefully watched Cunningham, absorbed ideas from him, and then went in her own direction. Brown's roots were in Aberdeen, Washington, and she had an early interest in dance and athletics. (The athletic quality of her compositions is still one of their outstanding features.) She began her studies with a local dance teacher Marian Hageage, who taught her a combination of tap, ballet, jazz, and acrobatics. Brown remembers her teacher dancing freely around the room with Brown, still a child, trailing behind. Beginning with this juvenile experience, Brown's most significant early dance instruction was marked by freedom, improvisation, and dance styles that stood outside the classical traditions.

From the early to the mid-1950s Brown was enrolled at Mills College, Oakland, California, which had a well-known dance program. There she studied dance methods that ranged from the more expressionist style of Martha Graham to the work of Louis Horst. Horst was famous for his workshops and classes in formal dance composition, and discouraged any sort of improvisational approach; ultimately, he figured as someone that Brown reacted against. During the summers of those years, Brown took dance workshops at Connecticut College. There she had contact with Horst, José Limon, and Merce Cunningham. The physicality of Limon's dance style meant something to Brown, although she eschewed his raw emotionalism. Even more than Cunningham's dance classes, Brown remembers John Cage's lecture "Indeterminacy." According to Brown, the lecture was "my first exposure to the idea of disrupting one's choices. Suddenly it made the material of dancing seem more like an object that one could play with in endless research into new relationships."[19] Already for Brown, Cage's theory of experimental, open-ended research had a more profound impact than the character of Cunningham's dances.

Doris Humphrey also taught advanced classes at Connecticut College and although Brown did not have the level of experience to take these classes, Humphrey had a long-term influence on her. Humphrey's early discoveries of "fall and recovery" (the process of falling away from and recovering equilibrium), breath rhythm (phrasing associated with the inherent patterns of breathing), natural movements, and reduction of dance to its basic elements all held significant, if indirect, implications for Brown's development as a dancer and choreographer. After Brown finished her studies at Mills College and Connecticut College, she accepted a teaching position at Reed College in Portland, Oregon in 1958, where she was responsible for creating the dance department. Although she remained at the college for two years, she soon found traditional methods of dance instruction constricting. Starving for new, fresh ideas, Brown turned to teaching based on improvisation. This was a daring step so early in her career and confirmed her desire for experimentation in dance.

During the summer of 1959, Brown attended Ann Halprin's six-week workshop on dance in Marin County, California. Brown's experience with Halprin had an important effect, one that is often underplayed in the literature, as is Halprin's general role in post-modern dance. In 1955, hoping to reinvest modern dance with spontaneity and vitality, Halprin had founded the San Francisco Dancers' Workshop, which rehearsed and performed on the deck of her home. Halprin's classes drew individuals from many walks of life including dancers, musicians, artists, architects, poets, and psychologists. Her multi-disciplinary approach was one of the sources for the Judson Dance Theater. In her classes, Halprin emphasized personal creativity and movement studies over dance as a perfected art form.[20] She discarded the predictability of cause and effect relationships and relied instead on sensory experiences. Halprin explored natural movements in her performances and often formed dances from such ordinary tasks as pouring water, changing clothes, and climbing down a rope, all of which were performed with an undramatic, workmanlike demeanor.

Such explorations in everyday activities and interactions with ordinary objects found their way through the Judson Dance Theater into Brown's choreography and Rauschenberg's performance pieces. Although Rauschenberg never met Halprin, she must be counted as a major indirect source for his performance ideas. Halprin also broke away from the proscenium stage, performing works outside, sometimes on sidewalks. When on stage, she expanded the performance space to include walls, ceilings, and aisles, all germane ideas for Brown's and Rauschenberg's later experiments with traditional proscenium space.[21] In a tradition carried on at Judson, Halprin's dance company consisted of individuals who came from many disciplines, not professional dancers, thus incorporating their movement experiences from everyday life into her pieces.[22]

At Halprin's workshop, Brown met young artists and dancers who were the key figures in the emerging world of post-modern performance. They included Simone Forti, Robert Morris, Terry Riley, Yvonne Rainer, and LaMonte Young. It was Forti who insisted that Brown had exhausted learning possibilities on the West Coast and that she must come to New York. Brown resigned her position at Reed College and arrived in New York in the fall of 1960. Brown has recalled, "I took a bus from Aberdeen and took Robert Dunn's classes. If I hadn't I probably would have stopped dancing."[23] Between 1960 and 1964 Robert Dunn gave a series of dance courses at Merce Cunningham's studio on 14th Street. The dancers and artists involved in those sessions became the core of the Judson Dance Theater. Some of those who met and interacted during those classes included – in addition to Brown – Judith Dunn, Simone Forti, Alex Hay, Deborah Hay, and Yvonne Rainer. Rauschenberg sat in on a number of the classes as did Robert Morris, who had a deep interest in dance and was then married to Forti. It was at these sessions that Rauschenberg had his first opportunity to see Brown's creative work.

Neither a dancer nor a choreographer, Robert Dunn was an accompanist for Cunningham and several other modern dance companies, and he was married to the Cunningham dancer Judith Dunn. It was Cage who had asked Dunn to teach the course, as Dunn believes, because he had a wide-ranging knowledge of several art forms and because Cunningham was not inclined to teach a composition course.[24] Cage may have also realized that Dunn was the correct choice precisely because he did not come from a choreographic tradition and would allow a latitude for invention in his classes that had little precedent in modern dance. Dunn had seen composition classes given by Louis Horst, Martha Graham's music director, and those given by Doris Humphrey. Dunn found the atmosphere in those classes oppressive for the young dancers. He recalled that they gave "recipes for things, which I thought were very stultifying recipes."[25]

Dunn had taken Cage's class in "Composition and Experimental Music" at the New School for Social Research, and his own classes followed, to some degree, the Cage model. They incorporated an eclectic variety of traditions, included individuals from many fields, and featured non-valuative discussions. In fulfilling assignments given in class, students were allowed a wide range in methods, materials, and structures. As in Cage's classes, discussion focused on how the choreographer had carried out his/her intentions rather than judging the results. Concerning the classes, Dunn recalled:

> But each assignment that I gave was only partly defined as to what I wanted and there were many, many choices up to the student. And in discussion, following John's [Cage] idea of discussing not evaluating, we concentrated on what we had seen. What was the structure, what were the materials, what were the methods. And it was very interesting to guess how the piece was put together, and to keep

throwing people off from evaluating statements to statements of what they had seen. The last person to confess what he had in mind was the choreographer himself. Often the choreographer's idea was much more narrow than what had come out of the class itself.[26]

The freedom of Dunn's teaching and his acceptance of experimental new ideas allowed, in his words, "the more sophisticated people to feed on the ideas of the less sophisticated." The non-evaluative interaction between audience and choreographer that he encouraged was another important model for both Brown's and Rauschenberg's approaches to dance. Brown recalled that the open-ended nature of Dunn's assignments was essential to her thinking, as was the creative interaction during the class. She has said:

> Through Simone I got into Robert Dunn's class on composition, so I was choreographing and working with all those people. There was a lot of chance and indeterminacy and that opened up new possibilities. But the thing that was most interesting about his class was that he would give a problem that was so vague that it was provocative, like "make a three-minute dance." You can think about that for a long time: what *is* a three-minute dance? Once the piece was completed, he directed criticism in terms of how did you make the piece, how did you make your decisions, so the *making* of the dance was important. You could quiz the audience about what they saw versus what you thought they saw and could find out what actually happened. It was a beautiful exchange of information.[27]

Brown's discussion of establishing broadly conceived problems and allowing maximum creative freedom in their solutions relates closely to methods that she later employed in her dances, and Rauschenberg's visual presentations utilize similar procedures.

In creating such freedom in his experimental dance classes, Dunn was aware, as perhaps was Cage, that he had included a level of improvisation that Cunningham was unwilling to tolerate. Dunn noted:

> Well, things about indeterminacy and letting people decide when to perform certain parts of their movement repertory in relation to somebody else's parts; and Merce said people would knock into each other on the stage. John and other people kept asking Merce why he didn't make an indeterminate dance. Well, Merce didn't think it was practical until he had seen the approaches to that through the Judson Dance Theater.[28]

Dunn was also indirectly aware that the independence he allowed in his classes had some parallels to the "improvisations of a very simple and repetitive nature" encouraged by Ann Halprin and because he knew that Halprin worked with, in his words, "non-proscenium things." The connecting link for Dunn was that Brown, Forti, and Rainer had worked with Halprin.[29]

Dunn recalled specifically the presence of Rauschenberg in his classes and Rauschenberg's use of everyday materials, which were also emphasized in Dunn's classes, as a way of generating dance situations. He said,

Rauschenberg and Morris did visit my classes. Rauschenberg said that he was not interested in happenings but he was interested in dances. Rauschenberg's things were situations and very striking. They were not so much lyric or dramatic movement things . . . I would say that the materials were very interesting . . .The understanding came from the art world not the entrenched music or dance world.[30]

An example of how close the aesthetic promulgated in Dunn's classes was to that of Rauschenberg is the piece developed during the class that Dunn considers its most "unforgettable," Lucinda Childs's *Street Dance*.[31] Originally developed in 1964, *Street Dance* was performed in a number of locations including a 1965 performance at and outside of Rauschenberg's studio at 809 Broadway. The dance consisted of a dialogue on tape describing the environment seen from the window of Rauschenberg's studio. The tape was played while two dancers descended in the elevator from the studio to the street outside. In a choreography that is timed to coordinate with the taped description, the dancers interacted with specified objects in the environment and with people on the street. The tape does not specify, however, the type of interaction in which the dancers engage. After six minutes the dancers returned to the studio, ending the piece. In *Street Dance*, Childs's minute observation of the environment and interest in its everyday aspects that reveal the passage of life are strikingly parallel to Rauschenberg's urban Combines and early Silkscreen Paintings, as discussed in Chapter 2. Like Rauschenberg's art, Childs's dance encourages attention to the urban environment in all its variety and engagement with the chance events of the street. A small section of Childs's tape recording reads like a description of one of Rauschenberg's paintings:

> I am concerned with the area between Bon Vivant Delicacies Store and Surplus Materials of Norbert and Hausknect. I am not concerned with either of these buildings specifically but with the area between. Old Europe Antiques Incorporated, a black sign with white letters, is framed in gold. The window below the sign displays various objects, presumably European: clocks, chandeliers, candelabras, various antiques labeled with white tags: B 103, Fa VR, another 64, another 20. The remaining tags remain overturned or blank or no information is on them.[32]

In 1961 Dunn's students organized an informal performance at the Living Theater in New York, and in 1962 they began to search for a location in which to show publicly their works. The Judson Memorial Church on West 4th Street had already featured several small exhibitions by the emerging Pop artists and had served as a space for "Happenings" by Claus Oldenberg, Jim Dine, and Allen Kaprow among others. The Judson Church building was a classical revival structure designed by Stanford White in the nineteenth century, but the congregation had been decreasing over several decades. Al Carmine, the new minister, believed that avant-garde artistic activities would encourage community involvement and thus welcomed the young dancers. The first performance, entitled "A Concert of Dances," was given on July 6, 1962 and lasted over three hours. It presented works by thirteen individuals including Deborah

74 *Parts of Some Sextets*, Yvonne Rainer choreographer (1965), left to right: Rauschenbeerg, Tony Holder, Steve Paxton, Deborah Hay, and Judith Dunn (on floor), photo by Phil MacMullan.

Hay, Steve Paxton, and Yvonne Rainer. Later concerts were numbered and the count finally reached sixteen in 1964 before the founding members took their activities in other directions.

From the beginning, the Judson Dance Theater (fig. 74) was regarded by its participants as an informal experimental laboratory for new ideas. Steve Paxton, who had already spent many years in the avant-garde dance world as one of Cunningham's major dancers, explained the motivations behind forming Judson and also emphasized Rauschenberg's notions of creatively using the objects or situations that were available as a major source for the dancers' ideas:

> The Judson meant that we could all do choreography which was simply unheard of. In the tight little world of modern dance most people have no chance to develop their own ideas. It took at least six weeks to make a dance and maybe a thousand dollars to get it performed – the restrictions were prohibitive. We began with this idea of Bob's that you work with what's available, and that way the restrictions aren't limitations, they're just what you happen to be working with.[33]

The works choreographed by participants in the Judson Dance Theater were oriented around collage methods, fragmentation, and loosely structured scores. They favored chance, pedestrian movement, and spontaneity. The Judson Dance Theater broke down the hierarchy between choreographer and dancers that still very much existed for Cunningham and other late-modern dancers. It also extended the Cage/Cunningham idea that there need be no hierarchy between dance, music, and visual presentation. Judson rejected the grandiosity of early-modern dance and instead sought interest in the ordinary. It shunned the idea of climax, treated each movement democratically, and evinced the important idea that dance could stem from curiosity about motion rather than an elaborately constructed narrative. All of these elements led to a new sense of engagement for the dancers and a heightened alertness on the part of the audience. Rauschenberg summarized the Judson Dance Theater:

> The original concept of the Judson was a movement clinic, or concept clinic. The dancers very generously made space in the concerts or workshops for nondancers, so painters and musicians became just as much a part of the dance. There was just one house rule: if someone asked you to do something, it made no difference whether you wanted to do it or not – you had to. And that was a very important rule, because with the nondancers you experienced a shyness, a reluctance, that had to be dealt with. That one simple rule got everybody together.
>
> To put shows on was almost an anti-climax. The original Judson concept was to have people to work with and some space to do it in. The performances were just an offshoot, never the intention.[34]

Early works by Brown and Rauschenberg provide examples of the inventions at Judson Church. *Trillium* (1962) was Brown's first piece at Judson. It was a structured improvisation that relied on high-speed movements. The rules that Brown gave herself were that "I could stand, sit or lie, and ended up levitating. In this dance I did not notify myself of my intentions in advance of the performance."[35] Brown

75 Trisha Brown and Steve Paxton rehearsing Brown's *Lightfall* (1963), Judson Memorial Church gymnasium, New York City, January 30, 1963. Photo by Sally Ritts.

broke the actions down into their basic mechanical structure, finding places of rest, power, and momentum in each action. In the studio she then went over and over the material accelerating all the actions, and with the increased speed mixing them up so that at one point lying down was done in the air. The high-energy movements deliberately involved curious timing, featuring relatively long periods of inactivity, so that she would suddenly stop all motion. The performance was accompanied by a tape of improvisational whistling by Simone Forti.

Another early piece by Brown, *Lightfall* (1963; fig. 75), was based on "contact improvisation," a term coined later by Steve Paxton who extensively developed the technique. *Lightfall* was a duet that Brown danced with Paxton, and contact improvisation, as it became known, is most often performed as a duet. In it, one dancer uses the momentum of the other to move in concert with the partner's weight, rolling, suspending, and thrusting; interest lies in the ongoing flow of energy. In addition to being a technique, contact improvisation is a philosophical model for the spontaneity of life and of human interdependence.[36] *Lightfall* was based on the position of waiting bent at the waist with hands on the knees (as do football players when resting). In this position, one dancer became the base for the other. In *Lightfall*, Brown and Paxton constantly exchanged positions, unbalancing then re-balancing, colliding and hopping on the backs of one another. Both *Trillium* and *Lightfall* were exemplary Judson pieces. They took seemingly simple problems with a minimum of rules and controls and allowed the dancers to maximize their creative and experimental responses to physical situations.

The importance of interaction with Steve Paxton for both Trisha Brown and Rauschenberg cannot be underestimated. During the Judson period, Paxton was a colleague and co-dancer with Brown, and between 1962 and 1970 Rauschenberg and Paxton were companions, as noted, sharing ideas on a daily basis. Rauschenberg's notion of incorporating everyday objects in his art and creating works based on the limitations of his materials certainly influenced Paxton, and Paxton's concept of performance as a venue for shared ideas and spontaneous inventions influenced Rauschenberg's own forays into choreography as well as his contemporary art works that moved and seemed to perform.

Paxton's revolutionary ideas about movement helped shape post-modern dance. Paxton was rigorously trained first as a gymnast then as a dancer. He became one of Cunningham's primary dancers and was known for his athletic performances and powerful stage presence. By 1962 his interests had shifted to searching for inspiration in everyday movements. He sought ways to involve non-dancers in dances and challenged the traditional separation between audience and performer. Like Rauschenberg, he sought more spontaneous approaches to art and found himself willing to accept the messiness of life and reflect it in his work. Paxton focused his attention on performers as people, not as technicians who only expressed the concept of the choreographer. Through simple instructions, he attempted to establish choreographic situations which maximize the inventiveness of the performers and wrench audiences away from traditional ways of looking at dance. Paxton's experiences at Judson and later as a founding member of Grand Union (1970), an impro-

visational company, led him from 1972 to focus exclusively on contact improvisation, which has formed a basis for his work ever since.

The first work Paxton choreographed, *Proxy* (1962), demonstrated the genesis of his ideas and also his early interactions with Rauschenberg. It is a sixteen-minute piece in three movements that begins with a long walking section in which the first performer circles the stage seven times carrying a white basin. For Paxton, walking was critical to dance. A movement that everyone performs, it provided a sympathetic link between the audience and dancers. At the same time, there is no single correct way of walking; it is a gesture of individualism. Simple actions like eating, drinking, smiling, and getting dressed also came to play major roles in Paxton's dances.

In *Proxy*, the performer places the basin down and stands behind it. Two other performers enter, one drinks a glass of water, and the other eats a piece of fruit. One thinks of the everyday objects in Rauschenberg's art and specifically of the photographs of a water glass and fruit that were recurring features in his contemporary silkscreen paintings. The second and third movements of *Proxy* are based on a "picture score" in which Paxton cut out photographs of athletes from magazines and pasted them on a board. The dancers respond to the pictures in their motions. This response would be like reacting in dance to one of Rauschenberg's paintings of the period, many of which were dominated by images of athletes in action. When *Proxy* was turned down at avant-garde dance spaces, it became a motivating factor in the search for alternative locations that eventually led to the Judson Church, and *Proxy* was performed at Judson in the first event, "A Concert of Dances."

77 Rauschenberg, Carolyn Brown, and Alex Hay performing *Pelican* at First New York Theater Rally (May 1965), photo by Elisabeth Novick.

Together with Steve Paxton, Rauschenberg spent a great deal of time with the Judson dancers. He went to all their workshops, worked backstage, and handled lighting for most performances. Considering this degree of involvement, it was perhaps inevitable that he would choreograph his own performance. That piece was *Pelican* (1963; fig. 76) which, suiting Rauschenberg's interest in chance events, was accidently commissioned. In 1963 an exhibition of paintings and sculptures titled "The Popular Image" was held at the Washington Gallery of Modern Art in Washington, D.C. and performance events under the rubric the "Pop Festival" were simultaneously scheduled. This was the first road tour for the Judson group. In the announcement, Rauschenberg was mistakenly listed as a choreographer rather than as technical crew. He decided to accept this twist of fate and rushed to choreograph his first piece. The festival was taking place at America On Wheels, a roller skating rink, so Rauschenberg decided that he would design a work to be danced on roller skates. This choice was an example of using "the limitations of materials as a freedom that would eventually establish form."[37]

Rauschenberg contacted his friend the Swedish artist Per Olof Ultveldt, who was visiting New York, and the two of them learned to roller skate at Rauschenberg's Broadway loft. The piece was conceived as a *pas de trois* also featuring Carolyn Brown, the most classically trained dancer in Cunningham's company. Rauschenberg assembled a musical score that was a collage of radio, music, and television sounds.

For the performance, Rauschenberg and Ultveldt entered the rink dressed in gray sweatsuits and balanced on their knees supported by axles attached to bicycle wheels.

In the kneeling position, they turned the bicycle wheels by hand. Their progress across the stage was extremely slow and difficult, consisting of short rolls and stops. As they moved laboriously across the rink, Carolyn Brown appeared, wearing a sweatsuit and toe shoes and took center stage. Rauschenberg had been insistent that Brown do traditional ballet moves in toe shoes. She proceeded to make a series of graceful arabesques across the open space approaching the two men on wheels; she also executed *jeté* and *chaîné* turns that made her seem to float in the air.[38]

Meanwhile, Rauschenberg and Ultveldt had moved to one side of the rink. They got off the bicycle wheels and put on backpacks to which were attached large pieces of fabric held by circular armatures so that they looked like parachutes. Skating around the rink with the parachutes spread behind them, they appeared to be a synthesis of great birds and the gliders used in early human flight. The men eventually skated up to Brown facing each other with their parachutes extended (fig. 77). As they circled around her, Brown, partly supported on their arms, extended her leg and arched her back toward Rauschenberg, allowing the circling men to rotate her *en pointe*. From the viewer position, Brown appeared and disappeared behind the veil of parachutes, creating an almost stroboscopic effect. To exit, Rauschenberg and Ultveldt took off their parachutes and knelt down again on the bicycle wheels. They slowly and arduously wheeled themselves 200 feet across the rink to exit where they had entered.

The work involves themes that have long been at the center of Rauschenberg's art. The wheel and the parachute are motifs, as discussed in Chapter 2, that he has used since the beginning of his career. They represent respectively his grounded connections to things of this world and his belief in the soaring character of imagination. Rauschenberg used the tire and parachute-like shapes in *First Landing Jump* (see fig. 34) and other Combines, and his space exploration works employed parachuting imagery that represented his hopes for the space program. *Pelican* features one of the most powerful uses of these motifs. Rauschenberg and Ultveldt literally crawling onto the stage is a visualization of the effort that the creative process sometimes takes: the piece begins with a creative but arduous motion. By comparison, Carolyn Brown's movements are graceful but also highly traditional, and she acts as a muse who provides inspiration to the males. When they rise to soar around her, they do so in a more modern, innovative, and energy-filled manner than even her highest leaps can attain. They represent a new and energized form of creativity achieved through technology and radical inventiveness. As mentioned earlier, the males resemble both birds in flight and glider planes. It was Trisha Brown who saw a rehearsal of the piece and suggested the name "pelican," recalling the bird that is awkward on the ground yet graceful in the air, and Brown remembers *Pelican* as one of the most compelling performances during the entire Judson period.

Technology, tied to inventiveness, is a major issue in *Pelican*. As mentioned earlier, among Rauschenberg's greatest heroes are Leonardo da Vinci, the artist/inventor who dreamed of human flight, and the Wright Brothers, American tinkerers and original thinkers, who first ventured into powered flight. Rauschenberg dedicated *Pelican* to the Wright Brothers. Shortly after choreographing it, Rauschen-

78 Rauschenberg and Lucinda Childs performing *Spring Training* at *Once Again Festival*, Ann Arbor, Michigan, (1965), photo by Ugo Mulas.

berg became intensely involved with engineers during the Experiments in Art and Technology, and this interest was followed closely by his space exploration works. In *Pelican*, Rauschenberg and Ultveldt envelope Brown in their fast-paced, swirling world of modern creativity, but the moment of flight does not last. The two males must return to earth and slowly crawl off the stage as if searching for the next soaring idea. For Rauschenberg, *Pelican* is an embodiment of creative activity including its difficulties, escape from tradition, and soaring ingenuity. One indication of the importance that he assigned *Pelican* is that he included an image of himself performing it as one of three panels in his monumental print *Autobiography* (1968), in which he attempted to summarize his artistic life.[39]

Rauschenberg's second choreographic work and the first in which Trisha Brown appeared was *Spring Training* (fig. 78). The piece premiered in 1965 as part of the First New York Theater Rally organized by Steve Paxton and Alan Solomon. For the performance, the audience sat on folding chairs close to the performers. While their position connected them more directly with the event, Rauschenberg has never advocated actual audience interaction as with the Happenings. Behind the viewers Brown and two other performers entered in bridal dresses with saltine crackers stuffed in their brassieres. They ate crackers as Rauschenberg entered pushing a shopping cart full of ticking alarm clocks. Another performer, Deborah Hay, emerged from the darkness. Above her, a white cardboard rectangle was supported on a shoulder harness, and as she moved, photographic images of New York were projected on this screen. The use of projected imagery was an important predecessor of the slide projections later employed by Rauschenberg in *Glacial Decoy* and of the movie images in *Set and Reset*.

As Hay got close to the audience, they could see that the bundle in her arms contained a photographic enlargement of John F. Kennedy's head. She lifted the corner of the coverlet to reveal that the bundle was actually a watermelon wearing diapers. As Hay moved back through the audience the house lights dimmed until the audience sat in total darkness. Meanwhile from the rear of the space, other performers maneuvered a large black box on wheels toward the front of the viewing area. Once in place, there were long moments of silence. Suddenly there was a splattering noise of something falling to the floor, and then another. Difficult to identify at first, these noises were caused by eggs being dropped from above the performance space and breaking on the floor.

Rauschenberg entered the now dimly lit stage walking clumsily on stilts, dressed only in a plaid shirt and jockey shorts. As he moved about, two performers began to take mysterious objects out of the box and spread them around the floor. The enigmatic things turned out to be forty turtles, each one with a flashlight strapped to its back. The turtles cast ghostly lights around the auditorium as they maneuvered slowly with their loads. When turned toward each other, they cast distorted reptilian shadows against the walls, and several other turtles came directly at the audience seated on the floor in the front rows. Amid this slow-moving drama, Rauschenberg continued to walk on his stilts, barely balanced, now in danger of both slipping on the broken eggs and tripping over the turtles.

At the end of this sequence, Rauschenberg commissioned a tap dance to the popular song "Telstar." He and Paxton had a duet in two parts; the rules of the first half were that one person could stand if the other were running. When one person altered this activity, the other also had to change. The second part consisted of a series of lifts. Rauschenberg and Paxton took turns stiffening their bodies while one carried the other horizontally at waist level. During this activity, Christopher Rauschenberg, the artist's son, sat on stage and tore pages out of a telephone book with a contact microphone to amplify the sounds.

Next, Rauschenberg designed a solo for Paxton to be danced with a tin can strapped to one leg. After a sequence during which Paxton danced on one leg with the can protruding on the other, he dropped down onto the can balancing on it and pivoting. Eventually, he rolled off the can as the lights went down. Finally, Rauschenberg came back onto stage dressed in slacks and a white dinner jacket with horizontal black lines drawn upon it and carrying a tin bucket suspended by a strap. He poured water into the bucket, which was filled with dry ice, and steam rose around him drifting across the stage. He then extended his left arm while placing his right across his chest. A sentimental recording of Hawaiian guitar music began. Thus Rauschenberg, with string-like stripes on his jacket, was the human guitar. The lights faded and the music stopped, ending the performance.

Spring Training embodies many of the ideas that remained essential to Rauschenberg's performance pieces. The artist began by carefully checking the character of the performance space and conditioned his work to the area. In this case, the vastness of the space and its darkness motivated the mysterious elements of *Spring Training*. Rauschenberg's care over the manner in which he organizes his presentations has often been underestimated in the literature on him. Like his paintings, his theatrical pieces are non-narrative. He has said about his choreographic procedures, "I begin working with separate ideas."[40] But also, like his paintings, they do revolve around general themes. In *Spring Training*, the overall theme is amorous surgings and disappointments in love that accompany the spring season. Love's prehistory, its modern nature, its mystery, silliness, and awkwardness are all explored by Rauschenberg.

The brides, who undermine their formal wedding garb by munching on crackers, provide a foil for the awkward male suitor, Rauschenberg, who clumsily attempts to demonstrate his athletic abilities on stilts in order to attract them. The drive for fecundity and fame through progeny are gently mocked in the Kennedy/watermelon baby. The broken eggs suggest the fragility of love while the haunting presence of the turtles, who slowly search for each other with their flashlights, reminds us of primal sources for our deep sexual drives. Rauschenberg's duet with Paxton is a serious reminder of one lover's support for another. *Spring Training*'s end, amid smoke and Hawaiian music, lends a romantic finale to Rauschenberg's amorous adventure. As suggested in Chapter 3, Rauschenberg views sexuality as part of the creative drive and rejoices in all of its richness and variety. He is an advocate of heterosexual and homosexual love, of love that is both profound and humorous.

In *Spring Training* and other Rauschenberg performances the materials or props are extremely important. Generally, Rauschenberg's stage situations are more varied and more complicated than those invented by other members of the Judson group, and perhaps this is to be expected of a visual artist. But there are other implications. Rauschenberg does not believe in pure improvisation. In his experience unguided improvisation leads to performers repeating habitual activities. Instead, through the materials that he selects, he establishes situations that determine what type of action is possible. While dealing with particular materials and conditions, his performers reveal the nature of those materials and expose their individual responses to varying situations. In this manner, Rauschenberg is able to provide structure for the performance and at the same time allow the performers wide latitude for personal expression. He has commented, "I write so that they are stockholders in the event, not simply performers."[41] Trisha Brown has called him "an ideal director" because he gives "just enough information to prevent the dancer from imitating his own movements."[42]

Rauschenberg's extensive use of objects to establish movement situations also masks the fact that he and some of his performers are not trained dancers. Through his emphasis on accomplishing tasks rather than complex dance moves, he turns the lack of dance experience into a positive condition by forcing his performers into unfamiliar situations where they will act in an original manner. He noted,

> I think I was lucky to pull something together like I do in a collage. I had so many extravagant ideas in my work to disguise the fact that I actually wasn't a dancer – thirty turtles, forty flashlights, six bushels of alarm clocks . . . If you're an intelligent choreographer, you've got to discover what's in the person himself that's unique, weaknesses and frailties.[43]

Indeed Rauschenberg's dances are generally marked by complex staging and simple, direct, and task-oriented movement. His visual effects also tend toward the dramatic – his use of movie projectors, lighting on turtles, and dry ice in *Spring Training* provide particularly striking visual events.

Two other aspects that mark Rauschenberg's choreography are his attitudes toward the audience and toward time. In his pieces the audience remains separate from the performance, which assures Rauschenberg a higher degree of control over its character, but he does promote what he calls "audience responsibility."[44] By this he means that he provides the minimum number of guarantees about satisfying audience expectations, and he assumes that the viewers will react to the often startling situations with open minds. This attitude fits his involvement with prosceniumbased works in the later collaborations with Brown, where the audience is stimulated and challenged but not directly involved in performances. Regarding the aspect of time in performance, Rauschenberg freely admits that it is his "weakest element."[45] In the studio, the artist need not consider timing as must a choreographer, and Rauschenberg's performances have been criticized for moving either too quickly or too slowly. His collaborations with Trisha Brown demonstrate his efforts to adjust this aspect of his theatrical work.

By 1965 the activities of the Judson Dance Theater had come to an end. Many reasons have been suggested, including some blame placed on Rauschenberg. In *Work 1961–73*, her personal dance history, Yvonne Rainer wrote,

> Upon Rauschenberg's entry – through no error in his behavior but simply due to his stature in the art world – the balance was tipped, and those of us who appeared with him became the tail of his comet. Or so I felt. It was not something I heard ever openly discussed, although I was aware of his sensitivity to the *possibility* that this might be occurring.[46]

In fact, the Judson group had grown much larger with the addition of many new members. The founders began pursuing individual directions to which Judson performances had led them. Paxton, Hay, Rainer, Rauschenberg, and others formed the short-lived Surplus Dance Theater. Later, Paxton and Rainer organized the improvisational group Grand Union. As noted, Paxton increasingly explored the involvement of people not trained in dance through contact improvisation. Rainer became an experimental filmmaker. Deborah Hay built her performances around establishing dance communities in different locales. Rauschenberg became committed to exploring the interaction of technology and art in the E.A.T. group.

Between 1965 and 1970 Brown created eleven new works and then formed her own company, the Trisha Brown Dance Company. Then from 1971 to 1975 she choreographed another eighteen works for the company, and although she and Rauschenberg did not see each other as frequently during these years, they kept track of each other's work. Brown's choreography suggests aspects of their shared aesthetic formed during the Judson years. Most of her dances during this period took place outside of traditional theater spaces. Like Rauschenberg's works, her interaction with the environment was essential as was creating unexpected physical situations for the audience. Brown was concerned with dealing in new ways with space and movement. To do so, she often employed inventive devices that provided tasks for her dancers to accomplish. Her pieces differed from Rauschenberg's earlier performances in that Brown focused more completely on new and often very difficult movements, while Rauschenberg was primarily concerned with the visual impact of simple activities.

Among Brown's most innovative pieces in terms of spacial and motion exploration were her "Equipment Dances." In *Man Walking Down the Side of a Building,* first performed in Lower Manhattan during April 1969, spectators were led through a tunnel to an inner courtyard. The piece began when a man dressed in street clothes was seen slowly falling, face forward, from the top of a seven-story building. When he was perpendicular to the wall of the building, he began to walk slowly down to the courtyard. As he reached the ground, he unfastened his mountain climbing equipment. The radical inventiveness of this piece, and the fact that it was performed in such a workmanlike manner, suited the aesthetics that Brown had developed with the Judson group.

Brown's exploration of the wall as a dance surface and the new type of motion required to negotiate it was elaborated in her *Walking on the Wall* piece done on two evenings in 1971 at the Whitney Museum of American Art. Tracking was placed on the ceiling of the museum above two walls that shared a common corner. Each track extended forty feet parallel to the wall surface. Attached to the track were cables of different lengths with harnesses on their other ends, and six dancers were suspended from the harnesses. The dancers stood, walked, and ran along the walls at different times and in different directions. When Rauschenberg heard this dance described by Brown, he funded all the equipment to make the performance possible. He has said, "Once I saw what she was up to and I knew she couldn't afford the right equipment, I knew I had to help her."[47] In another piece, *Planes,* performed six times between 1968 and 1971, dancers in black and white leotards, using hand and footholds, traversed a wall vertically, horizontally, and diagonally. A film of aerial footage was projected against the wall during some of the performances and the music consisted of a duet for vacuum cleaner and voice by Simone Forti.

The dance *Roof Piece* (1971; fig. 79) emphasizes Brown's connections with the urban environment and her interest in perceptions over time and through space and thus her affinities with Rauschenberg's preoccupations. It was performed twice along the rooftops of New York City, once with eleven dancers beginning on Wooster Street and ending on the roof of Rauschenberg's studio building at 381 Lafayette Street. The second performance took place in 1973 from West Broadway to White Street with fifteen dancers. The dancers were stationed on separate roofs spanning the nine- to twelve-block distances (or roughly one-half mile). The distances between them were unequal; some were short because of restricted sightlines while others were quite long. The piece began with one dancer initiating a sequence of movements that consisted of bends, twists, and arm rotations. That phrase was seen and copied by the next dancer and so on until it reached the end of the group. At that point, the sender ducked out of sight, and all dancers faced the opposite direction. The last receiver became the sender, passing the movements in the opposite direction.

The idea for *Roof Piece* probably came from practice sessions in basic ballet class. In that context, the teacher does the steps first and then the student copies them. In actuality, however, *Roof Piece* undermines this traditional system. Exact repetition of the movements was necessarily impaired by the distances between the buildings; the real space and time of the everyday world were primary forces. Details or nuances of movement were lost or incorrectly translated, forcing eventual distortion or disintegration of the original dance. The piece concerns the nature of human communication. With the misunderstandings inherent in *Roof Piece*'s spatial format, structure and improvisation interact in a way that mimics the processes of everyday life.

Another aspect of the interaction between art and everyday existence in *Roof Piece* is its relationship to the viewers. Although invited audience members were placed on several rooftops, no one could see the entire dance. Portions existed outside of any one person's perception, just as unseen events in life continue all around us. Thus, one viewer described the experience of seeing the motions re-emerge on their return route as "eerie, almost as if one were watching a radio transmission from outer space."[48] Another audience group consisted of the uninformed people on the street, involved in daily activities, who happened to notice part of the performance. Rauschenberg said of *Roof*,

> I think one of the reasons I can work with Trisha so much is that she thinks like a painter. Take *Roof Piece*, for example. It was gorgeous. It started with a movement. Then someone in the next block would pick it up as well as they could tell – relay it, you know – all the way up and back, downtown, from the rooftops. There was the power of understanding and misunderstanding in those ways of movement.[49]

From 1973 through the mid-1970s, Brown's work took on a more geometric and controlled character as she sought to investigate more precisely the underlying structure of movement. These more coolly logical investigations had sources in the use of rules, game theory, and exploration of everyday movements from the Judson days, but Brown now approached them in a more rigorous and systematic fashion. The sense of deliberate ambiguity and free play that continued to dominate even Rauschenberg's technology-oriented works was remote from the rigorous control exercised by Brown at this time. For this short period, Brown's explorations had greater affinities with the Minimalist artists of the era, such as Sol Lewitt and Donald Judd, who were exploring basic geometric shapes and spatial relationships.

Chief among Brown's works of this period were her "Accumulations" – *Accumulation*, *Primary Accumulation*, and *Group Accumulation*. The basic premise of these three pieces is adding motions to one another in order to create an entire sequence of movement. In *Accumulation*, which is a solo, a woman stands with her elbows at her sides and her forearms extended horizontally. The thumbs of both hands are extended upwards, then both are rotated one-quarter turn to point at each other. She then twists them outward so the thumbs point in opposite directions. Her arms then move forward and back and she drops her arms with palms facing outward. The hand motions continue as she adds these new movements. She then adds a step forward and a step back, and so forth. The simplicity of the gestures leads the viewer to think deeply about the development of movement. One is made aware of the adjustment of the human body for any motion and how these alignments can be linked to create a dance variation. In the Accumulations Brown continued to operate outside of traditional proscenium spaces and thus bring her experiments directly to the public. They were performed in parks, parking lots, gymnasia, and in boats on the water. The environment, however, did not play a role in altering the performances, which maintained their rigorous precision no matter what the locale. This provides an interesting contrast with Brown's works from the mid-1970s onward. While her more recent works are done in traditional proscenium situations, she constantly questions the limits of the performance environment. Both her dances and Rauschenberg's sets are based partly on the way our concepts of the proscenium stage may be altered and extended.

In 1978 Brown asked Rauschenberg to join the board of the Trisha Brown Dance Company; after he accepted she sent him a postcard which said, "Dear Bob, I just elected you president." Rauschenberg has remained in the position ever since. In 1979, she asked him to design the sets, lighting, and costumes for a dance that she was creating, *Glacial Decoy* (Rauschenberg also named the dance). Brown's new collaborations with Rauschenberg coincided with her beginning to choreograph dances for proscenium spaces. She recalls:

> My transition from alternative performance spaces to the proscenium theater in 1979 required expertise in the visual aspects of lighting, scenography, and costume. I turned to Bob. He knew the ropes. He had been wreaking havoc on the dress and behavior codes of conventional theater for decades through his work with Merce Cunningham, Paul Taylor, Viola Farber, and the Judson Dance Theater. He knows knee-jerk performance convention when he sees it and stomps the poor dormant thing to death as he replaces it.[50]

Brown recognized Rauschenberg's talent for undoing theatrical conventions, and her works were intent on challenging those same customs. Even as she was deciding to show her works in more traditional locations and with potentially more traditional audiences, the dances were developing in new directions. Her dance movements were becoming increasingly complex, gestures were fragmented and recombined in startling new manners, and she was exploring varied spatial orientations, unanticipated trajectories, landings, and traversals. Striking paradoxes began to play an important role in her work, and there was a new range of dancing skills requiring intricacies that contrasted to the more austere minimal works earlier in the decade. The new dances were not intended to represent idealized experiences as had the ones of the recent past. While still insisting on the primacy of articulated movement, they did not tell the viewer how and what to watch; instead they were composed of an assemblage of individual offerings. At the time, Brown noted the changes and spoke of her dances as generating instinctive reactions from the weight and movement of the body. She said, "I don't choose any way of looking at the dances. You go in and then your eye is distracted by something else. You follow one movement then lose track of the whole, then go back to a whole zillion combinations."[51]

Rauschenberg also noted the changes in Brown's work. He commented: "Trisha's gone from construction dances to conversation dances, which to me were sophisticated comedy, and those dances where she juggled physical actions in such extraordinary ways. Now it's as if they have been internalized more."[52] It was Rauschenberg's realization of the evolution in Brown's work that made him eager to collaborate with her. The time was also right for him. Since 1976, he had been primarily occupied with a new series of works, the Spreads. These were large, multi-panel solvent transfer and collage paintings that often utilized three-dimensional objects. Created after Rauschenberg's 1976 retrospective, the Spreads recalled his early signature Combine paintings but now on a grander scale. In addition to their sheer size, the Spreads often contained dramatically reflective metal surfaces and their own light sources. In short, they were theatrical in nature and their character must have led Rauschenberg toward renewed thoughts about stage design.

As mentioned above, Brown's collaborations with Rauschenberg coincided with her return to the proscenium stage after decades of working in alternative spaces. On one hand this change was certainly motivated by practical issues. Brown's company had grown, and her increasingly complex dances required more extensive funding. She had reached a point in her career where her public recognition in Europe was extensive, but she was less known in America. In America, the traditional stage remained the important venue for public recognition and thus funding both from ticket sales and from public and private grants.

On the other hand, the manner in which Brown approached the proscenium stage was not a bow to tradition but continued her predilection for challenging conventions. The stage itself became an important foil for her activities and a motivational force for invention. In her dances, Brown began to think about ways to undermine the conventions of the traditional stage. These included suggesting that the dance continues off-stage beyond audience view, eliminating the hidden sanctuary provided by the stage wings, designing a dance to be viewed simultaneously from horizontal and vertical perspectives, and designating certain portions of the stage as empty areas. Brown's use of the limitations of the proscenium to generate new ideas is reminiscent of Rauschenberg's aim to use "the limitations of materials as a freedom that would eventually establish form."

The first dance on which Brown invited Rauschenberg to collaborate was *Glacial Decoy* (fig. 80), which was performed initially at the Walker Art Center, Minneapolis on May 7, 1979. *Glacial Decoy* is a work that concerns the slippery world

of information, in this case information about movement, space, and vision. The dance suggests that things are going on all around us; we capture them with our attention for just a moment, and then they slip away, perhaps to appear a moment later in an altered form. Brown creates the illusion that the dancers we see on stage are only a small portion of a dance that continues beyond the boundaries of the proscenium. Her intention was to give the appearance of an infinite number of dancers. Also, because the dancers who are on stage do interact in a complex, non-linear fashion, the viewer must decide on what to focus. In addition, Rauschenberg's sets compete assertively for attention, so the viewer is constantly aware of making choices and of being able to comprehend only a portion of a complex, multifarious world.

Glacial Decoy is built around large scooping phrases in which each gesture requires a counter movement to balance it or to deal with the effects of gravity. Brown has said that her idea for motion in this dance came from "levers and pendulums."[53] Her dance motions often begin with rotation of the hips or a large swing of an arm or leg. Another part of the body must be activated to counter the imbalance created in the first gesture and the phrase is built out of these motions and counter motions. The dancers never pause for a classic moment of balanced stasis between gestures; the movement is constant and unceasing. A characteristic action that appears several times in the first few minutes of *Glacial Decoy* is a dancer running forward then throwing her upper torso ahead of her in a bending position from the waist. She then catches herself just before the sum of these forces topples her. Another consists of a dancer standing with her feet close together, leaning to one side and catching herself before she falls.

As *Glacial Decoy* progresses the relationships between individual dancers become increasingly complex. More dancers appear on stage and we are challenged to absorb more information, to use our memories to relate current phrases to ones we have seen a few minutes ago, and to imagine the next direction that the dance will take. We look for logically simple relationships but are forced to conclude that, as in life, they do not exist. The sequence in which the dancers appear is essential to the manner in which Brown structured *Glacial Decoy*. At the beginning of the piece, only one dancer occupies the stage at a time. Yet the single presence is derived from two dancers who appear in alternating patterns from opposite sides of the stage. Right away the illusion is created either that the same dancer has magically transformed herself from one side of the stage to the other or that there is an endless array of dancers performing in the wings one of whom occasionally pops into view. The dancers always appear in mid-phrase, never at the beginning of a phrase, when they come before the audience, so that the idea of a continuous dance beyond the viewer's visual field is planted. At 3:50 minutes into the performance, the single dancer takes center stage and at 4:15 she is replaced by the second of the two dancers at center stage for a solo. At 5:23 minutes three dancers appear for the first time at the edge of the stage. Then two of these three take center stage and begin a duet. The duet is opposed to the supporting roles two dancers assume in traditional ballet. The pair almost never touches and in fact there seem to be several near collisions (see fig. 80). The possible relations between the two dancers include identical movements, opposite movements (one jumps as the other crouches), near collisions, repetitions, symbiotic relationships (one dancer ducks as the other swings an arm past her), and no relationship. There is no perceivable linear or narrative pattern to these possibilities; they all co-exist as viable alternatives. With the two dancers, one's attention is divided. The viewer becomes aware that one cannot focus equally on both, and one dancer is no more significant, or interesting, than the other.

At 12:30 minutes into *Glacial Decoy* (fig. 81), a third dancer joins the other two. Attention is now divided three ways. The dancers begin a process of rotation at 13:50; one will disappear to stage-right as another is picked up from stage-left. Memory is brought into play as the viewer attempts to relate the three sets of phrases being executed on stage to the one completed by the departed dancer. At the moment of rotation a fourth dancer appears on stage, and thus the illusion of an endless line or of a circle of dancers, shifting in one direction then another, of which the audience sees only a small segment, is reinforced. At 15:20 minutes into *Glacial Decoy*, a row of four dancers shifts to the audience's right leaving three persons on stage. The row then shifts to the right a second time, as it is joined by yet another dancer from stage-left. She is the fifth member of the troupe. At once, the viewer realizes that this must be the final performer necessary to create the effects just seen yet wonders if Brown could endlessly add dancers.

For Brown as for Rauschenberg, there is no necessary contradiction between revealing how the work was made and inspiring imagination. For them, showing the materials that constitute a painting or a dance does not undermine its power. On the contrary, in the view of both Brown and Rauschenberg, it highlights the complex and interesting relationship between artistic creation and everyday life. At 17:50 minutes, *Glacial Decoy* is reduced to two dancers, and at 18:30 minutes the last dancer fades to the edge of the stage.

81 Trisha Brown Company, Inc., *Glacial Decoy*, 1981, visual presentation and costumes by Rauschenberg, dancers from left to right: Brown, Nina Lundborg, and Lisa Kraus, photo by Babette Mangolte.

Rauschenberg's costume and set designs for *Glacial Decoy* exist in a powerfully symbiotic relationship with Brown's dance. Misunderstandings about Rauschenberg's theater designs include the notions that they are not carefully considered, that there is virtually no communication between the choreographer and the artist, and that there is almost no relationship between the visual presentation and the dance. In fact, Rauschenberg gives his designs intense thought; the dialogue between him and Brown and his attention to the dance are essential, albeit informal; and there is a significant relationship between the visual presentation and the choreography. To a degree, these misunderstandings are due to the creators themselves. Beginning with Cunningham and Cage, the avant-garde choreographers, artists, and musicians were at pains to differentiate themselves from both traditional ballet and early modern dance where the visual decor, costume, and music were still largely at the service of the choreography and subject to the whims of the choreographer. Cage and Cunningham, and those influenced by them, dissolved this subservient relationship, making each element in concept separate and equal. The position that the elements had nothing to do with each other was necessary as a theoretical stance to differentiate the new dances, but independence and equality does not preclude relationship. The actual dances differ from the theoretical position.

In *Glacial Decoy*, the ideas of Brown and Rauschenberg remain independent yet strongly complementary. When Brown asked Rauschenberg to design the visual presentation, she explained her basic idea of extra dancers in the wings who would rotate onto the stage; Rauschenberg determined immediately that he wanted a moving, rather than still, set, and he called Brown's idea "painterly and kinetic."[54] Subsequently, he sat in on several rehearsals of *Glacial Decoy*, and over the period of a year he and Brown exchanged innumerable telephone calls and postcards about their developing ideas. More important than the amount of time that Rauschenberg spent communicating with Brown was his instinctive understanding of her investigations concerning the complexity and transitory nature of movement. One indication of his grasp of her ideas is that he chose the title for the dance. In "glacial" he was

197

82 Trisha Brown Company, Inc. *Glacial Decoy*, 1981, visual presentation and costumes by Rauschenberg, dancers from left to right: Brown, Nina Lundborg, and Lisa Kraus, photo by Babette Mangolte.

referring to the impermanence of ice, and "decoy" suggests deflection. In Brown's dance as well as Rauschenberg's sets, the eye is constantly being deflected or moved from one visual event to another.

Rauschenberg's revised costumes for *Glacial Decoy* demonstrate the care with which he thought about the dance. The original costumes were semi-transparent skirts and blouses with rumpled taffeta leggings in pastel hues. Brown later described these as being in the "shepherdess realm."[55] After the Minneapolis opening, Rauschenberg decided that the costumes hampered the body. On the airplane home from the performance, he created white A-frame dresses with wide vertical pleats running their entire length. Short sleeves were attached to the upper arms while part of the shoulder remained bare. The fabric was made from the semi-transparent material that had been used for silkscreen paintings. The idea of the white fabric, the amorphous partly seen bodies, and slippery flowing movement of the fabric as it billowed around the dancers coordinated with the theme of melting ice as a metaphor for changes of state.

Originally, Rauschenberg conceived of a mechanical stage set that would move during *Glacial Decoy*, but he discarded this idea because of the impracticality of having such a bulky set travel when the company went on tour. During decades of set design, Rauschenberg had learned the lesson of practicality. (In his early days with Merce Cunningham's company, all of the dancers, Cage, and Rauschenberg as well as the costumes and sets had to fit in a Volkswagen van.) For *Glacial Decoy*, Rauschenberg wanted to design "something weightless you can carry in your pocket."[56] His solution consisted of photographic images projected onto four immense twelve- by nine-foot screens that form the backdrop to the stage. Each photograph lasts for four seconds, then fades, and reappears on the next screen to the right (fig. 82). It is simultaneously replaced by a new image on the left. The constant movement of the photographic images is closely related to the movement of Brown's dancers. Just as Brown was suggesting an endless chain of dancers beyond

83 *Glacial Decoy Series: Etching II*, 1979, etching and photoetching on Swiss hand-made paper, 24 ³/₄ × 16 ³/₄", published by Universal Limited Art Editions, edition of 22.

the confines of the stage, so Rauschenberg intimated a limitless succession of visual images. *Glacial Decoy*, like the majority of Brown's works up to this time, contains no music. While the dancers' footsteps and breathing provide one level of audio information, Rauschenberg has suggested that the clicking of the slide projectors as they change images is part of the audio presentation for the dance, one that reveals the physicality of its procedures.

Rauschenberg's choice of four images parallels Brown's maximum number of dancers, minus the surprise fifth person. The four-second interval was selected so that the viewer can absorb but not analyze each image. Rauschenberg's four photographs, which always feature three that we have seen before and one new example, echo Brown's theme of continuity and discontinuity. We see the photographs often enough to allow us to speculate about relationships, but they are never so stable as to allow a linear or didactic reading. We realize that context means everything; the elements that attract our attention in each photograph depend on its changing relationship to its neighbors. To accomplish such sequencing, however, Rauschenberg was unable to realize his idea of a set that could be carried in the pocket. The system ultimately required eight slide projectors, fade instruments, and a computer to control the program.

The character of Rauschenberg's individual images counted as much as the overall design of his visual presentation. For the slides, he selected 620 images from 3,000 photographs that he took in the city of Fort Myers, Florida. (The playful irony of Florida photographs being used for a "glacial" dance was certainly not lost on either Brown or Rauschenberg.) The photographs are back and white, and Rauschenberg has noted that he especially chose an antique bichromate finish so that the photographs would have a particular sheen, like melting ice, that accompanied the impermanence of the images.[57]

Rauschenberg's use of his own photographs in *Glacial Decoy* marks his personal involvement in the piece as well as an important change in his art. He had begun to take photographs at Black Mountain College in 1948, and the medium became a life-long passion. Rauschenberg has stated that the camera functions for him as a sketchbook did for earlier artists, and at Black Mountain he expressed the desire to travel across America, photographing the nation foot by foot. This idea of recording his entire environment foretells Rauschenberg's ambitions, ones that were realized albeit in another manner in ROCI. While his early photographs were interesting, they were seldom included in his Combine paintings. For these works as well as his Silkscreen Paintings of the 1960s, which relied heavily on photographic imagery, commercial photographs were primarily used, a choice in keeping with the artist's desire to reveal the influence of the public media in these works. Once Rauschenberg used his own photographs in *Glacial Decoy*, his direction changed, and his own photographs became the staple for his art works. A selection of the photographs used in Brown's dance became a suite of five prints using photoetching and later a suite of four lithographs, the *Glacial Decoy Series* (1979–80; fig. 83). Subsequently, Rauschenberg has utilized his own photographs, through printmaking, silkscreening, and most recently computer imaging, in almost all of his works.[58]

The particular character of the photographs used in Brown's *Glacial Decoy* stands out. They were neither randomly taken nor haphazardly selected. In addition to the bichromate processing that tonally relates the photographs, they are linked by other formal characteristics. On the whole, the imagery is off center and not framed by surrounding elements. Many slides also feature large objects seen in close-up. Like the dancers, they are forceful and readable yet suggest impermanence rather than classical balance. The particular objects that Rauschenberg favored in his photographs have interested him throughout his oeuvre – old industrial machinery, handmade or worn signs, architectural elements (particularly windows and doors), chairs, sports figures, animals, scenes in nature, and fabric patterns.

Rauschenberg has stated that he "choreographed" these photographs for the dance, and indeed relationships can be found.[59] His overall aim was to establish contrasting patterns in the four images, so as to suggest surprising similarities but almost never to reveal a one-to-one relationship between them. In addition, Rauschenberg opens and closes the dance with visual puns. The opening sequence of photographs consists of an empty landscape, an empty room, a blank window, and an awning that looks like a stage curtain. One of the next photographs is a landscape containing four trees, hinting at the four dancers who will emerge in *Glacial Decoy* but not giving away the surprise fifth. One of the image sequences includes the following: a chair, a cow standing in profile so we can see her four legs, window panes in a pattern of four, and a door with vertical molding. This group has a surprising relationship in vertical and horizontal structure. In another sequence circular motifs are featured in a close-up photograph of a tiger lily flower, a bicycle wheel, round fabric patterns, and an automobile tire. The intricate pattern of a brick wall with an arrow painted on it, a clock with its pointing "hands" hung on an elaborately patterned metal grill, the hand of a piece of sculpture with pointing finger, and the pointed spire of a church steeple form another cluster of images.

In these cases, the formal relationships between seemingly incongruous objects spark our interest and lead us to speculate briefly as to what else these objects might have in common. Such surprising associations lead us to imagine, fantasize, and speculate. They open channels of thought, tweak our curiosity, and urge us to see the world in new ways, but each lasts for only a few seconds before we are intrigued by the next set of relationships. We find that the manner in which we see each object depends on its context, that is, how we visually relate it to the neighboring images. The method that Rauschenberg uses here is similar to that found in his paintings where surprising visual similarities encourage us to connect objects in new ways. Like the paintings, the photographic arrangements in *Glacial Decoy* do not add up to an iconography or narrative content, rather they represent intuitive choices made through Rauschenberg's ability quickly to spot visually interesting comparisons and contrasts. As a whole, they reveal his belief in an exciting multifaceted world, a message similar to that of Brown's dance.

Many other interesting relationships that Rauschenberg "choreographed" between his slides and Brown's dance could be highlighted but a few will suffice. The only slide that appears more than once in *Glacial Decoy* is the close-up photograph of a sign from an old ice machine, featuring the word "ICE," the leitmotif of the dance. Shortly after the four dancers emerge (approximately 14:20 minutes into the dance), Rauschenberg features his only use of four identical slides; they are four large, rectangular, industrial storage containers. Finally, the last four slides shown in *Glacial Decoy* are a chicken coop, a goat looking at us, a profile of a goat that appears in a sign, and the round traffic sign for a railroad crossing. The chickens and the goats are, of course, visual signatures for Rauschenberg because these animals were featured in his early Combines, particularly the goat in his most controversial and famous early work, *Monogram* (1955–59; see fig. 28), and the final photograph of the railroad crossing sign, of course, reads "RR."

As has been shown, Rauschenberg's sets are related to Brown's dance, yet they do stand as independent works. The idea of separating dance, visual presentation, and music was inherited from John Cage and Merce Cunningham, as noted above. There is, however, an essential difference between Rauschenberg's sets for *Glacial Decoy* and those he designed for Cunningham. Despite the theory of separate and equal in the Cunningham collaborations, Rauschenberg's sets and costumes remained secondary to the action of the dancers in Cunningham's works. This was precisely the source of controversy regarding Rauschenberg's design for Cunningham's *Story*. As mentioned earlier, during one performance, the living set consisting of Rauschenberg and Hay ironing their shirts garnered more audience attention than Cunningham's dancers. In *Glacial Decoy*, Rauschenberg's dynamic visual display attracts as much attention as the dancers. We cannot fully focus on its changing array and on the dancers at the same time. The visual presentation is an essential element in deflecting (or providing a decoy for) vision and making the audience aware of constant visual and intellectual choices. It is a mark of the trust that Brown and Rauschenberg had in each other, and the confidence of each in her/his own media, that they could allow such true diversity to exist.

The next dance project upon which Brown and Rauschenberg cooperated was *Set and Reset*, which premiered October 20, 1983 for the Next Wave Festival at the Brooklyn Academy of Music. In addition to the visual presentation by Rauschenberg, the dance featured music by Laurie Anderson. *Set and Reset* marked, up to that time, Brown's greatest success with the general public; all four performances of the 2,100 seat opera house were sold out, and reviews praised the originality of the piece.

Themes set forth in *Glacial Decoy* were continued in *Set and Reset*, whose connection to the earlier dance may be one reason that Brown again sought Rauschenberg's partnership. *Set and Reset* involves multiple experiences layered on top of one another. The dance provides layered events that happen all at once, and the spatial configuration of the dance encourages this reading. While the dancers in *Glacial Decoy* oriented themselves across the stage so that we could attempt to correlate their movements, those in *Set and Reset* often line up into depth so that the simultaneity of widely divergent actions is evident. Brown has called this dance one of her "molecular" works because the dynamic free flow resembles an "unstable molecular structure."[60] Rauschenberg's visual presentation coordinates with the

84 Trisha Brown Company, Inc., *Set and Reset*, 1983, visual presentation and costumes by Rauschenberg, dancers from left to right: Irene Hultman, Eva Karczay, and Vicki Schick, photo by Beatriz Schiller.

increased simultaneity of *Set and Reset*. He designed a three-dimensional set, the *Elastic Carrier (Shiner)* (fig. 84), that is placed in an unusual position for theater sets, suspended over the dancers. Projected on the *Elastic Carrier (Shiner)* are three overlapping films made from collage footage; Rauschenberg's multi-dimensionality parallels Brown's. In *Set and Reset*, Brown was exploring three different ideas. The first and most important was that each dancer was given a set of phrases, but the dancer her/himself determined when to begin, when to end, and whether to repeat a phrase or to move on to the next. This method allowed a higher degree of improvisation for the dancers than Brown had provided in any of her works since the Judson days. The movements in *Set and Reset* were among the most wide-ranging of Brown's career. They extended her signature gestures into acrobatic springs, into handstands, classical ballet lifts, and moves derived from the martial art T'ai Chi.[61]

In addition to the phrasing, Brown gave each of the dancers "rules" to aid their timing and movement patterns. These so-called rules were deliberately generalized concepts rather than specific edicts, so that each dancer was permitted a range of interpretations. Examples include "line up, keep it simple, and act on instinct."[62] Brown has commented on the underlying structure of the dance:

> In these works, a known phrase of the material is accompanied by a set of rules that further shape space and time, but the dancers act on their own impulses as to when they begin a phrase, or cut back, or jump forward. In this way, you get an overlay of action that is indecipherable; it's not made by the human mind, but something like you would see under a microscope: amoebas bobbing around in some random fashion.[63]

Brown's second overall idea in *Set and Reset* was exploring the edge of the stage. In essence, she traced the periphery of a stage area and used its edges, in her words, "like a conveyor belt" to deliver dancers into the central zone.[64] As Brown has pointed out, this is not at all the usual way for a choreographer to view the stage, but it complemented the improvisational character of her dance. Because of the

availability of all edges of the stage as entry and exit points, the dancers were freer to improvise knowing they could move on or off stage from any position near its edge.

The third concept in *Set and Reset* also relates to the more spontaneous nature of the dance; that notion is "visibility and invisibility."[65] By eliminating the "legs" (side curtains) at the wings of the stage, the dancers were visible at all times. This provided a dramatic physical and psychological change for the dancers, as Brown dramatically put it: "Our sanctuary is gone, invisibility dashed, downtime on display."[66] This modification was part of Brown's continuing challenge to the conditions of a proscenium stage, calling the wings "a space that made me uncomfortable."[67] But her alteration in stage conditions, which was worked out in tandem with Rauschenberg, is particularly suited to *Set and Reset* (fig. 85) because the dancers' improvisational gestures now became the sum total of their activities. We see the dancers finishing movements, waiting, resting, and preparing to re-enter the central stage area. Such movements as the mechanics of a catch when a dancer dives off stage were now visible. Interestingly, from the audience viewpoint, Brown's invention in *Set and Reset* is the opposite of *Glacial Decoy*. Rather than using the hidden area of the wings to suggest an infinite world of movement beyond what can be seen, the audience is privy to everything that the dancers do.

The intricacy of *Set and Reset* is closely related to ideas that Brown and Rauschenberg share about the improvisational character of life. They think that the best discoveries are often made intuitively without forethought. Basically, their belief is in the creative potential of the human mind once freed from the constraints of performing dictated activities. In the light of its improvisatory traits, the best way briefly to discuss the character of *Set and Reset* is to analyze a small section of the performance. The particular performance is Version I, filmed in 1984 for WGBH Television. One must bear in mind that Brown's choreographic guidelines led each performance to be different and that because of the speed and complexity of the dance this description would be impossible without the multiple playback opportunities that the filmed version allows. The dancers for this performance were Trisha Brown, Irene Hultman, Eva Karczag, Diane Madden, Stephen Petronio, Vicki Schicke, and Randy Warshaw.

In one sequence, the seven dancers line up behind one another from front to rear stage, a configuration related to Brown's earlier dance *Line Up*. In an instant, Warshaw spins out of line to the cameraman's left, as Hultman does a cartwheel breaking out of line to the right. At the same time, Madden, who is at the front of the line, walks through it with her back to the camera, scattering dancers as she touches them. Brown, who was at the back of the line, walks forward through the now cleared space with her eyes covered until she reaches the position of the cameraman. Brown then spins to the right edge of the designated stage rectangle. With two leaps, Petronio moves to the rear edge of the stage on the left side and stands still watching the action on stage, while Schicke dances in a circle around him. Madden skips forward and balances for a moment on one leg bending at the waist with both arms and other leg extended.

Karczag then leaps to the right side of the stage, reverses, and with two jumps returns to center stage. Petronio runs toward center stage and collides with Schicke, bumping her into the middle of the stage, and he then rotates directly behind her. Brown comes from the right and touches Madden who spins in a semi-circle ending in line behind Schicke and Petronio. All of the dancers momentarily move into line except for Warshaw who does a handspring through the line on the left side ending beyond it in a spread leg pose. The dancers have thus "reset" and another sequence of movements begins. The total elapse time for the above description is twenty seconds, and it provides some idea of the speed and variety of overlapping movements throughout *Set and Reset* (fig. 86).

The dance includes music by the composer and performer Laurie Anderson, a change for Brown, most of whose pieces had been done without a musical score. The composition features Anderson repeating the phrase "Long time no see" in various patterns and rhythms, and Richard Landry playing the alto saxophone and percussion. Anderson's music is characterized by steady states and contrasts. We can predict the type of sounds that are going to occur but never exactly which sounds. In this manner her music parallels Brown's choreography in which we recognize the phrases taught each dancer but can predict neither their order nor relationship to the phrases of other dancers. Anderson's music also features a strong beat. The beat emphasizes that, despite the seeming disorder of the dancers' movements, they are performing at the same rhythm. In a reversal of the usual situation where a dance is choreographed to pre-existing music, Anderson worked from a videotaped version of *Set and Reset*. After completing her first draft of the score, she found that she had to slow her tempo a little to match Brown's phrasing. Anderson's adjustments highlight the separate, but correlated, character of dance and music that is also found in the visual presentation.

When Brown asked Rauschenberg to collaborate on *Set and Reset*, she had only created the opening for the dance in which Diane Madden is carried horizontally around the stage and from this position "walks" along its exposed rear wall. The reference is to Brown's early celebrated piece *Walking on the Wall* (1971). Rauschenberg's immediate response to Brown's idea was to suggest a living set consisting of five or six people recruited and briefly trained at each location to which the dance traveled. The living set would occupy an upstage position with the dancers often performing behind them. Just as Brown was referring to her performance history, so Rauschenberg was rethinking one of his most controversial sets, the living set for Merce Cunningham's *Story*.

As Brown began to choreograph *Set and Reset* and to tell Rauschenberg of its development, his plans also evolved. Brown has commented on the remarkable profusion of ideas that Rauschenberg generates. She recalls about seventy different visual schemes that he developed over six months, often calling her in the middle of the night with a new idea.[68] One of his most interesting and eccentric ideas was based on phosphorus, which he encountered swimming at night near his Captiva studio. The effect, phosphorescence, makes the water sparkle when a swimmer splashes in it. Rauschenberg suggested a shallow pool of water across the entire stage. As the dancers sloshed through it, they would be lit from the waists down with sparkling light. While the scheme proved impractical, it demonstrates the richness and originality of Rauschenberg's inventions.

Rauschenberg's ideas for *Set and Reset* took on a more developed form when he observed the first rehearsal of the dance. Brown had arranged her practice studio with some pieces of hanging velour at either side in imitation of the fabric legs at the edges of a proscenium stage. Her initial intention was to get the dancers simply to touch and interact with the legs, eliminating the sacrosanct quality they have in traditional performances. Rauschenberg was particularly taken with the informal and impromptu character of the rehearsal. He recalled dancers crawling around him as they moved from spot to spot trying not to interfere with his visual field.[69] He wanted to preserve the casual effect of a rehearsal for the audience. Coordinating with Brown's developing ideas of the improvisational nature of *Set and Reset*, he proposed replacing the legs with transparent black scrims each edged with a vertical white satin stripe, only vague reminders of the concealing proscenium legs. As noted above, Brown commented, "Our sanctuary was gone," and all the actions of the dancers were revealed.

At the rehearsal, Rauschenberg also saw that Brown was beginning to use all sides of the stage as entry and exit points for her dancers, her "conveyor belt." Rauschenberg realized that Brown's choreographic idea would be spoiled by any sort of backdrop. Thus, the area remaining for his visual presentation was the vertical space above the dancers, and he designed *Elastic Carrier (Shiner)*. Although Rauschenberg has joked that he created this floating set to avoid "tripping" the dancers and to keep their shadows off his set, his idea is a significant solution to Brown's choreography. Hovering over the dancers, it provides a strong visual statement while in no way interfering with the manner in which they use all sides of the stage area.

The *Elastic Carrier (Shiner)* (see fig. 84) is a structure eleven by thirty-six feet consisting of two pyramids flanking a rectilinear box, all constructed of an aluminum armature. The entire structure is covered with a reflective silver fabric designed by NASA. Rauschenberg sought a surface that would accept projected images in such a manner that they would appear to be both on the surface and inside of the structure. At the beginning of the dance performance, the *Elastic Carrier (Shiner)* rests on the floor. As the theater darkens a film montage consisting of clips from newsreels (including children playing and a dog wagging its tail), television programs, and NASA footage of the moon landing and views of the earth from outer space is projected on the structure, creating in Rauschenberg's words "tonal vagaries."[70] Initially, there is also an audio tape containing a collage of sounds including text, music, instructions, and industrial noises. At precisely one minute and twenty seconds into the dance, the *Elastic Carrier (Shiner)* "lifts off," in Trisha Brown's words, and remains above the dancers with constantly changing film imagery but without sounds – at this point Laurie Anderson's music begins – for the remaining twenty-five minutes of the dance.

In addition, *Elastic Carrier (Shiner)* demonstrates Rauschenberg's understanding of the concepts behind Brown's dance. The structure emphasizes three-dimensionality, especially with its illusion of movies projected internally, just as Brown's dance is choreographed with the dancers overlapping into depth. Rauschenberg's progression from the sequential photographs used in *Glacial Decoy* to the four motion pictures overlapping each other in *Set and Reset* reveals his interpretation of the dance as a multi-layered and simultaneous experience.

The structure combines two of Rauschenberg's favorite themes – urbanism and space-age technology. They are both subjects suggested by the "molecular" character of Brown's choreography. On one hand, the seemingly chaotic movement of Brown's dancers suggests the speed and turmoil of pedestrians in a city. Suspended above the dancers, the rectangle and pyramids of *Elastic Carrier (Shiner)* look like building tops, especially those of shaped post-modern skyscrapers. The urban imagery used in some of the film footage as well as industrial noises in the initial soundtrack reinforce this impression of frantic urban energy. On the other hand, the space-age armature of *Elastic Carrier (Shiner)* and its shiny fabric surface resemble an exotic spaceship. In 1983 a variety of proposals for an American space station were made. The translucent film images and especially the NASA footage bolster this association. We are reminded that Rauschenberg keeps one eye on the gritty character of urban life and the other on technological dreams of the future.

Costumes for *Set and Reset* also express these dual themes. They consist of short-sleeved loose-fitting blouses with wide-legged pants for the women and pants only for the men. The thin gauzy material has a futuristic look similar to that of *Elastic Carrier (Shiner)*. The dancers are naked under the costumes so that the bodies are unhampered by underwear lines. Rauschenberg applied silkscreen images to the costumes consisting of photographs primarily of architectural details that he had taken in New York City. These pick up the urban theme of his visual presentation.

The creation of the costumes for *Set and Reset* also led Rauschenberg to a new series of works. The fabric for the costumes was so thin that some material had to be put under it to catch the left-over ink when it was silkscreened. The "left-over" compositions that were created from this process suggested that Rauschenberg should put canvas under the costumes and thus capture the images. His *Salvage* series (1983–85; fig. 87) fed directly out of his experiences in *Set and Reset*, conceptually as well as in technique. In *Set and Reset*, Brown combined references to her past works into an entirely new dance. The range of movements she had learned since her student days and the idea of chance procedures from the Judson period were incorporated into a "molecular" dance that had an entirely new appearance. Rauschenberg responded to this sensibility in his *Elastic Carrier (Shiner)* that was both industrial and futuristic.

Similarly, in the *Salvage* series, Rauschenberg sought to recapture his past at the same time as he thrust into the future. The "left-over" configurations embodied ideas of improvisation and fortuitous accidents in which Rauschenberg has always believed, while the application of the images was related to the techniques in Rauschenberg's celebrated Silkscreen Paintings of the 1960s. Rauschenberg then attacked the surfaces of the *Salvages* with vibrant brushwork, as he often had on his Combine paintings of the 1950s. Yet, in the *Salvages*, the images that bled onto the canvas were more amorphous and the colors and gestures of the brushwork were bolder than he had used in the past. In fact, the combination of bold splashes of color and the hazy changeable imagery had the look of early color computer screens that were just becoming popular. (The gaudy colors of the 1960s Silkscreen Paintings, by contrast, looked like the images on old color television sets.) In the *Salvages*, Rauschenberg's choice of subjects also looked simultaneously to the past and to the future. The artist self-consciously chose pictures from his personal development and ones that characterized his friendships, including Thomas Gainsborough's *Blue Boy* (the first significant piece of original art that Rauschenberg saw), a flag (for Jasper Johns), and soup cans (for Andy Warhol). At the same time, Rauschenberg incorporated recent photographs he had taken on his trips to Asia and to South America in preparation for his major new endeavor, the Rauschenberg Overseas Culture Interchange. In salvaging his past, Rauschenberg was simultaneously inventing his future.

The next collaboration between Brown and Rauschenberg was *Astral Convertible* (1989; fig. 88). The dance, which was commissioned by the Montpellier Festival in France, was premiered at the opening of the Rauschenberg Overseas Culture

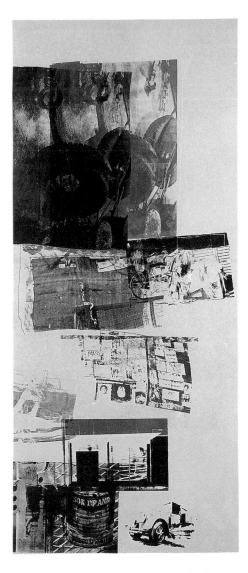

87 *Untitled (Salvage)*, 1984, acrylic and collage on canvas, 120 × 51 ", collection of the artist.

88 (*right*) Trisha Brown Company, Inc., *Astral Convertible*, 1989, visual presentation and costumes by Rauschenberg, dancers from left to right: Lance Gries, Carolyn Lucas, Gregory Lara, and Diane Madden, photo by Onyx/Mark Hanauer.

89 (*facing page*) Trisha Brown Dance Company, Inc., *Astral Converted (50″)*, 1991, visual presentation and costumes by Rauschenberg, premier performance in front of the National Gallery of Art, Washington D.C., photo by Dennis Brack/Black Star.

Interchange (ROCI) in Moscow, February 1–4. (*Glacial Decoy* and *Set and Reset* were also performed.) Rauschenberg designed the sets and costumes for *Astral Convertible* and Richard Landry composed the music. In 1991, Brown was asked by the National Gallery of Art in Washington, D.C. to choreograph a new work to present at the final ROCI exhibition to be held there. She chose to re-choreograph *Astral Convertible*, adding twenty minutes to its length and asking John Cage to compose music for the new version. It was titled *Astral Converted (50″)*, and it is the second, longer, version that primarily will be discussed here.

In contrast to either *Glacial Decoy* or *Set and Reset*, *Astral Converted (50″)* has a monumental character. The dance features traits of grandeur, solemnity, and structure suggesting that an avant-garde sensibility and classical dignity can simultaneously exist. The movements in the dance appear profound, forceful, and stately at the same time that they are highly inventive. The overall pacing of the dance is slower than most of Brown's recent works. The pendulum-like and rotational movement of the dancers' arms and legs remains an essential feature, but less pivoting of the hips is used so the movements appear less fleeting. Also, the interaction between the dancers is more direct as they touch, catch, lift, and support one another. Brown has commented about this change generally in her dance, connecting it with the introduction of male dancers into her company: "I thought for the first time about how

men actually moved, and used a series of drawings that I was making to translate geometric shapes into their bodies. I wanted forceful movement, huge arcs of energy that made great drawings in space."[71]

Since the days of the Judson Dance Theater, humor, puns, and a light-hearted playfulness had been one of the major factors in both Brown's choreography and Rauschenberg's art. The humor was a way of circumventing tradition by saying, in effect, "We are only having fun so we are free to invent as we like." *Astral Converted (50″)* demonstrates Brown's belief, as well as that of Cage and Rauschenberg, that an intense and mysterious dance need not preclude radical inventiveness.

The sub-theme of *Astral Converted (50″)* is cosmic events. Rauschenberg's fascination with outer-space themes is well known, and Brown shares that interest. The dancers react to one another like great stars exerting gravitational forces. The lights shining on their reflective, space-age costumes make them appear like nebula, and the aluminum towers that Rauschenberg invented to hold the lighting and sound systems have all the markings of futuristic structures. The fact that *Astral Converted (50″)* (fig. 89) premiered outdoors under the night sky on the Washington, D.C. Mall increased this effect, and one critic likened Rauschenberg's towers to rocket gantries and the overall look of the dance to a landing strip at an airport.[72] Rauschenberg named the dance "astral" to suggest "a passage through the sky" and originally "convertible" to indicate both that he had acquired many of the parts for his light towers from automobiles and more significantly that Brown "could make whatever changes she wants" in the dance.[73] When Brown "converted" the dance to its new format, her title equally indicated that change is always possible.

Two additional ideas inform Brown's choreography for *Astral Convertible* and *Astral Converted (50″)*.[74] The dance begins with a line of dancers at one edge of the stage who move across it and meet with another line mixed among the light towers at the opposite edge. As Brown watched early rehearsals of the opening sequences of the dance, she began, in her words, "to think of the half of the stage that was empty as beautiful, almost sacred."[75] Brown continued to choreograph *Astral Converted (50″)* around the idea of open space. Negative areas are extremely important, and Brown came up with innovative ways to move dancers across this space such as "sweeping" them off with a broom. The use of empty spaces in *Astral Converted (50″)* coordinates with the stellar references made in the dance.

Secondly, Brown designed *Astral Converted (50″)* as two dances – one seen horizontally from the orchestra and the other vertically from the balcony.[76] Much of the dance takes place on the floor where Brown invented a whole new variety of movements in which the dancers curl, stretch, extend, kneel, roll, and pivot. This notion can be extended back to the alternative audience views discussed with *Glacial Decoy*, but in *Astral Converted (50″)* it has a special effect. Strangely, the dancers on the floor do not seem earthbound. Instead, viewed from above, one reads the floor as open sky and the dancers seem to float amid this void in a gravity-defying manner. Brown herself has referred to this effect, saying that the dancers "mocked the floor," and that she wished to express "clear lines etched into the air."[77]

When Brown first contacted Rauschenberg about the visual presentation for the original *Astral Convertible*, she told him that, in his words, she "wanted a set that

could be used anywhere," and Rauschenberg wryly added "that's not a simple idea."[78] Specifically, Brown's notion was the opportunity to perform outdoors in small city squares in Europe that she found beautiful. Rauschenberg's first idea was inflatable towers, but this proved unworkable because of scale and wind considerations. (Steve Paxton had used an inflatable set in his well-known performance *Physical Things,* 1966.) Rauschenberg eventually arrived at the idea of eight towers constructed of openwork aluminum scaffolding, two each in heights of two, four, six, and eight feet (fig. 90). Each of the towers would be an entirely self-contained unit run by automobile batteries. Every tower would have automobile headlights that would act as the lighting system for the dance and a tape recorder that would provide the audio component. Later, Rauschenberg added the concept of light beams between the towers, so that when the beams were broken by the movements of the dancers the lights and the music would alternately shut off or turn on.

The towers turned out to be complicated to design. Rauschenberg worked on them for two months in collaboration with Billy Klüver and Per Biorn of E.A.T. and Ken Tabachnick, a third engineer, designed the lights. The different heights of the towers relate to the positions of the dancers who vary from lying on the ground to jumping high in the air. The largest tower is big enough to be a commanding presence without its scale overwhelming the dancers. The towers consist of grids of thin aluminum beams that have been bolted together; thus their structure is apparent, and we can see through them so that they obscure little of the dancers' movements. In relation to the towers' structure, one thinks of the grid designs that Rauschenberg has used throughout his career in paintings.

Each of the towers contains from four to six automobile headlights, which are mounted at different heights on all sides of the towers. However, they are all aligned in the same direction so that the towers do have a front and back, and the dancers know which way to point them to illuminate the performance. Thus the lighting has a random aspect, but it is also controlled because the light beams can be pointed. The predecessor for Rauschenberg's lighting system in *Astral Convertible* was his design for Cunningham's *Winterbranch*, a dance in which the lighting sequence was determined by chance, sometimes leaving the theater in total darkness and at others pointing spotlights directly at the audience. The piece premiered at Lincoln Center, New York where it was booed by the viewers primarily because they felt the lights to be a hostile gesture toward them. In *Astral Converted (50″)* the lights use random procedures but within more defined limits.

Each tower contains two audio speakers which are also mounted at different heights. Along the front of each tower, there are five to seven sets of invisible light-beam projectors and receivers. The base of each tower contains a tape recorder used to play the audio score, the control box for the light beams, and an automobile battery to power the tower; thus, each is an entirely self-sufficient unit. All of the electronics at the bases of the towers are enclose behind plexiglass sheets, which extend down over the wheels on which the towers roll, affording the equipment protection but leaving it visible to the audience. Just as Rauschenberg included electric cords as part of the experience of his early Combines, so the electronic workings of the light towers are an essential part of experiencing them. The electronic components are revealed, and their presence is meant to emphasize the artist's and engineers' creative work in designing the towers. Further, the wiring for each tower is deliberately not neatly bundled but runs loosely up through the center, giving the appearance of messy technology. Throughout his career, Rauschenberg has emphasized the human involvement in technological inventions by never allowing them to look too neatly constructed. Accordingly, we seem to be present at the moment a new idea is tried with a jumble of wires experimentally connected for the first time.

The thorniest problem for Rauschenberg, Klüver, and Biorn in the design of the towers was the placement of the light-beam receptors, and this problem involved Brown's choreography as well. Initially, each tower had only a single set of receptors. As the beam was broken a random sequencing box determined which lights on that tower would be turned on or off. The difficulty was that the random sequencing devices kept malfunctioning, and as the towers were moved it was extremely difficult for the dancers to line up the beam receptors so that they would catch the light beams and operate. The solution was a separate receptor for each light beam and one for the audio system. With so many beams being projected, many, if not all, would line up as the towers were moved about.

Brown's vertical and horizontal dance was coordinated with these towers. She was in the unusual position of knowing the concept of the lighting design for a full two months as she choreographed the piece. Creating dance phrases that varied from lying on the floor to jumping in the air, Brown tried to assure that a full range of lighting and music effects would occur. However, she did not have an opportunity actually to rehearse with the light towers until one day before the first performance of *Astral Convertible* in Moscow. She recalls, "I was given a gift and was hamstrung at the same time."[79] In Moscow, there were difficulties with aligning the towers so as to make them function at all. For subsequent performances and for the creation of *Astral Converted (50″)*, she thus simplified the movements of the dancers and restricted the changes of tower positions to fewer sections of the dance.

When Brown asked John Cage to provide the music for *Astral Converted (50″)*, Cage disliked what he termed "the one-to-one relationships" between the dancers' movements and the music because they turned the music off and on by breaking the light beams. In reality, the dancers' motions provided chance musical effects outside of Cage's control. Hence, Cage desired his music to be a continuous score not affected by the dancers' activities. As Brown wryly observed, "The master of chance wanted his *own* chance."[80]

The costumes that Rauschenberg designed for *Astral Convertible* reflect the themes of the dance. They are silver unitards with white stripes on them. The tight-fitting unitards reveal the mechanics of the body as the light towers show their working electronics. The silver color has a futuristic appearance like that of the towers, and the dancers shine like stars in the dark sky as they move about the stage. Realizing the dance would be done outdoors at night, Rauschenberg added white stripes to enhance further the visibility of the performers. The stripes also fit Brown's design of the dance as seen from two vantage points, because those on the male dancers are horizontal, while those on the female dancers are vertical. Rauschenberg further differentiated the female dancers by attaching fan-like pieces of transparent gauze between their legs, the gauze being a reference to the parachutes in Rauschenberg's own first choreographed work, *Pelican*.

A portion of *Astral Converted (50″)* (see fig. 89) reveals how Brown's choreography, Rauschenberg's set, lighting, and costume, and Cage's music create an integrated experience. The segment occurs at 5:50 minutes into the dance when a single male dancer enters on the left side of the stage. An eight-foot and a six-foot light tower stand stage-front at the far left-hand side, and a two-foot tower is behind the dancer. Two additional dancers push corresponding six- and eight-foot towers from the wings onto the right side of the stage. The dancers then shove the towers and allow them to roll freely onto the stage like futuristic dancers themselves. Another two-foot tower is already in place diagonally across the stage, facing the small tower behind the single dancer. The larger towers illuminate each other and angled lights irradiate the upper part of the male dancer. Because he dances behind them not breaking their light beams, the illumination is, for the moment, constant. The character of the automobile headlights is that of intensely bright areas with surrounding darkness. Thus the single dancer shimmers in his silver costume while the remainder of the stage, Brown's "almost sacred" space, is inky black.

The male dancer executes a series of spins extending a leg and arm around his torso as axis. The spirals are accompanied by traveling steps, and as he executes these he breaks the light beams of the small towers. As the headlamps of these towers go on and off, the lower half of his legs appear and disappear so that he seems to be floating off the ground as he whirls. After a two-minute solo, two female dancers enter from stage-right. They are both holding brooms before them. Brown described the sweeping motif, which occurs throughout *Astral Converted (50″)*, as a devise to have dancers exit across stage while not violating the empty central space. She recalled that her first desire was to float the dancers away by balloon, noting that this was a Judson-like concept.[81] She also knew that the notion was impractical, and the sweeping gesture was conceived as a substitute manner of moving the dancers across the stage, one that particularly suited the horizontal viewpoint of the dance.

Brooms play a frequent role in the art of Brown's generation, partly because they are a common item found in artist's and dancer's studios. One thinks of the brooms that have appeared in both Rauschenberg's and Jasper Johns's paintings, and of the well-known Yoko Ono *Sweeping Piece* (1962) that was an early Fluxus event. There is also the early story told by Yvonne Rainer of Brown's classes with Ann Halprin. One of Rainer's most emphatic memories is that of Brown diving across stage with a broom handle thrust ahead of her. In *Astral Converted (50″)*, the brooms are neither the common object of Johns, Ono, and Rauschenberg nor the instrument of dynamism in Brown's early gesture. Rather they are visionary. They lead us to focus on the empty space of the stage floor and make the floating motif even stronger; we imagine that floor as filled with unseen forces that are being shifted by the brooms as well as the dancers who actually realign themselves when touched by them.

At this point in *Astral Converted (50″)*, the two female dancers circle around the two light towers at stage-right as the male dancer rotates alone on the opposite side. As the females revolve they alternately duck, resting on the brooms, and stand. Therefore, they break different light beams and establish a more complicated pattern of changing light directed on the male dancer. The dance takes on a flickering quality. After the female dancers have made five different rotations of the light towers, two additional dancers enter from stage-right. They assume horizontal positions as they stretch, roll, pivot, and are swept across the open stage. Reaching the opposite side, they rise to their feet as the single male takes a horizontal position. Then he is swept off stage as a new duet begins.

John Cage's music runs during this sequence as throughout the dance. Cage's piece is marked by duration, pitch, and silence. While the music is not tied to specific movements in Brown's choreography, the long duration of most sounds, as well as the long silences often occurring between them, are counterparts to the relatively

slow movements of the dancers. The music is slow and majestic but not predictable. The long silences between many of the chords complement Brown's emphasis on the stage's empty space, and Cage's use of an electronic synthesizer for his music has a futuristic character in keeping with the dance. Cage's composition juxtaposes high and low pitches just as Brown's dancers rely on contrasting horizontal and vertical movements. In the same manner that the dancers allow us clearly to see variations and contrasts, which are nevertheless unexpected, so Cage never overlaps more than four chords at one time, but we are always surprised by their sound combinations. Thus, Cage's music is particularly appropriate to the combination of mystery and monumentality that is a leitmotif of *Astral Converted (50″)*. The complexity of *Astral Converted (50″)* was countered in 1994 by the directness of the most recent Brown/Rauschenberg collaboration, *If You Couldn't See Me* (fig. 91).

In the case of *If You Couldn't See Me*, Rauschenberg suggested the basic idea for the dance; the concept was that Brown perform it with her back to the audience.[82] As she recalls, he told her, "It's history, Trisha, no one has ever done it before. I'll make the music."[83] It was also Brown's first solo performance in fifteen years. Dancers traditionally use solo compositions to retrench, but Brown developed hers in order to explore new territory. Rauschenberg's suggestion to Brown shows his genius for startlingly new ideas but also his limitations in the dance field; that is, he has focused more on tasks conditioned by materials than inventions in sheer movement. As Brown observed, "He came up with the idea, but I had to make the dance."[84]

The dancer had reservations about the piece but enough respect for Rauschenberg and interest in a new idea to explore it. As she well knew, the first meaning of turning your back on an audience is rejection, so to her mind it would be very difficult to get beyond that message to address other implications.[85] Yet Brown was in a transitional period; her company was in repertory and new dancers were joining. It was an ideal moment for her to work on a solo performance. She had also been reading post-modern texts about the female gaze in art and advertising. While she found the texts themselves overwrought, she was interested in the idea of the averted female gaze in traditional painting as representing submissiveness and how the absence of eye contact could be used for other meanings.[86]

Brown decided that she would "accept" Rauschenberg's idea, write the best solo that she could, and simply turn it around. Brown recalls that when she first danced an early version of the piece she nearly cried because it was so difficult to lose eye contact with the audience. More serious issues arose when she tried the choreography on stage. During a tour with access to a proscenium, Brown had one of her dancers execute a trial run of the dance, noting that "everything looks different on stage."[87] To her, the dance appeared "exclusive, like I was busy with something upstage, and it looked indulgent."[88] Brown realized that taking a dance that was full of interesting turns and simply rotating it so that the dancer's back faced the audience yielded her worst fear, the appearance that she had rejected the audience. Subsequently, she re-choreographed *If You Couldn't See Me* so that the turns are truncated rather than completed. Throughout the dance, she launches into turns that could result in facing the audience, but then she does not execute them. She stops the turns mid-course and converts them into other types of movements. Brown noted, "For the second half of developing the dance I really paid attention to the back and discovered a wealth of new material."[89]

The movements in *If You Couldn't See Me* are based around weight redistribution throughout the body (see fig. 91). The spine is the center and the dress that Rauschenberg designed, with its low-cut back, emphasizes this fact. Movements are begun with a twist of the hips, swinging gesture of the arms or extension of one leg. While the movements are characteristic of Brown, they have never appeared as fully expressive as here. With huge sweeping movements of her limbs, Brown appears to be reaching deeply into the space around her. Often the full extension of both arms will be accompanied by a jump into space. In several of the movements, Brown, while balancing on one leg, bends at nearly a right angle and reaches with both arms and her other leg into the depth of the stage space. For a number of the truncated turns, Brown pivots and sweeps one leg in an arc across the axis of her body in a movement that should propel her into a turn. As the leg attains the far edge of the arc, she propels her upper body and her arms in the opposite direction, countering the force of the turn and moving her in exactly the reverse direction that we expect. The pace of the dance is kept relatively slow and reaching gestures are often held for several moments.

Rauschenberg has called *If You Couldn't See Me* one of Brown's most personal works, saying, "She has gotten just about as personal in her movements as anyone can afford. If she got any more intimate, it would be embarrassing."[90] While the dance is emotional, it is never overwrought or sentimental. The emotion in the dance comes from Brown's continued quest for new ideas. In this dance, that search is expressed by the relationship of her movements to the space around her. Instead of turning away from the audience, she is reaching into new territories as suggested by her stretches into the stage space. The lighting, executed by Spencer Brown, increases this effect. A bright spotlight occupies center stage, but Brown almost never enters it. Instead she remains on the periphery, lit indirectly and gesturing toward the black unknown on the rest of the stage.

The costume designed by Rauschenberg reveals the type of movements that occupy Brown during this dance. He had first considered an "open-work box" structure with gauze, but hearing Brown's ideas for the dance, designed a long one-piece garment of sheer fabric with a low back to emphasize the spine's essential function.[91] Slits up both sides of the long skirt allow full extension of the legs. The front and back panels of the skirt move in the breeze, highlighting the movements of the body, but they also hang between the legs, continuing the theme of the vertical axis formed by the spine. The theme of being centered but constantly expanding into new territories is highlighted by Rauschenberg's costume.

Rauschenberg also composed his first piece of music for *If You Couldn't See Me*. In keeping with the spirit of the dance, he intended the music to be evocative but not sentimental. He based the composition, in which the lingering notes seem to drift, on the fog rolling in and out of the bay at his Captiva Island studio.[92] Rauschenberg bought a synthesizer to compose the piece, and his score is related to Cage's compositions, especially that for *Astral Converted (50″)*. Like Cage's, the piece is based on slow alternating patterns of chords and silences, with almost no overlap. As in Cage's, we can predict the character of the music but never specifically the next note pattern. In a manner similar to the truncated turns and extensions in Brown's dance, Rauschenberg's music features elongations of sound events but no resolutions. Brown was especially sensitive to this feature. Upon hearing the first draft of Rauschenberg's composition, she found it too nostalgic. She noted that his final version contained a more straightforward 5,5,5 structure and a $2\frac{1}{2}$ minute silence, which suited her evocations of the unexplored empty territory of her environment.[93] Unlike Cage's composition for *Astral Converted (50″)*, Rauschenberg's piece relies less on pitch variations than on color changes. Because there are few pitch contrasts the music is less startling than Cage's and instead provides a melodious background of drifting sounds for Brown's dance. Rauschenberg commented that he wished the music to be "neither aggressive not apologetic."[94]

If You Couldn't See Me shows Brown and Rauschenberg, accomplished artists in their respective fields, continuing to seek new modes of invention. In this particular case, Rauschenberg's provocative idea of dancing with one's back turned to the audience led Brown to a whole series of movement discoveries, while the music demonstrates his continued willingness to experiment in new media. The expressiveness, associated with searching for new horizons, that Brown exhibits in the dance is part of her overall development, but it also results from her close relationship to Rauschenberg. Brown has said, "The dance is finally a communication between Bob and me. He is sending me a gift, and it is expressive."[95]

*   *   *

On the whole, Rauschenberg's work with Brown demonstrates how seriously the artist takes both his involvement in dances and collaborative process. In contrast to the often secondary role of these activities in the Rauschenberg literature, they are essential to Rauschenberg's oeuvre. His situation with Brown was pivotal for both artists. They had shared common backgrounds that included exposure to Merce Cunningham's discoveries about chance procedures and the separation of various media involved in dance performance, yet they both had sought to go beyond Cunningham. The experimental freedom of the Judson Dance Theater group had been essential to them, and they had watched and participated in each other's early choreographic experiments. While Rauschenberg has always sought "collaborators," including his studio assistants, engineers, and crafts people from a wide variety of cultures, they have seldom been his creative equals, as Rauschenberg certainly regards Brown.

Accordingly, because of their common backgrounds and the respect in which Rauschenberg holds Brown's works, his collaborations with her show his intent to understand the essential ideas behind her dances while never sacrificing his own artistic identity. Whether the dance involved the notion of simultaneous, seemingly unrelated, events as in *Set and Reset* or the mysterious poise of *Astral Converted (50″)*, Rauschenberg has attempted to cut to the core of Brown's choreography. His design procedures show him modifying and refining ideas as his understanding of each dance grew. In his visual presentations, he has tried neither to overwhelm the choreography nor be subservient to it. Instead Rauschenberg pursued parallel ideas in his own media, and sought, like Brown, to challenge the staid traditions of the proscenium stage. The visual presentations and the dances are separate but significantly related to one another. As such, the entire dance experience aims simultaneously at unity and variety.

Both Brown and Rauschenberg have grown through their collaborations. Since 1979, Brown has increased the degree of spontaneity and multiplicity in her dances, arguably a partial result of her increased contact with Rauschenberg. Rauschenberg's involvement with Brown has led to such specific changes in his works as the increased use of his own photographs following *Glacial Decoy*, and the discovery of the *Salvage* series from *Set and Reset*. More significantly, Rauschenberg's collaborations with Brown were an important part of the broadened artistic vision begun in the mid-1970s and encouraged by his first retrospective. The years between 1970 and 1974 had been hermetic in comparison with the rest of Rauschenberg's career. After the *Stoned Moon Series*, works that proposed a peaceful use of space technology, and the disappointing end to the 1960s expressed in his *Currents*, Rauschenberg had retreated to Captiva Island. By 1974 he had begun to travel and to make art inspired by foreign cultures, first in Israel then India. He had re-established contact with Merce Cunningham. In 1979, the year he accepted chairmanship of the Trisha Brown Dance Company, he also conceived of his most extensive art venture, the Rauschenberg Overseas Culture Interchange. Rauschenberg's collaborations with Brown, a powerful artistic equal whose works required his full inventive and critical attention, were an important step in the collaborative urges that have always been at the center of his art. It is certainly no coincidence that Rauschenberg linked one of the most politically charged of his ROCI venues, Moscow, with the performance of three Trisha Brown dances on which he collaborated, *Glacial Decoy*, *Set and Reset*, and *Astral Convertible*, an inclusion that emphatically restated the significance of his long history of collaborations with Brown.

five   ROCI in Chile

. . . a needed window on the world . . .

In 1984, Robert Rauschenberg began a seven-year and eleven-country art project, the Rauschenberg Overseas Culture Interchange (ROCI). His goal was to make art inspired by the eleven countries, to exhibit in each country the works motivated by it together with pieces created in the other venues, and thus to provide "a needed window on the world."[1] Of this complicated and ambitious venture, the most controversial venue was the second, Chile (1984–85; fig. 92). In Chile, Rauschenberg researched and exhibited his works in the midst of the dictator Augusto Pinochet's repressive regime, one that had become infamous for its human rights violations. Donald Saff, who oversaw the logistical operations for ROCI has recalled: "I never experienced as much anger about any artist's project with which I have been involved as about ROCI Chile. The reactions from friends, fellow artists, and others was absolute outrage that Bob would stage a show with Pinochet in control."[2]

Pinochet's violent overthrow of the elected government of Salvador Allende in 1973 had been followed by restrictions on free speech and the press and attacks on members of all opposing parties that resulted in the deaths of two to three thousand civilians. During the late 1970s, the violence had subsided with the repression of opposition to the government, and Chile had undergone a period of financial prosperity that limited further protests. But in the early 1980s, shortly before Rauschenberg planned his Chile venture, the Chilean economy collapsed and protests again erupted that were met with increasingly violent reprisals by government forces. It was into this volatile situation that Rauschenberg stepped. Arriving in Santiago, he recalled being shocked to see the army everywhere and to "hear the sounds of gunfire in the streets."[3] Rauschenberg remained in Chile for fifteen key days during which a state of siege was declared by Pinochet.

As stated, Rauschenberg undertook the Chile project despite the misgivings of most of his friends and advisors, who thought that his willingness to make art about Chile and exhibit there would be seen as a gesture of support for the dictatorship. In fact, the crisis in Chile forced Rauschenberg to devise a strategy through which his art could be exhibited in the context of a repressive society. The manner in which he dealt with Chile became a model for his other ROCI activities, which included works made in the context of such regimes as Cuba and the former Soviet Union. It is the strategy that Rauschenberg developed and the manner in which he attempted to express his viewpoint within these conditions that are the topics of this chapter.

Out of his Chilean experiences, Rauschenberg made a number of key decisions. He determined that it was essential that he not be identified as a representative of the United States or indeed any interest group. Accordingly, he undertook total control of the financial as well as creative aspects of ROCI, and he and his staff avoided to the greatest degree possible using American government help in arranging their projects. Second, even in the situations of dictatorships, Rauschenberg determined that he would be a guest of the government and would be exhibited under their auspices. On one hand, this decision was a matter of practicality. In an oppressive regime, the opportunity to exhibit art outside of official venues was extremely limited or impossible. On the other, Rauschenberg became convinced that his most radical gesture would be to show new and controversial art in the context of official venues.[4] Saff recalled, "For Bob, the most insidious idea was to show his art in their own museum, to use the government bureaucracy itself to encourage new openness."[5] One of the events that most struck Rauschenberg during the early ROCI years was a report from Spain just as the Chile exhibition was being mounted. The Spanish intellectual and cultural community was impressed by the Chilean show because they remembered being cut off during the Franco era.[6] They found that isolation from information in the form of a cultural embargo hurt the people and favored the dictator, rather than having the opposite effect.[7]

Rauschenberg had to find a way to express his views in the art works, while still having them exhibited in the context of government sponsorship. In his words, the pieces created in Chile are "apolitical" but that does not mean that they are "bipartisan."[8] Rauschenberg developed pictorial modes that explored the social situation without making direct political comments; he sought to collect and expose information without overtly condemning the existing system. His fundamental principle became that openness and availability of information can lead to change; the works call attention to the social situation while promoting peace and understanding through communication between different segments of the population. Rauschenberg's attitude was directly inspired by the situation of distrust he found in Chile; as he recalled, "We met with the intellectuals and we met with the politicians. They all had nothing in common except mutual hatred, anger and fear."[9]

The ROCI/Chile works and subsequent ROCI projects were based on the artist's profound belief that art can be a "social force and a conduit for new ideas."[10] Thus, ROCI/Chile proposes not a partisan position but an awareness of issues. As Rauschenberg officially announced ROCI at a United Nations press conference, he expressed these goals:

> Art is educating, provocative, and enlightening even when not at first understood. The very creative confusion stimulates curiosity and growth, leading to trust and tolerance . . . It was not until I realized that it is the celebration of the differences between things that I became an artist who could see. I know ROCI could make this kind of looking possible.[11]

Before discussing the background for Rauschenberg's Chilean works, it is necessary to examine the overall history of ROCI.

As mentioned earlier, ROCI was the most ambitious project of Rauschenberg's career and perhaps one of the most challenging undertaken by any twentieth-century artist. The project entailed researching and exhibiting art in quick succession in eleven countries, many of which were underdeveloped or had politically repressive governments. In chronological order, the countries were Mexico, Chile, Venezuela, Tibet, China, Japan, Cuba, the USSR, Germany, Malaysia, and the United States. The duration of ROCI from its announcement at the United Nations until the final exhibition at the National Gallery of Art, Washington, D.C. was only seven years. While the details of arranging and financing ROCI proved to be excruciatingly difficult, the overall plan was straightforward. Rauschenberg would travel to each country learning in an abbreviated time as much as he could about its culture and collecting materials and photographic images from that country to use in his pieces. The works that he produced as a result of those experiences would be exhibited in the country along with a small contextual overview of Rauschenberg's career and selected work from the other ROCI venues. Thus, in a constantly changing succession of exhibitions, the people of each ROCI country would be exposed to Rauschenberg's ideas about their environment and his notions of other countries. Rauschenberg's goal was to share ideas between countries, a number of which had limited opportunities for international communication.

Theoretically, the schedule for ROCI adhered to the following sequence. ROCI's logistical coordinator Donald Saff traveled to targeted countries to evaluate the interest of possible hosts, search for locations for the ROCI exhibition in that country, arrange for contacts between Rauschenberg and key intellectual and cultural figures, and suggest an author for a catalogue essay in each country. If the preliminary results were positive, Rauschenberg visited the country for between ten and fifteen days. He traveled extensively to selected areas, taking photographs that would eventually be used in the works, and his assistants made videos for documentation. Rauschenberg met with dignitaries and with local people. He also worked with local artists and artisans, often investigating new materials that were distinctive to that area. Afterwards, Rauschenberg returned to his Captiva studio to create the works. During that time he also supervised and attended the ROCI exhibition held in the previous country in which he had worked, and Saff and the artist's staff scouted out the next ROCI location. For the exhibition in each country, Rauschenberg personally supervised the installation. At each exhibition opening, he participated in events that ranged from formal dinners to open meetings with students. As part of ROCI, one work from each exhibition was given to the host country, and one work was given to the National Gallery of Art, Washington, D.C. to form a ROCI study collection there.

The origins for ROCI lie deep in Rauschenberg's career and world-view. Conceptually, the worldwide aspirations of ROCI began with the artist's participation in the world tour of the Merce Cunningham Dance Company during 1964. The itinerary throughout Europe and Asia that included thirty cities such as Paris, Vienna, Venice, Prague, Delhi, Chandigarh, Bangkok, Tokyo, and Osaka introduced Rauschenberg to an international cultural perspective. At the same time as that tour, Rauschenberg was awarded the Grand Prize in Painting in the Venice Biennial. As a result of this extensive travel and of his first substantial international recognition, Rauschenberg began to view himself with international commitments and interests. In 1973 he traveled overseas for the first time specifically to work with artisans abroad. This project, Pages and Fuses, involved shaped and cast works from paper pulp made at Moulin à Papier Richard de Bas in Ambert, France, an area that had produced handmade paper since the fourteenth century. The French collaboration led to activities that were more fully developed in ROCI. In May 1974, Rauschenberg was scheduled to have an exhibition at the Israel Museum in Jerusalem. In preparation for the show, the artist lived at the Jerusalem Foundation's Mishkenot Sha'ananim, a residence for artists and scholars, where he spent three weeks gathering materials for the sculptures titled Made in Israel. From this event, the idea for gathering material from a foreign culture for art works that explore that culture was born.

In 1975 Rauschenberg worked for a month at an ashram in Ahmadabad, India, a textile center and the birthplace of Mahatma Gandhi, creating Bones and Unions – the invitation had come as a result of contacts Rauschenberg made on the Cunningham world tour. Rauschenberg's Indian experience highlighted the stimulation that foreign cultures could provide because not only did it result in the pieces executed there but colorful Indian silks also influenced his Jammers series (1975–76). His 1976 retrospective at the National Collection of American Art, Washington, D.C. further increased the social role that he envisioned for his art. At that exhibition, he was praised by director Joshua Taylor as "an artist who is also a great citizen, who is engaged in political dialogue and discourse, takes public stands . . ."[12] With these events in his immediate background, Rauschenberg first conceived during the fall of 1978 a traveling overseas exhibition of his work.

The final and perhaps most significant event that led Rauschenberg toward ROCI was the 1982 experience of working at the Xuan Paper Mill in Jingxian, China. Through the print atelier Gemini G.E.L., he was invited to work in the Anhui province of China, an area that housed the world's oldest paper mill. The project resulted in Rauschenberg's Seven Characters, seven suites of seventy-four works each containing silk, ribbon, paper pulp relief, ink, and gold on handmade Xuan paper. But the experience of the insular character of the society in China's provinces shocked Rauschenberg. The episode also demonstrated his ability and that of his staff to work despite the most severe bureaucratic restrictions. When Rauschenberg and his colleagues arrived, they were held for days in the Yellow Mountains by Chinese officials. So afraid were the officials, for reasons never explained, of letting them work at the paper mill that they even had all posters referring to the town where the mill was located removed from the areas near where Rauschenberg stayed. Rauschenberg recalled:

> There we sat getting frustrated because I had only limited time to do my project . . . They kept us in the Yellow Mountains or were trying to keep us there one day too long. I refused to stay. I don't know what I was going to do but I refused to stay. I wanted to get to work. They had no choice. Also it was one of the first times you could be on a bus and stop it and get off in these places that had been closed to foreigners for forty years.[13]

Don Saff remember that when the Rauschenberg team finally got to Jingxian they discovered to their horror that the residents could not travel without permission and that they seldom got more than twenty-five miles from their village:

> In China the idea developed that the project would have to extend beyond simply a retrospective and it would have to have some relevance to countries with sensitive problems. By the time we arrived back in Beijing, the concept was there. You can effect change by taking imagery that they use in a very traditional way and you use it in your own way. Perhaps in doing so you give them the license to think more openly."[14]

Rauschenberg commented, "I think they were really just beaten down. They had exhausted any initiative, any hope of anything changing. Once you kill the curiosity, everything else goes."[15] He recalled that the most potent symbol of the entire China trip was a photograph that he took of a water buffalo that had been blindfolded with an old rag and was walking around in circles to power a mixing machine in a brick factory. As Rauschenberg commented, "that was his whole life. If one isn't moved by that . . ."[16] It was through these experiences that Rauschenberg concluded that ROCI had to be an evolving exhibition based on the culture of each country. He conceived the plan to go to each country and immerse himself in the imagery and materials of that society and through his interpretation to try to "create an opening in how they saw themselves and how they saw others."[17]

The major criticism that has been leveled against ROCI was that Rauschenberg could not possibly learn enough about a country to represent it accurately in the time allotted, and that the works created were too much Rauschenberg and not enough the culture of the host country.[18] A corollary of this argument is that the artist brought with him on each trip such a powerful set of American-based democratic ideals combined with the prejudices of the European and American avant-garde movements that he could not fully appreciate disparate cultural and social values. For instance, in China, the imitation of a master's work with only subtle variations, an idea essential to Chinese art but anathema to the European avant-garde, was lost on Rauschenberg.

The opposite argument, however, may also be made: that Rauschenberg's lack of deep familiarity with the different cultures allowed him a fresh approach. The immediacy and intensity of his exposure to non-familiar situations yielded observations and insights that might have been lost on those numbed by repetitive experiences. From this perspective, Rauschenberg's disposition toward lateral thinking and intuitive working procedures, explored in the first chapter, is essential to the manner in which ROCI was conceived and executed.

In any case, Rauschenberg's approach to ROCI, whether sound or flawed, was consistent with his art-making career as demonstrated in the following aspects. Once underway, the speed of ROCI was a prime feature; Rauschenberg shifted rapidly from visiting foreign countries in order to collect information to creating the works to installing exhibitions, sometimes overlapping as many as three countries at once. There was little time for reflection. Instead, the artist relied on instinct and immediate response, as has been his custom throughout his career. As always, Rauschenberg believed that surface knowledge, rather than exhaustive research, provided fresh perspectives. In accordance with the interactive and performance aspects of his work, he felt that all the experiences of organizing ROCI, not just the art objects themselves, were parts of the work. In this regard, Rauschenberg wrote to his friend Pontus Hulten, the newly appointed director of the Los Angeles Museum of Contemporary Art, "I conceive of the tour as a giant creative piece on the hoof, supported by intrigue, deceptions, misunderstandings, and para-political maneuvers."[19]

Another way in which ROCI was in keeping with Rauschenberg's career was the heavy reliance on collaborators. These individuals ranged from his staff, who organized and coordinated events, to local craftspeople who introduced the artist to new materials and techniques, to museum directors and even political figures who made the exhibitions possible. Despite the collaborative aspects, Rauschenberg insisted on maintaining final and unequivocal control of the product, whether it was the creation of individual works, the hanging of the exhibitions, or the production of the accompanying catalogues.

The features just listed were simultaneously ROCI's strengths and its weaknesses. The personal collaborative relationships and understandings that Rauschenberg had traditionally relied upon in his smaller projects did not translate well into the enormous scale and managerial complexity that ROCI required, and the speed at which ROCI proceeded made it difficult to structure coherently. At certain points, the political intrigues, financial debacles, and misunderstandings that plagued ROCI were so severe that Rauschenberg held the project together only by sheer determination. Writing an interim summary of ROCI's history in 1987, Donald Saff concluded that despite outstanding artistic success because the tour had already visited six countries,

> The result has been ten years [including pre-ROCI preparation] of uncertain efforts, promises unrealized and a general lack of cohesive organization. To date, in spite of efforts pursued by many individuals at enormous expense to Mr. Rauschenberg, there is no substantial sponsorship for the program nor are there presently any prospects for such outside contributions.[20]

The ground rules originally set by Rauschenberg for financing ROCI included abstention from any form of government support and avoidance of financial relationships that would dilute his control of the project. Rauschenberg demanded carte blanche discretion in the utilization of all funds. This decision made it difficult to enlist significant support either from private institutions or from a sponsoring museum, whose directors felt they would in some way profit materially or have rights to exercise control in the evolution of the project. Despite these restrictions, which one advisor to Rauschenberg characterized as making fund-raising "a thousand-to-one effort," Rauschenberg went so far as to construct a list of companies from whom he would not accept funding because he did not approve of their products and public policy stances. ROCI's inability to secure funding led to serious difficulties in fixing firm exhibition dates and locations. Also, in its early stages, ROCI had no clear managerial structure. As mentioned above, the informal relationships and professional acquaintances that Rauschenberg had relied on so successfully in smaller projects did not serve the scale and complexity of ROCI, and because of his involvement in the studio the artist was unable to exercise the day-to-day supervision of events that was required to give ROCI cohesiveness. As a result, exploratory ideas were presented to potential sponsors as if they were concrete agreements, giving the entire project, in Saff's words, "an air of instability and unpredictability."[21]

During the conception of ROCI, Rauschenberg and his staff recognized the advantage of having a major sponsoring museum. They first approached the Fort Worth Art Museum, but that endeavor was abandoned in 1978 and interest was directed toward the Los Angeles Museum of Contemporary Art. The curator Ann Livet, who had been working as a coordinator for ROCI, had just accepted a position at the museum where the new director was Rauschenberg's longtime friend Pontus Hulten, as noted. In spite of these personal connections, the relationship with the museum is illustrative of the early problems with ROCI. Once contacted, the museum proceeded to search for venues and solicit funds as if the arrangements with Rauschenberg had been finalized, which they had not. Eventually, it appeared to Rauschenberg that Los Angeles MOCA felt obliged to play a decisive role in the decision-making process. Materials were sent by the museum to a variety of potential sponsors which gave the impression that Los Angeles MOCA was the supporting institution and that site selections had been made and were in the process of being confirmed. Outlines of the venues and tentative dates were presented as if the tour was planned and in place, which it was not. Finally, in February of 1982, Rauschenberg sent a letter to Hulten terminating their negotiations, stating his philosophy concerning ROCI's independence, and asserting his sole control of all aspects of the project from its organizational structure to the subject matter of its art:

> If you have wondered about the amount of time that has passed since I received your letter initiating contractual areas of responsibility, rights and restrictions, all of course to be discussed and mutually agreed on with adjustments, it is because I have realized that working in and through an institution will inhibit all of the inprocess, spontaneous reactions and decisions that cannot be filtered through a bureaucracy or legal contract.
>
> It seems to me that if the RR Round the World Tour is going to succeed or fail, the entire exhibition has to be a series of my decisions. I want to assume full responsibility. I am setting up my own foundation for this project only.[22]

Following the breakdown of negotiations with Los Angeles MOCA and the unavailability of outside funding for the project, Rauschenberg determined that he would provide the funding necessary to initiate ROCI. He and his staff began to organize corporations designed solely for administrating and financing the tour. In 1982 Rauschenberg's friends from the corporate world, including his accountant and advisor Rubin Gorewitz, Theodore Kheel, who was then President of the Center for Non-Broadcast Television, and Frank Saunders, the Vice President for Corporate Relations and Communications at Philip Morris, put together a corporate structure through which ROCI could be managed. However, confusions about whether the corporation could seek non-profit status and thus whether donations to it could be tax-deductible were never resolved. As a result, the corporate structure was never used and funding continued to be provided solely by Rauschenberg.

With the idea of bringing ROCI to Italy, Count Giuseppe Panza, who had made a fortune in real estate and manufacturing and had a major art collection specializing in the 1960s and 1970s, was contacted. Panza expressed a willingness to be on the ROCI board and suggested that financial support from such companies as Fiat,

Martini & Rossi, and Olivetti would be forthcoming, yet there were no positive results. Also notable for their absence of support for ROCI were Rauschenberg's longtime friends and dealers Leo Castelli and Ileana Sonnabend. In fact, Castelli was quoted as saying that monies due Rauschenberg had been delayed because he worried that Rauschenberg might "waste" them on ROCI.[23]

In the meantime, Rauschenberg had contacted Frederick R. Weisman, an entrepreneur and American art collector, and received a promise for funding that would support ROCI. Contracts were drawn up with the Frederick R. Weisman Foundation of Art, and Rauschenberg agreed to exchange art for three million dollars of support from the foundation. Since it seemed that funding for ROCI had become a certainty, Rauschenberg decided to announce formally the launch of ROCI in the Delegates Lounge at the United Nations on December 13, 1984. The arrangements to present ROCI at the United Nations had been made by Theodore Kheel through the American ambassador Jean Kirkpatrick, and the day before the announcement Rauschenberg had presented a print to Secretary General Xavier de Cuellar to mark the occasion. As final preparations for the ceremony were being made, Rauschenberg and his staff discovered that Weisman disapproved of the press release, which he felt did not sufficiently emphasize the funding provided by his foundation. Through his agents, Weisman demanded a rewritten press release and drafted a legal statement of joint control of ROCI's future operations. Literally as Rauschenberg was arriving at the United Nations to make his presentation, he decided that all arrangements with Weisman had to be severed. Thus Rauschenberg's announcement at the United Nations was made in the absence of any funding to support ROCI. He recalled:

> My United Nations announcement, which I admit was not too soberly presented, happened on the very day that three million dollars' worth of ROCI support, for which I had exchanged works, was taken away in a dispute. I had to pay for ROCI again later with works. So I got confused and disillusioned, yet I knew ROCI was good. So I guess all those years traveling with Merce Cunningham and working with the Judson Dance Group paid off. The old idea that the show must go on really proved itself, because the show did go on.[24]

Immediately after the United Nations announcement, the funding situation was so bleak and the spirits of Rauschenberg and his staff were so low that discussions were held about terminating ROCI after its first venue in Mexico City, the only stop for which definite arrangements had been made.[25] While attempts were made over the next several years to interest a variety of corporations in the support of ROCI, the die had been cast. Rauschenberg's desire to control the project artistically and conceptually made such sponsorship impossible to find. Every company that was approached wanted to use ROCI in some way to enhance its image and to control decisions made during the project. As a result of this painful and chaotic period of failed negotiations with potential patrons, Rauschenberg came to believe that ROCI's credibility depended on avoiding corporate or government ties. So he took a positive view of the string of financial disasters:

Absolutely nobody was interested, which was terrific because, if you have a really thorough rejection, then you have to act realistically. As I said, I think our failures in making ROCI run smoothly gave it a lot more honor and integrity. With the exceptions of contributions from personal friends, we never took a dime from anyone. That protected us from one side of criticism.[26]

In order to fund ROCI personally, Rauschenberg mortgaged his studio and home on Captiva Island and, more significantly, decided to sell paintings that had been given to him by his closest artist friends. The decision was terrible because the paintings were not simply objects but key memories of his own early history. For those attached to visual culture, even in ways less thorough than Rauschenberg's deep involvement, such works become like family members; they are containers for one's past. In Rauschenberg's reminiscences, the personal associations are clear:

> Yes, I sold my big black and white Cy Twombly that he had done in my studio on Fulton Street. And I sold the first cartoon, *Alley Oop*, the first non-monocolored Jasper Johns. That had a kind of family history because he lived above me and came down one Sunday morning and said, "I can't paint more than one color at a time." And that's serious; that's a serious problem.

> One of the other pieces I hated to part with was a very early Andy Warhol, *Dick Tracy*, but I had to see what could bring the most money. I placed all three in important collections where the public has access. That fact, too, helped me not to miss them.[27]

Rauschenberg's decision to part with these personal objects demonstrates his absolute commitment to ROCI. Simultaneously, he decided that there would be no sales of ROCI works during the tour so that he could not be accused of financial motivations.[28] As mentioned above, Rauschenberg discovered that his financial control of ROCI became an essential condition for the integrity of the project because it reduced suspicions that there were hidden backers who controlled his art and stood to gain from the exhibitions:

> I think it did prevent a lot of confusion about the function of ROCI because, in dialogues with the public in various countries, one of the first questions was, "Who is paying for this? Who is behind this?" The whole world is very suspicious, still, even after ROCI. Somehow ROCI maintained my integrity by my being able to say, "I did it through my work or selling my collection of favorite things." Continuing ROCI was definitely worth it and this was a decision I had to re-make every time that I parted with something that I loved so much.[29]

Naturally, the artist hoped to recoup some of his losses by selling ROCI works after the world tour ended, but the sales of these works, perhaps because they are quite large and their imagery is so heavily based on foreign cultures, have never been strong in either the American or European markets.[30]

One important logistical arrangement did work out just as ROCI began: the project secured museum sponsorship. While Rauschenberg suggested approaching the Metropolitan Museum of Art or the Museum of Modern Art in New York as sponsors, Donald Saff favored the National Gallery of Art. In January 1985, Rauschenberg gave a talk on ROCI at the National Gallery and was interviewed by the curator Nan Rosenthal. Meanwhile Saff and Rauschenberg's archivist David White met with Jack Cowart, the curator of twentieth-century art, to discuss the possibility of the National Gallery hosting the final American venue of the ROCI tour. A major stumbling block was that the National Gallery had never permitted a one-person exhibition of the works of a living artist. Once Rauschenberg learned of this archaic rule, he became more determined to break a precedent that implicitly indicated that artists did not merit significant attention from the nation's museum until they were dead.[31] Jack Cowart conceived the idea of Rauschenberg donating a body of work from the ROCI project, which would strengthen the museum's collection in contemporary art, as a way of circumventing the prohibition on an exhibition of a living artist.[32] By the middle of January, Carter Brown, the Director of the National Gallery, had taken Rauschenberg's proposal to the board of the museum, and they had agreed to support the exhibition, in principle, if a major donation from the ROCI project were made to the National Gallery.

Initially, the directors of the National Gallery had been suspicious that Rauschenberg would donate only less significant pieces so they demanded that Cowart have control over the selection process. The first work that Rauschenberg donated, however, was the *Copperhead Grande* (1985; see fig. 99). As discussed below, this work is certainly one of the most significant pieces done during ROCI/Chile. After that the National Gallery realized that Rauschenberg's intent was not to hoard works but to create a study collection, and it allowed him to make the remainder of the choices unimpeded. In the context of these gifts to the museum, Rauschenberg conceived of a small informal gathering in which the ambassadors from all ROCI host countries could meet. His thought, like the overall idea for ROCI, was that bringing these diplomats together in an unusual context might foster discussion and understanding. Rauschenberg noted, "I didn't think I was going to create peace or anything, but perhaps just getting them together in a new context would be good."[33]

The Rauschenberg Overseas Culture Interchange opened first at the Museo Rufino Tamayo in Mexico City on April 17, 1985. Mexico had been chosen as a starting point because of the geographic ease of access to the country and its relatively good relationship with the United States. The exhibition was an enormous success; it included twelve new Mexican works featuring collage and silkscreen images of scenes around Mexico City, all in hot Mexican colors, as well as a selection of Rauschenberg's other works since 1972. The exhibition was organized so that the thousands of Mexicans who visited the opening saw the works from their own country first. The stone walls of the Tamayo museum echoed with live saxophone music played by Dickie Landry. Rauschenberg commented that he found the exhibition opening like avant-garde theater. A poem in the catalogue was written by Octavio Paz, who had just won the Nobel Prize for literature, and Colombia's Nobel Laureate Gabriel García Márquez visited the show just before the formal opening. Ironically, the success of this first ROCI exhibition might have carried the seeds of demise for all of ROCI. Nearly all of Rauschenberg's friends advised him that the events in Mexico were so perfect that they filled ROCI's goals; and that in view of the logistical and financial difficulties ahead, it was time to stop.

Rauschenberg's response was to return to his studio in Captiva to begin working on the Chilean pieces. From the beginning Chile had been a situation opposite to Mexico. Saff, who went in early October 1984 to scout out the locale, recalled, "The night I arrived there was a riot. Tires were burning in the street and all of that. It was very frightening, but I never hesitated for a moment. It just seemed right."[34] He immediately contacted Rauschenberg, who was in retreat in Tobago devising the overall principles for ROCI that he would present at the United Nations, and urged him to make Chile the next venue for ROCI. Rauschenberg spent from October 25 until November 10 in Chile. As he later said, "I was here for the first time in October with my assistant, took a car and drove on as many roads as we could find, sometimes on no roads. I left Chile with my whole body filled with that country."[35]

Before discussing Rauschenberg's specific experiences in Chile and the works that resulted, some background on the country and the events into which Rauschenberg thrust himself is necessary. This summary attempts to duplicate the information that Rauschenberg would have had as he arrived. It is based on a "Briefing Paper" on Chile prepared for Rauschenberg by his staff and preserved in the ROCI archives.[36] That paper determined a number of the experiences that Rauschenberg sought in Chile, and in other cases its dearth of specific information allowed aspects of the country to startle the artist. The Briefing Paper opened with a discussion of the special geographic conditions of Chile by stating that the country is eighty percent mountainous land dropping into the sea and covers thirteen climatological regions. Interestingly, it emphasized the northern region, as opposed to the south, which has since been favored for popular ecological tours. It stated,

> The Atacama Desert is one of the driest areas in the world, a place few Chileans go . . . Contrary to the monochrome barrenness that most people expect, the landscape is spectacular, criss-crossing hills of all shapes and sizes and of many colors . . . On the Andean Plain shallow saline lakes form during the spring, and they are home to such unusual birds as enormous herons.

This description may partly account for Rauschenberg's unusual decision to spend six of his fifteen days in Chile touring the Atacama, an arduous journey from which even his Chilean friends tried to dissuade him, but one that resulted in prominent nature imagery in his ROCI/Chile works.

The Briefing Paper also assserted that the Chilean people seem very European compared with those of other South American countries but that the major native group is the Araucan people in south central Chile. Rauschenberg dedicated one of his Chilean works, the *Araucan Mastaba* (1985), to this group. The paper emphasized the special position of Santiago in Chile's infrastructure, highlighting the enormous size of the city and explaining that thirty-nine percent of the total Chilean population lives there. The paper pointed out that Santiago is the center of commerce and mentioned its classical architecture as well as skyscrapers, both of which appear in

Rauschenberg's Chilean works. But the huge shantytowns that ring the city were also discussed. While the paper did not describe the horrid squalor of the shantytowns or indicate that they were hotbeds of civil unrest, Rauschenberg discovered these facts first-hand when he visited and photographed them, against the advice of Chilean friends, and included those photographs in his works.

The Briefing Paper stressed the important role of the Roman Catholic church in Chile, accenting the fact that it had been an important social and moral force in the country since the 1930s. It pointed out that during the 1960s Chilean Catholic leaders gave tacit support to Salvador Allende, despite his Communist background, because of his enlightened social programs. During the Pinochet years, the Catholic Church had been often the only force aiding those who had suffered humans rights abuses. These statements and Rauschenberg's personal experiences in Chile had a profound impact. Rauschenberg's works throughout his career show a marked absence of Western religious themes, yet images from the Catholic church are by far the most common in his Chilean pieces.

While the Briefing Paper was reasonably detailed concerning the subjects just discussed, it was surprisingly brief about the political situation in Chile. It noted that in 1973 Pinochet took over the government from Allende in a violent coup and that Allende committed suicide. Only when he arrived in Chile did Rauschenberg find that nearly all of his liberal Chilean acquaintances believed Allende's death was an assassination, an event about which they remained bitter. The Briefing Paper went on to note that "significant human rights abuses" had occurred during Pinochet's years in power, but that "the situation had improved over the last several years and the United States was working toward a condition of normalcy in Chile."[37] The Briefing Paper's summary report of Pinochet's time in power and its mild ending left Rauschenberg unsuspecting of how devastating Chile's recent history had been and largely ignorant of how volatile was its current situation. Despite his discussions with Saff about the latter's experiences in Chile, Rauschenberg later confided, "If I had been aware of how dangerous things were there I might have stayed away, and that would have been a shame."[38]

As mentioned, the Briefing Paper did not discuss the extreme violence that marked Pinochet's initial assumption of power. Under Pinochet, the military junta put officers in all positions of power, and the government treated the legitimately elected Popular Unity Party, which was the Marxist-oriented party of Allende, not simply as a rival but as an enemy to be wiped out. The Chilean Congress was disbanded, news media were censored, books burned, the universities purged of any left-wing professors, union activities were banned, and most political parties outlawed. Communist leaders were hunted down, and thousands of civilians were murdered, jailed, tortured, brutalized, or exiled. Through the actions of Pinochet's secret police, the National Intelligence Directorate (DINA), all dissidents lived in fear of torture or murder. Rauschenberg learned from student radicals when he arrived in Chile that the common term used by both sides was "disappearance," because it was impossible to obtain any information about many of those taken away by the secret police, even to learn if they were dead or alive.

The Briefing Paper also did not point out that the "situation of normalcy" to which it referred was not a matter of resolution of the human rights abuses but rather based on Chile's spectacular economic growth during the mid-Pinochet years. Having felt that he had defeated his political enemies, Pinochet switched his attention to Chile's economy. Between 1976 and 1981 a combination of partly secured foreign loans, mostly from the United States, and increased export of non-traditional items produced what became commonly known as the "Chilean miracle."[39] On average, there was a yearly eight percent growth in Chile's economy. While this figure ignores the fact that unemployment was still in the double digits and that the poor lacked almost all social services, the regime felt so confident that it moved to legitimize itself with a plebiscite that established Pinochet's "constitutional" power until 1989. The economic assistance to Chile increased spectacularly during the Nixon and Ford presidencies. Despite sour relations during the Carter years, because of that administration's emphasis on human rights, Chilean economic success remained dominant in American thinking. During the Reagan presidency, increased support of economically successful right-wing dictatorships returned Chile to full American good graces.

In 1982, however, the seemingly invincible Pinochet regime was shaken by a severe economic crisis. An economy that had been growing substantially had a fourteen percent decline that year, and unemployment rose to fifteen percent. The Chilean peso was devalued by twenty-three percent and some prices of goods rose by fifty-five percent.[40] In May of 1983, the country's union leaders called for a "National Social Protest." The first major protest since Pinochet had come to power, it left two protesters dead and two hundred arrested. Rudolfo Sequel, who was head of the copper workers' union, emerged as leader of the strike. It is no coincidence that Rauschenberg chose to visit the copper mines in northern Chile during his research trip one year later and to make the majority of his Chilean works on large copper sheets in order "to show," as he put it "my hope for Chile."[41] On June 14, 1983 a national day of protest with work stoppages all over the country was called and hundreds of thousands of people responded. Up to this point the protesters had been relatively peaceful and the Chilean army had shown some degree of restraint. The early marches were dubbed the "pots and pans" protests because of the banging of kitchen utensils that accompanied them. Pinochet appeared on television to announce that he would not resign, and a coalition of student and union leaders called for monthly national protest days. At this point, it appeared to many Chileans that Pinochet might be toppled peacefully.

By early 1984, the year that Rauschenberg arrived, the level of violence had increased radically as a result of organized terrorist activities from members of the radical left, who were convinced that Pinochet could only be eliminated by violent overthrow. On March 2, nineteen car bombs exploded in the cities of Santiago, Valparaiso, and Concepción. On March 18, eighteen bombs exploded in six cities, and on March 31 the bombing of a police bus in Santiago coincided with bombs set at the country's power stations, an event that caused black-outs in Santiago as well as seven hundred miles of central Chile. These events gave the government the excuse it needed for violent reprisals. Commando raids were launched against all Communist centers, and any protest was met with increasing hostility. It was into this situation that Rauschenberg arrived to research ROCI/Chile between October 25 and November 10, 1984.

Rauschenberg flew into Chile with Terry Van Brunt, his studio assistant, and he was greeted by Saff and his assistant Brenda Woodward, translator Monica Gelcich, and Mario Stein, the representative for Schenker-Elmac shipping, the agency ROCI used throughout its South American venues. Saff and Woodward only spent the evening with Rauschenberg and departed for Buenos Aires on the next day to negotiate another ROCI venue. Stein acted as the major contact person for Rauschenberg's time in Santiago.[42] As Stein conducted the group through the airport, he observed that the terrorist activities had been so prevalent over the past several months that the airport was heavily guarded by soldiers with machine guns. Rauschenberg recalled on the way into Santiago that the road was lined with armed military convoys, and he could hear occasional shots being fired in the distance.[43] He did not yet know that these shots were the sounds of early armed incursions into the shantytowns that he later visited. Their first night in Santiago, the group had to retire early because a nightly curfew was in effect.

In fact, Rauschenberg had come at one of the most tense moments in Chile's recent history. On October 26, the day after he arrived, a car bomb exploded in the center of Santiago near the building where Pinochet gave his annual "state of the union" address, injuring four people. During a day of national protest on October 29, two young protesters were killed in Santiago by the police, and twelve car bombs exploded in cities throughout Chile. As a result of these events, 140 people were arrested and sent into internal exile in secret prisons in northern Chile. On November 1, the Roman Catholic Archbishop of Santiago issued the church's first public condemnation of human rights and civil liberties abuses since Pinochet had come to power. Pinochet issued sweeping restrictions on the freedom of the press on November 2, and on November 5 Chile's entire cabinet resigned so that, in their words, "the President [Pinochet] can make whatever decisions he believes necessary."[44] As a result, on November 6 Pinochet declared "a state of siege," the equivalent of martial law, allowing him to use the military at will and to hold all terrorist suspects indefinitely without trial.[45]

To a visitor just arrived, the depth of the impending crisis could not be immediately absorbed. When Stein took Rauschenberg on his first tour of the city, he recalled, the artist's initial reaction was to the modernity and cleanliness of Santiago. "I took Bob to see the Santiago subway, you can eat off of the spotless floors and impeccably clean trains, everybody's clean, well dressed, smelling of Armani, crime zero, drugs zero."[46] To Stein's surprise at the end of this initial excursion, Rauschenberg engaged him in a discussion about the nature of oppression. Stein recalled that Rauschenberg's basic question was, "Can you feel so safe and still be repressed, and what did you have to give up for this safety?"[47] Rauschenberg photographed the shining skyscrapers of downtown Santiago, and those photographs appear in his Chilean work *Caryatid Cavalcade II* (see fig. 98). But even here they are merged with an image of Santiago Cathedral which is reflected in their surfaces. More than just a clever photograph, Rauschenberg revealed in this picture that he was already thinking of the moderating force of the Catholic church and its call for peace in Chile. On the day of this photograph, the archbishop, who celebrated mass at the cathedral shown in Rauschenberg's photograph, made an official plea for a peaceful resolution of the growing conflict in Chile. Five days later, as mentioned above, the archbishop with his fellow bishops published a letter to the government calling for an end to human rights abuses.[48]

After seeing briefly the center of Santiago, Rauschenberg was more interested, as Stein remembers, in the small shops and the street vendors on the edge of the business district or, in Rauschenberg's words as Stein remembers them, "everyday people who were the heart of Chile."[49] A wide range of the images appearing in ROCI/Chile, like the worker carrying a stack of boxes, one of which is labeled "Chile," in *Altar Peace Chile* (see figs. 93 and 104) and people in front of a roadside shop in *Copperhead Bite IX*, document this interest. Stein explained to Rauschenberg that many of the individuals whom he photographed lived in the shantytowns surrounding Santiago and that their jobs, which were often only several hours per week, were grouped as "informal occupations" by the government to keep the unemployment figures lower. Stein then spent the next two days trying to dissuade Rauschenberg from visiting the shantytowns.[50]

On his second day in Santiago, Rauschenberg visited the Museo Nacional de Bellas Artes where he was planning to hold the ROCI exhibition. He was delighted by the look of the museum, a turn-of-the-twentieth-century Neoclassical structure that had giant re-creations of the caryatids from the Acropolis in Athens supporting its second-story porch. These caryatids appear in a number of Rauschenberg's Chilean works, and they are the centerpiece of *Caryatid Cavalcade I* (see fig. 97). The interior of the museum contained a hundred-foot-long courtyard covered with a glass and iron-truss vault that Rauschenberg noted "looked so good that it should have been designed by Gustave Eiffel."[51] Rauschenberg decided to show his Chilean works in this gallery. In fact, the space was so important to him that when it was partly damaged by an earthquake in March 1985, shortly before his exhibition, he paid to have it restored. Rauschenberg's meeting with the director of the museum, Nena Ossa, was of a different order. While Ossa was enthusiastic about the exhibition, Rauschenberg recognized her immediately as a civil servant and thus part of the established order. Ossa recalls, "He was always very friendly on the outside. He kissed me and made a fuss, but I was aware from the beginning that there were certain things I wasn't being told, things that should be done without me there. This was especially true after he had discussions with José Donoso."[52]

On his third day in Santiago, Rauschenberg met with José Donoso, the most prominent Chilean novelist of the twentieth century and a staunch opponent of the Pinochet regime. Donoso was suggested by Don Saff and chosen by Rauschenberg to write the catalogue essay for ROCI/Chile precisely because of his combination of public celebrity and his dissident status, which reinforced the message of change delivered by Rauschenberg's Chilean paintings. In 1980 Donoso had returned to

Chile after nearly twenty years abroad in order to face the situation in his homeland. Shortly before coming back, he wrote the novel *Casa de campo* which was an allegory about the collapse of Chile, complete with fragments of speeches by Allende and Pinochet. The story ends with a leveling of all social orders that metaphorically calls for cooperation in the face of national chaos, a message also central to Rauschenberg's Chilean works. Donoso's play *Sueños de mala muerte* (1982) captured the despair that hung over the country which was strangled by a dictatorship and economic depression. Donoso was thus well positioned to communicate to Rauschenberg the emotional gravity of the situation in Chile.

The translator Monica Gelcich remembers that the primary discussion between Rauschenberg and Donoso concerned the location of the exhibition, but this discussion, like an allegory, took on added levels of meaning.[53] Donoso did not understand why Rauschenberg wanted to show his ROCI works in the national museum, a location that seemed to indicate support for Pinochet. He suggested holding it in a church because, in his view, the church was the only institution that the people still respected.[54] Rauschenberg remembers, "I had to persuade him like crazy . . ."[55] Rauschenberg's argument was that the church did not need the art. The translator remembers Rauschenberg repeating over and over that the museum needed the art whereas the church did not. To her mind, the "need" that she was being asked to translate was not about filling space on the walls, it concerned "a deeper idea of necessity." María del Pilar, artist, critic, and Donoso's wife, recalled that Rauschenberg and Donoso "spoke a great deal about open exchange of ideas and creative freedom."[56] It seemed to her that "without a direct statement being made, the two men had reached an understanding about common goals."[57]

Donoso's essay for the ROCI exhibition followed the lead that his conversations with Rauschenberg set. It discussed the need for receptivity to new ideas and the willingness to change, and Donoso labeled Rauschenberg as the "Great Transgressor." The essay examined his art in terms that do not make specific reference to Pinochet's rule in Chile, yet the underlying message is that Rauschenberg's art encourages fresh evaluation. Donoso began: "Views age easily. From time to time they have to be revitalized, exposed to horror, or to scandal, or to the tremblings of renewed tenderness, to prove if they can still bound over their shadows and enter the world of the imagination." In this context, "everything in Rauschenberg's art, needs to threaten us from time to time with its definitive crumbling down." For Donoso, Rauschenberg as the Great Transgressor "rises against the single history" and "proposes to turn us from mere contemplators into transgressors also . . ."[58]

While all of Donoso's language is couched in general terms of formal and visual appreciation for Rauschenberg's works, his call for historical re-evaluation is clear. The approach that Donoso took in his essay was comparable to that found in Rauschenberg's Chilean works. By presenting a wide variety of information in these works and by juxtaposing the incongruities in Chilean society, Rauschenberg expressed his belief that openness can lead to change. He did so without specifically condemning the existing political and social structure. In essence Donoso's essay and Rauschenberg's paintings follow parallel courses.

As part of their discussion, Donoso suggested to Rauschenberg that he should meet students in Chile and learn their views. Also, Rauschenberg had already developed the idea that he might use copper as one material in his Chilean works, and Donoso, through his daughter who was also involved in the visual arts, promised to arrange a meeting with an artist at the university who worked in copper. Donoso was well aware that the university was a seat of much of the unrest in Chile and that Rauschenberg would be exposed to the imperatives for political change in a forceful manner.[59] Stein offered to take Rauschenberg to the Universidad de Chile the next day. Rauschenberg's photographs of the university buildings appear in *Caryatid Cavalcade I* and other works. While to the non-Chilean viewer these buildings appear as sedate Neoclassical structures, any resident of Santiago would immediately recognize them as representing one of the locales of radicalism during this period. At the university, Rauschenberg first met with the artist Benito Rojo, who was an expert in treating and enameling copper surfaces. Rauschenberg was especially interested in the acids that Rojo used to patinate surfaces. In a morning, Rauschenberg learned of a variety of acids and other tarnishing agents that would discolor and corrode copper, giving effects that were visually rich but also dark and foreboding in character. It was this use of acids on copper sheets that came to dominate Rauschenberg's *Copperhead Bite* series, his largest group of Chilean works.

During the afternoon, Rauschenberg attempted to meet with students whose names Donoso had given him. He discovered that they were "terribly afraid" and in his words, "They told me of the 'disappearances.' They had lost friends and family members and wondered if they would be next."[60] Many of the students were too nervous to speak to Rauschenberg at the university, and they insisted on meeting him in a nearby church. He recalled, "It was the only place that they felt safe. They believed that the church would provide sanctuary." After these meetings, Rauschenberg began to photograph the interiors of churches in Chile, and such religious objects as crucifixes, images of saints (fig. 94), and priests' vestments. For Rauschenberg, these items were inextricably bound not to traditional religion but to the moderating and protective role that the church might play in Chile and to the fact that it provided one of a few common denominators for this dangerously divided people.

Rauschenberg insisted on seeing the shantytowns that surrounded Santiago; it was a somewhat risky decision. The shantytowns had for decades fostered the most miserable living conditions in Chile and more recently had become a center of radical protest against Pinochet. The army was convinced that the Communist terrorists responsible for the recent bombings were hiding there. On October 29, just one day before Rauschenberg visited, the residents of the largest shantytown, La Victoria, had set up fiery barricades to discourage the army from entering. But this maneuver failed, and supported by armored vehicles and helicopters, soldiers arrested 140 people and sent them into internal exile.

The origin of the shantytowns in Santiago dates from the 1950s. They resulted from the poverty of the lower classes in Chile combined with the explosive growth of Santiago. Between 1920 and 1960 the population of Santiago went from five million

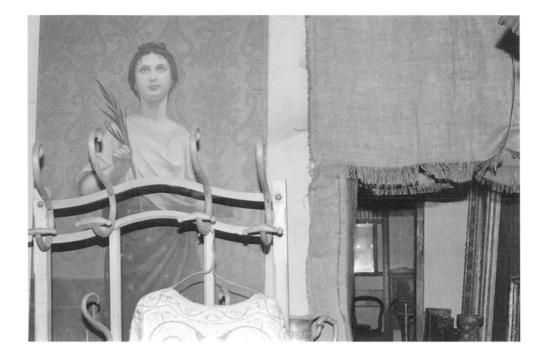

93 (*above left*) *Chile*, 1984, gelatin-silver print, sheet: 20 × 16", collection of the artist.

94 (*above right*) *Chile*, 1984, gelatin-silver print, sheet: 16 × 20", collection of the artist.

to twenty million people and the government was unable to provide housing. In 1956 several thousand of Santiago's poorest citizens, who had been living in misery along the San Miguel River, staged a *tomba* (an illegal seizure of land) that started the first of the shantytowns, La Victoria.[61] By 1984 it was estimated that some twenty percent of Santiago's population, or 3.6 million people, lived in the shantytowns, most in horrid conditions. There the huts with dirt floors were made of left-over wood and corrugated metal from construction sites in the city. Most consisted of only one room and had no plumbing. Only occasional buildings had electricity, and several extended families often lived in one structure. La Victoria alone consisted of ninety-six blocks of such huts. When Rauschenberg went to the shantytowns, Mario Stein recalled, "All the art patrons, mostly well-to-do people who lived in Chile thought he was crazy. His equipment would be stolen. He would be attacked. But he wanted to go out among the people, to see the other side."[62]

Rauschenberg remembers, "I went to the edge of La Victoria, the largest shantytown, with Terry [Van Brunt] and our translator. We were frightened to go any further than the outer edges (fig. 96). I have seen some terrible living conditions, but this was one of the worst. I took photographs of the shacks. Through the translator, we talked to a few people. They were totally discouraged because they felt no connection with the rest of Chile and had no hope that anything would ever change."[63] Rauschenberg included eight of his photographs of the shantytown dwellings in the *Copperhead Bite* works to increase awareness among the Chilean people of this aspect of their society.

By November 2 the political situation in Santiago had further deteriorated. The day-long strike of October 30 had closed most businesses and slowed traffic movement in the city to a near standstill. At the end of that day, Pinochet radically curtailed freedom of the press. Nationwide, six newspapers were shut down, all reports of political protests had to be passed by government censors, and photographs of demonstrations were forbidden. Ever since using newspapers in his Combines of the

95 (*above*) *Chile*, 1984, gelatin-silver print, sheet: 16 × 20", collection of the artist. (See fig. 103.)

96 (*right*) *Chile*, 1984, gelatin-silver print, sheet: 16 × 20", collection of the artist.

1950s, Rauschenberg has conducted a career-long dialogue with the popular press, and the accumulation of varied information on the surface of his works has been compared to the front page of a newspaper.[64] Not surprisingly, some of the most common images in Rauschenberg's Chilean works are newspapers which, as discussed below, have special meaning because of the curtailment of freedom of the press.

Pinochet's restrictions, which as noted above eventually led him to declare a state of siege in Chile on November 6, made it difficult for Rauschenberg to move around the city and to see more than he already had. As a result, he decided to leave Santiago. His choice was to go north to the Atacama Desert, a decision that again upset his well-to-do acquaintances in Santiago. A typical outing for a Chilean would be to go southwest along Chile's beautiful beach-lined coast. The northern mountain region is remote and rugged, and it is said that few Chileans ever visit it. Rauschenberg's decision to go to the northern desert was motivated by three factors. First, the fact that so few Chileans visited there meant he could fulfill his goal of revealing the country to itself. Second, copper, a material symbolic of Chile, had caught the artist's attention, and the country's major copper mine at Chuquicamata was in the northern desert. The copper mine had been the greatest historical source of Chilean economic prosperity, but it was also the location of some of the country's most abusive labor practices and was currently a stronghold of anti-government protests. Finally, as had been highlighted in the Briefing Paper that Rauschenberg consulted on his way to Chile, the northern desert was one of the most dramatically beautiful areas in all of Chile – as I have said, a concern with ecology and the beauty of the natural world, as humankind's common heritage, had long been a central theme Rauschenberg's art.

The Atacama Desert is more than 600 miles long. It is divided from the sea by a mountain range that drops in sheer cliffs to the ocean. The dominant part of the desert, the area for which Rauschenberg was headed, is the Atacama Plateau, which

97 *Caryatid Cavalcade I/ROCI Chile*, 1985, acrylic on canvas, 138 × 260 ³/₄", collection of the artist.

reaches heights of 13,000 feet. Of this area, Rauschenberg recalled, "Chile, I think, is one of the most beautiful places in the world. In the north are the deserts and copper fields."[65] Rauschenberg, Terry Van Brunt, and Monica Gelcich rented a car and started on the two-day drive north. Gelcich remembers, "I was apprehensive because, like most Chileans, I had never been north but Robert's enthusiasm was overwhelming."[66] As Gelcich remembers, within hours of leaving the city they had climbed several thousand feet and connected with the high desert road. Along the road are small towns often having no more than two hundred residents. Gelcich recalled, "It seems that these towns have not changed in two hundred years."[67] The exception to their stasis is electricity that was run into this area during the Allende presidency. The towns have subsistence economies; they grow their own food in the difficult climate, keep animals, and one of their few exports is the colorful woven woolens made by the local women. Rauschenberg stopped at a number of these towns and took photographs of rural settings, including one of a desert cemetery (fig. 95). His depictions of a woman weaving in *Caryatid Cavalcade II* (fig. 98) and of another woman cooking in *Copperhead Bite X* come from these villages, as does the traditional stone oven and the ropes from a weaving loom in *Caryatid Cavalcade I* (fig. 97). Rural animals like the hens in *Copperhead Grande* (fig. 99) and *Copperhead Chica* (fig. 101) also come from these villages. Gelcich remembers that Rauschenberg was particularly taken with the seemingly tranquil lifestyle of the village people and the fact that they so readily welcomed outsiders. He remembers, "We were never refused for being strangers. They welcomed us in every town."[68] The harmony contrasted dramatically with the upheavals he had just experienced in Santiago. Each small town was dominated by a church. Combined with the role of

church officials trying to end hostility in Santiago, the prominence of these village churches solidified in Rauschenberg's mind the central role that the Catholic faith might play in reuniting Chile. Rauschenberg was fascinated by the folk art carvings and painted altarpieces in these churches, and such images as the Madonna with flowers in *Caryatid Cavalcade II*, the image of Christ crucified in *Copperhead Bite V*, and the altar in *Copperhead Bite XII* come from these churches.

At the same time, Rauschenberg avoided treating the villages nostalgically. He was aware that they were subject to modernity and change albeit in a different manner from the city. For instance, the village of Nacota interested him because it contained both an elaborately decorated church and a roadside Coca Cola stand. There, Rauschenberg photographed the electric wires running into the traditional town center along with the humorous image, shown in *Copperhead Bite VIII*, of a wooden horse meant for tourists to sit upon in order to have their souvenir travel pictures taken.

Approaching the great Atacama Plain, the villages became widely spaced and considerably smaller. Gelcich remembers traveling up to seventy kilometers without seeing another car. In this area, the view became spectacular because the immense plain is backed by the Andes mountains. Llamas are the most common large animals, and Rauschenberg saw them both grazing along the hillside and coming up to the car. The desert is full of beautiful color contrasts. Because of mineral deposits, one distant hill will appear copper-colored while another is rust and yet another is emerald-toned. The colors of the desert – copper, brown, rust red, and olive green – are those that dominate Rauschenberg's *Copperhead Bite* series. Despite being one of the driest places on earth, the desert has shallow lakes formed by mountain snow run-off during early spring, the time Rauschenberg was there. Rauschenberg showed the edge of such a lake, contrasted with the cracked desert, in *Copperhead Bite VI* (see fig. 102). Because of mineral content, these lakes are also spectacularly colored. They often have crusty white shorelines from the accumulated saline, and some have hot springs bubbling up through their surfaces. The lakes support a variety of desert vegetation, like the huge blooming thistle Rauschenberg depicted in *Copperhead Grande*. The desert also features enormous cacti, some 100 years old, like those depicted in *Caryatid Cavalcade II* and *Altar Peace Chile*. Birds, like the Chilean heron appearing in *Copperhead Bite VI*, were also photographed by Rauschenberg. The landscape is so rich with minerals that semi-precious stones lie right on the surface, and Rauschenberg remembers picking up "three big turquoise stones just lying in this desert."[69] These stones became the source for the minerals that the artist included in *Araucan Mastaba*. Overall, Rauschenberg's feeling about the desert was one of "deep love for its wild beauty" and hope that all Chileans would see that natural beauty as a unifying element in their society.[70]

Fifty miles from the copper mines at Chuquicamata, the mood of the trip changed. The group passed through a ghost town, its landscape ruined by mining. The town had been one of the centers of nitrate mining, the mineral originally used to make dynamite until a synthetic substitute was invented after World War I. Gelcich told Rauschenberg that more recently the town had been used as a detention center for the political prisoners who "disappeared" during Pinochet's early years and that a number of other detention centers were at secret locations in the northern desert.[71] As Gelcich recalled, this information gave a new sobriety to the trip. The copper town Chuquicamata is more a small city than a village. The copper industry is entirely controlled by the government as are all of the city's services, and in rows of ugly concrete buildings, the government provides for housing, hospitals, schools, supermarkets, and clubs and thus attempts to regulate the workers' lives.

Even though Rauschenberg had carefully made arrangements to visit the mines through applications to the government before he left Santiago, he found that he was held up at Chuquicamata for nearly two days before permission was granted. Gelcich recalls that the wait was very boring and frustrating because, although the town was a center of union opposition to the government, everyone was afraid to speak to Rauschenberg since he was a stranger.

Rauschenberg viewed copper as an ambiguous but central symbol for the Chilean condition. The beautiful reflective sheets became dark and portentous when tarnished. The copper industry had been the mainstay of the Chilean economy for nearly a century, and the country could not survive without it. But the copper mines were also the location of some of the worst government authoritarian practices and labor abuses. The mining of the copper and particularly the smelting process provided exciting high drama, but the industry was coming under increasing attack for its hazards to the environment and its total lack of concern for ecology. When Rauschenberg depicted the copper mines and processing factory, he tried to reflect this conflicted situation.

The immense open-pit mine, one of the largest in the world, is recorded in *Caryatid Cavalcade I*; the distant photograph portrays the overwhelming scale of the operation, both awesome to view and devastating to the natural environment.[72] The mine is contrasted, however, with more intimate views of worn dump trucks decorated with graffiti and the old loading cars on railroad tracks that carry the minerals to the smelting area. Rauschenberg had been interested in machinery humanized by long use since his Combines of the 1950s. In *Copperhead Bite III* he showed the exhausted workers resting between shifts.

The most dramatic event for Rauschenberg was entering the fire-refining factory itself. He said, "I felt like Dante descending into the inferno."[73] The fire-refining process takes place within a single enormous building. The copper ore, once extracted from the ground and sorted from other minerals, is placed in large ovens. The refining process consists of two stages. The crude copper is heated first under oxidizing conditions to remove impurities and then reducing conditions to decrease the oxygen content. Visually, the most dramatic process is a final reheating of the copper to over one thousand degrees celsius in order to pour it into molds. Once the copper has reached the melting point, the oven is opened by operators in their silver heat-protective suits, who seem in Rauschenberg's words "like visitors from another planet."[74] Great buckets are lowered into the molten copper from chain hoists, and lifted high to the ceiling of the immense shed so that the copper can be poured into capillary tubes. The whole process must be conducted at high speed so the copper does not prematurely solidify. During this operation buckets swing, and gleaming molten copper splashes onto the floor briefly exploding into flames as it hits any surface. Capillary tubes connect to molds that shape the liquid copper into six-by-four foot sheets. Streaming down these tubes, the liquid copper looked like rivers of light.

The copper pour provided a highlight of Rauschenberg's Chilean voyage and solidified his determination to reflect the drama of his experiences in Chile. After leaving the mines and making the two-day return trip to Santiago, Rauschenberg found the city in deep crisis. As noted earlier, since his departure, the Chilean cabinet had resigned giving Pinochet full dictatorial powers, and a state of siege had been declared. In this context, it became impossible for Rauschenberg to learn much more, and he left Chile, traveling first to the opening of ROCI in Mexico City and then to his studio in Captiva to make the ROCI/Chile works. Later he said of his Chilean experience, "we just talked to as many people as we could find; and looked until our eyes swelled shut . . ."[75]

Before investigating five of Rauschenberg's Chilean works in detail, it would be helpful to have an overview of the types of imagery that he included in these works because categorizing the images reveals the issues that preoccupied him. Rauschenberg used eighty-five images in his Chilean works; twelve of the images were repeated twice, one of newspapers three times, and a mural depicting the Chilean War of the Pacific (1879–83) was repeated four times. Another photograph of a hen was repeated six times. Most of these images can be divided into seven overall themes. In order of frequency, they are: religious images, depictions of women, representations of commerce in the city and urban workers, newspapers and posters, the shantytowns, nature and animals, and the copper mines.

The most frequent of the images, fifteen in all, involve Roman Catholic depictions, including crucifixes, sculptures of saints, church windows, and representations of the Virgin Mary. Since Rauschenberg's work typically contains relatively little Christian subject matter, the predominance of this subject comes as a surprise. More than simply a result of frequently seeing religious objects throughout Chile, it derives from the prominent role the church was playing as peacemaker. As discussed earlier, the church's role as protector of those whose disagreed with the Pinochet regime was reinforced by frightened students who would speak freely with Rauschenberg only inside of churches.

The second most recurrent subject in Rauschenberg's Chilean works is women, who appear in eleven different instances. This theme is also a departure for Rauschenberg. During his career males including John F. Kennedy, astronauts, and athletes have dominated the art. The female figures in Rauschenberg's Chilean works vary from the caryatids on the porch of the Museo Nacional de Bellas Artes to peasant women, to female saints, to a child's drawing of her mother. From Rauschenberg's contacts in Chile, he learned that the women of Chile were among the most active, vocal advocates for human rights and for social services to aid the poor.[76] Pinochet's government had actively courted women in their traditional roles as mothers and as the spiritual center of the family. Ironically, when women put together some of the first anti-Pinochet organizations – Families of the Detained and Disappeared and Families of Political Prisoners – in order to demand information, visitation rights, and the return of these prisoners to their families, the government was reluctant to oppose their emotional arguments, which were made in the name of family unity. Women continued to be particularly active in opposition to the government, and eventually the large number of women who voted against Pinochet in the plebiscite of 1989 contributed to his downfall.

The next most common subjects are urban scenes and depictions of workers. Urban imagery has always dominated Rauschenberg's art, and it is not surprising that he should seek this subject in Chile. With the exception of the photograph of a glass skyscraper with Santiago Cathedral reflected on it, the majority of Rauschenberg's images concern the working people. They include vendors, day laborers, a man carrying boxes of fruit, and a street cleaner. In Chile, these depictions had a special meaning because of the problem with so-called "informal" jobs. As Mario Stein informed Rauschenberg, most of the people in such jobs made only a pittance for part-time work and lived in the shantytowns. While the government insisted on counting them as fully employed, outside estimates were that as much as eighty-five percent of the shantytown population was employed in "informal" occupations and that two-thirds of the population of Santiago was involved in part-time service. This issue was a major source of the political unrest in Chile.[77] Stein remembers discussing the plight of these people with Rauschenberg, and certainly every resident of Santiago who saw Rauschenberg's Chilean works would have been aware of the problem.[78] The eight images that Rauschenberg included of the shantytowns would have been obvious to both Chileans and foreigners as representations of substandard living, but to Chileans these photographs had a

99 *Copperhead Grande/ROCI Chile*, 1985, acrylic with corrosives and polishes on copper sheet sealed in lacquer, 91 $^7/_8$ × 144 $^3/_4$", collection of the National Gallery of Art, Washington, D.C.

special resonance as representations of the Pinochet government's worst social failure and a core area of civil strife in their country.

Another eight representations in Rauschenberg's Chilean works involve newspapers, broadsides, and posters. Since the 1950s Rauschenberg had been using newspaper fragments in his art, a sign of his active involvement with the events of everyday life and his desire to view his works as collecting points for a wide variety of information. Their use in these Chilean works takes on added significance because of the restrictions on freedom of the press imposed by the Pinochet government. These constraints reached a high-water mark during Rauschenberg's stay in Chile, as said earlier. Such censorship flew directly in the face of open access to information that is at the core of ROCI.

As an example of Rauschenberg's use of the news media, *Caryatid Cavalcade II* (fig. 98) depicts an urban wall with broadsides that have been torn off and layered over one another. There, the layering is so complex that none of the broadsides can be made out clearly; only isolated words like "Circo" (circus) and "L'Hombre" (the man) appear. Such fragmented posters had been used before by Rauschenberg to signal the complexity of modern life, but here they may refer specifically to the chaos in Chilean society at this time. Another newspaper page that appears prominently in Chilean works, like *Copperhead Grande* (fig. 99), is an advertisement for the Chilean national lottery. Besides expressing a lighthearted side to the society and the fact that, to some extent, everyday life continued, Rauschenberg commented, "that particular photograph represented hope. Someone was going be lucky and perhaps someday all Chileans would share good fortune."[79]

A third photograph of a wall of newspapers used by Rauschenberg, and featured in such works as *Copperhead Bite IV* (fig. 100), ranks among the most direct political commentary in his Chilean works. The three most prominent images in this photograph are the banner page from the Santiago newspaper *La Segunda*, announcing the assassination of Indira Gandhi, the second page of the same paper, indicating that two hundred people had been detained during Chilean protests of the previous several days, and a magazine cover for an essay on Napoleon Bonaparte, featuring *Napoleon I on His Imperial Throne* (1806, Musée de l'Armeé, Paris) by the nineteenth-century French painter Jean-Auguste-Dominique Ingres. Rauschenberg used this particular photograph in three different Chilean works for emphasis. The "200 Detenidos" (200 arrested) page which appears next to Ingres's painting of Napoleon as the autocratic ruler completely disconnected from reality makes a comparison to Pinochet unavoidable. In this context, the feature story on the assassination of Gandhi is not a call for the assassination of Pinochet but exactly the opposite. Rauschenberg had deep admiration for Indira Gandhi, and he was heartbroken when he learned of her death. The byline for the newspaper discusses the chaos in Indian society that had been caused by her assassination. Rauschenberg's selection of a photograph that included the Indira Gandhi headline should be seen in context with another photograph that he used in several Chilean works, including *Caryatid Cavalcade I*. It shows statues of Jawaharlal Nehru, Mahatma Gandhi, and Deendranath Tagore from Parque Forestal in Santiago. Here, Rauschenberg presents three great politicians and peacemakers who brought degrees of stability to Indian society. His reference to these leaders suggests that a peaceful transition in Chile might be guided by their principles, the very opposite of either violent overthrow or assassination.

Another major subject category in Rauschenberg's Chilean works is that of rural life – the people, nature, and animals. As discussed earlier, these photographs were based on the artist's trip to the Atacama Desert, thirteen images from which were eventually used. After the discord and violence in Santiago, Rauschenberg found solace in the beauty of the desert and the seeming concord of rural life. The photographs that he chose do not ignore the slow arrival of technology, like the electric lines running into villages, but on the whole they show harmony in the villages. His close-up photographs of looms, adobe ovens, and walls are some of the most artistic images in the Chilean works. On the whole, Rauschenberg tended to ignore the grinding poverty that was also a reality of rural life. Although these small peasant farmers had received "parcelas" of land during the Allende reforms, they were overwhelmed by the large farms of the Pinochet era, and poverty was rapidly increasing among the peasant landowners.[80] Gelcich remembers, "My family was from a small village in the south with similar problems, and I tried to tell Robert of their difficulties, but he did not seem too interested. I think he was exhausted from his experiences in Santiago."[81]

100 *Copperhead-Bite IV/ROCI Chile*, 1985, acrylic with corrosives and polishes on copper sheet sealed in lacquer, 96 × 51 $\frac{1}{4}$", collection of the artist.

The last major theme in the ROCI/Chile works was the copper mines of which eight representations appear in the Chilean works. These photographs, which are found in the monumental ROCI/Chile works *Caryatid Cavalcade I*, *Copperhead Grande*, and *Copperhead Bite IV*, depict the mines and workers as well as the dramatic smelting process. Photographs of workers resting from their labors contrast with the overwhelming scale of the open mining pit. The photographs suggest the difficult working conditions for which the mines were notorious as well as ecological concerns, found in such images as the smoke stacks shown in *Altar Peace Chile* (see fig. 104). Rauschenberg's double-edged meaning for copper, and by extension for all of the ROCI/Chile works, comes out in the title of the series, "Copperhead Bite." It refers to the poisonous North American snake and makes an analogy between its bite and the bite of acid into the copper. Thus the danger of the Chilean situation as Rauschenberg perceived it was highlighted. Yet at the same time Rauschenberg affirmed that he used copper in these works "to show my deep identification with the Chilean people."[82]

The largest ($138 \times 260^{3}/_{4}$ inches each) and most intricate of the ROCI/Chile works were *Caryatid Cavalcade I* and *Caryatid Cavalcade II* (figs. 97 and 98). Because *Caryatid Cavalcade I* was the first of the Chilean works that Rauschenberg executed, it serves as a springboard for ideas explored throughout the series. It is also the most boldly colored of Rauschenberg's Chilean works: the painting sets off hot red, yellow, and pink tones against black paint that is splashed onto the center of the canvas in a manner that anticipates the acids that Rauschenberg used on the slightly later copper works. The painting is divided into five panels in the mode of "Old Master" altarpieces, giving it an aura of complexity and authority. The two dominant images are the caryatids from the balcony of the Museo Nacional de Bellas Artes. They introduce women as a theme in the Chilean pieces. In the context of their original position in the museum, they were seen by many Chileans as representing the haughty removal of that government institution. By contrast, Rauschenberg brings them down onto the street, having them interact with his vision of the multifaceted Chilean culture, just as he wanted to make the museum into a people's museum.[83] Accordingly, the caryatid to the right is placed near an adobe oven, a representation of the work of everyday women. Below the caryatid, the artist positioned a well-known commercial sign, located in downtown Santiago, for sparkling Chilean wine. The oven with its orifice and the exploding cork of the wine bottle make a sexual pun that further humanizes the caryatid.

The panel to the left of this caryatid consists of four vertical sections, each in a different color. They deal with the contrasts in Chile that Rauschenberg hoped to reconcile. Using black pigment, the bottom section shows the shantytowns, the worst living conditions in Chile. The flame-like red forms partly overlapping the images of these buildings may represent the violence, including burnings, that took place in the shantytowns. Directly above the shantytown photograph and colored sunny yellow, there are classical buildings that might be occupied by the privileged. A sweeping red brushstroke connects these two radically different building complexes. An additional charge is given to the classical buildings because they are part of the university – a fact every Santiago resident would recognize – which was a hotbed of protests against the Pinochet government. So these very different-looking pieces of architecture are more connected than an outsider would suspect. Above the horizontal arrangement of the university buildings is a horizontal line of simple woolen threads stretched in preparation for weaving by village artisans. The visual similarity suggests the need for greater connection between city and country in Chile. At the top of this panel are sculptures of the three Indian peacemakers mentioned before – Nehru, Gandhi, and Deendranath Tagore, the nineteenth-century Hindu reformer who purged the religion of divisive practices. The statues are a tribute to Chile's historic tolerance toward immigrants, including the small Indian community in Santiago, as well as Chilean admiration for these leaders as "reformers and men of advanced political and social ideas."[84] Rauschenberg's inclusion of these statues expresses his desire for such nonviolent reform in contemporary Chile.

The left side of *Caryatid Cavalcade I* features the second caryatid, who like her sister overlays and thus unites urban and country themes, a combination that makes her more accessible to the viewer. Behind her upper torso is the northern Chilean desert with colored minerals strewn across its surface, alternatives to the white classical stone from which she is carved. On her lower torso, a stack of Coca-Cola bottles forms an impromptu sculpture, further undermining the caryatid's formality. As seen in the early Combine *Curfew* (see fig. 27), Coca-Cola has long been a favorite representation of the common person for Rauschenberg. Also, the two faucets at the caryatid's feet press together in a gesture filled with humor and sexual suggestion.

In the far left panel of *Caryatid Cavalcade I*, Rauschenberg also contrasts seemingly irreconcilable subjects. Three of the images concern the copper mines, while the two others show tranquil horses in a field and a handmade graveside shrine. Yet there are visual similarities among the images. The pattern of the horses across the field resembles the arrangement of hauling machinery in front of the giant torta mine at Chuquicamata, shown in the lower-left corner. The worn mining trucks to the upper-left side, one of which has simple paintings made by the workers on it, relate to the human presence found in the handmade shrine at the center. The visual similarities suggest that these very different experiences may not be irreconcilable, or at the very least that they must all be contemplated to understand Chile.

Rauschenberg is sufficiently realistic to know that the visual and thematic connections made in *Caryatid Cavalcade I* will not be easy to achieve, and the center panel of the painting sounds a warning. In the upper section of the panel, an outdoor crucifix has been splattered with a large area of black pigment. Rauschenberg's violent and expressionistic gesture of flinging paint across the surface is uncharacteristic and more resembles the paint handling of the Abstract Expressionists. It is also reminiscent of the dramatic explosions of blood from Christ's wounds found in the art of the Counter-Reformation. The emotional effect certainly signals Rauschenberg's response to the violence, hatred, and anger he found in so many aspects of Chilean society.

The final element in *Caryatid Cavalcade I* is the dominant image of the black hen set against a red ground at the lower center. This photograph is the most frequent

101 *Copperhead Chica/ROCI Chile*, 1985, acrylic and enamel with corrosives and polishes on copper sheet sealed in lacquer, 48 ³/₄ × 59 ³/₄ × 1", collection of Mr. and Mrs. Jeff Tarr.

image – it appears six times – in Rauschenberg's Chilean works. Fowl have been included in Rauschenberg's works going back to the 1950s, and their appearance has been related to the animals that Rauschenberg kept as a child. Of course, he would also have seen many chickens on the farms in the Chilean countryside, but the prominence of the hen in his Chilean works suggests deeper connections. As curator and longtime Rauschenberg friend, Walter Hopps once noted, "For Rauschenberg, animals are the sentient innocent witnesses to human affairs and follies."[85] The outstanding feature of the photograph is the alertness of the creature. She stands neck erect, head high, and feathers ruffled. In *Copperhead Chica* (fig. 101), the same hen confronts us four times: she stands on guard, wary of dangers. From his contact with hens as a child, Rauschenberg knew that they have a keen ability to identify predators and warn the flock of danger, a fact that has been confirmed in recent cognitive studies.[86] In *Caryatid Cavalcade I* and other Chilean works by Rauschenberg, the hen's vigilance warns the viewer that alertness, care, and prudence will be necessary to return stability to Chile.

The largest number of Rauschenberg's Chilean works were executed directly on copper plates, including the twelve *Copperhead Bite* works as well as *Copperhead Grande* and *Copperhead Chica*. These mark the first time that Rauschenberg had executed a series of pieces on metal, and they are the predecessors for such series on metal as the Borealis (1990) and the Night Shades (1991). Rauschenberg was attracted by the rich color of the copper – the only metal other than gold that possesses a natural color – and by its reflective character. Pure copper has a salmon tone that varies to deeper reddish tints depending on the amount of oxide film in it. Yet, in working with the four by eight foot sheets sent from Chile, Rauschenberg became increasingly interested in more somber tonalities that occurred as the copper oxidized. Accordingly the silkscreen images he painted on these sheets tend toward more muted colors. In a significant number of these images, Rauschenberg used negative rather than positive screens so that the highlights were not bright-toned paint but rather the oxidized copper surface itself. This procedure gives the images a less substantial effect, as if they are fading away before our eyes. The negative printing suited the moody, evocative character of the Chilean works which is simultaneously pointing to hope for the future and recognizing the present crisis.

In addition to silkscreen painting, Rauschenberg worked the copper surfaces with a variety of acids, utilizing the techniques he had learned from Benito Rojo at the Universidad de Chile. It was the first time that Rauschenberg had used tarnishing agents in his work. The acids varied from relatively powerful nitric acid and hot sulphuric acid to less potent hydrochloric acid and ammonium hydroxide.[87] With combinations of these tarnishing agents, Rauschenberg could create a range of colors and intensities of oxidization. These variations went from the thin washes of hydrochloric acid used all over the surface of *Copperhead Bite IV* to give it a weathered look to the intense splatters of nitric acid that suggest generative forces in *Copperhead Bite VI*. In each of the works discussed below, corrosive agents were used for different effects.

In contrast to the encyclopedic character of *Caryatid Cavalcade I*, the *Copperhead Bite* works focus more narrowly on specific themes. For instance, *Copperhead Bite IV* (see fig. 100) concerns different types of information systems, and by extension the ways that Rauschenberg gathered information in Chile. The types of data shown in this work include popular culture, the reality of the daily news, and the artist's first-hand experiences. The copper plate has been washed all over with ammonium hydroxide, giving it – except for the photograph at the bottom right – a bleached look, and all the images are arranged as if they were faded broadsides on a wall. Above is a menu of popular foods representing connecting links through popular culture. According to Nena Ossa, "They are foods that everyone loves to eat, although they might not admit it."[88] The foods include *guatitas* (stomach), *perniles* (German ham hocks), and *patitas de puerco* (pigs' feet). Below this restaurant card is a group of idealized photographs from a shop window including a young girl with a chicken (the innocent offspring of Rauschenberg's alert hens), a beautiful landscape, a representation of Christ, and a young boy and girl. The innocence of these images is the dominant topic. To the lower-left side of these idealized photos is the wall with current newspapers and periodicals attached to it. As discussed above, the periodicals contain direct references to the detention of two hundred protesters by the Chilean police as well references to the political chaos caused by the assassination of Indira Gandhi and an allusion, through Napoleon, to Pinochet as a despotic figure. The wall of current events represents another type of information that Rauschenberg collected.

In the lower-right corner of *Copperhead Bite IV*, Rauschenberg placed one of the most dramatic photographs taken in Chile, the pouring of molten copper in Chuquicamata. The photograph forcefully represents the power of the experiences that Rauschenberg had in Chile. This depiction is almost theatrical in its immediacy compared to the reproductions and texts around it. Rauschenberg has connected the fiery copper ovens to the wall of newspapers, and by extension to the other images in the work, through a sweeping gesture of acid in the lower-left quadrant that looks simultaneously like splashed copper from the processing plant and dirt thrown on an old city wall to which all these newspapers might be attached.

The two works *Copperhead Bite VI* and *Copperhead Bite VII* act as pendants. Using women and nature as dominant themes, *Copperhead Bite VI* (fig. 102) suggests the potential for healing and growth in Chile. The role of women as peacemakers and the moral conscience of the country, as well as Rauschenberg's ideas about the unifying character of the natural environment, have been discussed. At the bottom of the copper sheet are two corresponding images of women. One is a classical sculpture by the artist Rebecca Matte from the Parque Forestal in Santiago, and the other is a child's drawing, perhaps of her mother. These gentle feminine images act as a seedbed for images of nature above them. The cracked earth of the Atacama Desert, a beautiful pattern in itself, is overlaid with the vine of a trumpet flower. Thus, the desert comes alive, mirroring Rauschenberg's experiences during his trip to the Atacama. The acid on these sections of the copper plate is applied in drip patterns that are seed-like in appearance. An elegant Chilean heron appears in the top register of *Copperhead Bite VI*, and thus seems to stand on the desert and in front of a simple stone wall. Next to the heron is a piece of organically shaped ironwork in green that looks like a growing plant. The heron is one of those that Rauschenberg saw in the saline lakes of the desert, of which he recalled, "They were so grand. It seemed like they could survive anywhere and that their spirit would never be broken."[89]

The second work, *Copperhead Bite VII* (fig. 103) initially seems also to show reassuring images. The largest photograph, to the lower left, is a benign scene of Chileans sunbathing at one of the coastal resorts that Rauschenberg briefly visited on his way to the northern desert. The scene is transformed, however, by the more disturbing images that surround it. Directly above the beach are crosses that are gravemarkers in a desert cemetery (see fig. 95) with crosses protruding from the sand that resemble the shapes of the bathers on the beach. In addition, the image is kept from being

102 *Copperhead-Bite VI/ROCI Chile*, 1985, acrylic with corrosives and polishes on copper sheet sealed in lacquer, 96 $^7/_8$ × 51 $^1/_4$", collection of the artist.

103 *Copperhead-Bite VII/ROCI Chile*, 1985, acrylic with corrosives and polishes on copper sheet sealed in lacquer, 96 $^7/_8$ × 51 $^1/_4$", collection of the artist.

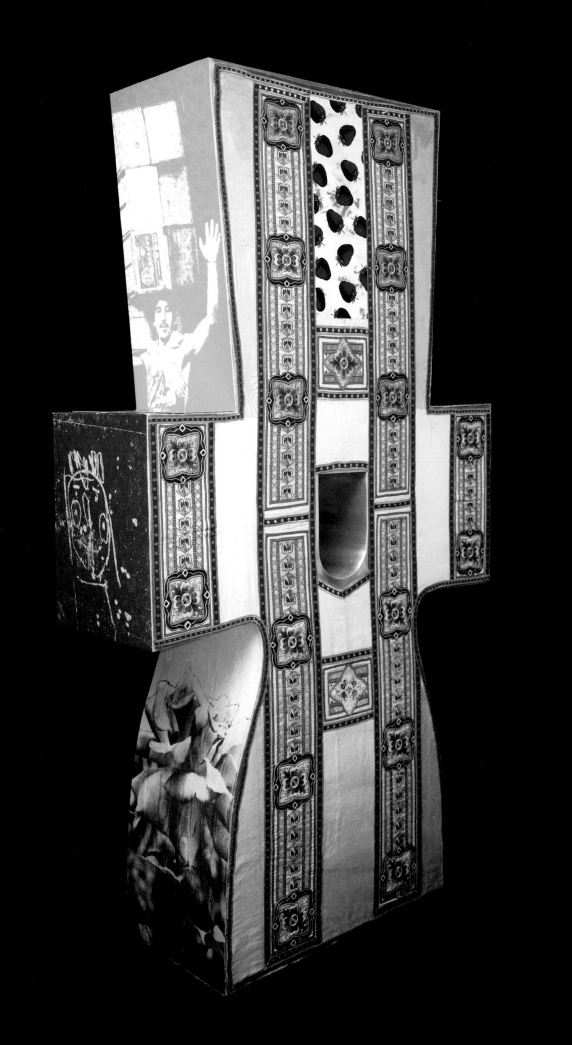

tranquil by the rough application of tarnishing agents over this part of the sheet. The effect is to suggest a stormy turbulent landscape. Even the country oven, overlapping this image, appears in this context like a tomb chamber or perhaps like the ovens where many people believe the bodies of the "disappeared" were burned to destroy incriminating evidence.[90] Suddenly, the image of playful relaxation is transformed into an ominous reminder of death, alluding to the needless deaths that have occurred under the Pinochet regime.

From the belief of many Chileans that the executions of civilians took place near the internment camps in the northern desert, Rauschenberg's image gained an emotional charge.[91] In the lower-right corner of *Copperhead Bite VII*, Rauschenberg placed a photograph of an interior courtyard whose dominant feature is a striped pattern formed by light shining through an exterior grill. The emptiness of the space is foreboding and the grill pattern looks distinctly like jail-cell bars. With these associations, the red abstract patterns, partly covering the bathers to the lower left, seem to be reminders of bloodshed.

In *Copperhead Bite VII*, as in Rauschenberg's other Chilean works, references to the violence in Chile are indirect. The artist never shows actual riots, protestors, or armed Chilean police. The works function by allusion and visual association. Such a strategy, which parallels that used by Donoso in his essay on Rauschenberg, allowed the works to be exhibited without censorship but provided evidence to carefully observant viewers of Rauschenberg's convictions.

A work that Rauschenberg may regard as among most important was *Altar Peace Chile* (fig. 104), because he selected it to represent his Chilean creations at his 1998–99 retrospective exhibition. With the exception of the multiple *Araucan Mastaba*, *Altar Peace Chile* is the only three-dimensional work made for ROCI/Chile. It consists of a large shaped cross ($79\frac{1}{2} \times 44\frac{5}{8} \times 15\frac{1}{4}$ inches) constructed of aluminum with acrylic paint and collage fabrics. At the center of the cross is an open area. A hidden light-bulb within the cross projects colored light onto that center cavity. *Altar Peace Chile* ties together themes that had been occupying Rauschenberg since his visit to Chile and some currents that have run through his career.

Overall, the cross-shaped configuration is related to Rauschenberg's experiences with the Catholic church in Chile. As mentioned before, Rauschenberg's personal contacts with Chilean students, fearful of the Pinochet government, took place in the churches which they felt provided sanctuary. Donoso had expressed his desire to have the ROCI/Chile exhibition held in a church because he felt, as Rauschenberg recalled, "that it was the only institution that the people still respected."[92] In addition to these experiences, Rauschenberg was aware from the press and his conversations that the Catholic church was acting increasingly, as a force for peaceful change in Chile. Accordingly, as outlined earlier, religious imagery was the most frequent subject of Rauschenberg's Chilean works. Of course, the title of *Altar Peace Chile* is a pun on altarpieces, the paintings and sculptures traditionally placed on Christian altars. But, more deeply, it expresses Rauschenberg's plea for peace in Chile.

Despite the infrequency of direct religious imagery in Rauschenberg's work, his connections to formal religion and more significantly informal spirituality throughout his career should be noted. It is well known that he was raised in an evangelical household and that as a child he even considered becoming a minister. Less well-known is the fact that Rauschenberg continued to attend church regularly during his early years in New York City. Rauschenberg's earliest works, like *Mother of God* (c. 1950, San Francisco Museum of Modern Art), occasionally made direct religious references, and even such Combines as *Hymnal* and *Co-Existence*, the latter of which contains a saint's tooth in a reliquary case, have religious associations. Early in the 1950s, Rauschenberg replaced his interest in formal religion with a broader and more loosely defined belief in the potential of humankind and the creativity of individuals, a belief that is essential to his world-view. Such a broad-based faith plays a role in *Altar Peace Chile*, which is as secular as it is sacred.

The shape of *Altar Peace Chile*, as much as resembling a cross, looks like a human figure with outstretched arms. The sculpture's proportions are on a human scale, and its curves, including the bowing outward of the lower torso and the triangular expansion of the upper section, are unlike the geometric rigidity of traditional crosses. They give the work a particularly anthropomorphic feel. The outstretched arms of the cross are, in human terms, a welcoming gesture, and they are a primary indicator of the openness and tolerance that Rauschenberg sought in Chile. A figure with outstretched arms is also a measure of human potential as found in Leonardo da Vinci's *Vitruvian Man* (c. 1487; Accademia, Venice), an image that particularly interests Rauschenberg.[93]

The overall design of *Altar Peace Chile* supports this reading of Catholicism mixed with broad humanist implications. The proportions of the sculpture, in fact, are determined by the shape of a priest's chasuble. Flattened but otherwise unaltered, chasubles were attached to the front and rear surfaces of the sculpture; the opening in the center of the work is the location of the head-hole in the garment. Rauschenberg was certainly attracted to the rich gold, red, and green pattern of the chasuble's cloth. In addition, the liturgical season of these vestments is Christmas, a time of hope and new beginnings. The beautifully handcrafted character of the vestments expresses the connection between craftspeople and the church in Chile. In addition to the priest's robes, the front and rear surfaces of *Altar Peace Chile* contain pieces of brightly colored ordinary fabrics. Here again the sacred and secular allusions of the work are related, and Rauschenberg reminds the viewer of his life-long interest in fabrics as an expression of individual integrity.

The outer edges of *Altar Peace Chile* are silkscreened with six images that function in opposition to each other on opposite sides of the sculpture. On the left side one finds a Chilean worker balancing a massive stack of crates on his shoulder but still having the energy to give the photographer a friendly wave and a smile. For Rauschenberg, he epitomized the spirit of the Chilean people.[94] Below him, the artist placed the child's drawing, perhaps of her mother; also found in *Copperhead Bite VI*. Finally, on the bottom panel there is an image of flowers in full bloom. On the opposite edge of *Altar Peace Chile*, Rauschenberg positioned a triad of more difficult images. On top, one finds smoke stacks from the copper mines. In the center, there appears a close-up view of a shantytown shack, and below one finds a cactus with its dangerously protruding needles. While none of these three images condemns Chile, each alludes to the thorny problems that the country faces.

The top of *Altar Peace Chile* and the top edge of each arm contain no silkscreen images but rather consist of the reflective aluminum surface. The effect, particularly on the arms, is that the viewer sees herself reflected in the work when walking around it. While Rauschenberg has used reflective surfaces, including mirrors, in his works since the 1950s so that they actively respond to their environments, the horizontal location of these surfaces and the close-up position in which one sees them in *Altar Peace Chile* assures that the human presence dominates. The Chilean viewers coming to see Rauschenberg's exhibition about their country would see themselves literally reflected in this work.

The most mysterious aspect of *Altar Peace Chile* lies at its center. The sculpture has been perforated in a horse-shoe configuration, and the lower curved edge consists of polished aluminum while the hidden upper surface is open. Inside the sculpture, Rauschenberg has concealed a red-toned light bulb. The shining light creates a multi-colored effervescent glow that is reflected in the polished aluminum. The glowing core of the sculpture is reminiscent of the glowing heart of Jesus, a symbol of the Jesuit religious order, found in traditional religious art. In more secular terms, it might represent the spirit of this figure-shaped sculpture. Such deliberately mystical effects are unusual in Rauschenberg's art. When he wanted to illuminate a work, like *First Landing Jump*, he typically showed the bulb in order to emphasize its objective nature. In contrast, the effect in *Altar Peace Chile* resembles the hidden light sources intended to create a dramatically spiritual impression in such works as Gianlorenzo Bernini's *Ecstasy of Saint Teresa* (1645–52, Cornaro Chapel, Santa Maria della Vittoria, Rome). While one may discuss the success of the light's effect, it seems clear that Rauschenberg was driven to such overt drama by his desire to heal Chile's social and political wounds.

Rauschenberg had arrived in Chile relatively unaware of the dangerous political situation, and when he realized the situation it took a certain amount of courage not to pack up immediately and head for home. He learned from people like Mario Stein and from the artists and students about the abuses of the Pinochet regime, saw riots from a distance, and heard car-bomb explosions and police gunshots. On the second night that Rauschenberg was in Chile, a small earthquake occurred, and he and his staff took refuge in the bathroom of their high-rise hotel. Fate seemed to be against him, but he stayed. Rauschenberg traveled throughout Santiago, including visiting the periphery of the shantytowns. One afternoon driving with Terry Van Brunt down a country road on the outskirts of the city, he was suddenly surrounded by soldiers. Inadvertently, he had wandered onto the road leading to Pinochet's private compound. Rauschenberg recalled, "I had the distinct feeling that if I'd continued they would have shot us."[95] He also made the difficult trek to the northern desert to see the infamous copper mines.

In the face of these experiences, the ROCI/Chile works, perhaps surprisingly, do not depict violence. Generally, they do not contain images of authoritarian figures, policemen, or soldiers, which were the essence of Pinochet's rule. There is a single, rather benign, depiction of a policeman, taken from a poster, in *Caryatid Cavalcade II* (see fig. 98). The only representation of armed individuals, which Rauschenberg used four times, is derived from a mural of the War of the Pacific (1879–83) that Chile conducted with Bolivia, and even this representation shows the peaceful settlement at the end of the war. As mentioned above, the absence of such imagery is, on one hand, a practical matter. Rauschenberg rightly believed that the government censors would never allow him to exhibit the works in Chile with such subjects included.[96] On the other hand, the artist's choice was also part of his worldview, one that emphasizes understanding over conflict.

Instead of violence, Rauschenberg's ROCI/Chile works concern reconciliation through open communication. They are intended to give the Chilean people a way to look at themselves, using the information Rauschenberg was able to gather during his short stay. Chile's problems are not glossed over; for instance, the shantytowns with their devastating living conditions and the open-pit copper mine with its ecological problems and difficult working conditions were shown. In addition, disguised references were made to the horrors of the Pinochet years, like the innocent beach bathers juxtaposed with gravemarkers in *Copperhead Bite VII*. (In fact, many of the representations, like those of the university where anti-Pinochet sentiments were strong, were addressed directly to Chileans, and the implications of such depictions would be understood fully only by them.) Rauschenberg's emphasis, however, was on the elements of Chilean society that he found potentially restorative. These included the church, women, and nature. The material out of which he chose to make the majority of the Chilean works – copper – was a forceful symbol of the society.

The end of Pinochet's reign came in a peaceful manner that surprised everyone. During the summer of 1988, Pinochet's advisors convinced the aging leader to conduct a second plebiscite that would further legitimize his position. The plebiscite was scheduled only five weeks away on October 5. Based on a decision that the only way to beat Pinochet was by his own rules, fourteen opposition parties gathered around a "no" vote. Their primary goal became to register voters, and an amazing ninety-two percent of the electorate voted. The "no" campaign had been denied access to the media until just before the election. When finally given last-minute television time, the coalition stunned the nation with "its unity and a series of upbeat, appealing advertisements that stressed harmony and joy in a reunited Chile," a message similar to the one found in Rauschenberg's works.[97] By contrast, the government's grim advertisements reminded people of the violence and disorder before Pinochet's coup and suggested more was to come. Despite the plebiscite that officially removed Pinochet from the presidency, his legacy has proved more difficult to resolve.

Before leaving office, the general rearranged the constitution to strengthen the role of the military and appointed himself its commander in perpetuity. Not until 1998 were legal barriers cleared for the arrest of Pinochet on charges of human rights abuses. The former dictator, who was in London seeking medical aid, fought extradition to Chile for over a year, but twenty-five of his generals were arrested. While some of the officers have been brought to trial, the legal battle to try Pinochet is still being fought. To this day Chile attempts to deal with the physical and psychological scars of the Pinochet years. Despite his optimistic character, Rauschenberg is too much a realist to think that his Chilean works had a large effect in leading that country to a peaceful resolution. Instead, he has stated that "perhaps a little something happened."[98] When asked about the final aim of the ROCI/Chile works, the artist, who usually loves to tell a long story, answered simply that they were intended "to show my solidarity with the Chilean people."[99]

remarks

This study has attempted to provide an in-depth investigation of several Rauschenberg ideas and projects. Its goal has been to understand better the artist's creative process and from that understanding to provide surer interpretations of his works in relationship to modern history. The chapters have used different approaches, ranging from observations of Rauschenberg working in the studio to detailed considerations of the sociopolitical situations in which he found himself. In each of these studies, context has been important. Efforts have been made to detail the environments in which Rauschenberg existed as well as to explore the kinds of information he collected, what he rejected, what he learned from his collaborators and associates, and finally how he transformed that information in his art works.

Rauschenberg has revealed himself to be a much more complicated and thoughtful artist than typically portrayed in the literature, and his work is certainly not random as has often been stated. Rather the artist has an innate, and perhaps physiological, disposition to accumulate vast amounts of information and to make associations between images that others often miss. On one level, Rauschenberg's art is a model for the late-modern world, where each of us is required to absorb during each day a plethora of new information. It is interesting, for instance, to note that Rauschenberg's Silkscreen Paintings of the 1960s, an era when television was new to many households, look somewhat like the overlapping "windows" found on today's computer screens. Rauschenberg's art demonstrates manners of seeing and thinking generic to our era; in his words to the dancer Steve Paxton, "I tend to see everything."[1]

Rauschenberg also sorts information. While his art does not lend itself to linear narratives or to simple iconographic interpretations, it does gathers around identifiable focal points. The types of materials that Rauschenberg uses and the images that he selects show consistency within individual works and particularly within series of works. Although viewers are allowed some latitude for interpretation because of the rich associative values of the things that Rauschenberg selects, the works do express his world-views. The way that he organizes his studio, the energy with which he gathers source materials, and his use of expert collaborators are signs of the organization behind his seemingly spontaneous art. Yet, even these organizational systems are geared toward capturing the surface of life. Rauschenberg's dislike of detailed analysis is both his strength and weakness. While his intuitive approach often allows him to see associations bypassed by others, he can also miss connections that might become apparent with more prolonged consideration.

Whatever the successes or flaws of his procedure, Rauschenberg sees himself as an artist citizen, and the development of his beliefs and values may be traced from his 1950s urban-based Combines to the more national concerns of the Silkscreen Paintings. A culmination of his progressive vision is found in his international Rauschenberg Overseas Culture Interchange. On one hand, Rauschenberg's evolving position is a measure of the ambitions he has for his art. On the other, it is the sign of an activist who thinks that the world can change for the better and that art can participate in, or even lead, such change. In an era often dominated by cynicism, this viewpoint appears refreshing rather than naive. Rauschenberg's desire is to reach out to the multifaceted world, learn from it, and give back to it in the form of his art. Once asked what he feared most, the artist responded, "That I might run out of world."[2]

notes

introduction

1   Jasper Johns quoted by Donald Saff, interview with the author, August 18, 2000. Tape recording in the author's files, Easton, Penn.

2   For instance, see Julius S. Held, *Rembrandt Studies* (Princeton University Press, 1991); and Elizabeth Johns, *Thomas Eakins: The Heroism of Modern Life* (Princeton University Press, 1983).

3   Rauschenberg, interview with the author, November 4, 1993. Tape recording in the author's files, Easton, Penn.

4   Ibid.

one

1   Rauschenberg in Faye Hirsh, "Robert Rauschenberg's Ground Rules Series," *Journal of Prints, Drawings, and Photography* 2 (November–December 1997), 14.

2   Rauschenberg in Richard Kostelanetz, "A Conversation with Robert Rauschenberg," *Partisan Review* 35 (winter 1968), 94.

3   See esp. Andrew Forge, *Rauschenberg* (1969; New York: Abrams, 1972).

4   See e.g. Rosalind Krauss, "Rauschenberg and the Materialized Image," *Artforum* 13, no. 4 (December 1974), 36–43; and Douglas Crimp, "On the Museum's Ruins," *October* 13 (summer 1980), 41–57.

5   Charles F. Stuckey, "Reading Rauschenberg," *Art in America* 65, no. 2 (March–April 1977), 74–84.

6   Charles F. Stuckey, "Rauschenberg's Everything, Everywhere Era," *Robert Rauschenberg: A Retrospective* (New York: Solomon R. Guggenheim Museum of Art, 1997), 38.

7   G. R. Swenson, "Rauschenberg Paints a Picture," *Art News* 62, no. 2 (April 1963), 44–47, 65–67. The film sources include: "The American Image," May 26, 1967, television broadcast, produced by NBC Television, New York; "Rauschenberg Pieces," February 22, 1981, television broadcast, produced by CBS News, New York; "Robert Rauschenberg: Inventive Genius," 1999, co-produced by Thirteen/WNET and Film Odyssey Inc., New York.

8   Barbara Rose, *Rauschenberg* (New York: Vintage, 1987), 86.

9   Ibid., 86–87.

10 Rauschenberg, interview with the author, November 4, 1993.

11 Swenson, "Rauschenberg Paints a Picture," 45–46; and Calvin Tomkins, *Off the Wall: Robert Rauschenberg and the Art World of Our Time* (Garden City, New York: Doubleday, 1980), 211–19.

12 Rauschenberg in John Richardson, "Epic Vision," *Vanity Fair* (September 1997), 281.

13 In 1994, Rauschenberg's assistants began recording his photographs digitally for preservation. They also acquired an Iris printer to print the digitally mastered photographs. Rauschenberg was concerned that the color dyes used to reproduce these photographs would be toxic. The manufacturer informed him that the dyes were vegetable-based and water soluble. This information gave Rauschenberg the idea of placing the printed photographs face down on a larger piece of paper, wetting their surfaces, and thus transferring their images onto larger sheets of paper. In this manner, portions of the photographs could be used and multiple images could be conjoined and overlapped. This technique is related to Rauschenberg's early transfer drawings of the 1960s, and it has spawned a wide variety of recent works, including *Anagrams* (1995–96) and *Arcadian Retreats* (1996). In the latter, photographic images were transferred onto wet plaster in a technique resembling that of traditional fresco painting.

14 Rauschenberg, interview with the author, November 6, 1993.

15 Ibid.

16 Ibid., November 5, 1993.

17 Author's discussion with Darryl Pottorf, artist and Rauschenberg's primary studio asistant, September 20, 2000. Notes in author's files, Easton, Penn.

18 See the author's *Masterworks in the Robert and Jane Meyerhoff Collection* (New York: Hudson Hills Press, 1995), 124–26; *Photographic Views of New York City 1870s–1970s from the Collection of the New York Public Library* (Ann Arbor: University Microfilms International, 1981).

19 The photograph was first used in *Cuban Acre*, ROCI/Cuba, 1988.

20 Rauschenberg, interview with the author, November 5, 1993.

21 Ibid., November 6, 1993.

22 Rauschenberg in *Rauschenbergsculpture*, exh. cat.(Modern Art Museum of Fort Worth, 1995), 52–54.

23 See Edward de Bono, *The Mechanism of Mind* (New York: Simon and Schuster, 1969) and *Lateral Thinking: Creativity Step by Step* (New York: Harper and Row, 1974).

24 Edward de Bono, *Lateral Thinking: Textbook of Creativity* (London: Ward Lock Educational, 1970), 39.

25 Sigmund Freud, "A Note on the Unconscious in Psychoanalysis" (1912) in *A General Selection From the Works of Sigmund Freud*, ed. John Rickman, M. D. (Garden City: Doubleday Anchor Books, 1937), 46–69. C. G. Jung, "Psychoanalysis and Associated Experiments" in *The Psychoanalytic Years: C. G. Jung*, trans. F. C. Hull (Princeton University Press, 1973), 3–32.

26 Rauschenberg, "The Artist Speaks: Robert Rauschenberg," interview with Dorothy Gees Seckler, *Art in America* 54, no. 3 (May–June 1966), 81.

27 Robert Rauschenberg, "Robert Rauschenberg: An Audience of One," interview with John Gruen, *Art News* 76, no. 2 (February 1977), 48.

28 Maxime de la Falaise McKendry, "Robert Rauschenberg talks to Maxime de la Falaise McKendry," *Interview* 6, no. 5 (May 1976), 34.

29 Steve Paxton in *Robert Rauschenberg: A Retrospective*, 262–63.

30 Macdonald Critchley and Eileen A. Critchley, *Dyslexia Defined* (London: William Heinemann Medical Books, 1978); T. J. Wheeler and E. J. Watkins, "Dyslexia: A Review of Symptomology," *Dyslexia Review* 2, no. 1 (1979), 12–14.

31 Bobbie H. Jones, "The Gifted Dyslexic," *Annals of Dyslexia* 36 (1986), 301–17.

32 Priscilla L. Vail, "Gifts, Talents and the Dyslexias: Wellsprings, Springboards, and finding Foley's Rocks," *Annals of Dyslexia* 40 (1990), 3–17.

33 Susan Hampshire, *Susan's Story: An Autobiographical Account of My Struggle with Dyslexia* (New York: St. Martin's Press, 1982), 12.

34 Rose, *Rauschenberg*, 85.

35 J. F. Stein, "Developmental Dyslexia, Neural Timing and Hemisphere Later-

alism," *International Journal of Psycho-physiology* 18 (1994), 247.

36 Thomas G. West, "Appendix A: Symptomology," *In the Mind's Eye* (Buffalo: Prometheus Books, 1980), 257–959; Wheeler and Watkins, "Dyslexia," 15.

37 P. G. Aaron, "Is There a Visual Dyslexia?" *Annals of Dyslexia* 43 (1993), 110–24; S. K. Reed, "Structural Descriptions and the Limitations of Visual Images," *Memory and Cognition* 2 (1974), 329–36.

38 Stein, "Developmental Dyslexia," 254. See also A. J. Richardson and J. F. Stein, "Personality Characteristics of Adult Dyslexics," in S. F. Wright and R. Groner, eds, *Facets of Dyslexia and Its Remediation* (London: Elsevier Science, 1993), 411–21.

39 Stein, "Developmental Dyslexia," 246.

40 William H. Berdine and A. Edward Blackhurst, eds, *An Introduction to Special Education* (Boston: Little, Brown, 1981), 414–23.

41 Rauschenberg cited in Calvin Tomkins, "Profiles: Moving Out," *New Yorker* 40, no. 2 (February 29, 1964), 101.

42 Swenson, "Rauschenberg Paints a Picture," 44–46.

two

1 Robert Rauschenberg, "Random Order," *Location* 1, no. 1 (spring 1963), 27–31.

2 In 1965 Rauschenberg moved to a studio on Lafayette Street near Astor Place, which he still owns. By that time the influence of the neighborhood was much less consequential.

3 Brian O'Doherty, "Robert Rauschenberg and the Vernacular Glance," *Art in America* 61, no. 5 (September–October 1973), 82–87. This article was later expanded as "Robert Rauschenberg: The Sixties," *American Masters: Voice and Myth* (New York: Random House, 1974), 188–225.

4 O'Doherty, "Robert Rauschenberg: The Sixties," 201.

5 Rauschenberg quoted in Peter Conrad, *The Art of the City: Views and Versions of New York* (New York and Oxford: Oxford University Press, 1984), 301.

6 Rauschenberg, interview with the author, November 4, 1993.

7 Harold Rosenberg, "Tenth Street: A Geography of Modern Art," *Discovering the Present* (University of Chicago Press, 1960), 101–09.

8 Dore Ashton, *The New York School: A Cultural Reckoning* (Harmondsworth, Middlesex and New York: Penguin, 1973), 198.

9 *Indiana, Kelly, Martin, Rosenquist, Youngerman at Coenties Slip*, essay by Mildred Glimcher, exh. cat. (New York: Pace Gallery, January 16–February 13), 1993.

10 *New York City Guide* (1939; New York: Octagon Books, new ed. 1970), 81.

11 Rauschenberg, interview with the author, November 4, 1993.

12 John I. Griffin, *The Port of New York* (New York: City College Press, 1959), 133.

13 Barbara Mensch, *The Last Waterfront* (New York: Freundlich Books, 1985), 101.

14 Rauschenberg, interview with the author, November 4, 1993.

15 The last link to the East Side Highway, the South Street Elevated Highway, was being built in 1953–56 only a few blocks from Rauschenberg's studio. Its impact on his work will be discussed below.

16 Rauschenberg, interview with the author, November 4, 1993.

17 Charles Grutzner, "Plan to Rebuild Downtown Area Outlined to City," *New York Times* (October 15, 1958), 1.

18 See particularly "Photographic Views of New York City", archive on microfiche, New York Public Library.

19 Ben H. Bagdikian, "Endings, Beginnings, and Endings: Media in the 1950s," in Sidra Stich, *Made In U.S.A.* (Berkeley and Los Angeles: University of California Press, 1987), 228–33.

20 Robert Rauschenberg, "Random Order," 27–31.

21 Rauschenberg, interview with the author, November 5, 1993.

22 Gay Talese, *New York: A Serendipiter's Journey* (New York: Harper & Brothers, 1961). Talese's book, which is both humorous and factual, concerns the history of garbage in New York City.

23 Edgar M. Hoover and Raymond Vernon, *Anatomy of a Metropolis* (Cambridge, Mass: Harvard University Press, 1959), 33, 70, 88.

24 Rauschenberg, interview with the author, November 6, 1993.

25 *Manhattan Address Telephone Directories* from *New York City Telephone Directories* (Ann Arbor: University Microfilms International, 1984).

26 Mattison, *Masterworks in the Robert and Jane Meyerhoff Collection*, 114.

27 Raymond Vernon, *Metropolis 1960: An Interpretation of the Findings of the New York Metropolitan Region Study* (Cambridge, Mass: Harvard University Press, 1960), 108.

28 Sidney Kobre, *The Development of American Journalism* (Dubuque, Ia: Wm. C. Brown Publishers, 1969), 570–71.

29 Edwin Emery, *The Press and America: An Interpretive History of the Mass Media* (Englewood Cliffs, N.J: Prentice-Hall, 1972), 741.

30 The pledge was clearly not upheld in the case of the April 1961 attempted invasion of Cuba.

31 Cited in Kobre, *Development of American Journalism*, 724.

32 John Cage, "On Robert Rauschenberg, Artist, and His Work," *Metro* 2 (May 1961), 37.

33 The most extensive study of the Black Paintings, and a model for the examination of Rauschenberg's work, is Walter Hopps, *Robert Rauschenberg: The Early 1950s*, exh. cat. (Houston: The Menil Collection and Houston Fine Art Press, 1991). Hopps divides the Black Paintings into five sub-groups.

34 Martin Duberman, *Black Mountain: An Exploration in Community* (New York: Dutton, 1972).

35 John Cage quoted in Hopps, *Robert Rauschenberg*, 65.

36 Rauschenberg, interview with the author, November 4, 1993.

37 Hopps, *Robert Rauschenberg*, 65.

38 Judith E. Bernstock, "A New Interpretation of Rauschenberg's Imagery," *Pantheon* 46 (1988), 149–64.

39 Swenson, "Rauschenberg Paints a Picture," 44.

40 This arrangement also resembles the predellas and pinnacles in traditional European panel paintings of the late medieval and early Renaissance periods.

41 The literature on *Collection* mistakenly identifies the article about Patterson as a get-rich-quick scheme by a citizen not

connected with the government. The error was made initially in Roni Feinstein, "Random Order: The First Fifteen Years of Robert Rauschenebrg's Art, 1949–1964," Ph.D. diss. (New York University, 1990), 168, and repeated in Bernstock, "A New Interpretation."

42 Joel Schwartz, *The New York Approach: Robert Moses, Urban Liberals, and the Redevelopment of the Inner City* (Columbus: Ohio State University Press, 1993), 249 and 253.

43 Tomkins, *Off the Wall*, 118.

44 Ibid., 111.

45 Jasper Johns to Leo Steinberg, "Jasper Johns: The First Seven Years of His Art," *Other Criteria: Confrontations with Twentieth-Century Art* (New York: Oxford University Press, 1972), 31.

46 Nan Rosenthal and Ruth E. Fine, *The Drawings of Jasper Johns*, exh. cat. (Washington, D.C: National Gallery of Art, 1990), 94.

47 J. K. Galbraith, *The Affluent Society* (1958; Boston: Houghton Mifflin, 1969).

48 Talese, *New York*, 110.

49 *New York Times* (September 15, 1955), 6C.

50 Rauschenberg, interview with the author, November 5, 1993.

51 Ibid.

52 Tomkins, *Off the Wall*, 136.

53 Robert Hughes, *The Shock of the New* (New York: McGraw-Hill, 1980), 335. In a less convincing argument, Hughes also discusses *Monogram* as "one of the few great icons of male homosexual love in modern culture."

54 Calvin Tomkins quoting Rauschenberg in "Sistine on Broadway" in Roni Feinstein and Calvin Tomkins, *Robert Rauschenberg: The Silkscreen Paintings 1962–64*, exh. cat. (New York: Whitney Museum of American Art, 1990), 14.

55 *Manhattan Address Telephone Directory*, 1958.

56 Unsigned, "South Street Overpass Due to Open in Late Fall," *New York Times* (April 28, 1958), 31.

57 Grutzner, *New York Times* (October 15, 1958), 1.

58 Editorial, "A New Downtown Manhattan," *New York Times* (October 15, 1958), 38.

59 Rauschenberg in "The Emperor's Combine," *Time* (April 18, 1960), 92.

60 Hans Hofmann, *Search for the Real and Other Essays* (Cambridge, Mass: M.I.T. Press, 1948 and 1967).

61 Swenson, "Rauschenberg Paints a Picture," 328.

62 Rauschenberg's interests parallel Jasper Johns's investigations of the "impossibility of sufficient visual memory to transfer from one like object to another the memory imprint." Quoted in John Cage, "Jasper Johns: Stories and Ideas," *Jasper Johns*, exh. cat. (New York: The Jewish Museum, 1964), 23–24. Typically, Johns investigates this idea with the rigor of a philosophical construct while Rauschenberg does so more intuitively.

63 Rose, *Rauschenberg*, 56.

64 Hoover and Vernon, *Anatomy of a Metropolis*, 27.

65 "Metropolis in a Mess," *Newsweek* 54, no. 4 (July 27, 1959), 29–31.

66 Fred J. Cook and Gene Gleason, "The Shame of New York," *Nation* 189, no. 14 (October 1959).

67 Later studies have shown that cities with less extensive slum clearance and highway programs suffered a similar fate to that of New York City. The dispersion of industry, flight of the middle class, influx of racial minorities, FHA-assisted mortgages for single-family dwellings which urged suburban growth were all part of larger national forces.

68 Schwartz, *New York Approach*, 143.

69 Jane Jacobs, *The Death and Life of Great American Cities* (New York: Random House, 1961), ch. 3. For significant commentary on the opposition between Moses and Jacobs, see Robert A. M. Stern, *New York 1960: Architecture and Urbanism between the Second World War and the Bicentennial* (New York: Monacelli Press, 1995), 37–46.

70 Rauschenberg, "Random Order," 28.

71 David Rockefeller, "Development of City Piers," letter to the editor, *New York Times* (Novemeber 23, 1959), 30.

72 Charles C. Bennett, "Fulton St. Change Leads to Clash," *New York Times* (May 7, 1959), 35.

73 *Manhattan Address Telephone Directory*, 1960.

74 Rauschenberg quoted in Esther Sparks, *Universal Limited Art Editions* (New York:

Art Institute of Chicago and Abrams, 1989), 219.

75 Kobre, *Development of American Journalism*, 716.

76 Mitchell Stephens, *A History of News from the Drum to the Satellite* (New York: Viking, 1988), 281.

77 Ibid., 280–88.

78 Rauschenberg, interview with the author, November 6, 1993.

79 Tomkins, "Sistine of Broadway," 15.

80 Rauschenberg titled a series of his later large Combines "Spreads," in reference to the cowboy slang for a sizable piece of land. *Estate* provides an urban parallel to this reference.

81 Rauschenberg, interview with the author, November 4, 1993.

82 George E. Mowry and Blaine A. Brownell, *The Urban Nation 1920–1980* (New York: Hill and Wang, 1981), 225.

three

1 Rauschenberg, [untitled], *Studio International* 178, no. 917 (December 1969), 246–47.

2 These articles include Kenneth Bendiner, "Robert Rauschenberg's *Canyon*," *Arts Magazine* 56, no. 10 (June 1982), 57–59; Roberta Bernstein, "Robert Rauschenberg's *Rebus*," *Arts Magazine* 52, no. 5 (January 1978), 138–41; and Stuckey, "Reading Rauschenberg," 74–84.

3 Robert Wohl, *A Passion for Wings: Aviation and the Western Imagination 1908–1918* (New Haven and London: Yale University Press, 1994), 7.

4 Ibid., 173.

5 Ibid., 175.

6 Pablo Picasso, *Nature morte: "Notre Avenir est dans l'Air"* (1912, private collection).

7 The umbrella in *Charlene* also resembles an artist's color wheel. Rauschenberg never shows umbrellas being held or as protection from the rain. Instead he focuses on their open canopy, often displayed as if floating in the air.

8 Lawrence Alloway, Introduction, *Rauschenberg: Graphic Art*, exh. cat. (Philadelphia: Institute of Contemporary Art, University of Pennsylvania, April 1–May 10, 1970), 9.

9 Max Kozloff, "American Painting During the Cold War" (1973), in Francis Frascina, ed., *Pollock and After: The Critical Debate* (New York: Harper & Row, 1985), 120.

10 Christin J. Mamiya, *Pop Art and Consumer Culture* (Austin: University of Texas Press, 1992), and "We the People: The Art of Robert Rauschenberg and the Construction of American National Identity," *American Art* 7, no. 3 (summer 1993), 41–63.

11 Ibid., 52.

12 Mary Lynn Kotz, *Rauschenberg: Art and Life* (New York: Abrams, 1990), 176.

13 Interview with James Dean, former Director of the NASA Art Program, July 31, 1998, Alexandria, Va. Tape recording of interview in the author's files, Easton, Penn.

14 Ibid.

15 John M. Logsdon, *The Decision to Go to the Moon: Project Apollo and the National Interest* (Cambridge, Mass., and London: M.I.T. Press, 1970), 14 and 16.

16 Ibid., 102.

17 "Special Issue: The Space Age," *Newsweek* 60, no. 15 (October 8, 1962), 85.

18 William L. O'Neill, *Coming Apart: An Informal History of America in the 1960s* (Chicago: Quadrangle Books, 1971), "Profile: Space," 51–59.

19 The precedent for the use of a broken lithographic stone in Rauschenberg's work was *Accident* (1963).

20 *Time* (April 12, 1961), 22. "But following the course of technological developments some military space enthusiasts see improved methods of warfare as the primary goal of research in space."

21 The batter in *Brace* is the Yankee player Roger Maris (number 9) who made headlines in 1961 when he outperformed his teammate Mickey Mantle to break Babe Ruth's record for the most home runs hit in a season.

22 Interview with Billy Klüver, October 9, 1997, Berkeley Heights, N.J. Tape recording in the author's files, Easton, Penn.

23 This photograph was also used in Rauschenberg's most important published, early theoretical statement, "Random Order," 27–31.

24 *Die Hard*'s three panels form a triptych. Given the almost religious zeal expressed in the work, this reference to the format of traditional Northern European altarpieces may be deliberate.

25 The fruit can be found at the bottom of *Persimmon* (1964, Jean-Christophe Castelli Collection).

26 The entire football scene with players and the ball highlighted with a circle drawn around it appears in *Echo* (1962, private collection).

27 "Editor's Notes," *Newsweek* 60, no. 15 (October 8, 1962), 6–12.

28 Ibid., 24.

29 Klüver, interview with the author, October 3, 1997.

30 Ibid.

31 Kotz, *Rauschenberg*, 178.

32 *E.A.T. News* 2, no. 1 (March 18, 1968), n.p.

33 Ibid.

34 James Dean, "The Artist and Space," *Interdisciplinary Science Reviews* 3, no. 3 (1978), 244. This article is the most extensive source on the entire NASA Art Program.

35 Dean, interview with the author, July 31, 1998.

36 Ibid.

37 Ibid.

38 In the letter, Rauschenberg discussed the possibility of trading art with anyone who had been given one of these rocks. Rauschenberg also expressed an interest in acquiring heat shield tiles from the exterior of the space capsules and moon dust – all presumably to use in art works. None of these requests was possible. James Dean files, Alexandria, Va.

39 Walter Cronkite quoted in O'Neill, *Coming Apart*, 58.

40 Rauschenberg, *Studio International*, 246–47.

41 Feinstein, *The Silkscreen Paintings*, 78.

42 "Booster rocket" is listed as one of 100 new words entering the English language in *The New Webster Encyclopedic Dictionary of the English Language*, Virginia S. Thacher, ed. (Chicago: Consolidated Book Publishers, 1970), xii.

43 Chairs are among the most frequently recurring motifs in Rauschenberg's art. While he admires the simplicity and structural stability of these unadorned chairs, he often puts them in situations that involve their opposite, movement. Use of chairs in his works include the early photographic depiction *Quiet House* (1949, collection of the artist), done at Black Mountain College; the chair attached to the Combine *Pilgrim* (1960, Museum Folkwang, Essen); the illusion of tumbling chairs in the electronic piece *Soundings* (1968, Museum Ludwig, Cologne); the chair attached to Merce Cunningham's back in the dance *Antic Meet* (1958); and the chairs, both illusory and real, in *Big D Ellipse (Shiner)* (1990, collection of the artist).

44 See *Life* (September 27, 1963), 76–93.

45 For a more extensive discussion of this topic, see the author's "Robert Rauschenberg's *Autobiography*: Context and Meaning," *Wallraf-Richartz-Jahrbuch* 59 (1998), 297–305.

46 Lisa Susan Wainwright, "Reading Junk: Thematic Imagery in the Art of Robert Rauschenberg from 1952 to 1964," Ph.D. diss. (University of Illinois at Urbana-Champaign, 1993), 107–32.

47 As reported in ibid., 107, n. 50.

48 Interview with Sidney Felsen, Director of Gemini G. E. L., June 4, 1998, New York City. Tape recording in the author's files, Easton, Penn.

49 Interview with Kenneth Tyler, Director of Tyler Graphics, August 4, 1998, Mount Kisco, N.Y. Tape recording in the author's files, Easton, Penn.

50 Ibid.

51 Ibid.

52 Ibid.

53 Dean, interview with the author, July 31, 1998.

54 *Dam* also contains a parachutist jumping from a plane in its upper-right corner.

55 Special Issue, "The Space Age," *Newsweek*, 60, no. 5 (October 8, 1962), 30.

56 A similar theme appears in the print *Post*. It depicts the astronauts being comical during jungle survival training in Panama.

57 Brian Harvey, *Race into Space: The Soviet Programme* (Chichester: Ellis Horwood, 1988), 188.

58 Rauschenberg had been suspicious of organized religion since his experiences with the fundamentalist church in Port Arthur. He is quoted in Calvin Tomkins as saying, "Finally, I decided I couldn't spend the rest of my life thinking everybody else was going to hell, but I kept on going to church . . . Giving it up was a major

change in my life." Tomkins, *Off the Wall*, 15.

59 The print *Moon Rose (Stoned Moon Series)* also shows this cosmonaut.

60 Harvey, *Race into Space*, 70–72.

61 Special Section, *New York Times* (July 17, 1969), 34.

62 Ibid.

63 Ibid.

64 The first print Rauschenberg made from an accidentally broken stone was *Accident* (1963), for which he won the Grand Prize at the international print exhibition, Moderna Galerija, Ljubljana, Yugoslavia. The joyful mood of *Accident* is the opposite of *Brake*.

65 O'Neill, *Coming Apart*, 51–60.

66 Another use of clear diagrams by Rauschenberg is the dual trajectory diagrams showing the mission route to the moon and back in *Loop (Stoned Moon Series)*.

67 Rauschenberg has been a constant supporter of environmental issues. In 1970, he created the official Earth Day poster for the April 22 nationwide demonstration. The poster presents a considerably bleaker appraisal than that found in the *Stoned Moon Series*. In *Earth Day* almost all of the images are of wasted, contaminated, and environmentally damaged areas. The only two living creatures in the poster are endangered species. One is a gorilla, and at the center there is a bald eagle which is printed ominously in black and brown ink, a dark symbol of America.

68 Dean, interview with the author, July 31, 1998.

69 In the print *Sky Rite*, Rauschenberg contrasts the same photograph of Wernher von Braun with a photograph of the entire staff of the Launch Control Room looking up from their instruments to watch a launch. In the breakdown of roles at NASA, Von Braun, as the director of the center in Huntsville, Alabama where the rockets were built, was in charge of constructing and delivering the rocket to Cape Canaveral. When it arrived, Launch Control at Cape Canaveral took over responsibility; about ten minutes after launch Mission Control in Houston took over the flight, and the individuals in

Launch Control could go home. James Dean (interview July 30, 1998) recalls explaining this pattern of changing responsibilities to Rauschenberg and having him be particularly interested in it because of the collaboration and shared responsibility.

70 Ironically, Rauschenberg had won the Venice Biennale six years earlier, when his entry was the first that the United States government had officially sponsored.

71 Kotz, *Rauschenberg*, 176.

72 Tyler, interview with the author, August 4, 1998.

73 Ibid.

74 John Canaday, "Rauschenberg Art: A Chance to Catch Up," *New York Times* (July 10, 1970), 16.

75 Paul Richard, "Apollo 11 As an Art Form," *Washington Post* (October 30, 1970), B1.

76 Donald H. Karshan, "Robert Rauschenberg," *Art International* 58, no. 6 (November–December 1970), 48–49.

77 Joseph E. Young, "Los Angeles Letter," *Art International* 14, no. 3 (March 1970), 87.

78 Kotz, *Rauschenberg*, 180

79 Rauschenberg also witnessed the last launch of the Apollo program, a spectacular night launch, that he viewed with Cy Twombly. James Dean, interview with the author, July 31, 1998.

80 Robert Schulman, telephone interview with the author, July, 29, 1998. Notes in the author's files, Easton, Penn.

81 Ibid.

82 *New York Times* (September 30, 1988), 1A.

four

1 Rauschenberg statement in the lithograph *Autobiography* (1968).

2 Trisha Brown, "Collaboration: Life and Death in the Aesthetic Zone," *Robert Rauschenberg: A Retrospective*, exh. cat. (New York: Solomon R. Guggenheim Museum of Art, 1997), 269.

3 Recent essays include Steve Paxton, "Rauschenberg for Cunningham and Three of His Own," 260–67, and Trisha Brown in ibid. These first-hand accounts are among the most significant essays in the catalogue. An important earlier study is Nina Sundell, *Rauschenberg/Performance*

1954–1984, exh. cat. (New York: Arthur A. Houghton, Jr. Gallery, Cooper Union for the Advancement of Science and the Arts, December 7–22, 1983).

4 Rauschenberg in Richard Kostelanetz, *The Theater of Mixed Means* (New York: Dial Press, 1968), 80 and 94.

5 Don Shewey, "'We collaborated by postcards': An Interview with Robert Rauschenberg," *Theatre Crafts* 18, no. 4 (April 1984), 38.

6 Not included in this study are Rauschenberg's sets for *Lateral Pass* (1985, Naples, Italy performance), which he created when the original sets by Nancy Graves failed to arrive, and his visual presentation for *Foray Forêt* (1990).

7 Trisha Brown quoted in Geoff Gehman, "Longtime duo agree on taking chances," *Morning Call* (Sunday, February 13, 1994), F4.

8 Tomkins, *Off the Wall*, 221–33.

9 Ibid., 228–33.

10 David Sears, "A Trisha Brown–Robert Rauschenberg Collage," *Ballet Review* 22 (fall 1982), 47.

11 David Vaughan, *Merce Cunningham: Fifty Years* (Denville, N.J: Aperature, 1997), 128.

12 *Trophy I (For Merce Cunnningham)* (1959, Kunsthaus, Zurich) expresses similar ideas. The Combine is a homage to Cunningham but adds notes of chance and vulnerability with the inclusion of incomplete floorboards, a sign reading "Caution, Watch Your Step," and the image of a fallen horse. Cunningham had recently broken his foot, and Rauschenberg's work commemorates accidental events as well as the precision of Cunningham's dance technique.

13 Rauschenberg, interview with the author, November 6, 1993.

14 Vaughan, *Merce Cunningham*, 131.

15 Ibid., 130.

16 Tomkins, *Off the Wall*, 230.

17 Vaughan, *Merce Cunningham*, 134.

18 Steve Paxton quoted in Tomkins, *Off the Wall*, 228.

19 Hendel Teicher, "Trisha Brown Free Measures: Drawings," exh. cat. (New York: The Drawing Center's Drawing Room, 1998), n.p.

20 Ann Halprin interview in Kostelanetz, *Theatre of Mixed Means*, 66–77.

21 Don McDonagh, *The Complete Guide to Modern Dance* (New York: Doubleday, 1972), 381–82.

22 Richard Schechner, interview, "Ann Halprin: A Life in Ritual," *Tulane Drama Review* 33 (1989), 67.

23 Trisha Brown quoted in David Bourdon, "Living in the Moment of the Next Move," *New York Times* (September 8, 1996), 62.

24 Sally Banes, *Democracy's Body: Judson Dance Theater, 1962–1964* (Ann Arbor, Mich: UMI Research Press, 1980), ch. 2. Banes's book is the most thorough study of the Judson Dance Theater.

25 Robert Dunn interview in Don McDonagh, *The Rise and Fall and Rise of Modern Dance* (New York: Outerbridge & Deinstfrey, 1970), 79.

26 Ibid., 81–82.

27 Sally Sommer, "Equipment Dances: Trisha Brown," *The Drama Review*, 16, no. 3 (September 1972), 136.

28 Robert Dunn quoted in McDonagh, *Rise and Fall and Rise of Modern Dance*, 90.

29 Ibid., 90–91.

30 Ibid., 85.

31 Robert Ellis Dunn, "Judson Days," *Contact Quarterly* 4 (winter 1989), 11.

32 Lucinda Childs's *Street Dance*, section quoted in McDonagh, *Complete Guide to Modern Dance*, 146.

33 Steve Paxton quoted in Tomkins, *Off the Wall*, 226.

34 Sears, "A Trisha Brown–Robert Rauschenberg Collage," 48.

35 Sally Banes, "Gravity and Levity: Up and Down with Trisha Brown," *Dance Magazine* 52, no. 3 (March 1978), 62.

36 Cynthia Novack, *Sharing Dance: Contact Improvisation and American Culture* (Madison: University of Wisconsin Press, 1990), 8–25.

37 Hopps, *Robert Rauschenberg*, 184.

38 Paxton, "Rauschenberg for Cunningham and Three of His Own," 264.

39 See the author's "Robert Rauschenberg's Autobiography," 297–306.

40 Rauschenberg interview in Kostelanetz, *Theater of Mixed Means*, 85.

41 Richard Kostelanetz, "A Conversation with Robert Rauschenberg," *Partisan Review* 35, no. 1 (winter 1968), 104.

42 Gehman, "Longtime duo agree on taking chances," F4.

43 Sears, "A Trisha Brown–Robert Rauschenberg Collage," 48.

44 Rauschenberg in Kostelanetz, *Theater of Mixed Means*, 89.

45 Ibid., 92.

46 Yvonne Rainer, *Work 1961–73* (Halifax and New York: The Press of Nova Scotia College of Art and Design and New York University Press, 1974), 9.

47 Sears, "A Trisha Brown–Robert Rauschenberg Collage" 48.

48 McDonagh, *Complete Guide to Modern Dance*, 345.

49 Sears, "A Trisha Brown–Robert Rauschenberg Collage," 48.

50 Brown, "Collaborations," 269.

51 Trisha Brown, interview with the author, February 16, 1994. Video tape in the author's files, Easton, Penn.

52 Sears, "A Trisha Brown–Robert Rauschenberg Collage," 50.

53 Brown, interview with the author, February 16, 1994.

54 Sears, "A Trisha Brown–Robert Rauschenberg Collage," 49.

55 Trisha Brown in *Robert Rauschenberg: A Retrospective*, 269.

56 Ibid.

57 Rauschenberg, interview with the author, November 6, 1993.

58 Rauschenberg's decision was also influenced by a copyright infringement lawsuit that was initiated by a professional photographer, one of whose images Rauschenberg had used in his works. Rauschenberg eventually won the lawsuit.

59 Rauschenberg, interview with the author, November 6, 1993.

60 Bourdon, "Living in the Moment of the Next Move," 62.

61 Steve Paxton used martial arts movements in several of his early works at the Judson Dance Theater.

62 Brown, interview with the author, February 18, 1994. Tape recording in the author's files, Easton, Penn.

63 Roslyn Sulcas, "Trisha Brown: Choreography," *Dance Magazine* 69, no. 4 (April 1995), 47.

64 Brown, interview with the author, February 18, 1994.

65 Ibid.

66 Brown in *Robert Rauschenberg: A Retrospective*, 271.

67 Brown, interview with the author, February 16, 1994.

68 Ibid.

69 Ibid.

70 Rauschenberg quoted by Brown in *Robert Rauschenberg: A Retrospective*, 271.

71 Sulcas, "Trisha Brown," 47.

72 Ann Kisselgoff, "Trisha Brown: Simplicity within Complexity," *New York Times* (May 5, 1994), C18.

73 Rauschenberg, interview with the author, November 6, 1993.

74 Brown, interview with the author, February 18, 1994.

75 Ibid.

76 Ibid.

77 Ibid.

78 Rauschenberg, interview with the author, November 4, 1993.

79 Ibid.

80 Ibid.

81 Ibid.

82 Ibid.

83 Brown in *Robert Rauschenberg: A Retrospective*, 269.

84 Brown, interview with the author, February 18, 1994.

85 Ibid.

86 Ibid.

87 Ibid.

88 Ibid.

89 Ibid.

90 Sears, "A Trisha Brown–Robert Rauschenberg Collage," 50.

91 Rauschenberg, interview with the author, November 6, 1993.

92 Ibid.

93 Brown, interview with the author, February 16, 1994.

94 Rauschenberg, interview with the author, November 6, 1993.

95 Brown, interview with the author, February 16, 1994.

five

1 Rauschenberg, interview with the author, November 4, 1993.

2 Donald Saff, interview with the author, August 18, 2000, Oxford, Md. Tape recording in the author's files, Easton, Penn.

3 Rauschenberg, interview with author, November 4, 1993.

4   Rauschenberg, interview with the author, November 5, 1993.

5   Saff, interview with the author, August 18, 2000.

6   "ROCI: An Incomplete History of the Rauschenberg Overseas Culture Interchange," compiled by Donald Saff (1987), n.p. Rauschenberg Archives, New York City.

7   Ibid.

8   Rose, *Rauschenberg*, 107.

9   Ibid., 106.

10 Rauschenberg, interview with the author, November 6, 1993.

11 Rauschenberg, "The Tobago Statement." See *Rauschenberg Overseas Culture Interchange*, exh. cat., introduction Jack Cowart (Washington, D.C: National Gallery of Art, May 12 – September 2, 1991), 154.

12 *Robert Rauschenberg: A Retrospective*, 574.

13 Rauschenberg, "A Conversation about Art and ROCI: Robert Rauschenberg and Donald Saff" in *Rauschenberg Overseas Culture Interchange*, exh. cat. (Washington, D.C.: National Gallery of Art, 1991), 160.

14 Saff, interview with the author, August 18, 2000.

15 Rauschenberg, "A Conversation about Art and ROCI," 161.

16 Ibid.

17 Rauschenberg, interview with the author, November 5, 1993.

18 See e.g. Robert Hughes, "The Arcadian as Utopian: Robert Rauschenberg's Rhapsodic Energies Fill Four Manhattan Shows," *Time* 24 (January 1983), 74–77; and John Perrault, "Rauschenberg: The World Is His Studio," *Geo* 5, no. 11 (November 1983), 64–71, 98.

19 Rauschenberg, "A Conversation about Art and ROCI," 156.

20 Saff, "ROCI," n.p.

21 Ibid.

22 Letter to Pontus Hulten, February 12, 1982, Rauschenberg Archives, New York City.

23 Leo Castelli quoted in note in Rauschenberg Archives, New York City.

24 Rauschenberg, "A Conversation about Art and ROCI," 164.

25 Rauschenberg, interview with the author, November 5, 1993.

26 Rauschenberg, "A Conversation about Art and ROCI," 156.

27 Ibid., 156–57.

28 Rauschenberg, interview with the author, November 5, 1993.

29 Rauschenberg, "A Conversation about Art and ROCI," 157.

30 Rauschenberg, interview with the author, November 6, 1993.

31 Once the board of trustees of the National Gallery decided to break the precedent, the first exhibition was a retrospective of the drawings of Jasper Johns, which was held before the Rauschenberg Overseas Culture Interchange exhibition.

32 Saff, interview with the author, August 18, 2000.

33 Rauschenberg, interview with the author, November 6, 1993.

34 Saff, interview with the author, August 18, 2000.

35 Rauschenberg, "A Discussion with Students, Artists, and Writers," July 13, 1985. Typescript in Rauschenberg Archives, New York City.

36 "Briefing Paper on Chile," Rauschenberg Archives, New York City.

37 Ibid.

38 Rauschenberg, interview with the author, November 6, 1993.

39 Leslie Bethell, ed., *Chile Since Independence* (Cambridge University Press, 1995), 177–86.

40 *New York Times* (November 11, 1984), 4A.

41 Rauschenberg, interview with the author, November 6, 1993.

42 While all other individuals close to Rauschenberg in Chile were interviewed, Terry Van Brunt, who accompanied him for the entire journey, is now estranged from him and refuses to discuss any topic involving him.

43 Rauschenberg, interview with the author, November 6, 1993.

44 *New York Times* (November 6, 1984), 1A.

45 *New York Times* (November 7, 1984), 1A.

46 Mario Stein, electronic mail to the author, August 14, 2000.

47 Stein, electronic mail to the author, August 22, 2000.

48 For an overview of this topic, see Michael Fleet and Brian H. Smith, *The Catholic Church and Democracy in Chile and Peru* (South Bend: University of Notre Dame Press, 1997), ch. 4.

49 Stein, electronic mail to the author, August 22, 2000.

50 Ibid.

51 Rauschenberg, interview with the author, November 6, 1993.

52 Nena Ossa, interview with the author, October 10, 2000, Philadelphia. Tape recording in the author's files, Easton, Penn.

53 Monica Gelcich, electronic mail to the author, May 6, 2001.

54 Maria del Pilar, letter to the author, October 25, 2000.

55 Rauschenberg, "A Conversation about Art and ROCI," 166.

56 Pilar, letter to the author, October 25, 2000.

57 Ibid.

58 José Donoso, "Rauschenberg: El Transgressor," *ROCI: Rauschenberg Overseas Culture Interchange*, exh. cat. (Santiago: Museo Nacional de Bellas Artes de Chile, July 17 – August 18, 1985), 8–10.

59 Pilar, letter to the author, October 25, 2000.

60 Rauschenberg, interview with the author, November 6, 1993.

61 Simon Collier and William F. Sater, *A History of Chile: 1908–1994* (Cambridge University Press, 1995), 374.

62 Kotz, *Rauschenberg*, 26.

63 Rauschenberg, interview with the author, November 6, 1993.

64 John Cage, "On Robert Rauschenberg, Artist, and His Work," *Metro* 2 (May 1961), 37.

65 Rauschenberg, "A Conversation about Art and ROCI," 167.

66 Gelcich, electronic mail to the author, May 6, 2001.

67 Ibid.

68 Rauschenberg, interview with the author, November 6, 1993.

69 Rauschenberg, "A Conversation about Art and ROCI," 167.

70 Rauschenberg, interview with the author, November 6, 1993.

71 Gelcich, electronic mail to the author, May 6, 2001.

72 This type of mining is called *torta* (cake) mining by the Chileans because the earth is removed in concentric rings that resemble the negative form of a layer cake.

73 Rauschenberg, interview with the author, November 6, 1993.

74 Rauschenberg, interview with the author, November 6, 1993.

75 Rauschenberg, "A Discussion with Students, Artists, and Writers," n.p.

76 Paul W. Dreak and Ivan Jaksic, eds, *The Struggle for Democracy in Chile* (Lincoln, Nebr. and London: University of Nebraska Press, 1995), 162ff.

77 *New York Times* (April 25, 1983), 1A. See also Collier and Sater, *History of Chile*, 374.

78 Stein, electronic mail to the author, August 22, 2000.

79 Rauschenberg, interview with the author, November 6, 1993.

80 Collier and Sater, *History of Chile*, 367–69.

81 Gelcich, electronic mail to the author, May 6, 2001.

82 Rauschenberg, interview with the author, November 6, 1993.

83 Rauschenberg, "A Discussion with Students, Artists, and Writers," n.p.

84 Ossa, interview with the author, October 10, 2000.

85 Hopps, *Robert Rauschenberg*, 6.

86 See Lesley J. Rogers, *The Development of Brain and Behavior in the Chicken* (Wallingford: CAB International, 1995), 214–19; Rene Zayan and Ian J. H. Duncan, eds, *Cognitive Aspects of Social Behavior in the Domestic Fowl* (Amsterdam: Elsevier, 1987), esp. Robert Bryan Jones, "Social and Environmental Aspects of Fear in the Domestic Fowl," 82–87.

87 Darryl Pottorf, discussion with the author, September 20, 2000.

88 Ossa, interview with the author, October 10, 2000.

89 Rauschenberg, interview with the author, November 3, 1993.

90 Ossa, interview with the author, October 10, 2000.

91 Ibid.

92 Rauschenberg, interview with the author, November 5, 2000.

93 Mattison, "Robert Rauschenberg's Autobiography," 297–300.

94 Rauschenberg, interview with the author, November 4, 1993.

95 Ibid.

96 Ibid.

97 Rex A. Hudson, ed., *Chile: A Country Study* (Washington, D.C: Federal Research Division, Library of Congress, 1994), 211.

98 Rauschenberg, interview with the author, November 6, 1993.

99 Ibid.

remarks

1 Paxton in *Rauschenberg: A Retrospective*, 262.

2 Rauschenberg, "A Conversation about Art and ROCI," 179.

selected bibliography

published interviews, writings, and statements by the artist

1959
Statement in Dorothy C. Miller, ed. *Sixteen Americans*, exh. cat. (New York: The Museum of Modern Art, 1959), 58.

1963
"Random Order," *Location* 1, no. 1 (spring 1963), 27–31.

1966
Seckler, Dorothy Gees, "The Artist Speaks: Robert Rauschenberg," *Art in America* 54, no. 3 (May–June 1966), 72–84.

1968
Kostelanetz, Richard, "A Conversation with Robert Rauschenberg," *Partisan Review* 35, no. 1 (winter 1968), 92–106. Expanded and published as "Robert Rauschenberg," chapter in Kostelanetz, *The Theatre of Mixed Means: An Introduction to Happenings, Kinetic Environments, and Other Mixed-Means Performances* (New York: Dial Press, 1968), 78–99.

1973
Statement in "Robert Rauschenberg: Technology as Nature," chapter in Douglas Davis, *Art and the Future: A History/Prophecy of the Collaboration between Science, Technology and Art* (New York: Praeger Publishers, 1973), 143–45.

1975
Statement in James Klosty, ed, *Merce Cunningham* (New York: Saturday Review Press, E.P. Dutton, 1975), 83.

1976
McKendry, Maxime de la Falaise, "Robert Rauschenberg Talks to Maxime de la Falaise McKendry," *Interview* 6, no. 5 (May 1976), 34–36.

1977
Gruen, John, "Robert Rauschenberg: An Audience of One," *Art News* 76, no. 2 (February 1977), 44–48.

1978
Perry Arthur, "Vancouver: A Conversation between Robert Rauschenberg and Arthur Perry," *Artmagazine* 10, no. 4 (November–December 1978), 31–35.

1981
Klüver, Billy, and Robert Rauschenberg. "Art en mouvement: Souveniers conjugés"/"Kunst in beweging: Een gekombineerde herinnering," in *Le Moderna Museet de Stockholm a Bruxelles*, exh. cat. (Brussels: Palais des Beaux-Arts, 1981), 35–40.

1982
Photos In + Out City Limits (New York: ULAE), 1982.

1984
Shewey, Don, "We Collaborated by Postcards: An Interview with Robert Rauschenberg," *Theatre Crafts* 18, no. 4 (April 1984), 36–38, 72–75.

1987
Rose, Barbara, *Robert Rauschenberg* (New York: Vintage Books, 1987).

1990
Taylor, Paul, "Robert Rauschenberg," *Interview* 20, no. 12 (December 1990), 142–47.

1991
With Donald Saff, "A Conversation about Art and ROCI," In *Rauschenberg Overseas Culture Interchange*, exh. cat. (Washington, D.C.: National Gallery of Art, 1991), 155–79.
Statement in Donald J. Saff, "Conservation of Matter: Robert Rauschenberg's Art of Acceptance," *Aperture* no. 125 (fall 1991), 26.
"Tobago Statement," in *Rauschenberg Overseas Culture Interchange*, exh. cat., (Washington, D.C.: National Gallery of Art, 1991), 154.

1995
Turrell, Julia Brown, "Talking to Robert Rauschenberg," in *Rauschenbergsculpture*, exh. cat., (Fort Worth: Modern Art Museum, 1995), 49–82.

books and dissertations

Banes, Sally, *Democracy's Body: Judson Dance Theater, 1962–1964*, Studies in the Fine Arts: The Avant-Garde, no. 43 (Ann Arbor: University Microfilms International Research Press, 1983).
Bethell, Leslie, ed, *Chile Since Independence*, (Cambridge University Press, 1995).
Bono, Edward de, *Lateral Thinking: Textbook of Creativity* (London: Ward Lock Educational, 1970).
Bono, Edward de, *Lateral Thinking: Creativity Step by Step* (New York: Harper and Row, 1974).
Collier, Simon, and William F. Sater, *A History of Chile: 1908–1994* (Cambridge University Press, 1995).
Critchley, Macdonald, and Eileen A. Critchley, *Dyslexia Defined* (London: William Heinemann Medical Books, 1978).
Davis, Douglas, "Robert Rauschenberg: Technology as Nature," chapter in *Art and the Future: A History/Prophecy of the Collaboration between Science, Technology and Art* (New York: Praeger Publishers, 1973), 141–45.
Dreak, Paul W., and Ivan Jaksic, eds, *The Struggle for Democracy in Chile* (Lincoln and London: University of Nebraska Press, 1995).
Feinstein, Roni, "Random Order: The First Fifteen Years of Robert Rauschenberg's Art, 1949–1964," Ph.D. dissertation (New York University, 1990).
Fineberg, Jonathan, "Robert Rauschenberg," section of chapter in *Art Since 1940: Strategies of Being* (Englewood Cliffs, N.J.: Prentice Hall, 1995) 176–86.
Fleet, Michael, and Brian H. Smith, *The Catholic Church and Democracy in Chile and Peru* (South Bend: University of Notre Dame Press, 1997).
Forge, Andrew, *Rauschenberg* (1969; New York: Abrams, 1972).
Hoover, Edgar M., and Raymond Vernon. *Anatomy of a Metropolis* (Cambridge, Mass.: Harvard University Press, 1959).
Jacobs, Jane, *The Death and Life of Great American Cities* (New York: Random House, 1961).
Kostelanetz, Richard, *The Theater of Mixed Means* (New York: Dial Press, 1968).
Kotz, Mary Lynn, *Rauschenberg: Art and Life* (New York: Abrams, 1990).
Logsdon, John M., *The Decision to Go to the Moon: Project Apollo and the National Interest* (Cambridge, Mass. and London: M.I.T. Press, 1970).
Mamiya, Christin J., *Pop Art and Consumer Culture* (Austin: University of Texas Press, 1992).
Mattison, Robert S., "Robert Rauschenberg," chapter in Mattison, *Masterworks in the Robert and Jane Meyerhoff Collection: Jasper*

Johns, Roy Lichtenstein, Robert Rauschenberg, Ellsworth Kelly, and Frank Stella (New York: Hudson Hills Press, 1995).

McDonagh, Don, *The Rise and Fall of Modern Dance* (New York: Outerbridge & Dienstfrey, 1970).

Mensch, Barbara, *The Last Waterfront* (New York: Freundlich Books, 1985).

O'Doherty, Brian, "Robert Rauschenberg: The Sixties," chapter in *American Masters: The Voice and the Myth* (New York: Random House, 1974), 188–225. Expanded version of "Rauschenberg and the Vernacular Glance," *Art in America* 61, no. 5 (September–October 1973), 82–87.

O'Neill, William L., *Coming Apart: An Informal History of America in the 1960s* (Chicago: Quadrangle Books, 1971).

Rauschenberg, Robert, *Rauschenberg: XXXIV Drawings for Dante's Inferno*, commentary by Dore Ashton (New York: Abrams, 1965).

Sandler, Irving., "Rauschenberg and Johns," chapter in *The New York School: Painters and Sculptors of the Fifties* (New York: Harper and Row Publishers, 1978), 174–95.

Schwartz, Joel, *The New York Approach: Robert Moses, Urban Liberals, and the Redevelopment of the Inner City* (Columbus: Ohio State University Press, 1993).

Smith, Mark Lesley, "Image and Word in the Prints of Robert Rauschenberg, 1951–1981," Ph.D. diss. (The University of Texas at Austin, 1992).

Stich, Sidra, *Made in U.S.A.* (Berkeley and Los Angeles: University of California Press, 1987).

Tomkins, Calvin, "Robert Rauschenberg," chapter in *The Bride and Her Bachelors: The Heretical Courtship in Modern Art* (New York: Viking Press, 1965), 185–237.

Tomkins, Calvin, *Off the Wall: Robert Rauschenberg and the Art World of Our Time* (Garden City, N.Y.: Doubleday, 1980).

Vaughan, David, *Merce Cunningham: Fifty Years* (New York: Aperture, 1997).

Wainright, Lisa Susan, "Reading Junk: Thematic Imagery in the Art of Robert Rauschenberg from 1952 to 1964," Ph.D. diss. (University of Illinois at Champaign-Urbana, 1993).

Wissman, Jürgen, *Robert Rauschenberg: Black Market* (Stuttgart: Philipp Reclam, 1970).

articles and exhibition catalog essays

Alloway, Lawrence, Françoise Choay, Gillo Dorfles, Alain Jouffroy, Michel Ragon; statement by John Cage; and previously published interview with Rauschenberg by André Parinaud, *Rauschenberg: Première Exposition (Oeuvres 1962–1963); Rauschenberg: Seconde Exposition*, exh. cat. (Paris: Galerie Ileana Sonnabend, 1963).

Alloway, Lawrence, *Robert Rauschenberg*, exh. cat. (Washington, D.C.: National Collection of Fine Arts, 1976).

Ashton, Dore, "Thirty-four Illustrations for Dante's Inferno," *Metro*, no. 2 (May 1961), 52–61.

Bendiner, Kenneth, "Robert Rauschenberg's Canyon," *Arts Magazine* 56, no. 10 (June 1982), 57–59.

Bernstein, Roberta, "Robert Rauschenberg's Rebus," *Arts Magazine* 52, no. 5 (January 1978), 138–41.

Bernstock, Judith E, "A New Interpretation of Robert Rauschenberg's Imagery," *Pantheon* 46 (1988), 149–64.

Brown, Trisha, "Collaborations: Life and Death in the Aesthetic Zone," *Rauschenberg: A Retrospective*, exh. cat. (New York: Solomon R. Guggenheim Museum of Art, 1997).

Cage, John, "On Robert Rauschenberg, Artist, and His Work," *Metro*, no. 2 (May 1961), 36–51.

Cowart, Jack, *Rauschenberg Overseas Culture Interchange*, exh. cat. (Washington, D.C., National Gallery of Art, 1991).

Cranshaw, Roger and Adrian Lewis, "Re-Reading Rauschenberg," *Artscribe*, no. 29 (June 1981), 44–51.

Crimp, Douglas, "On the Museum's Ruins," *October*, no. 13 (summer 1980), 41–57.

Donoso, José, Donald Saff, and Robert Hughes, *Rauschenberg Overseas Culture Interchange ROCI Chile*, exh. cat. (Santiago: Museo Nacional de Bellas Artes, 1985).

Eigo, Jim, "Trisha Brown and Robert Rauschenberg," *Dance Ink* 5, no. 1 (spring 1994), 22–25.

Feinstein, Roni, "The Unknown Early Robert Rauschenberg: The Betty Parsons Exhibition of 1951," *Art Magazine* 59, no. 5 (January 1985), 126–31.

Feinstein, Roni, "The Early Work of Robert Rauschenberg: The White Paintings, the Black Paintings, and the Elemental Sculptures," *Art Magazine* 61, no. 1 (September 1986), 28–37.

Feinstein, Roni, and Calvin Tomkins, *Robert Rauschenberg: The Silkscreen Paintings 1962–64*, exh. cat. (New York: Whitney Museum of American Art, 1990).

Forge, Andrew, *Robert Rauschenberg*, exh. cat. (Amsterdam: Stedelijk Museum, 1968).

Gemini, G.E.L., Los Angeles, *Booster and 7 Studies*, 1967.

Hopps, Walter, *Robert Rauschenberg: The Early 1950s*, exh. cat. (Houston: Menil Collection and Houston Fine Art Press, 1991).

Hopps, Walter, "Introduction: Rauschenberg's Art of Fusion," *Robert Rauschenberg: A Retrospective*, exh. cat. (New York: Solomon R. Guggenheim Museum of Art, 1997).

Hughes, Robert, "The Most Living Artist," *Time* 108, no. 22 (November 29, 1976), 54–62.

Katz, Jonathan, "The Art of Code: Jasper Johns and Robert Rauschenberg," In Whitney Chadwick and Isabelle de Courtivron, eds., *Significant Others: Creativity and Intimate Partnership* (London: Thames and Hudson, 1993), 188–207.

Klüver, Billy, "Theater and Engineering: An Experiment: 2. Notes by an Engineer," *Artforum* 5, no. 6 (February 1967), 31–33.

Klüver, Billy, and Julie Martin, "Four Difficult Pieces," *Art in America* 79, no. 7 (July 1991), 80–99, 138.

Klüver, Billy, and Julie Martin, "Working with Rauschenberg," *Robert Rauschenberg: A Retrospective*, exh. cat. (New York: Solomon R. Guggenheim Museum of Art, 1997).

Kostelanetz, Richard, "The Artist As Playwright and Engineer," *The New York Times Magazine*, October 9, 1966, 32–33, 109–110, 119–24. Revised and published as "Robert Rauschenberg: Painting in Four Dimensions," chapter in Kostelanetz, *Master Minds: Portraits of Contemporary American Artists and Intellectuals* (Toronto: The MacMillan Company, 1967), 251–69.

Kotz, Mary Lynn, "Robert Rauschenberg's State of the Universe Message," *Art News* 82, no. 2 (February 1983), 54–61.

Kotz, Mary Lynn, "Rauschenberg's Tour de Force," *The New York Times*, May 3, 1987, sec. 2, 30, 33.

Kotz, Mary Lynn, "Working Habits: Robert Rauschenberg Builds a Painting," *Art News* 89, no. 8 (October 1990), 123–28.

Kozloff, Max, "American Painting during the Cold War," *Artforum* 11, no. 9 (May 1973), 43–54.

Krauss, Rosalind, "Rauschenberg and the Materialized Image," *Artforum* 13, no. 4 (December 1974), 36–43.

Krauss, Rosalind, "Perpetual Inventory," *Robert Rauschenberg: A Retrospective*, exh. cat. (New York: Solomon R. Guggenheim Museum of Art, 1997).

Mamiya, Christin J., "We the People: The Art of Robert Rauschenberg and the Construction of American National Identity," *American Art* 7, no. 3 (summer 1993), 41–63.

Mattison, Robert Saltonstall, *Breaking Boundaries: Robert Rauschenberg Prints from the Robert and Jane Meyerhoff Collection*, exh. cat. (Easton, Penn.: Art Gallery of Lafayette College, 1994).

Mattison, Robert Saltonstall, "Robert Rauschenberg's *Autobiography*: Context and Meaning," *Wallraf-Richartz Jahrbuch*, no. 59 (1998), 297–305.

Owens, Craig, "The Allegorical Impulse: Toward a Theory of Postmodernism (Part 2)," *October*, no. 13 (summer 1980), 59–80.

Paxton, Steve, "Rauschenberg for Cunningham and Three of His Own," *Robert Rauschenberg: A Retrospective*, exh. cat. (New York: Solomon R. Guggenheim Museum of Art, 1997).

Perrone, Jeff, "Robert Rauschenberg," *Artforum* 15, no. 6 (February 1977), 24–31.

Rose, Barbara, "Rauschenberg: The Art as Witness," *Vogue* 167, no. 2 (February 1977), 174–75, 220, 226.

Roth, Moira, "The Aesthetic of Indifference," *Artforum* 16, no. 3 (November 1967), 46–53.

Saff, Donald J., "Conservation of Matter: Robert Rauschenberg's Art of Acceptance," *Aperture*, no. 125 (fall 1991), 24–31.

Solomon, Alan R. *Robert Rauschenberg*, exh. cat. (New York: The Jewish Museum, 1963).

Steinberg, Leo, "Reflections on the State of Criticism," *Artforum* 10, no. 7 (March 1972), 37–49. Revised and published as "Other Criteria" in Steinberg, *Other Criteria: Confrontations with Twentieth-Century Art* (New York: Oxford University Press, 1972), 55–91.

Stuckey, Charles F,. "Reading Rauschenberg," *Art in America* 65 no. 2 (March–April 1977), 74–84.

Stuckey, Charles F., "Rauschenberg's Everything, Everywhere Era," *Robert Rauschenberg: A Retrospective*, exh. cat. (New York: Solomon R. Guggenheim Museum of Art, 1997).

Sundell, Nina, *Rauschenberg/Performance*, exh. cat. (New York: Arthur A. Houghton Jr. Gallery, The Cooper Union for the Advancement of Science and the Arts, 1983).

Swenson, G[ene], "Rauschenberg Paints a Picture," *Art News* 62, no. 2 (April 1963), 44–47, 65–67.

Whitman (Forti), Simone, "Theater and Engineering: An Experiment: 1. Notes by a Participant," *Artforum* 5, no. 6 (February 1967), 99–106.

index